PEARSON TEST PREP SERIES
AP® U.S. HISTORY

BY THE PEOPLE
A HISTORY OF THE UNITED STATES

AP® Edition

James W. Fraser
New York University

Prepared by
Gary Roldan

PEARSON

Boston Columbus Indianapolis New York San Francisco Upper Saddle River
Amsterdam Cape Town Dubai London Madrid Milan Munich Paris Montréal Toronto
Delhi Mexico City São Paulo Sydney Hong Kong Seoul Singapore Taipei Tokyo

PEARSON

ISBN 10:   0-13-136619-X
ISBN 13: 978-0-13-136619-0

PearsonSchool.com\Advanced

CONTENTS

PART I

INTRODUCTION TO THE *AP U.S. HISTORY EXAMINATION*

This section overviews the advanced placement program, introduces the types of questions you will encounter on the exam, and provides helpful test-taking strategies. It also explains the grading procedure used by the College Board. Finally, a correlation chart is provided that shows where key information commonly tested on the examination is covered in *By the People: A History of the United States*. Review this section carefully before sample items in the following parts.

INTRODUCTION

THE ADVANCED PLACEMENT PROGRAM

The AP program offers thirty-five college-level courses to qualified high school students. If you receive a grade of 3 or higher on an AP exam, you may be eligible for college credit, depending on the policies of the institution you plan to attend. Approximately 3,000 college and universities around the world grant credit to students who have performed well on AP exams. If you are taking several AP courses and if you score well on multiple AP exams, you may even be eligible to enter college as a sophomore. Some institutions grant sophomore status to incoming first-year students who have demonstrated mastery of many AP subjects. In addition, the College Board confers a number of AP Scholar Awards on students who score 3 or higher on three or more AP exams. Additional awards are available to students who receive very high grades on four or five AP exams.

WHY TAKE AN AP COURSE?

You may be taking one or more AP courses simply because you are thirsty for knowledge. Of course, the fact that colleges look favorably on applicants who have AP courses on their secondary school transcripts is another powerful incentive! Because AP classes usually involve rigorous lessons, a great deal of homework, and many tests, they signal to college admissions officers that AP students are willing to work hard to get the most from their education. Because AP course work is more difficult than average high school work, many admissions officers evaluate AP grades on a kind of curve—if you receive a *B* in an AP class, for example, it might carry the same weight as an *A* in a regular high school class.

Your AP U.S. History course prepares you for many of the skills you will need in college. For example, your teacher may assign research papers and encourage you to use resources outside the scope of your textbook. Some of these resources may be primary sources that permit you to analyze events as a historian would. Other class assignments may require you to write longer-than-usual essays on historical subjects. The AP U.S. History course will challenge you to gather and consider information in new—and sometimes unfamiliar—ways. You can feel good knowing that your ability to use these methods and skills will give you a leg up as you enter college.

Each college or university decides whether or not to grant college credit for an AP course, and each bases this decision on what it considers satisfactory grades on AP exams. Depending on what college you attend and what area of study you pursue, your decision to take the AP U.S. History Exam could end up saving you tuition money. You can contact schools directly to find out their guidelines for accepting AP credits.

TAKING AN AP EXAMINATION

Your AP teacher or school guidance counselor can give you information on how to sign up for an AP exam. Remember, the deadline to sign up and pay the fees for the exam is usually in January, four months before the actual date of the exam in May. If, after taking the exam, you want to have your score report sent to additional schools besides those you named on your registration—or if you want to withhold or cancel your score—you will need to notify the College Board by mid-June. You should check with the AP website for the exact date in June for notifying the College Board. The College Board's pamphlet, *Bulletin for AP Students and Parents*, is an excellent source for exam information: https://apstudent.collegeboard.org. Your exam grades will be sent to you by mail in early July. However, for an additional fee, Educational Testing Service (the organization that develops and scores tests for the College Board) will release your score to you over the phone around July 1st. If your school does not administer the AP exam, your teacher or guidance counselor can help you find a nearby school that does. If you continue to have difficulty determining what schools in your region offer the exam, you can always visit the College Board's website (*www.collegeboard.com*) for more information. The cost of the exam frequently changes and can differ depending on the number of exams taken. If you feel that you cannot afford this fee, you may apply to the College Board for a fee reduction based on your financial need.

TEST-TAKING STRATEGIES FOR AP U.S. HISTORY EXAMINATION

Below is a brief list of basic tips and strategies to think about *before* you arrive at the exam site.

- It's a good idea to arrive at the exam site thirty minutes before the start time. This saves you additional worry about arriving late. You should plan your schedule so that you get *two* very good nights of sleep before exam day. On the day of the exam, make sure that you eat good, nutritious meals. These tips may sound corny or obvious, but your body must be in peak form in order for your brain to perform well.

- It's a good idea to have a photo I.D. with you when you arrive at the exam site. (It is essential if you are taking the exam at a school other than your own.) Carrying a driver's license or a student I.D. card will allow you to prove your identity, if anyone needs such proof.

- You should bring at least two pencils for the multiple-choice section, as well as two black or dark blue pens for the essay sections of the exam. Take a moment to make sure that your pencils are labeled #2 and that they have good erasers. After all, the machine that scores Section I of the exam cannot recognize marks made by other types of pencils. Also, it cannot read a correct answer if a previous answer has not been erased completely.

- If possible, it's helpful to have a watch with you at the exam. It's true that most testing rooms will have clocks and that most test administrators will give you periodic reminders of how much time you have remaining. Still, having your own watch makes it easy to keep close track of your own pace. The watch cannot have a calculator or an alarm, however, as these are not permitted in the exam room.

- There are a few other things that are not allowed in the exam room. Do not bring books of any kind, laptop computers, cameras, or portable radios. If you must bring a cellular phone with you, prepare to turn it off and give it to the test proctor until you are finished with your exam. Educational Testing Service prohibits the objects listed above in the interest of fairness to all test-takers. Similarly, the test administrators are very clear and very serious about what types of conduct are not allowed during the examination. Below is a list of actions to avoid at all costs, since each is grounds for your immediate dismissal from the exam room.

  - Do not consult any outside materials during the three hours and five minutes of the exam period. Remember, the break is technically part of the exam—you are not free to review any materials at that time either.
  - Do not speak during the exam, unless you have a question for the test proctor. Raise your hand to get the proctor's attention.
  - When you are told to stop working on a section of the exam, you must stop *immediately.*
  - Do not open your exam booklet before the test begins.
  - Never tear a page out of your test booklet or try to remove the exam from the test room.

- Do not behave disruptively—even if you're distressed about a difficult test question or because you've run out of time. Stay calm and make no unnecessary noise. Remember, too, the worst-case scenario: if you are displeased with your performance on test day, you can always cancel your exam scores.

STRATEGIES FOR MULTIPLE-CHOICE QUESTIONS

Having a firm grasp of U.S. history is, of course, the key to your doing well on the AP U.S. History Examination. In addition, being well-informed about the exam itself increases your chances of achieving a high score. Below is a list of strategies that you can use to increase your comfort, your confidence, and your chances of excelling on the multiple-choice section of the exam.

- Pace yourself and keep track of the remaining time as you complete the multiple-choice section of the exam. Remember, you have fifty-five minutes to answer all eighty questions. It's important that you don't get stuck on one question for too long.
- Make a light mark in your test booklet next to any questions you can't answer. Return to them after you reach the end of Section I. Sometimes questions that appear later in the test will refresh your memory of a particular period, and you will be able to answer one of those earlier questions.
- Always read the entire question carefully, and underline key words or ideas. You might wish to double underline words such as *NOT* or *EXCEPT* in that type of multiple-choice question.
- Read each and every one of the answer choices carefully before you make your final selection.
- Trust your first instinct. Since it has been proven statistically that your first choice is more likely to be correct, you should replace it only if you are completely certain that your second choice is correct.
- Use the process of elimination to help you home in on a correct answer. Even if you are quite sure of an answer, cross out the letters of incorrect choices in your test booklet as you eliminate them. This cuts down on distraction and allows you to narrow the remaining choices even further.
- If you are able to eliminate two or more answer choices, it is better to make an educated guess at the correct answer than to leave the answer blank.
- Remember that the multiple-choice section of the AP U.S. History Exam is designed so that easier questions appear at the start of the test. Try to answer the easy questions as quickly as you can without sacrificing care and thoroughness. If you are able to rack up many correct answers at the start of the section, you will conserve time (and mental energy) for the more difficult questions toward the end of the test.
- About a month prior to the test date, you should begin doing drills to prepare for the multiple-choice section of the test. Ask your teacher for copies of old AP U.S. History Exams, and answer the multiple-choice questions. Answer the sample questions in Part II of this book, and take the sample tests in Part IV. After you've answered the questions, check your answers and use the answer explanations to determine any content areas that you need to study or review more thoroughly.
- Make yourself completely familiar with the instructions for the multiple-choice

questions *before* you take the exam. You'll find the instructions in this book. By knowing the instructions cold, you'll save yourself the time of reading them carefully on the day of the test.

■ In the week before the exam, do a comprehensive review of the history you've studied. However, don't dwell on obscure details. Focus on the larger issues that you might confront in the exam. It's a good idea to revisit with your teacher any major themes that you have found confusing or that you feel you don't know as well as you should. You can review using information in the Part I correlation chart and in Part II chapter content summaries of By *the People*, as well as in your textbook.

■ Try to grow as familiar as you can with the format of Section I. The more comfortable you are with the multiple-choice format and with the kinds of questions you'll encounter, the easier the exam will be. Remember, Part II and Part IV of this book provide you with invaluable practice on the kinds of multiple-choice questions you will encounter on the AP U.S. History Exam.

STRATEGIES FOR SHORT AND LONG ESSAY QUESTIONS

Below is a list of strategies that you can use to increase your chances of excelling on sections II (Short Answer Questions) and III (Long Essay Question) of the exam.

■ Since you have just two hours and ten minutes to outline and write three essays in the free-response sections of the AP U.S. History Exam, you must manage your time carefully.

■ Be careful not to stray from the focus of the question being asked. As you read a question, underline any directive words that indicate how you should address and focus the material in your essay. Some of the most frequently used directives on the AP U.S History Exam are listed below, along with descriptions of what you need to do in your writing to answer the question.

- *Analyze* (show relationships between events; explain)
- *Assess/Evaluate* (give an opinion of; appraise; discuss advantages and disadvantages)
- *Compare* (address similarities and differences between two or more things)
- *Contrast* (examine to illustrate points of difference or divergence)
- *Defend/Refute* (argue for or against a specific statement or position, using factual support to back up your argument)
- *Describe* (give a detailed account)
- *Discuss* (consider or examine; debate)
- *Explain* (clarify; tell the meaning)
- *To what extent and in what ways* (tell how much and how)

■ As you formulate your thesis, always consider whether or not it will answer the essay question directly.

STRATEGIES FOR THE DOCUMENT-BASED QUESTION (DBQ)

The following strategies will help you conceive, organize, and write your response to the DBQ.

- During the fifteen-minute reading period, begin by reading carefully the DBQ and the historical background provided along with it.
- Underline key words and make a note of any outside information you might be able to connect to the question or to the historical background material.
- Then read each of the historical documents in order, reviewing some for more in-depth analysis, and flagging any phrases or words that connect that document to the main theme of the DBQ.
- Although some documents will be more crucial to an understanding of the topic than others, each document is relevant to the question. Make a mark next to those documents that you feel are the most pertinent and that you will use most extensively to support your argument.
- Take note of the date of each source and identify the author's position or point-of-view (including any potential bias).
- If the reading period allows, decide on a thesis statement and plan an outline that will enable you to analyze and interpret as many of the documents as possible into a cohesive essay.
- Keep in mind that successful DBQ responses incorporate analysis of the majority of documents. However, you do not need to cite every document to get a high score. Specific mention of individual documents should always occur in the context of the overall topic and should help to illustrate or organize arguments made in your essay. In short, documents should *never* be cited or summarized without analysis. One key to your success on the DBQ portion of the exam is a seamless integration of the documents into the body of your essay.
- Whenever you make use of documents in your DBQ response, ask yourself how they function with respect to your thesis and to the DBQ question itself. It is important also to address any documents that directly refute your thesis. Readers will be as interested to see how you handle material that contradicts your main argument as they will be to see your use of documents that support your thesis.
- Remember to refer to individual documents by author name and/or by the document number. If time allows, you may want to write a conclusion to your DBQ essay that reflects on how the documentary evidence illustrates your thesis.
- If you have time, try to proofread your essays for any inconsistencies or weaknesses.

Here is an abbreviated version of the kind of DBQ you will encounter on your AP U.S. History Exam. In this sample DBQ, you will have four historical documents to consider and integrate into your response. A sample analysis of the documents and the manner in which you should proceed to write your essay follows.

Document-Based Question

1. *To what extent and in what ways did sixteenth-century Spanish attitudes toward the lands and people conquered in the New World affect government policy?*

Background History: The fifteenth century witnessed the beginning of Western Europe's expansion into unknown lands. A quest for gold and spices dominated these initial adventures at sea. Christopher Columbus's voyage of 1492 marked the beginning of the Spanish dominance of a vast American territory. Subsequently, Spaniards set up satellite governments in North America and South America, and they recruited and enslaved native Indians to assist them in mining, agriculture, and other endeavors aimed at creating a New World economy to profit Spain.

DOCUMENT 1 Source: Hernán Cortés, Spanish conqueror, second letter to Charles V, 1520

In the place of these I put images of Our Lady and the Saints, which excited not a little feeling in Montezuma and the inhabitants, who at first remonstrated, declaring that if my proceedings were known throughout the country, the people would rise against me; for they believed that their idols bestowed on them all temporal good, and if they permitted them to be ill-treated, they would be angry and without their gifts, and by this means the people would be deprived of the fruits of the earth and perish with famine. I answered, through the interpreters, that they were deceived in expecting any favors from idols, the work of their own hands, formed of unclean things; and that they must learn there was but one God, the universal Lord of all, who had created the heavens and earth, and all things else, and had made them and us …

DOCUMENT 2 Source: Bartolomé de las Casas (1474–1566), Dominican missionary, "A Brief Account of the Destruction of the Indies," ca. 1542

That which led the Spaniards to these unsanctified impieties was the desire of Gold, to make themselves suddenly rich … In a word, their covetousness, their ambition, which could not be more in any people under heaven, the riches of the Country, and the patience of the people gave occasion to this their devilish barbarism. For the Spaniards so condemned them … that they used them not like beasts, for that would have been tolerable, but looked upon them as if they had been but the dung and filth of the earth, and so little they regarded the health of their souls, that they suffered this great multitude to die without the least light of Religion …

DOCUMENT 3 Source: "The New Laws of the Indies," laws and ordinances made by Charles V for the government of the Indies and treatment of the Indians, 1542

As we have ordered provision to be made that from henceforward the Indians in no way be made slaves, including those who until now have been enslaved against all reason and right and contrary to the provisions and instructions thereupon, We ordain and command that the Audiencias having first summoned the parties to their presence, without any further judicial form, but in a summary way, so that the truth may be ascertained, speedily set the said Indians at liberty unless the persons who hold them for slaves show title why they should hold and possess them legitimately. And in order that in default of persons to solicit the aforesaid, the Indians may not remain in slavery unjustly, We command that the Audiencias appoint persons who may pursue this cause for the Indians and be paid out of the Exchequer fines, provided they be men of trust and diligence.

DOCUMENT 4 Source: Anonymous, "The Gold of the Indies," from the Court of Philip II of Spain, 1559

[G]reat quantities of gold and silver are no longer found upon the surface of the earth, as they have been in past years; and to penetrate into the bowels of the earth requires greater effort, skill and outlay, and the Spaniards are not willing to do the work themselves, and the natives cannot be forced to do so, because the Emperor has freed them from all obligation of service as soon as they accept the Christian religion. Wherefore it is necessary to acquire negro slaves, who are brought from the coasts of Africa, both within and without the Straits, and these are selling dearer every day, because on account of their natural lack of strength and the change of climate, added to the lack of discretion upon the part of their masters in making them work too hard and giving them too little to eat, they fall sick and the greater part of them die.

Analysis

This sample DBQ question asks you to consider *how* Spanish attitudes toward lands and peoples in the New World contributed to government policy and *how much* they contributed. By narrowing the focus to Spanish attitudes in the sixteenth century, and by relying on documents exclusively from that period, this question provides you with much of the equipment that you will use in formulating your response.

As you read through each of the documents, pay attention to the author of each work. You should recognize Hernán Cortés, the author of **DOCUMENT 1**, as the Spanish conquistador who brutally defeated the Aztecs of Mexico in 1521 and reclaimed the region as New Spain. Here, Cortés relates his efforts to convert the Aztecs to Christian worship, and he characterizes their worship of idols as wrong. It is worth noting that Cortés' primary objective in his dealing with the Aztecs was not religious conversion, but the vast quantities of gold held by the Aztec ruler, Montezuma. Cortés and his soldiers brutally conquered the city of Tenochtitlán, killing thousands of Aztecs and asserting Spanish control of the region. Any analysis of this document (and its benevolent but paternalistic attitude toward the Indians) must take into account Cortés's brutality against the Aztecs.

You may be familiar with Bartolomé de las Casas, the author of **DOCUMENT 2**, the Dominican missionary who waged a campaign against the exploitative aspects of conquest in the Americas. You may also recall that the ideas of Las Casas led to new royal regulations of conquest. In this excerpt, you should detect Las Casas' anger at the greed of the Spanish, as well as his frustration at their debasing treatment of the Indians.

His emphasis on religion is clear in his condemnation of the Spanish massacre of Indian societies and of the failure to offer Native Americans religious enlightenment.

The third document reflects new royal laws about the treatment of Indians, and it demands their liberty from slavery. The authorship of this official document from the court of Charles V is unclear, but the sentiments expressed reflect a significant departure from the conditions described by Las Casas **DOCUMENT 2** and call for freedom for the Indians under Spanish control.

The fourth document, from the court of Philip II of Spain, alludes to the problem of carrying out some of the labor-intensive mining of gold and silver that has been done in the past by Indians. The author contends that Indians were freed from forced labor as soon as they converted to Christianity, and that African slaves will be necessary to carry out the difficult work. It is worth noting that though the Indians were released from forced servitude, they gained their liberty only by converting to a new faith—hardly the liberty and freedom described in **DOCUMENT 3**.

As you develop a strong thesis that answers the question and enables you to discuss these works in detail, you will want to respond to the "To what extent and in what ways," portion of the question. If you don't know much about this period in history, you can rely on some of the details provided in the documents. You should make use of most of the documents in your response, and you should explain authorial bias whenever you detect it. You should glean the following basic ideas from the documents and keep them in mind as you compose your thesis:

- Christianity was important to sixteenth-century Spaniards, many of whom were concerned that the natives in the lands they conquered were not believers.
- Natives experienced significant bloodshed and brutality at the hands of the Spanish. Many of the natives were treated by the Spanish as if they were worthless creatures who had no basic rights as human beings.
- In the sixteenth century, new laws released natives from enslavement, but these laws were conditional on the natives' conversion to Christianity.
- Among the primary motives of sixteenth-century explorers and discoverers was the acquisition of gold and other riches in the New World. This ambition to gain access to more minerals and wealth, coupled with new laws prohibiting native slavery, led Spaniards to seek other unrestricted labor markets, such as those in Africa.

One way to address the question in thesis form would be as follows:

> Spanish greed to acquire the riches of the New World at any cost competed with a desire to convert to Christianity the peoples it conquered; the result of these conflicting desires was sixteenth-century legislation that sought to protect the rights of natives but that led ultimately to the exploitation of natives in Africa.

In your first paragraph, you might want to back up your thesis statement by discussing the Spanish quest for riches of the New World. You could cite passages from Bartolomé de Las Casas and from **DOCUMENT 4**, and you could describe the quest of

Hernán Cortés to find the gold of the Aztecs. This would be an excellent place in the essay to demonstrate your outside knowledge on the subject, as you could refer to other explorers whose conquests you recall. Using details, you should develop the idea that this quest for wealth led to tremendous exploitation of the natives.

In your second paragraph, you could address the Spanish desire to impart Christian faith in the lands they conquered, and you could cite the Cortés passage. You would want to acknowledge the bias implicit in this document—that is, that Cortés was a brutal conquistador who could liken himself to the Indians and make claims of their being made by the same God, but who could then go on to destroy their civilization. You could also refer to Las Casas' concern that the natives were killed without the benefit of religious enlightenment, and you could allude to the fact (noted in **DOCUMENT 4**) that natives who converted were granted freedom from slavery. You could assert that the campaign of Las Casas and other reformers persuaded Emperor Charles V that Spanish exploitation of natives was wrong, and that the campaign resulted in the legislation (indicated in **DOCUMENT 3**) that granted natives their freedom from slavery. You might feel that it is worth acknowledging that by 1542, much damage had already been done to these native civilizations, as Columbus had arrived in the New World fully fifty years earlier.

You might close the essay by saying that while Spanish concern for the religious faith of the peoples they conquered was significant, it was overwhelmed by their desire for the wealth of the New World. As **DOCUMENT 4** suggests, though new legislation protected the natives (provided that they agreed to convert—in itself a kind of enslavement, one might argue), it did not compel the Spanish to check their desire to seize the region's riches. The policies of the Spanish government had changed over time as a result of demands from religious organizations seeking human rights assurances, and exploitation of the natives had slowed by the middle of the sixteenth century. However, greedy Spanish colonials sought new labor markets in other continents and displayed a similar disregard for the rights of natives on the African continent.

A response that has a strong thesis statement, develops its ideas clearly, integrates information from most of the documents, identifies and explains any bias demonstrated by those documents, and directly answers the actual Document-Based Question will earn a high score.

CORRELATION OF *BY THE PEOPLE* TO THE AP U.S. HISTORY CURRICULUM FRAMEWORK

Upon publication, this text was correlated to the College Board's U.S. History Course Description beginning for the 2014–2015 school year. We continually monitor the College Board's AP Courses Description for updates to exam topics. For the most current correlation for this textbook, visit PearsonSchool.com/AdvancedCorrelations.

AP US HISTORY CURRICULUM		Chapter and Page References
Period 1 **1491–1607**	On a North American continent controlled by American Indians, contact among the peoples of Europe, the Americas, and West Africa created a new world.	Chapters 1, 2, 3, 4
Key Concept 1.1	Before the arrival of Europeans, native populations in North America developed a wide variety of social, political, and economic structures based in part on interactions with the environment and each other.	Chapter 1
	I. As settlers migrated and settled across the vast expanse of North America over time, they developed quite different and increasingly complex societies by adapting to and transforming their diverse environments.	pp. 1–16
Key Concept 1.2	European overseas expansion resulted in the Columbian Exchange, a series of interactions and adaptations among societies across the Atlantic.	Chapters 1, 2
	I. The arrival of Europeans in the Western Hemisphere in the 15th and 16th centuries triggered extensive demographic and social changes on both sides of the Atlantic.	pp. 17–23, 29–38
	II. European expansion into the Western Hemisphere caused intense social/religious, political, and economic competition in Europe and the promotion of empire building.	pp. 33–35, 41–54
Key Concept 1.3	Contacts among American Indians, Africans, and Europeans challenged the worldviews of each group.	Chapters 2, 3, 4
	I. European overseas expansion and sustained contacts with Africans and American Indians dramatically altered European views of social, political, and economic relationships among and between white and nonwhite peoples.	pp. 29–34, 37–38, 78–89, 92–104
	II. Native peoples and Africans in the Americas strove to maintain their political and cultural autonomy in the face of European challenges to their independence and core beliefs.	pp. 78–81,88–89, 97–104

Period 2 1607–1754	Europeans and American Indians maneuvered and fought for dominance, control, and security in North America, and distinctive colonial and native societies emerged.	Chapters 3, 4
Key Concept 2.1	Differences in imperial goals, cultures, and the North American environments that different empires confronted led Europeans to develop diverse patterns of colonization.	Chapters 3, 4
	I. Seventeenth-century Spanish, French, Dutch, and British colonizers embraced different social and economic goals, cultural assumptions, and folkways, resulting in varied models of colonization.	pp. 63–75, 83–90, 116–119
	II. The British-American system of slavery developed out of the economic, demographic, and geographic characteristics of the British-controlled regions of the New World.	pp. 91, 97–104
	III. Along with other factors, environmental and geographical variations, including climate and natural resources, contributed to regional differences in what would become the British colonies.	pp. 66–71, 73–77
Key Concept 2.2	European colonization efforts in North America stimulated intercultural contact and intensified conflict between the various groups of colonizers and native peoples.	Chapters 3, 4
	I. Competition over resources between European rivals led to conflict within and between North American colonial possessions and American Indians.	pp. 65–66, 71–73, 75–77, 83–85, 109–120
	II. Clashes between European and American Indian social and economic values caused changes in both cultures.	pp. 78–83, 88–89, 116–119
Key Concept 2.3	The increasing political, economic, and cultural exchanges within the "Atlantic World" had a profound impact on the development of colonial societies in North America.	Chapter 4
	I. "Atlantic World" commercial, religious, philosophical, and political interactions among Europeans, Africans, and American native peoples stimulated economic growth, expanded social networks, and reshaped labor systems.	pp. 95–119
	II. Britain's desire to maintain a viable North American empire in the face of growing internal challenges and external competition inspired efforts to strengthen its imperial control, stimulating increasing resistance from colonists who had grown accustomed to a large measure of autonomy.	pp. 95–97, 109–116

Period 3 1754–1800	British imperial attempts to reassert control over its colonies and the colonial reaction to these attempts produced a new American republic, along with struggles over the new nation's social, political, and economic identity.	Chapters 4, 5, 6, 7
Key Concept 3.1	Britain's victory over France in the imperial struggle for North America led to new conflicts among the British government, the North American colonists, and American Indians, culminating in the creation of a new nation, the United States.	Chapters 5, 6, 7
	I. Throughout the second half of the 18th century, various American Indian groups repeatedly evaluated and adjusted their alliances with Europeans, other tribes, and the new United States government.	pp. 131–136, 155–156, 169–171, 203–205
	II. During and after the imperial struggles of the mid-18th century, new pressures began to unite the British colonies against perceived and real constraints on their economic activities and political rights, sparking a colonial independence movement and war with Britain.	pp. 134–145, 149–158
	III. In response to domestic and international tensions, the new United States debated and formulated foreign policy initiatives and asserted an international presence.	pp. 207–215
Key Concept 3.2	In the late 18th century, new experiments with democratic ideas and republican forms of government, as well as other new religious, economic, and cultural ideas, challenged traditional imperial systems across the Atlantic World.	Chapters 4, 5, 6, 7
	I. During the 18th century, new ideas about politics and society led to debates about religion and governance, and ultimately inspired experiments with new governmental structures.	pp. 113–116, 137–139, 149–151, 178–179
	II. After experiencing the limitations of the Articles of Confederation, American political leaders wrote a new Constitution based on the principles of federalism and separation of powers, crafted a Bill of Rights, and continued their debates about the proper balance between liberty and order.	pp. 178–189, 194–199, 205–215
	III. While the new governments continued to limit rights to some groups, ideas promoting self-government and personal liberty reverberated around the world.	pp. 171–174, 182–184, 207

Key Concept 3.3	Migration within North America, cooperative interaction, and competition for resources raised questions about boundaries and policies, intensified conflicts among peoples and nations, and led to contests over the creation of a multiethnic, multiracial national identity.	Chapters 6, 7
	I. As migrants streamed westward from the British colonies along the Atlantic seaboard, interactions among different groups that would continue under an independent United States resulted in competition for resources, shifting alliances, and cultural blending.	pp. 90, 167–169, 203–205
	II. The policies of the United States that encouraged western migration and the orderly incorporation of new territories into the nation both extended republican institutions and intensified conflicts among American Indians and Europeans in the trans-Appalachian West.	pp.167–171, 210
	III. New voices for national identity challenged tendencies to cling to regional identities, contributing to the emergence of distinctly American cultural expressions.	pp. 171–219
Period 4 1800–1848	The new republic struggled to define and extend democratic ideals in the face of rapid economic, territorial, and demographic changes.	Chapters 7, 8, 9, 10, 11, 12, 13
Key Concept 4.1	The United States developed the world's first modern mass democracy and celebrated a new national culture, while Americans sought to define the nation's democratic ideals and to reform its institutions to match them.	Chapters 7, 8, 9, 10, 11, 12
	I. The nation's transformation to a more participatory democracy was accompanied by continued debates over federal power, the relationship between the federal government and the states, the authority of different branches of the federal government, and the rights and responsibilities of individual citizens.	pp. 211–218, 230–231, 245, 279–280, 286–288, 302–307, 328–332, 383–384
	II. Concurrent with an increasing international exchange of goods and ideas, larger numbers of Americans began struggling with how to match democratic political ideals to political institutions and social realities.	pp. 307–316, 357–364, 370–375
	III. While Americans celebrated their nation's progress toward a unified new national culture that blended Old World forms with New World ideas, various groups of the nation's inhabitants developed distinctive cultures of their own.	pp. 277–278, 289, 310–313, 364–379
Key Concept 4.2	Developments in technology, agriculture, and commerce precipitated profound changes in U.S. settlement patterns, regional identities, gender and family relations, political power, and distribution of consumer goods.	Chapters 9, 10, 12

	I. A global market and communications revolution, influencing and influenced by technological innovations, led to dramatic shifts in the nature of agriculture and manufacturing.	pp. 260–277
	II. Regional economic specialization, especially the demands of cultivating southern cotton, shaped settlement patterns and the national and international economy.	pp. 262–266, 272–276, 286–287, 294–300
	III. The economic changes caused by the market revolution had significant effects on migration patterns, gender and family relations, and the distribution of political power.	pp. 267–269, 272–279, 286–287, 300–307, 360–362
Key Concept 4.3	U.S. interest in increasing foreign trade, expanding its national borders, and isolating itself from European conflicts shaped the nation's foreign policy and spurred government and private initiatives.	Chapters 8, 10
	I. Struggling to create an independent global presence, U.S. policymakers sought to dominate the North American continent and to promote its foreign trade.	pp. 251–255, 330–334
	II. Various American groups and individuals initiated, championed, and/or resisted the expansion of territory and/or government powers.	pp. 245–247, 302–307, 331, 336
	III. The American acquisition of lands in the West gave rise to a contest over the extension of slavery into the western territories as well as a series of attempts at national compromise.	pp. 262–266, 280–282
Period 5 1844–1877	As the nation expanded and its population grew, regional tensions, especially over slavery, led to a civil war—the course and aftermath of which transformed American society.	Chapters 11, 12, 13, 14, 15, 16
Key Concept 5.1	The United States became more connected with the world as it pursued an expansionist foreign policy in the Western Hemisphere and emerged as the destination for many migrants from other countries.	Chapter 11, 12, 13
	I. Enthusiasm for U.S. territorial expansion fueled by economic and national security interests and supported by claims of U.S. racial and cultural superiority, resulted in war, the opening of new markets, acquisition of new territory, and increased ideological conflicts.	pp. 321–322, 336, 343, 362–363, 380, 385–386
	II. Westward expansion, migration to and within the United States, and the end of slavery reshaped North American boundaries and caused conflicts over American cultural identities, citizenship, and the question of extending and protecting rights for various groups of U.S. Inhabitants.	pp. 313, 357–364, 487, 489
Key Concept 5.2	Intensified by expansion and deepening regional divisions, debates over slavery and other economic, cultural, and political issues led the nation into civil war.	Chapters 10, 12, 13

17

	I. The institution of slavery and its attendant ideological debates, along with regional economic and demographic changes, territorial expansion in the 1840s and 1850s, and cultural differences between the North and the South, all intensified sectionalism.	pp. 302–306, 366–367, 374–375, 384–389, 396–397
	II. Repeated attempts at political compromise failed to calm tensions over slavery and often made sectional tensions worse, breaking down the trust between sectional leaders and culminating in the bitter election of 1860, followed by the secession of southern states.	pp. 385–396, 398–399, 402–409
Key Concept 5.3	The Union victory in the Civil War and the contested Reconstruction of the South settled the issues of slavery and secession, but left unresolved many questions about the power of the federal government and citizenship rights.	Chapters 13, 14, 15
	I. The North's greater manpower and industrial resources, its leadership, and the decision for emancipation eventually led to the Union military victory over the Confederacy in the devastating Civil War.	pp. 406–409, 414, 440
	II. The Civil War and Reconstruction altered power relationships between the states and the federal government and among the executive, legislative, and judicial branches, ending slavery and the notion of a divisible union, but leaving unresolved questions of relative power and largely unchanged social and economic patterns.	pp. 440, 451–471
	III. The constitutional changes of the Reconstruction period embodied a Northern idea of American identity and national purpose and led to conflicts over new definitions of citizenship, particularly regarding the rights of African-Americans, women, and other minorities.	pp. 453, 457–459, 465–472
Period 6 1865–1898	The transformation of the United States from an agricultural to an increasingly industrialized and urbanized society brought about significant economic, political, diplomatic, social, environmental, and cultural changes.	Chapters 16, 17, 18, 19
Key Concept 6.1	The rise of big business in the United States encouraged massive migrations and urbanization, sparked government and popular efforts to reshape the U.S. economy and environment, and renewed debates over U.S. national identity.	Chapter 17
	I. Large-scale production—accompanied by massive technological change, expanding international communication networks, and pro-growth government policies — fueled the development of a "Gilded Age" marked by an emphasis on consumption, marketing, and business consolidation.	pp. 510–520, 525–527, 531–536

	II. As leaders of big business and their allies in government aimed to create a unified industrialized nation, they were challenged in different ways by demographic issues, regional differences, and labor movements.	pp. 461–465, 527–530, 540–546, 555–565
	III. Westward migration, new systems of farming and transportation, and economic instability led to political and popular conflicts.	pp. 548–554, 586–588
Key Concept 6.2	The emergence of an industrial culture in the United States led to both greater opportunities for, and restrictions on, immigrants, minorities, and women.	Chapters 16, 17, 19
	I. International and internal migrations increased both urban and rural populations, but gender, racial, ethnic, religious, and socioeconomic inequalities abounded, inspiring some reformers to attempt to address these inequities.	pp. 527–534, 578–581
	II. As transcontinental railroads were completed, bringing more settlers west, U.S. military actions, the destruction of the buffalo, the confinement of American Indians to reservations, and assimilatory policies reduced the number of American Indians and threatened native culture and identity.	pp. 480–498
Key Concept 6.3	The "Gilded Age" witnessed new cultural and intellectual movements in tandem with political debates over economic and social policies.	Chapters 17, 18, 19
	I. Gilded Age politics were intimately tied to big business and focused nationally on economic issues—tariffs, currency, corporate expansion, and laissez-faire economic policy—that engendered numerous calls for reform.	pp. 543–546, 558–560, 574–578, 585–586
	II. New cultural and intellectual movements both buttressed and challenged the social order of the Gilded Age.	pp. 519, 546–547, 569–570, 581–583
Period 7 1890–1945	An increasingly pluralistic United States faced profound domestic and global challenges, debated the proper degree of government activism, and sought to define its international role.	Chapters 17, 18, 19, 20, 21, 22, 23
Key Concept 7.1	Governmental, political, and social organizations struggled to address the effects of large-scale industrialization, economic uncertainty, and related social changes such as urbanization and mass migration.	Chapters 17, 19, 22

	I. The continued growth and consolidation of large corporations transformed American society and the nation's economy, promoting urbanization and economic growth, even as business cycle fluctuations became increasingly severe.	pp. 512–520, 531–536, 664–668
	II. Progressive reformers responded to economic instability, social inequality, and political corruption by calling for government intervention in the economy, expanded democracy, greater social justice, and conservation of natural resources.	pp. 570–572, 583–595
	III. National, state, and local reformers responded to economic upheavals, laissez-faire capitalism, and the Great Depression by transforming the U.S. into a limited welfare state.	pp. 668–669, 671, 675–679, 681–682, 689
Key Concept 7.2	A revolution in communications and transportation technology helped to create a new mass culture and spread "modern" values and ideas, even as cultural conflicts between groups increased under the pressure of migration, world wars, and economic distress.	Chapters 20, 21, 23
	I. New technologies led to social transformations that improved the standard of living for many, while contributing to increased political and cultural conflicts.	pp. 641–646, 651, 655–657
	II. The global ramifications of World War I and wartime patriotism and xenophobia, combined with social tensions created by increased international migration, resulted in legislation restricting immigration from Asia and from southern and eastern Europe.	pp. 619, 621–622, 634–635, 651–653
	III. Economic dislocations, social pressures, and the economic growth spurred by World Wars I and II led to a greater degree of migration within the United States, as well as migration to the United States from elsewhere in the Western Hemisphere.	pp. 646–647, 672–675, 697-704
Key Concept 7.3	Global conflicts over resources, territories, and ideologies renewed debates over the nation's values and its role in the world, while simultaneously propelling the United States into a dominant international military, political, cultural, and economic position.	Chapters 20, 21, 22, 23

	I. Many Americans began to advocate overseas expansionism in the late 19th century, leading to new territorial ambitions and acquisitions in the Western Hemisphere and the Pacific.	pp. 602–609
	II. World War I and its aftermath intensified debates about the nation's role in the world and how best to achieve national security and pursue American interests.	pp. 617–629, 686–689
	III. The involvement of the United States in World War II, while opposed by most Americans prior to the attack on Pearl Harbor, vaulted the United States into global political and military prominence, and transformed both American society and the relationship between the United States and the rest of the world.	pp. 697–707, 710–721
Period 8 1945–1980	After World War II, the United States grappled with prosperity and unfamiliar international responsibilities, while struggling to live up to its ideals.	Chapters 24, 25, 26, 27, 28
Key Concept 8.1	The United States responded to an uncertain and unstable postwar world by asserting and attempting to defend a position of global leadership, with far-reaching domestic and international consequences.	Chapters 24, 25, 26, 27, 28
	I. After World War II, the United States sought to stem the growth of Communist military power and ideological influence, create a stable global economy, and build an international security system.	pp. 741–744, 751–753, 762–768, 813–823, 831–832
	II. As the United States focused on containing communism, it faced increasingly complex foreign policy issues, including decolonization, shifting international alignments and regional conflicts, and global economic and environmental changes.	pp. 763–765, 843–846, 848–851, 871–873
	III. Cold War policies led to continued public debates over the power of the federal government, acceptable means for pursuing international and domestic goals, and the proper balance between liberty and order.	pp. 747–751, 762, 818–819
Key Concept 8.2	Liberalism, based on anticommunism abroad and a firm belief in the efficacy of governmental and especially federal power to achieve social goals at home, reached its apex in the mid-1960s and generated a variety of political and cultural responses.	Chapters 25, 26, 27

	I. Seeking to fulfill Reconstruction-era promises, civil rights activists and political leaders achieved some legal and political successes in ending segregation, although progress toward equality was slow and halting.	pp. 778–791, 808
	II. Stirred by a growing awareness of inequalities in American society and by the African-American civil rights movement, activists also addressed issues of identity and social justice, such as gender/sexuality and ethnicity.	pp. 796, 806, 833–837, 840
	III. As many liberal principles came to dominate postwar politics and court decisions, liberalism came under attack from the left as well as from resurgent conservative movements.	pp. 793–794, 797–799, 806–813, 842
Key Concept 8.3	Postwar economic, demographic, and technological changes had a far-reaching impact on American society, politics, and the environment.	Chapters 24, 26, 27
	I. Rapid economic and social changes in American society fostered a sense of optimism in the postwar years, as well as underlying concerns about how these changes were affecting American values.	pp. 731–738, 793–799, 840–842
	II. As federal programs expanded and economic growth reshaped American society, many sought greater access to prosperity even as critics began to question the burgeoning use of natural resources.	pp. 702–704, 796–798, 811
	III. New demographic and social issues led to significant political and moral debates that sharply divided the nation.	pp. 827–828, 833–835, 840–842
Period 9 1980– PRESENT	As the United States transitioned to a new century filled with challenges and possibilities, it experienced renewed ideological and cultural debates, sought to redefine its foreign policy, and adapted to economic globalization and revolutionary changes in science and technology.	Chapters 27, 28, 29, 30
Key Concept 9.1	A new conservatism grew to prominence in U.S. culture and politics, defending traditional social values and rejecting liberal views about the role of government.	Chapters 27, 28
	I. Reduced public faith in the government's ability to solve social and economic problems, the growth of religious fundamentalism, and the dissemination of neoconservative thought all combined to invigorate conservatism.	pp. 842–852, 882–884
	II. Conservatives achieved some of their political and policy goals, but their success was limited by the enduring popularity and institutional strength of some government programs and public support for cultural trends of recent decades.	pp. 864–865, 882–884

Key Concept 9.2	The end of the Cold War and new challenges to U.S. leadership in the world forced the nation to redefine its foreign policy and global role.	Chapters 28, 29, 30
	I. The Reagan administration pursued a reinvigorated anti-Communist and interventionist foreign policy that set the tone for later administrations.	pp. 868–869, 873–874
	II. Following the attacks of September 11, 2001, U.S. foreign policy and military involvement focused on a war on terrorism, which also generated debates about domestic security and civil rights.	pp. 922–926, 928–934
Key Concept 9.3	Moving into the 21st century, the nation continued to experience challenges stemming from social, economic, and demographic changes.	Chapters 28, 29, 30
	I. The increasing integration of the U.S. into the world economy was accompanied by economic instability and major policy, social, and environmental challenges.	pp. 878–880, 895–896, 899, 911–917
	II. The U.S. population continued to undergo significant demographic shifts that had profound cultural and political consequences.	pp. 884–885, 904

PART II

TOPICAL REVIEW WITH SAMPLE QUESTIONS AND ANSWERS AND EXPLANATIONS

This section is keyed to chapters 1 through 30 in *By the People*.
Part II overviews important information in bullet
form. Use the practice questions to arm yourself thoroughly
for the kinds of test items you will encounter on the AP exam.

Chapter 1
THE WORLD BEFORE 1492

THE PEOPLING OF NORTH AMERICA

- Anthropologists have traced the migration of the first Americans from Asia either by crossing the Bering Strait or by utilizing small boats. This migration occurred between 36,000 and 14,000 years ago during an ice age. Essentially, this ice age created a land strip between Asia and North America that allowed hunters chasing wild game to cross into the new world.
- The migration into the Americas occurred over the course of thousands of years thus resulting in a very diverse and complex pattern of settlement.
- In some regions such as the southwest (present-day United States), spear tips such as those belonging to the Clovis people could be found. In this same region, the Anasazi cultivated crops such as corn and constructed large buildings made of adobe.
- In the eastern region of present-day United States, the Cahokia or Moundbuilders established a settlement that is estimated to have a population of 20,000 to 40,000 and featured agriculture to sustain this population.

THE DIVERSE COMMUNITIES OF THE AMERICANS IN THE 1400s

- The diverse migration patterns of the early Americans resulted in the formation of many different languages and cultures. Yet despite this diversity these settlers shared the same sacred approach to all aspects of life and shared in the concept of community over the individual. Nevertheless, the differing patterns of migration combined with the physical diversity of these settlements led to a different way of life of each region.
- Due to the dry climate in the Southwest, people such as the Pueblos and Hopis used intricate irrigation systems to water their crops. Climate also played a role in the decline of the Cahokia people in that a "Little Ice Age" sapped them of their agricultural producing ability. This in turn led to a struggle between the smaller remaining chiefdoms who wrestled for control of the Mississippi Valley.
- In the Pacific Northwest, the cedars and salmon allowed for housing and food, and in California the abundance of wild foods actually hindered the promotion of settled agriculture and advanced civilization.
- Along the Atlantic Coast, the Iroquois dominated and centered themselves around the area of present-day Syracuse, New York, and in creating a council of five tribes, otherwise known as the Iroquois Confederation, peace was able to prevail under this arrangement (at least among these tribes).
- Another large tribe that occupied the Atlantic Coast was the Algonquian with the Powhatans being the largest within this tribe. The Algonquians developed a sense of permanency with their houses and agriculture.
- South of border of what is now the United States, the three notable civilizations that dominated this region included the Aztecs, the Mayans, and the Incas. Centered in

Tenochtitlan (today Mexico City), the Aztecs created a warlike civilization that used captured enemies as human sacrifices.

- The Mayan civilization in the Yucatan Peninsula of Mexico and became noted for its calendar and written language. The civilization reached its highpoint before the Aztecs.
- Despite the language differences and distances between the peoples of North and South America, trading networks existed and some even expanded over great distances. However, not all of the natives lived in harmony. Given that each tribe believed it represented the center of life, no overall sense of unity amongst the natives as a whole. This lack of unity helped to pave the way for a devastating European invasion.

A CHANGING EUROPE IN THE 1400s

- Long before Columbus was even born, the Vikings had already sailed westward across the Atlantic Ocean, first settling in Greenland and Iceland. Subsequently, Leif Erickson established Vineland in present-day Newfoundland (North America) in 1001. Eventually this colony vanished along with the knowledge that the Vikings had been the first Europeans to make contact with North America.
- The years prior to Columbus's voyage would bring great change that made the prospects of exploring more within the realm of possibility. Yet before these changes occurred, Europeans found themselves recovering from the devastating effects of the Black Death and Hundred Years War.
- The aura of conflict and death that dominated Europe in the 1300s gave way to a flourishing trade with Asia that increased the significance of city-states along the Mediterranean such as Venice, Genoa, and Florence. The Ottoman Turks severely hindered this trade once they captured Constantinople and controlled the surrounding Middle East.
- The result of this trade restriction led Europeans to seek new ways to reach Asia. The Portuguese, under the direction of Prince Henry "the Navigator" led the way in exploring for new routes to Asia. The Portuguese routes would follow the coast of Africa and eventually Vasco de Gama reached India in 1498.
- Through this interaction with Africa, the Portuguese would trade for slaves and perpetuate an institution that had long existed before their arrival. As the Portuguese solidified their trade routes to Asia and led Europe in the realm of exploration, England and France were crippled by the effects of war.
- Meanwhile, Spain also saw conflict as Christians tried to free Spain of Muslim rule which had dominated the Iberian Peninsula for hundreds of years. This dominance was not without its benefits however as the Arabic culture and scientific developments flourished in Spain.
- Nevertheless, the *Reconquista* would finally be achieved in 1492 as the last vestiges of Muslim rule were eradicated from Spain under the monarchy of Ferdinand and Isabella. These same monarchs commissioned Christopher Columbus to find a route Asia that differed from that of the Portuguese.

- Contact with Africa and the Mediterranean civilization had long existed before the Portuguese ventured along this continent. Thousands of years before this, the Romans had attached Northern Africa into its grand empire.
- The Kingdom of Ghana centered at the heart of a lucrative trade route that would see the exchange of slaves, gold, and ivory in return for salt, silk, and other goods. Thereafter, the Kingdom of Mali would see a conversion to Islam, highlighted by the pilgrimage to Mecca by the Malian king, Mansa Musa. Under Musa's reign, scholarship flourished culminated by the establishment of an Islamic university at Timbuktu.
- The strongest military and economic power in West Africa proved to be Songhay, a Muslim empire that respected the traditional customs of those within the kingdom. Like the kingdoms of Mali and Ghana, the strength of Songhay centered on its trade that ultimately reached Egypt, the Middle East, and Europe.
- Below the Kingdom of Songhay were the Kingdoms of Congo and Benin. Congo, through Portuguese missionaries, would actually feature Catholicism mixed with some local traditional beliefs.
- Due to the centrality of the Congo, the Portuguese had a very difficult time invading this region through traditional military means as they were matched by the skilled maneuverings of West Africans in canoes. Consequently, the Portuguese dealt with these inhabitants through trade and commerce instead of conquest.
- A significant portion of the Portuguese trade with West Africa involved the transaction of slaves, though the trafficking of human beings had existed before the Portuguese arrived by at least one thousand years. Since each tribe considered itself to be the center of life, the capturing and selling of other African tribe members did not faze African slave traders. Nevertheless, the Portuguese slave trade not only saw the displacement of African slaves from their homes, but from their cultures as well, especially those headed to the Americas.

ASIA IN THE 1400S

- Unlike other regions of the world where division was strong in the 1400s, China boasted a unified empire that had existed for more than 2,000 years. Under the Emperor Zhu Di, Chinese explorers sailed to South Asia, India, and East Africa, but with a high cost. To be sure, vast amounts of trees were used and many of the sailors never returned.
- In 1424, all Chinese sailing expeditions came to a halt and China would enter a period of isolation for the next 200 years. As a result, China would not be a participant in the exploration and settling of the Americas. This would not be the case with Spain as it prepared to unknowingly change the lives of millions beginning in 1492.

MULTIPLE CHOICE QUESTIONS

1. The earliest people who migrated into North America did so by
   A. Traveling across the Atlantic in large ships.
   B. Crossing the Atlantic from Africa as slaves.
   C. Crossing the Bering Strait during an ice age.
   D. Migrating from South America.

2. The Moundbuilders at Cahokia were known for
   A. Engaging in war with neighboring tribes and using captured soldiers for human sacrifice.
   B. Living in dispersed settlements throughout the Southwest.
   C. Establishing a council of five powerful tribes in the Northeast.
   D. Establishing a settlement with a population that ranged from 20,000 to 40,000 people.

3. What purpose did the Green Corn Dance serve?
   A. to give thanks for the gifts of food amongst the Algonquian-speaking tribes
   B. to signify the importance of irrigation amongst the Anasazi people
   C. to celebrate the unity of Native American and European trade
   D. to rejoice in the introduction of corn to the Iroquois nation

4. Which of the following was NOT true of the Aztecs, Mayans, and Incas?
   A. They all used human sacrifice as part of their religion.
   B. They all featured a high degree of democracy.
   C. They all featured advanced forms of civilization.
   D. They all featured a hierarchal form of government.

5. The fall of Constantinople to the Ottoman Turks in 1453 resulted in
   A. a vast network of open trade that included Europe, Asia, and Africa.
   B. the restriction of land and sea routes across the eastern Mediterranean.
   C. the emergence of Catholicism in Eastern Europe.
   D. war between the Ottoman Empire and a coalition of European and Asian traders.

6. Spanish and English authorities were surprised with slaves from Kongo because
   A. their religious leaders served as intermediaries between divine and human affairs.
   B. they had Catholic beliefs and knowledge of the Catholic Mass.
   C. their directed their warlike nature towards other tribes.
   D. they had vast knowledge of European languages including Spanish and English.

7. The following can be said of African societies EXCEPT
   A. by the threat of superior armies they were forced to engage in a slave trade.
   B. despite the introduction of Catholicism and Islam, traditional beliefs and customs were preserved.
   C. they establish vast trading networks.
   D. their resources attracted outsiders such Europeans and Arabs.

8. What stopped the China from exploring the Americas?
   A. the vast expanse of the Pacific Ocean
   B. the absence of wood for shipbuilding
   C. the presence of several competing rulers
   D. the decision to stop all voyages and business abroad

9. Where did the largest and most sophisticated civilizations exist in the new world before Columbus arrived?
   A. in the Northeast where the Iroquois Nation presided
   B. in the Southwest where Anasazis presided
   C. in Mexico and South America where the Incas, Aztecs, and Mayans presided
   D. in Cahokia within the Mississippi Valley

10. What features best highlight the Anasazi communities?
    A. irrigation networks and large adobe buildings
    B. capturing and sacrificing of enemy tribes
    C. vast network of berry and acorn production
    D. first Natives to introduce the concept of private ownership

11. Which of the following was NOT a characteristic of the North American Indians?
    A. They were very spiritualistic.
    B. They considered themselves to be unified under one Native American race.
    C. They believed in the communal ownership of land.
    D. They adapted to their physical environment to create unique cultures.

12. Why do historians consider the Vikings to be the first to Europeans to reach New World instead of Columbus?
    A. They colonized in Greenland and Iceland between the 800s and 900s.
    B. Their navigation skills landed them in San Salvador in the 1400s.
    C. They established the impermanent settlement of Vineland in 1001.
    D. Columbus never actually reached the New World but settled in Asia instead.

Questions 13-14 refer to the following visual:

13. The settlement of Cahokia refutes the notion that
   A. all Native Americans were spiritual.
   B. all Native Americans were nomadic.
   C. Native Americans could be civilized.
   D. Native Americans were organized.

14. At the apex of Cahokia, the population stood at
   A. less than one thousand.
   B. more than one hundred thousand.
   C. between 20,000 and 40,000.
   D. approximately 1 million.

Questions 15-17 refer to the following excerpt.

In those same days the Onondagas had no peace. A man's life was valued as nothing... At night no one dared leave their doorways...Such was the condition when there was no Great Law...South of the Onondaga town lived an evil-minded man...Moreover, this monster was a devourer of raw meat, even of human flesh...Adodarhoh was the name of the evil man...Notwithstanding the evil character of Adodarhoh the people of Onondaga, the Nation of Many Hills, obeyed his commands. . . .Dekanawida requested some of the Mohawk chiefs to call a council, so messengers were sent out among the people and the council was convened...Dekanawida said, "...We have obtained the consent of five nations. These are the Mohawks, the Oneidas, the Onondagas, the Cayugas, and the Senecas. Our desire is to form a compact for a union of our nations. Our next step is to seek out Adodarhoh. It is he who has always set at naught all plans for the establishment of the Great Peace... " ....Then Dekanawida taught the people the Hymn of Peace ...When the time had come, Dekanawida summoned the chiefs and people together and chose one man to sing the songs before Adodarhoh . . .Then Dekanawida himself sang and walked before the door of Adodarhoh's house. When he finished his song...Adodarhoh was made straight and his mind became healthy...Dekanawida addressed the three nations. "We have now overcome a great obstacle. It has long stood in the way of peace....Now indeed may we establish the Great Peace..."Before we do firmly establish our union each nation must appoint a certain number of its wisest and purest men who shall be rulers, Rodiyaner..." . .Then calling each chief to him he said: "...Now you are Rodiyaner, each of you... You must be patient and henceforth work in unity. Never consider your own interests but work to benefit the people...You have pledged yourselves to govern yourselves by the laws of the Great Peace. All your authority shall come from it. . . .Then did Dekanawida repeat all the rules...devised for the establishment of the Great Peace...Then in the councils of all the Five Nations he repeated them and the Confederacy was established.

15. According to the story, what conditions led to a call for unity?
   A. invasion of the Spanish
   B. the threat of French dominance
   C. constant warfare amongst the natives
   D. preparations for war with the Algonquians

16. Who proved to be the obstacle for peace?
    A. Dekanawida
    B. Rodiyaner
    C. The Five Nations
    D. Adodarhoh

17. The result of this call for unity proved to be
    A. the Five Nations of the Iroquois.
    B. Tecumsuh Confederation.
    C. the Algonquian Tribe.
    D. short term peace.

Questions 16-18 refer to the following excerpt.

After the creation of the earth, all the other animals withdrew into the places...When the first ones died, the Great Hare caused the birth of man from their corpses...These first men...whom hunger had weakened...broke off a branch from a small tree, made a cord with the fibers of the nettle...and armed its end with another sharp stone, to serve them as an arrow; and thus they formed a bow [and arrows] with which they killed small birds. After that, they made viretons [crossbow arrows], in order to attack the large beasts; they skinned these...But as they found only the fat savory, they tried to make fire, in order to cook their meat... they used softer wood, which yielded them fire. The skins of the animals served for their covering. As hunting is not practicable in the winter on account of the deep snows, they invented a sort of racket [snowshoe]...and they constructed canoes...to cross the river...these men...while hunting found the footprints of an enormously tall man...They went on into his territory...they were astonished at seeing there the feet and legs of a man so tall that they could not descry his head; that inspired terror in them... This great colossus...saw the man who had discovered him, whom fear had driven to hide himself in a thicket...The giant said to him, "My son, why art thou afraid? Reassure thyself; I am the Great Hare, he who has caused thee and many others to be born from the dead bodies of various animals. Now I will give thee a companion." Here are the words that he used in giving the man a wife: "Thou, man...shalt hunt, and make canoes, and do all things that a man must do; and thou, woman, shalt do the cooking for thy husband, make his shoes, dress the skins of animals, sew, and perform all the tasks that are proper for a woman." Such is the belief of these peoples in regard to the creation of man.

18. According to the excerpt, the creator of man is
    A. God.
    B. the Great Hare.
    C. all of earth's animals.
    D. the Universe.

19. According to the excerpt, the Great Hare can be considered
    A. fearful.
    B. deceiving.
    C. righteous.
    D. dangerous.

20. Through this version of creation, one can infer
    A. the Indians had a great deal of respect and reverence for all beings of life.
    B. the Europeans would respect this version of creation.
    C. the Europeans would supplement this version of creation with their own.
    D. the roles of Indian men and women would not be clearly defined.

Questions 21-24 refer to the following excerpt.

Precious feather, child,
Eagle woman, dear one,
Dove, daring daughter,
You have labored, you have toiled,
Your task is finished.
You came to the aid of your Mother, the noble lady, Cihuacoatl Quilaztli.
You received, raised up, and held the shield, the little buckler that she laid in your hands: she
your Mother, the noble lady, Cihuacoatl Quilaztli.
Now wake! Rise! Stand up!
Comes the daylight, the daybreak:
Dawn's house has risen crimson, it comes up standing.
The crimson swifts, the crimson swallows, sing,
And all the crimson swans are calling.
Get up, stand up! Dress yourself!
Go! Go seek the good place, the perfect place, the home of your Mother,
your Father, the Sun,
The place of happiness, joy,
Delight, rejoicing.
Go! Go follow your Mother, your Father, the Sun.
May his elder sisters bring you to him: they the exalted, the celestial women,
who always and forever know happiness, joy, delight, and rejoicing, in the company and in the
presence of our Mother, our Father, the Sun; who make him happy with their shouting.
My child, darling daughter, lady,
You spent yourself, you labored manfully:
You made yourself a victor, a warrior for Our Lord, though not without consuming all your
strength; you sacrificed yourself.
Yet you earned a compensation, a reward: a good, perfect, precious death.
By no means did you die in vain.
And are you truly dead? You have made a sacrifice. Yet how else could you have become worthy
of what you now deserve?
You will live forever, you will be happy, you will rejoice in the company and in the presence of
our holy ones, the exalted women. Farewell, my daughter, my child. Go be with them, join them.
Let them hold you and take you in.
May you join them as they cheer him and shout to him: our Mother, our Father, the Sun;
And may you be with them always, whenever they go in their rejoicing.

--Anonymous Aztec "The Midwife has Addressed the Woman who has died in Childbirth"

21. The woman who has died
    A. is criticized for leaving earth too early.
    B. is mourned for leaving her child motherless.
    C. is praised as being brave.
    D. is considered to have died in vain.

22. The use of the term "warrior" to describe the fallen woman
    A. refers to the warrior-like mentality of the Aztecs.
    B. does not reflect women who give birth.
    C. is not used to praise the fallen woman.
    D. is in reference to the woman fighting in the Aztec army.

23. The term "sacrifice" in the poem
    A. is in reference to a literal sacrifice of the woman by Aztec priests.
    B. identifies as a necessary ritual inherent in the Aztec society.
    C. relates to the sacrifice of the child for the Aztec gods.
    D. occurred for an unworthy cause.

SHORT ANSWER QUESTIONS

The development of European exploration in the New World was an event that did not occur quickly.

   a. Choose ONE of the following and explain why your choice represents the event that hindered European exploration in the New World.

   * The Black Death
   * The Hundred Years War
   * The Fall of Constantinople

   b. Contrast your choice against ONE of the other options, demonstrating why that option in not as significant as your choice.

LONG ESSAY QUESTION

What major achievements occurred in Africa, China and the Americas prior to the European exploration of the New World in the 1400s?

ANSWERS AND EXPLANATIONS

Multiple Choice Questions

1. C The last ice age lowered the waters around the Bering Strait essentially creating a land strip between Asia and North America.
2. D Cahokia was considered to be one of the largest settlements in present-day United States before Columbus arrived.
3. A The Algonquians celebrated this dance to give thanks for their harvests.
4. B These civilizations were very hierarchical.
5. B Muslims controlled the land routes to Asia.
6. B The Portuguese had earlier introduced Catholicism in the Kongo.
7. A African societies had long engaged in the slave trade before more powerful forces arrived.
8. D The Chinese decided to be a closed empire prior to the exploration of the Americas.
9. C The Incas, Aztecs, and Mayans all were advanced civilizations.
10. A The Anasazis were well known for irrigating their crops and using adobe to build their dwellings.
11. B Each tribe believed it was the center of importance.
12. C The Vikings reached Vineland which is considered to be part of North America.
13. B Cahokia proved to be a well-established settlement.
14. C Cahokia had a large population.
15. C Warfare led to a constant state of danger amongst the Iroquois.
16. D Adodarhoh stood in the path of peace.
17. A With the unifying efforts of Dekanawida, the Iroquois united into a confederation.
18. B The Great Hare created man from dead animals.
19. C The Great Hare is good to man.
20. A Indians regarded all beings as having spirits.
21. C Giving birth was seen as a very brave act by the Aztecs.
22. A Constant warfare with enemy tribes created a warrior-like mentality amongst the Aztecs.
23. B A woman who sacrificed her life in delivering a child was praised by the Aztecs.

Long Essay Question

What major achievements occurred in Africa, China and the Americas prior to the European exploration of the New World in the 1400s?

(Key topics to focus and elaborate on)
- The extensive trading network established by the Muslims in Africa
- The unified empire of China
- The technology and government of the Aztecs, Mayans, and Incas

Chapter 2
FIRST ENCOUNTERS, FIRST CONQUESTS, 1492-1607

COLUMBUS: THE COLUMBIAN EXCHANGE, AND EARLY CONQUESTS

- The premonition of Columbus towards the natives was clear: They would be exploited to serve the purposes of the crown
- Columbus truly believed he had reached Asia and so named the people he encountered, Indians, after those inhabitants of the East Indies
- The voyages and administration of Columbus probed not to be fruitful because the Tainos rebelled against the Spanish, and the Spanish arrivals complained about the difficulty of living in the New World
- The voyage of Columbus inspired others to follow suit including the Portuguese. In fact, in 1494, the Spanish and Portuguese agreed to the Pope's line of division that split South America between them. After Columbus' journey, Amerigo Vespuccis through his own voyages for Spain and Portugal, claimed that the Europeans had reached a new continent, thus in his honor a new map of the world with the new continent would bear his name, America.
- The treatment of the Indians worsened after Columbus's voyages, and the Spanish brutally murdered many of them. The real threat and overall killer of the native population were diseases carried by the Spaniards. Since the Indians didn't have the immunity to these diseases, they died by the millions.
- The oceanic trail set by Christopher Columbus spurred a shift in trade patterns that dramatically shifted the world. Essentially, the use of oceanic routes that included the Atlantic, Pacific, and Indian Oceans opened up a vast intercontinental network of trade between Europe, Africa, Asia and the Americas that previously seemed unimaginable.
- The heavy trade between Europe and the Americas came to be known as the Columbian Exchange; a trade that would come to include diseases that devastated the Indian population, food that literally changed the diet of the world, and cultures that through intermixing would generate a whole new breed of Americans
- Soon after the Spanish voyages of discovery reached the Americas, a period of armed conquest would see great civilizations such as the Aztecs and Incas destroyed by the 1530s. With the assistance of enemy tribes, Hernan Cortes conquered the Aztec capital of Tenochtitlan led by Montezuma in 1521. Thereafter, on top of this capital, Cortes laid the foundation for a new capital, Mexico City that served as capital of New Spain.
- Shortly after the conquest of the Aztecs, Francisco Pizarro conquered the Incas in South America by 1532. The superiority of weapon technology became very apparent as a much smaller Spanish force defeated a mighty Inca force. Yet, disease played a larger role, as small pox and other ailments ravaged the Aztec and Inca population.
- The most famous criticisms of the Spanish treatment of the Indians came from Bartolome de Las Casas, a Spanish priest who wrote about this mistreatment in Latin America for

over 50 years and urged the Spanish crown to stop the abuses of the conquistadores. Unintentionally, instead of bringing about major reforms, he fueled the Protestant's criticism of Catholic Spain by introducing the concept of the "Black Legend."

A DIVIDED EUROPE: THE IMPACT OF THE PROTESTANT REFORMATION

- In 1517, a German monk named Martin Luther began a massive religious revolution when he questioned the practices of the Catholic Church with his doctrine, Ninety Five Theses. The result of this questioning led to a religious split that became known as the Protestant Reformation
- Protestantism arose along with the rise of nation-states. After years of fighting between Catholics and Protestants, came the Treaty of Westphalia: rulers of each nation-state would choose what religion that state would follow. In effect this created a sense of religious unity within each nation-state, and this in turn affected the pattern of settlement in the Americas.

EXPLORATION AND ENCOUNTER IN NORTH AMERICA: THE SPANISH

- Eventually, various Spanish explorers sought to find riches by exploring North America. Ponce de Leon explored Florida bringing with him African slaves and Puerto Rican Indians, and though he died by an enemy arrow, he helped to establish a Spanish tie to this region.
- The ill-fated Narvaez expedition found by accident the region of Texas, and a few of its survivors, including Alvar Nunez Cabeza de Vaca eventually made their way down to Mexico City fueling the desire for greater exploration and expectations of finding wealth.
- In the Southwestern regions of present-day Arizona and New Mexico, Francisco Coronado and his expedition were met with hostility (1540) and they later fled to parts of Texas, Oklahoma, and Kansas only to be disappointed in not finding any gold.
- Under Hernando De Soto in 1541, Spaniards again explored Florida, and then moved through Tennessee, Alabama, and Arkansas. Like the other Spanish explorers, the De Soto expedition found little that interested them.
- Along the coast of California, Juan Cabrillo found California to be a great place for settlement, and even discovered Monterrey Bay. Yet like the other expeditions, the Cabrillo explorers did not find gold (though they were a lot closer than the other explorers to achieving this) nor did they find a shorter route to China.
- Spain began preparations for settlement in North America but only after rival nations showed interest in this continent. Led by French Protestants, a colony had been established along the St. Johns River in Florida bringing an immediate rebuke from Spanish authorities.
- Menendez de Aviles founded St. Augustine for the Spanish in 1565 making it the oldest European city in present-day United States. Subsequently, Spanish authorities eradicated all traces of French occupation, making Florida solely a Spanish settlement.
- The spirit of Reconquista manifested itself in Florida as those who settled wanted the freedom they enjoyed as soldiers fighting Muslims in Spain. At the same time, St. Augustine would be home to other Europeans who looked to escape religious persecution. Whereas some came to St. Augustine for religious freedom, Franciscans

arrived in Florida to bring about religious conversion amongst the Indians. In general, Florida was left alone as a settlement until it was ceded to the U.S. in 1821.

- Further west, the achievements of Englishman Francis Drake and his presence on the west coast led the Spanish to seize New Mexico. Led by Don Juan de Onate, a group of 400 claimed New Mexico and proceeded to divide it into districts led by priests. Yet peace between the Spanish and the Pueblo Indians didn't last and bloodshed arose in 1598 and continued for decades.

EXPLORATION AND ENCOUNTER IN NORTH AMERICA: THE FRENCH

- In not wanting to be left out by, in 1524 the French commissioned Italian sailor, Giovanni de Verrazano to explore the Atlantic Coast and find a new route to Asia. Through his travels, Verrazano mapped out land between North Carolina and Newfoundland.
- In addition, Jacques Cartier explored the St. Lawrence River in present-day Canada and established a long-lasting trade between the French and the Indians.

EXPLORATION AND ENCOUNTER IN NORTH AMERICA: THE ENGLISH

- The first explorer for the English was John Cabot who explored what was probably Newfoundland and Maine in 1497.
- A few decades later, Henry VIII in seeking dissolution of his marriage to Catherine of Aragon, embraced the Protestant Reformation as a tool to annul this union. Though a new church emerged in England, it was distinctly Catholic.
- Ultimately, Henry's daughter Elizabeth would rule England in a Protestant manner. Alongside Elizabeth's rise to power was her counterpart rival in King Philip II of Spain, and the two grew to be bitter Protestant/Catholic rivals. The defeat of the Spanish in 1588 led England to dominate the Atlantic Ocean, and licensed pirates who worked for the English stole gold and silver indiscriminately from Spanish ships.
- As a launching point for Drake to strike, Sir Walter Raleigh attempted to establish a settlement in North Carolina called Roanoke in the 1580s. Unfortunately for Raleigh, after a few years of no contact with it suppliers, the colonists disappeared and England's first attempt at permanent settlement failed.

MULTIPLE CHOICE QUESTIONS

1. The goal of the Spanish explorations into North America was to
   A. expand the Spanish Empire to include more inhabitants.
   B. seize settlements established by the French.
   C. convert Indians to the Protestant faith.
   D. find treasures in gold and silver.
2. The impact of Columbus's voyages in the New World included
   A. a new oceanic trade amongst all of the continents.
   B. an exchange of disease that wiped out 1/3 of Europe.
   C. a depression in Spain's economy due to the expense of these voyages.
   D. the empowerment of Portugal who sponsored the venture of Columbus.

3. Martin Luther based his protest against the Catholic Church on
    A. the belief that profits of indulgences should remain local.
    B. the Church's insistence that only bishops could interpret the Bible.
    C. the interpretation of what constituted as "good works."
    D. the center of the Catholic Church should be based in Germany.

4. The effect of the Protestant Reformation in Europe was that
    A. a new crusade emerged to remove Muslim forces from the Holy Land.
    B. a Catholic Counter-Reformation would lead to devastating war in Europe.
    C. a link between national unity and religious uniformity became stronger amongst nation-states.
    D. England and the Papacy would establish closer bonds.

5. The critical writings that Bartolome de Las Casas reported on the abuses of the Indians and led to
    A. dramatically better treatment of the Indians by Spanish conquistadores.
    B. the establishment of an international commission geared to eliminate mistreatment of the Indians.
    C. the creation of the "Black Legend" which highlighted the uniqueness of Spanish cruelty.
    D. no response by the Spanish monarchs including Queen Isabella.

6. Instead of finding a "Fountain of Youth" in Florida, Ponce de Leon
    A. coordinated one of the first meetings in present-day US of Native Americans, Africans, and Europeans.
    B. founded a safe haven for the Jews of Portugal.
    C. founded St. Augustine, the first European settlement in present-day U.S.
    D. found large amounts of gold and silver.

7. The exploration of Jacques Cartier along the St. Lawrence River led to
    A. the establishment of English claims in present-day Canada.
    B. a lucrative fur trade with the Indians in that region.
    C. the discovery of New York and Manhattan Island.
    D. a shortcut to Asia.

8. Queen Elizabeth supported the ventures of Francis Drake because
    A. his piracy enriched the English government at the expense of the Spanish.
    B. he established claims to California for the English.
    C. his discovery of North Carolina led to the establishment of England's first settlement.
    D. he established control and English settlement of St. Augustine.

9. The Columbian Exchange did all of the following EXCEPT
    A. decimate the Indian population.
    B. introduce the horse to the Native Americans.
    C. produce offspring in the Americas from vastly different parts of the world.
    D. introduce spiritual deism into the practices of Catholics and Protestants.

10. The intention of Christopher Columbus in sailing west was to
    A. find gold and silver that the Vikings were rumored to have found in North America.
    B. establish a Spanish Empire in the New World that would be based on agriculture.
    C. spread Catholicism to the natives of East India.
    D. find a shorter sea route to Asia.

11. The exploration of Cabeza de Vaca proved that
    A. the natives were eager to establish permanent friendly relations with the Europeans.
    B. gold and silver was plentiful in land north of Mexico.
    C. a great harbor existed in northern California.
    D. the natives ultimately did not trust the Europeans and wanted no permanent contact with them.

12. Under the Treaty of Tordesillas the Pope held that
    a. South America would be divided between Portugal and Spain.
    b. the new land discovered by Columbus would be named America.
    c. Catholicism would replace the religion of the natives in America.
    d. St. Augustine was in fact a Portuguese settlement.

Questions 13-14 refer to the following visual.

How the Savages Roast Their Enemies

13. How would one describe the treatment of their enemies by these Native Americans?
    A. an eye for an eye
    B. brutally savage
    C. fair and justified
    D. somewhat excessive

14. In what way could the Europeans utilize this savagery to meet their own agenda?

41

A. They could conquer enemies within Europe with this same savagery.
B. The Europeans could bring the principles of civility to the New World.
C. Europeans can brutally conquer the Native Americans with this same savagery.
D. They could use this as actions to avoid in their behavior.

Questions 15-17 refer to the following excerpt.

On the Island Hispaniola was where the Spaniards first landed…Christians perpetrated their first ravages and oppressions against the native peoples. This was the first land in the New World to be destroyed and depopulated by the Christians, and here they began their subjection of the women and children, taking them away from the Indians to use them and ill use them…Among these gentle sheep, gifted by their Maker with the above qualities, the Spaniards entered as soon as soon as they knew them, like wolves, tiger and lions which had been starving for many days, and since forty years they have done nothing else; nor do they afflict, torment, and destroy them with strange and new, and divers kinds of cruelty, never before seen, nor heard of, nor read of. . . . . The Christians, with their horses and swords and lances, began to slaughter and practice strange cruelty among them. They penetrated into the country and spared neither children nor the aged, nor pregnant women, nor those in child labour, all of whom they ran through the body and lacerated, as though they were assaulting so many lambs herded in their sheepfold… They made bets as to who would slit a man in two, or cut off his head at one blow: or they opened up his bowels. They tore the babes from their mothers' breast by the feet, and dashed their heads against the rocks. Others they seized by the shoulders and threw into the rivers, laughing and joking, and when they fell into the water they exclaimed: "boil body of so and so!" They spitted the bodies of other babes, together with their mothers and all who were before them, on their swords… They made a gallows just high enough for the feet to nearly touch the ground, and by thirteens, in honour and reverence of our Redeemer and the twelve Apostles, they put wood underneath and, with fire, they burned the Indians alive.

--Bartolomé de Las Casas, "On the Island of Hispaniola"

15. The account of Bartolomé de Las Casas described
    A. the total disregard the Indians had for the well-being of the Spanish.
    B. the methods of torture the Indians would use against their Spanish captives.
    C. the monotheistic nature of the Indian religion.
    D. the willingness of the Spanish to use sheer brutality to subdue the Indians.

16. According to de Las Casas
    A. the natives never resisted the Spanish.
    B. not even women and children were spared of the Spanish brutality against the Indians.
    C. the Spanish only resorted to flogging to subdue the Indians.
    D. the Spanish only used the theme of Biblical obedience to control the Indians.

17. The irony of the Spanish treatment of the Indians according to de Las Casas was

A. the Spanish instructed the essence of Christianity on the very people they terrorized.
B. the Indians already expected to be tortured by a strange people and thus accepted it.
C. English Protestants would use this mistreatment as deterrence for mistreatment of the Natives in North America.
D. despite this mistreatment, the Spanish never found the gold and silver riches they were seeking.

Questions 18-20 refer to the following excerpt.

The people of this island, and of all the others that I have found and seen, or not seen, all go naked, men and women, just as their mothers bring them forth; although some women cover a single place with the leaf of a plant, or a cotton something which they make for that purpose. They have no iron or steel, nor any weapons; nor are they fit thereunto; not be because they be not a well-formed people and of fair stature, but that they are most wondrously timorous. They have no other weapons than the stems of reeds in their seeding state, on the end of which they fix little sharpened stakes. Even these, they dare not use; for many times has it happened that I sent two or three men ashore to some village to parley, and countless numbers of them sallied forth, but as soon as they saw those approach, they fled away in such wise that even a father would not wait for his son. And this was not because any hurt had ever done to any of them:-but such they are, incurably timid. It is true that since they have become more assured, and are losing that terror, they are artless and generous with what they have, to such a degree as no one would believe but him who had seen it. Of anything they have, if it be asked for, they never say no, but do rather invite the person to accept it, and show as much lovingness as though they would give their hearts. And whether it be a thing of value, or one of little worth, they are straightways content with whatsoever trifle of whatsoever kind may be given them in return for it. I forbade that anything so worthless as fragments of broken platters, and pieces of broken glass, and strapbuckles, should be given them; although when they were able to get such things, they seemed to think they had the best jewel in the world. . . .

--Christopher Columbus, Letter to Luis de Sant' Angel

18. In terms of military strength, Columbus views the Indians as
    A. extremely powerful due to their population.
    B. weak because of their primitive weapons.
    C. formidable because of overbearing persona.
    D. invincible because of their use of iron and steel.

19. In terms of material items, Columbus regards the Indians as
    A. extravagant with their well-designed wardrobes.
    B. pompous with the use of their gold and silver jewelry.
    C. innocent with their lack of clothing and appreciation of trifle gifts.
    D. arrogant with their rejection of Spanish gifts.

20. An overall impression that Columbus had of the Indians was

A. they were timid and respectfully fearful of the Spanish.
B. they were unapproachable.
C. they were belligerent towards the Spanish.
D. they were more arrogant than the French or English.

Questions 21-23 refer to the following excerpt.

...wee sawe two companies of boates of wilde men going from one land to the other: their boates were in number about fourtie or fiftie. One part of the which came to the said point, and a great number of the men went on shore making a great noise, beckening unto us that wee should come on land, shewing us certaine skinnes upon pieces of wood, but because we had but one onely boat, wee would not goe to them, but went to the other side lying in the Sea: they seeing us flee, prepared two of their boats to follow us, with which came also five more of them that were comming from the Sea side, all which approched neere unto our boate, dancing, and making many signes of joy and mirth, as it were desiring our friendship, saying in their tongue Napeu tondamen assurtah, with many other words that we understood not. But because (as we have said) we had but one boat, wee would not stand to their courtesie, but made signes unto them that they should turne back, which they would not do, but with great furie came toward us: and suddenly with their boates compassed us about: and because they would not away from us by any signes that we could make, we shot off two pieces among them, which did so terrifie them, that they put themselves to flight toward the sayde point, making a great noise...The next day part of the saide wilde men with nine of their boates came to the point and entrance of the Creeke, where we with our ships were at road. We being advertised of their comming, went to the point where they were with our boates: but so soone as they saw us, they began to flee, making signes that they came to trafique with us, shewing us, such skinnes as they cloth themselves withall, which are of small value. We likewise made signes unto them, that we wished them no evill: and in signe thereof two of our men ventured to go on land to them, and cary them knives with other Iron wares, and a red hat to give unto their Captaine. Which when they saw, they also came on land, and brought some of their skinnes, and so began to deale with us, seeming to be very glad to have our iron wares and other things, stil dancing with many other ceremonies, as with their hands to cast Sea water on their heads. They gave us whatsoever they had, not keeping any thing, so that they were constrained to goe backe againe naked, and made us signes that the next day they would come againe, and bring more skinnes with them....

--Journal of Jacques Cartier on meeting the Micmac Indians

21. Upon encountering the Micmac Indians on their boats, Cartier regarded them to be
    A. highly civilized and sophisticated.
    B. essentially wild men.
    C. as advanced as the Spanish or French.
    D. extremely aggressive and warlike.

22. According to Cartier, the weapons of the French

A. did not deter the Micmac's from approaching the French.
B. were inferior to that of the Micmacs.
C. terrified the Micmacs once they were sounded off.
D. only made the Micmacs more curious of the French.

23. The impression that Cartier had from the exchange of gifts with the Micmacs was
    A. they were extremely generous people
    B. they did not appreciate the French offerings
    C. they could not be trading partners
    D. the Micmacs were reluctant to trade gifts

SHORT ANSWER QUESTIONS

England proved to be much slower in exploring the New World than the Spanish.

a. Choose ONE of the following and explain why your choice represents the event that most significantly impacted this slow development:

- The Black Death
- Ongoing war between England and France
- The Protestant Reformation

b. Contrast your choice against ONE of the other options, demonstrating why that option is not as significant as your choice.

LONG ESSAY QUESTION

Why didn't the Spanish settle extensively in North America as they did in Central America, South America, and in the Caribbean?

ANSWERS AND EXPLANATIONS

Multiple Choice Questions

1. D The Spanish did not hide their pursuit for valuable metals.
2. A The discovery of the New World opened up a vast world-wide trading network.
3. B Protestants wanted congregations to have local control of interpreting the Bible.
4. C Nation-states would embrace the Catholic or Protestant faith.
5. C Protestants used the writings of de Las Casas to criticize the Catholic country of Spain.
6. A Ponce de Leon brought together a mixture of races into Florida.

7. B Cartier's discovery led to a rich fur trade with the Indians.
8. A Drake stole fortunes of gold and silver from Spanish ships.
9. D Christians did not accept the deism of the Indians.
10. D Columbus believed he could find a shorter route to Asia by sailing across the Atlantic Ocean.
11. D The natives did what they could to force the Europeans out of their domains
12. A The Treaty of Tordesillas split South America between Portugal and Spain.
13. B The Europeans believed the Indians were truly savages even without scenes such as that in the illustration.
14. A The Europeans used this savagery to justify their own brutal treatment of the Indians.
15. B The Spanish stopped at nothing to subdue the Indians.
16. B Indian women and children also suffered the brutal wrath of the Spanish.
17. A After slaughtering the Indians into submission, they taught whoever was left Christianity.
18. B Columbus as well as the Spanish in general regarded the Indians and their weapons to be weak and easily penetrable.
19. C Columbus marveled at how easily pleased the Indians could be when given small gifts.
20. A Columbus believed the Indians would be easily subdued.
21. B Cartier first description of the Indians he encountered was essentially "wilde."
22. C Weapons that were fired by the French made the Micmacs turn back.
23. A Like all natives, they were easily pleased by whatever gift they received from the Europeans.

Long Essay Question

Why didn't the Spanish settle extensively in North America as they did in Central America, South America, and in the Caribbean?

(Key topics to focus and elaborate on)
- Spanish exploration in the Southwest
- Spanish exploration in Florida
- Spanish exploration of the Mississippi Valley

Chapter 3
SETTLEMENTS, ALLIANCES, AND RESISTANCE 1607-1718

Throughout much of the 1500s, much of North America was ignored by Europeans. By the late 1600s, England and France had laid the framework for vast settlement along the east coast, Canada, and Mississippi River regions. Meanwhile, the Native Americans developed mixed relations with these new coming Europeans.

THE ENGLISH SETTLE IN NORTH AMERICA

- In 1607, the Virginia Company sent 105 men to find riches, a shortcut to Asia, and to build settlements in North America. The location of this settlement known as Jamestown proved to be disastrous and because of previous experience with Europeans, the natives did not display friendly overtures to these settlers.
- Fortunately, through the leadership of John Smith, the Powhatan did not destroy Jamestown and actually assisted in its early survival. Yet, between 1609-1610, the colonists of Jamestown went through a starving time that almost completely wiped out the colony.
- Frustration continued to loom amongst the Virginia Company until the colony began to cultivate tobacco as a cash crop. This cultivation marked a shift from trade with the Indians to agriculture based on the hands of English servants and African slaves.
- As the need for agricultural labor emerged in North America, King James saw a need for Protestant extremists, known as Puritans and Separatists, to leave England. The Pilgrims became the first such group to leave England and settle in Plymouth in 1620.
- Their initial struggles became much easier when an Indian named Squanto introduced the Pilgrims to the various food sources in the region, marking a period of peace celebrated by the first Thanksgiving in 1621.
- The Puritans, with their Massachusetts Bay Company, migrated to North America near present-day Boston. Led by John Winthrop, the intentions of this group aimed a creating a "City upon a Hill" to serve as a model religious colony for those in England. Since the basis of the colony consisted of understanding the Bible, the Puritans highly stressed the importance of education and literacy.
- Dissension within the Massachusetts Bay Colony emerged as Puritans across the Connecticut River formed their own colony, Roger Williams was banished for promoting the concept of separation of church and state, and Anne Hutchinson met the same fate as Williams when she claimed she received direct revelations from God.
- The strict nature of church membership eventually gave way to a Halfway Covenant that ultimately expanded church membership thereby allowing more in Massachusetts to vote.
- North of Virginia, George Calvert established the first proprietary colony that served as a haven for Catholics. In order to attract more settlers, Maryland granted freedom of

worship to all Christians including Protestants. Following the lead of Virginia, Maryland also utilized a headright system to cultivate tobacco.

- Throughout the colonial period, various colonies would merge with others such as Plymouth being absorbed by Massachusetts Bay.
- The colony of New York was actually a Dutch colony (named New Netherland, with Manhattan Island being named New Amsterdam) that essentially served as a trading base for the fur trade. The colony eventually became diverse with various languages and religions.
- In 1664, the Duke of York (brother of King Charles II) sent a fleet to seize New Amsterdam with little resistance of this English takeover. With this takeover New York-- as it was renamed quickly--became one of England's most valuable North American colonies.
- Just west of New York, William Penn established the proprietary colony of Pennsylvania as a safe haven for Quakers in 1682. The Quakers practiced a form of Christianity that featured no formal clergy, equal rights of women, and pacifism.
- In the lower region of the colonies, Charles II established Carolina as a way to both reward his supporters and to thwart Spain from expanding into the realm of the English colonies. Essentially, Carolina had two sections: a northern section that consisted of small farmers, and a southern section that consisted of large rice plantation owners. In 1729, Carolina officially split into North Carolina and South Carolina.
- Georgia was founded by James Oglethorpe as a second-chance colony for debtors in England in 1733. The colony also served as a buffer between Spanish Florida and the rest of the English colonies.
- Throughout the English colonization of North America, slavery existed and was first introduced in 1619 at Jamestown. Initially, the fate of an African slave in the North American colonies was unclear as to whether he/she would remain a slave for life. Some African slaves such as Anthony Johnson would eventually own land. In the north, slavery became an urban institution with work that was servant-like.

ENGLAND'S WARS, ENGLAND'S COLONIES

- The tensions that erupted into Civil Wars in England fueled the English migration into the Americas. Yet tension and violence also erupted in the English colonies in North America.
- Charles I's strict adherence to Angelicalization was at odds with the Puritan-dominated Parliament which in turn led to a civil war in England in the 1640s. The beheading of Charles I culminated the war and thereafter England was without a monarch until 1660.
- Charles II reestablished the monarchy in 1660 and a number of British colonies in North America emerged during his reign.
- Not long after settlement, the Puritans at the Massachusetts Bay Colony clashed with neighboring Indians. These tensions between English could be with intermarriage being rare between the two groups, a reluctance of the natives to convert to Christianity, and the ever-growing European population in the New World.
- King Philip's War displayed the voracity the English and natives had towards each other. The war quickly spread into mass bloodshed as seen at the Great Swamp Fight in 1675.

Essentially the struggle became a conflict of annihilation with the intent of each side to destroy each other.

- Virginia also saw conflict, but the tension rose more due to economic tensions than to the conflicts seen in New England. When clashing between natives and Virginian colonists arose in 1675, Nathaniel Bacon led a retaliatory militia that the governor William Berkeley did not support.
- Thus, a civil war broke out between the forces of Berkeley and Bacon ending with Bacon and his men's defeat. Since Bacon's forces in part consisted of dissatisfied indentured servants, landowners subsequently looked to slave labor to tend to their crops.

FRANCE TAKES CONTROL OF THE HEART OF THE CONTINENT

- A demand for beaver furs accelerated the settlement of the French in North America. In effect, this trade inflamed rivalries between the Natives who now had European weapons to destroy each other.
- The rise of the fur trade spurred the rise of French settlements such as Quebec and Montreal. New France, as it came to be known, was constantly under the threat of the English-allied Iroquois.
- In the 1670s, Louis Joliet and Jacques Marquette travelled along the Mississippi River and discovered such villages as Chicago. Robert De La Salle travelled along the Mississippi River and named the region of the mouth of the river Louisiana after King Louis XVI.
- In bolstering their claim to the mouth of the Mississippi River, France developed the settlements at La Mobile (Mobile, Alabama) and New Orleans, a settlement that saw the emergence of slavery within it quarters.

DEVELOPMENTS IN SPANISH COLONIES NORTH OF MEXICO

- The Spanish controlled Santa Fe and the surrounding area with an iron hand and this ultimately led to the Pueblo Revolt in 1680. Eventually, through compromise, the Spanish regained control of Santa Fe.
- To deter the threat of a French invasion in Texas, the Spanish established the city of San Antonio, and to deter the incursion of the English and Russians, the Spanish established a series of forts in California.

MULTIPLE CHOICE QUESTIONS

1. The settling of Jamestown faced numerous obstacles including all of the following EXCEPT
    A. the pollution of salt and swamp water with fresh water.
    B. a lack of community responsibility.
    C. uneasy alliance with the Powhatans.
    D. constant attack from the Spanish.

2. The Mayflower Compact represented
    A. an agreement by the Pilgrims to get along with each other.
    B. a contract to divide land according to wealth.
    C. the establishment of a hierarchy at Plymouth.
    D. the Puritans code of living.

3. The colony of Maryland proved to be England's first
    A. permanent colony in North America.
    B. proprietary colony in North America.
    C. colony established for Quakers.
    D. colony established for Puritans.

4. The colony of New York previously belonged to
    A. the French.
    B. the Quakers.
    C. the Spanish.
    D. the Dutch.

5. King Philip's War represented
    A. the growing tension between Protestants and Catholics.
    B. a war fueled by the rivalry of Queen Elizabeth and King Philip.
    C. the tension between freedmen and landowners.
    D. growing tensions between the Indians of New England and English settlers.

6. The Pueblo Revolt proved to be
    A. a telling sign to the Spanish that Santa Fe would be difficult to control
    B. major warfare amongst the rival tribes in the Southwest
    C. a slave uprising near St. Augustine
    D. rebellion of the Indians in the Caribbean

7. In exploring for the French, Robert de La Salle
    A. established Quebec.
    B. established Montreal.
    C. claimed the settlement of Chicago.
    D. claimed land that would be named Louisiana.

8. Bacon's Rebellion reflected
   A. animosity between freed indentured servants and land owners.
   B. a rift in church leadership in Massachusetts.
   C. the dissatisfaction with Governor Andros.
   D. a slave rebellion in South Carolina.

9. The Restoration in England resulted in
   A. the placement of Oliver Cromwell into power.
   B. the coronation of James II.
   C. the establishment of several British North American colonies.
   D. the beheading of Charles I.

10. The colony that proved to be a buffer between the English colonies and Spanish Florida, and also a second chance colony for debtors was
    A. South Carolina.
    B. Georgia.
    C. Delaware.
    D. Pennsylvania.

Questions 11-12 refer to the following visual.

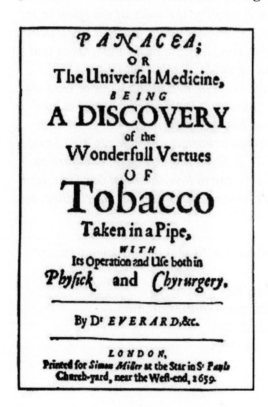

11. The tobacco from which this advertisement is based on stemmed from
    A. Georgia.
    B. Virginia.
    C. Massachusetts.
    D. New York.

12. The glorification of tobacco ultimately resulted in
    A. the extinction of the Native Americans.
    B. better health amongst Europeans.
    C. heavy diversification of food crops in the Chesapeake.
    D. extreme economic gap between the wealth and poor in the Chesapeake.

Questions 13-15 refer to the following excerpt.

Now the only way to avoid this shipwreck and to provide for our posterity is to follow the counsel of Micah, to do justly, to love mercy, to walk humbly with our God. For this end we must be knit together in this work as one man, we must entertain each other in brotherly affection, we must be willing to abridge ourselves of our superfluities for the supply of others' necessities, we must uphold a familiar commerce together in all meekness, gentleness, patience, and liberality, we must delight in each other, make others' conditions our own, rejoice together, mourn together, labor and suffer together, always having before our eyes our commission and community in the work, our community as members of the same body So shall we keep the unity of the spirit in the bond of peace...For we must consider that we shall be as a city upon a hill, the eyes of all people are upon us. So that if we shall deal falsely with our God in this work we have undertaken and so cause Him to withdraw His present help from us, we shall be made a story and byword throughout the world, we shall open the mouths of enemies to speak evil of the ways of God and all professors for God's sake, we shall shame the faces of many of God's worthy servants, and cause their prayers to be turned into curses upon us till we be consumed out of the good land whither we are going...And to shut up this discourse with that exhortation of Moses, that faithful servant of the Lord in His last farewell to Israel, Deut. 30., Beloved there is now set before us life and good, death and evil, in that we are commanded this day to love the Lord our God, and to love one another, to walk in His ways and to keep His commandments and His ordinance, and His laws, and the articles of our covenant with Him...

--John Winthrop "A Model of Christian Charity"

13. John Winthrop intended to shape the Massachusetts Bay Colony
    A. in a manner that the settlers would work for the good of the community.
    B. to promote individual profit through commercialism.
    C. to inspire piety through personal divine inspiration.
    D. so that church and state would be separated.

14. "…we shall be a city on a hill" refers to
   A.   Winthrop's belief that the Puritans will rise to new heights of financial success.
   B.   the argument that Heaven can be attained in Massachusetts.
   C.   the notion that no matter what transgressions the Puritans in Massachusetts make, they will still be superior to those in England.
   D.   the belief that the Puritans in Massachusetts will provide a model of Christian faith for the world to see.

15. In "City on a Hill" Winthrop is urging the colonists to
   A. be frugal, self-sufficient, and not a burden to society.
   B. be a model example of the Anglican Church.
   C. honor the covenant to follow the Ten Commandments.
   D. incessantly follow the rituals of the Catholic Church.

Questions 16-18 refer to the following excerpt.

That the Heathen people amongst whom we live, and whose Land the Lord God of our Fathers hath given to us for a rightfull Possession, have at sundry times been plotting mischievous devices against that part of the English Israel which is seated in these goings down of the Sun, no man that is an Inhabitant of any considerable standing can be ignorant. Especially that there have been (nec injuria) jealousies concerning the Narragansets and Wompanoags, is notoriously known to all men. And whereas they have been quiet until the last year, that must be ascribed to the wonderful Providence of God, who did (as with Jacob of old, and after that with the Children of Israel) lay the fear of the English [colonists] and the dread of them upon all the Indians. The terror of God was upon them round about. Nor indeed had they such advantages in former years as now they have in respect of Arms and Ammunition, their bows and arrows not being comparably such weapons of death and destruction as our guns and swords are, with which they have been unhappily furnished. Nor were our sins ripe for so dreadful a judgment until the Body of the first generation was removed, and another Generation risen up which hath not so pursued, as ought have been, the blessed design of their Fathers, in following the Lord into this Wilderness, whilst it was a land now sown. . . .

--Increase Mather

16. Mather believed that the English had "rightfull Possession" of land in New England because
   A. they purchased it from the local native tribes.
   B. their neighboring Indian tribes were heathen.
   C. the jealousies of the Indians nullified their right to own territory.
   D. God gave the Indians possession of the land but their fall from grace thwarted their legal possession.

17. According to Mather, a factor that led to warfare included all of the following EXCEPT
    A. the Indians possessed arms and ammunition.
    B. jealousy of the Narragansets.
    C. jealousy of the Wampanoags.
    D. sins of the English in New England.

18. According to Mather, the generation that followed the first
    A. did not have the same religious zeal as the first.
    B. was far more pious than the first.
    C. was equal to the task in following the Lord into the wilderness.
    D. was without sin.

Questions 19-21 refer to the following excerpt.

Now we all found the losse of Captain Smith, yea his greatest maligners could now curse his losse: as for corne, provision and contribution from the Salvages, we had nothing but mortall wounds, with clubs and arrowes; as for our Hogs, Hens, Goats, Sheepe, Horse, or what lived, our commanders, officers & Salvages daily consumed them, some small proportions sometimes we tasted, till all was devoured; then swords, armes, pieces, or any thing, wee traded with the Salvages, whose cruell fingers were so oft imbrewed in our blouds, that what by their crueltie, our Governours indiscretion, and the losse of our ships, of five hundred within six moneths after Captain Smiths departure, there remained not past sixtie men, women and children, most miserable and poore creatures; and those were preserved for the most part, by roots, herbes, acornes, walnuts, berries, now and then a little fish: they that had startch in these extremities, made no small use of it; yea, even the very skinnes of our horses. Nay, so great was our famine, that a Salvage we slew, and buried, the poorer sort tooke him up againe and eat him, and so did divers one another boyled and stewed with roots and herbs: And one amongst the rest did kill his wife, powdered [salted] her, and had eaten part of her before it was knowne, for which hee was executed, as hee well deserved; now whether shee was better roasted, boyled or carbonado'd [grilled], I know not, but of such a dish as powdered wife I never heard of. This was that time, which still to this day we called the starving time; it were too vile to say, and scarce to be beleeved, what we endured.

--John Smith "The Starving Time"

19. After Smith left Jamestown, he described the trade between the settlers and the Indians as
    A. the same as when he occupied the colony.
    B. not cordial and unfriendly.
    C. better than when he was there.
    D. suspicious but still prosperous.

20. "…but of such a dish as powdered wife I never heard of…" refers to
    A. the cannibalistic nature of the Powhatans.
    B. the acceptable solution to famine.
    C. the desperation of the famished colonists.
    D. a form of execution for heresy.

21. The "Starving Time" that Smith describes
    A. was a result of the settlers intentions for moving to Jamestown.
    B. was an exclusive result of the Powhatan's suspicion toward the settlers at Jamestown.
    C. was a tragedy that could not be avoided.
    D. was a failed covenant for community by the Jamestown settlers.

SHORT ANSWER QUESTIONS

The establishment of slavery in the Chesapeake Bay region became well entrenched by the 1700s.

  a. Choose ONE of the following and explain why your choice represents the event that most significantly impacted this establishment.

   - Bacon's Rebellion
   - The development of the slave trade to the Americas
   - The development of tobacco

  b. Contrast your choice against ONE of the other options, demonstrating why that option is not as significant as your choice.

LONG ESSAY QUESTION

Why didn't the English colonies in North America follow a pattern of uniformity such as that of the Spanish colonies in the Americas?

ANSWERS AND EXPLANATIONS

Multiple Choice Questions

1. B Initially, the Powhatans helped the settlers at Jamestown to survive.
2. A Being outside of England's jurisdiction, the Pilgrims created their own agreement to get along.
3. B Lord Baltimore became the first proprietor of England's North American colonies.

4. D   The Dutch established a lucrative fur trading colony known as New Netherland.
5. D   Tensions between New Englanders and Indians grew in the late 1600s.
6. A   Maintaining control of Santa Fe (even losing it at one point) was a challenge.
7. D   Land around the mouth of the Mississippi River would be name after King Louis.
8. A   Nathaniel Bacon represented freed indentured servants who had little hope for financial prosperity.
9. C   Charles II distributed land in the New World to those who were loyal to his father Charles I.
10. B   Georgia was wedged between Spanish Florida and the British colonies and became a place for debtors from England as well.
11. B   Virginia was the first English colony in North America to have tobacco.
12. D   The wealthy owned most of the land that contained the tobacco.
13. A   The Puritans led by Winthrop worked to benefit the community as a whole.
14. D   Winthrop wanted the make the Puritan colony a model for other Christians to follow.
15. C   In being a Christian model for others, the Puritans in Massachusetts had to follow the Ten Commandments.
16. B   Mather essentially believed that New England was made for the Puritans.
17. E   The English were never really successful in converting the Indians to Christianity.
18. A   Time and commerce influenced New Englanders to be less pious.
19. B   John Smith's absence influenced relations with the Powhatans in a negative way.
20. C   Extreme hunger led to cannibalism in Jamestown.
21. A   The colonists intended to get rich and not establish a surviving settlement.

Long Essay Question

Why didn't the English colonies in North America follow a pattern of uniformity such as that of the Spanish colonies in the Americas?

(Key topics to focus and elaborate on)
- Different motives to migrate.
- Different climate amongst the colonies.
- No system of protocol for colonization amongst the British monarchs.

Chapter 4
CREATING THE CULTURE OF BRITISH NORTH AMERICA, 1689-1754

- The libel case against John Peter Zenger ended in Zenger's right to freedom of the press spurring a network of newspapers that promoted a sense of unity amongst the British colonies.
- As the colonies matured, a sense of distrust of British rule began to emerge.

ENGLAND'S GLORIOUS REVOLUTION AND "THE RIGHTS OF ENGLISHMEN," 1689

- The ouster of James II during the Glorious Revolution in 1689 sparked a demand for more rights in both England and its colonies as the new monarchs, William and Mary, had to rule England within the limits of Constitutional law.
- As a supporter of the Glorious Revolution, John Locke argued that people would support or reject governments depending on whether these governments protected their rights.
- The effect of the Glorious Revolution in the colonies would be the ouster of a hated governor in the Dominion of New England, the dissolution of this dominion, and a liberty of conscience in Massachusetts.
- Under this revolution, Catholicism suffered in that New England did not allow for its practice in its region and ironically Catholics could not hold public office in Maryland.

THE PLANTATION WORLD: FROM A SOCIETY WITH SLAVES TO SLAVE SOCIETY

- By the late 1600s, slavery became a dominant institution in the South and the status of slaves became permanent for Africans. Even children of white fathers but African mothers were subject to a life of slavery.
- Despite the dominance of slavery in the Southern colonies, only a small percentage of the slave trade found its way to the North American British colonies because most slave traders directed the transfer of slaves to the Caribbean and South America.
- The sale of slaves became a brutal as all traces of humanity disappeared with the transit of slaves through the Middle Passage from Africa to the New World. This horror is vividly described by African slave, Olaudah Equiano.
- Life in the South was not much better for slaves because they were subject to torture, floggings, and even death.
- Slave owners constantly lived in fear of revolts such as the Stono Rebellion in which slaves in South Carolina rose up in attempts to reach Spanish Florida in 1739.

STABILITY AND INSTABILITY IN AMERICAN AND BRITISH WORLDS

- The British American colonies created a great sense of wealth especially those owing plantations in the South. Yet despite this prosperity, there proved to be a great sense of instability in the colonies.

THE SALEM WITCH TRIALS OF 1692

- The Salem Witch Hunts had underlying tensions that served as a volatile background to this hysteria. Fear of Indian attacks, jealousy of the poor towards the prosperous, and the role of women in New England society provided the context of these witch hunts.
- In total, 20 people were executed during the Salem Witch Hunts in 1692, but after closer examination of the hysteria, colonial leaders in Massachusetts halted the proceedings, thereby bringing an end of executions for religious purposes in North America.

WOMEN'S LIVES

- Although there were opportunities for social interaction amongst women in the cities, most of the North American colonists lived in isolated farms.
- Yet even in rural areas, women did have the chance to interact with each other.
- Often times, women discussed issues of medical care and child-rearing.
- Some women had tremendous responsibilities because their husbands were often travelling extensively.

THE GROWTH OF CITIES: PHILADELPHIA, NEW YORK, BOSTON, CHARLESTON

- After 1700, the population in the colonies exploded with cities such as Boston, Philadelphia, New York, and Charleston experiencing tremendous growth. These cities served as important centers of trade and culture for the colonies.
- The trade between England and the British West Indies proved to be very lucrative, and with vaccination for small pox, these cities became safer as well.

COMMERCIAL ATTITUDES, COMMERCIAL SUCCESS-MERCANTILISM AND THE NEW TRADING ECONOMY

- England's intent was to establish a mercantilist system that would draw raw materials from the colonies and establish colonial markets for English manufactured goods. As a result, the British passed the Navigation Acts in the 1660s to ensure that only British trade would find its way to the colonies and American raw goods would only be sent to England.
- The mercantilist system eventually created a Triangular Trade that involved the British colonies of North America, England, and Africa. This trade did not favor the colonies and

thus loopholes in the system (legal and illegal) would be found and utilized to generate colonial wealth.

- Within this trading system, a wealth of information was exchanged as the colonies became an international center point of ideas, and common interests amongst the colonists also developed.

CHANGING SOCIAL SYSTEMS

- Colonial development nurtured a hierarchical trend of deference in which a gentlemen class dominated over a class of mechanics (people who worked because they had to support themselves/families), servants, and slaves.
- This rise of deference was not without its critics as a new middle class emerged by 1720.

A CHANGING RELIGIOUS LANDSCAPE-FROM THE HALFWAY COVENANT TO THE FIRST GREAT AWAKENING

- The belief that the colony served as a basis for a divine mission evolved into a period where diversity of Protestant sects became prevalent and the intellectual pursuits of the Enlightenment led many to seek reason rather than faith.
- Amidst this waning of religious interest lay a new divine presence that came to be known as the Great Awakening.
- This awakening consisted of a series of religious revivals led by Jonathan Edwards who convinced many to convert to a new relationship with God, and George Whitefield who came from England to spread the word of God.
- The Great Awakening cut across many societal lines and led to creation of religious institutions such as Yale, Dartmouth, and Princeton.

ONGOING WARS IN EUROPE AND BRITISH NORTH AMERICA

- The rivalry between England and France continued from 1689 to 1815 and found its way into North America as the English feared the encirclement of their colonies by the French. Essentially, war proved to be a fact of life for the English colonists, especially since the French allied themselves with Indians who attacked during various episodes of this conflict.
- King William's War and Queen Anne's War highlighted how tensions between European rivals, in particular England and France, could be played out in the colonies and how Native Americans such as the Iroquois could become entangled in these conflicts.
- By the 1700s, many natives tried to distant themselves from this rivalry, and some Iroquois even switched to the French influence in Canada.
- In the Carolinas, resistance of the Tuscaroras against white settlement and then later the Yamasee and Creeks would be thwarted when the English allied with the Cherokees who relied on British goods through trade.
- Whereas the War of Jenkin's Ear saw England dominate Spain in the Atlantic and Caribbean in 1739. King George's War between England and France saw more fighting between European colonists in North America along with their Indian allies. Thereafter the French and Indian War between 1754 and 1763 saw more of the same type of fighting

but with a convincing British victory that earned England the claim to all of French Canada.

THE UNIFYING EFFECTS OF THE WARS ON BRITISH COLONIES

- The wars in the 1700s promoted a sense of patriotism amongst the British colonists, but also generated a sense of independence amongst the colonies through both the rise of colonial militias and the strengthening of independent colonial governments.
- Benjamin Franklin tried to build a sense of unity amongst these colonies with his Albany Plan, but both the colonies and England feared the consequences of this unity. However, as a consequence of the French and Indian War, the union between England and her British colonies in North America would deteriorate to the point of no return.

MULTIPLE CHOICE QUESTIONS

1. The case of John Peter Zenger resulted in
   A. the execution of Zenger for treason.
   B. the banning of colonial newspapers.
   C. a key victory for freedom of the press.
   D. the destruction of colonial assemblies

2. The group that suffered the most during the Glorious Revolution was
   A. Puritans in Parliament.
   B. Catholics in England and the colonies.
   C. Colonial assemblies in New England.
   D. Protestants in Maryland.

3. In his *Second Treatise on Government*, John Locke argued that
   A. powers of monarchs are justified by divine right.
   B. the people can remove a legislative power that is distrustful.
   C. the powers of a nation's government must be separate.
   D. the Glorious Revolution represented unbounded tyranny.

4. The story of Olaudah Equiano represents
   A. the suffering that slaves faced while on the Middle Passage.
   B. the transition from being a slave in Africa to indentured servitude in America.
   C. the flourishing slave trade in West Africa.
   D. the culture of Brazilian slavery.

5. The following all proved to be underlying tensions of the Salem Witch Trials EXCEPT
    A. Indian attacks against English settlers in New England.
    B. tensions between poor residents in Massachusetts and their prosperous counterparts.
    C. the societal roles of assertive women in New England.
    D. previous experiences with massive hysterical witch hunts.

6. The growth of cities such as New York, Philadelphia, Boston, and Charleston can be attributed to all of the following EXCEPT
    A. the presence of deep harbors.
    B. the dominance of British trade.
    C. the demand for goods from the British West Indies.
    D. the rise of inter-colonial trade.

7. England passed the Navigation Acts in order to
    A. free the colonies to allow more trade and generate more revenue.
    B. flow the direction of wealth from the colonies to England.
    C. only allow the colonies to receive raw materials from England.
    D. ensure that colonial goods would be sold only from colonial ships.

8. Mechanics in the British North American colonies were
    A. indentured servants from England.
    B. slaves who worked in the cities.
    C. workers such as farmers and tradespeople.
    D. gentlemen who served in colonial assemblies.

9. The preaching of Jonathan Edwards during the First Great Awakening
    A. made individuals ignore their sinful ways.
    B. led many to undergo deeply emotional conversion experiences.
    C. embraced anti-intellectual religion.
    D. encouraged individuals to seek out religious truths by pure faith alone.

10. The wars between European rivals between 1689 and 1815
    A. entangled the Native Americans into allied partnerships with England and France.
    B. were fought exclusively on European soil.
    C. were fought solely by England and France.
    D. had no impact on the British North American colonies.

11. During the early 1700s, conflict with Native Americans in Carolina led colonial officials to
    A. seek an alliance with the Creeks.
    B. reward the Tuscarora for their loyalty to the colony.
    C. seek an alliance with the powerful Cherokees.
    D. establish a safe haven for the Yamasees.

12. The purpose of Benjamin Franklin's Albany Plan of Union was to
   A. prepare the colonies for independence.
   B. encourage the independent nature of the colonies.
   C. create a unified government with a 'president general" to oversee the colonies.
   D. send a list of grievances to England's Parliament.

Questions 13-14 refer to the following illustration.

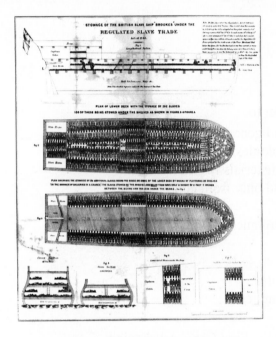

13. The slave ship shown represents
   A. a ship headed towards England.
   B. the horrors of the Middle Passage.
   C. the desire to pack in families within these ships.
   D. the inefficient nature of the Portuguese.

14. The illustration depicts all of the following EXCEPT
   A. the value of the slaves for traders.
   B. the inhumane nature of the slave trade.
   C. the misery of being captured and sold into slavery.
   D. opportunity in the New World for a better life.

Questions 15-17 refer to the following excerpt.

The first object that saluted my eyes when I arrived on the coast was the sea, and a slave ship, which was then riding at anchor, and waiting for its cargo. These filled me with astonishment, that was soon converted into terror, which I am yet at a loss to describe...I was immediately handled and tossed up to see if I was sound, by some of the crew; and I was now persuaded that I had got into a world of bad spirits, and that they were going to kill me. Their complexion too, differing so much from ours, their long hair, and the language they spoke, which was very

different from any I had ever heard, united to confirm me in this belief...I asked...if we were not to be eaten by those white men with horrible looks, red faces, and long hair...
In a little time after, amongst the poor chained men, I found some of my own nation...They gave me to understand we were to be carried to these white people's country to work for them....we were landed up a river a good way from the sea, about Virginia county, where we saw few of our native Africans, and not one soul who could talk to me.

--Olaudah Equiano

15. Olaudah Equiano's description of the slave ship
    A. reflected the horrors of the slave trade.
    B. symbolized a slave trade that was exclusively stayed in Africa.
    C. displayed the familiarity that African slaves had with the Europeans.
    D. illustrated the sense of humanity that slave traders had towards Africans.

16. The journey of Olaudah Equiano
    A. would see a total unification of African slaves from the same tribes in America.
    B. ended in a lifetime of slavery in Virginia.
    C. reflected the ease towards freedom that most Africans could obtain in America.
    D. described the loneliness that African slaves in America often felt.

17. Equiano's experience of the Middle Passage demonstrated
    A. the desire for Europeans to convert the Africans to civilized beings.
    B. the rise of indentured servitude in the Americas.
    C. the demand for slave labor in the Americas.
    D. the desire of Africans to discover a new world.

Questions 18-20 refer to the following excerpt.

Almost every natural man that hears of hell, flatters himself that he shall escape it: he depends upon himself for his own security; he flatters himself in what he has done, in what he is now doing, or what he intends to do. Every one lays out matters in his own mind how he shall avoid damnation, and flatters himself that he contrives well for himself, and that his schemes will not fail. They hear indeed that there are but few saved, and that the greater part of men that have died heretofore are gone to hell; but each one imagines that he lays out matters better for his own escape than others have done. He does not intend to come that place of torment; he says within himself, that he intends to take effectual care, and to order matters so for himself as not to fail...But the foolish children of men miserable delude themselves in their own schemes, and in confidence in their own strength and wisdom; they trust to nothing but a shadow...

--Jonathan Edwards, "Sinners in the Hands of an Angry God"

18. According to Edwards, why does every natural man believe he will escape hell?
    A. Because he has received divine intervention.
    B. Because God has already saved him.
    C. Because the natural man is entitled to Christianity.
    D. Because the natural man lays out schemes for himself that will not fail.

19. According to Edwards, there are *"but few saved"* because
    A. those that were not saved already knew their fate.
    B. the unsaved did not properly lay out matters for himself.
    C. the unfortunate who were not saved didn't have confidence in their fate.
    D. the unsaved adopted the deism of the surrounding Native Americans.

20. The inference of Edwards's "Sinners In the Hands of an Angry God" is that
    A. man is doomed to damnation.
    B. man cannot pave their own way to Heaven through his own means.
    C. man can actually live a life that is too holy to be saved.
    D. man can actually outwit death with the right scheme.

Questions 21-23 refer to the following excerpt.

The reason why men enter into society, is the preservation of their property; and the end why they chuse and authorize a legislative, is, that there may be laws made, and rules set, as guards and fences to the properties of all the members of the society, to limit the power, and moderate the dominion, of every part and member of society...whenever the legislators endeavor to take away, and destroy the property of the people, or to reduce them to slavery under arbitrary power, they put themselves into a state of war with the people, who are thereupon absolved from any farther obedience, and are left to the common refuge, which God hath provided for all men, against force and violence. Whensoever therefore the legislative shall transgress this fundamental rule of society; and either by ambition, fear, folly or corruption, endeavor to grasp themselves, or put into the hands of any other, an absolute power over the lives, liberties, and estates of the people; by this breach of trust they forfeit the power the people had put into their hands...and it devolves to the people, who have a right to resume their original liberty, and by the establishment of a new legislative, provide for their own safety and security...

--John Locke *The Second Treatise of Government*

21. Locke's excerpt reflects his belief that
    A. legislative bodies reign supreme.
    B. legislative bodies can be replaced.
    C. monarchs are protected by divine right.
    D. once legislative bodies are formed the people are powerless.

22. According to Locke, the purpose of a *legislative* is to
    A. impose taxation for war.
    B. empower the purse of the monarch.
    C. protect the property of the people.
    D. ravage the coffers of foreign nations.

23. The context of Locke's excerpt from the *Second Treatise of Government* is
    A. the Glorious Revolution.
    B. Bacon's Rebellion.
    C. Queen Anne's War.
    D. imposition of the Navigation Acts

SHORT ANSWER QUESTIONS

The events known as the Salem Witch Trials resulted in the executions of twenty in Massachusetts.

a. Choose ONE of the following and explain why your choice represents the event that most significantly impacted these trials and executions:
   - Indian attacks in New England
   - Emergence of class resentment
   - The establishment of strict gender roles in New England

b. Contrast your choice against ONE of the other options, demonstrating why that option is not as significant as your choice.

LONG ESSAY QUESTION

How did the events such as the Glorious Revolution and wars in Europe affect the colonies in North American?

ANSWERS AND EXPLANATIONS

Multiple Choice Questions

1. C The Zenger Trial planted the seeds of freedom of the press, but not without risks.
2. B New England banned Catholicism and Catholics lost political power in Maryland.
3. B Locke argued that people can replace governments that do not protect their rights.
4. A Slaves such as Equiano suffered horrific treatment during their Middle Passage journey.
5. D Although executions for witchcraft had occurred in the colonies prior to 1692, the hysteria of these executions never matched that of the Salem Witch Trials.
6. D Early forms of industrialism had not existed yet.
7. B These acts were part of England's mercantilist plan to enrich the mother country at the expense of the colonies.

8. C   Mechanics had to work in farming and trading to earn a living.
9. D   Through his religious logic, Edwards aimed to move listeners to convert.
10. A   Native Americans found partnerships with either England and France to inevitable and to their advantage.
11. C   By allying with the Cherokees, Carolina officials were able to remove enemy Indian tribes.
12. C   Franklin dreamed of uniting the colonies but still under the auspices of England.
13. B   Slave ships traveling along the Middle Passage were very often inhumanely packed.
14. D   Enduring the Middle Passage only guaranteed most often than not a life of slavery.
15. A   Equiano's description of his journey put words to the horrors of slave ships.
16. D   Slaves from different tribes often couldn't speak to each other.
17. C   Equiano's journey represented that of millions who would be slaves in the Americas.
18. D   According to Edwards, man thinks he always has the perfect plan to get to Heaven.
19. B   Man believes that to be saved, one must plan better than others.
20. B   Even with planning, Edwards believes one must live a holy life as well.
21. B   According to Locke, legislative bodies that don't protect property can be replaced.
22. C   People are entitled to protection of property by legislative bodies.
23. A   Locke wrote his treatise in support of the Glorious Revolution.

Long Essay Question

How did the events such as the Glorious Revolution and wars in Europe affect the colonies in North American?

(Key topics to focus and elaborate on)
- Catholics face discrimination.
- Dominion of New England dissolved.
- Wars created alliances amongst the Native Americans.

Chapter 5
THE MAKING OF A REVOLUTION, 1754-1783

PRELUDES TO REVOLUTION

- The struggle for the Ohio Valley between the French and English culminated in a war that was fought on several continents. The result of this war led to British dominance in North America as the French lost control of Canada and land east of the Mississippi River. However the debt incurred during this war would leave several countries, especially England, in deep and severe debt.
- For Native Americans, the result of this French and Indian War proved to be devastating in that there was no longer a European rival to take advantage for each tribe's well-being and security. Furthermore, struggles such as Pontiac's Rebellion highlighted the conflict that continued between Indians and white settlers.
- In trying to protect commitments the English made to several tribes, the English established a Proclamation Line to keep colonial settlement east of the Appalachian Mountains. No doubt, this drew the immediate ire of land-hungry colonists.
- By the 1760s, for many such as the Paxton Boys, the Indians were seen as a race that had to be eliminated.
- In the 1760s, British authorities agreed that the colonies should pay their fair share of the cost of war against the French. The colonists disagreed.

THE REVOLUTION WAS IN THE MINDS OF THE PEOPLE

- The call for independence did not happen overnight because many colonists opposed the American Revolution and stayed loyal to England, and others had different conclusions as to what independence would translate to.
- Undoubtedly, John Locke and French philosophers influenced the minds of those seeking independence or engaging in rebellion against authorities such as England or royal governors.
- Ultimately, the American Revolution led to other revolutions such as those in Europe and Latin America.
- The spirit of revolution even extended to religion as the Great Awakening resulted in a direct challenge to the leaders of the major Protestant denominations.
- The open nature of the sea seemed to inspire the road to revolution as acts of rebellion occurred throughout the eastern seaboard. No doubt, the British practice of impressment drew fierce opposition from the colonists.
- The 1760s brought a host of Parliamentary acts that fueled colonial resistance, including the Sugar Act, the Stamp Act, the Revenue Acts, the Tea Act of 1773, and the Intolerable Acts.

- The Stamp Act brought spirited resistance since it affected the cost of legal and commercial documents. The act also led to the formation of the Sons of Liberty which led heated protests against colonial officials. Essentially, for the first time, the protest created a sense of unity amongst the colonists throughout the thirteen colonies.
- Following the repeal of the Stamp Act, in 1767 Parliament passed the Revenue Act that imposed a new round of taxes on various items. In a display a of force and to encourage obedience to this act, the British sent troops to cities such as New York and Boston. The presence of British Redcoats in Boston ultimately led to fatal incident known as the Boston Massacre in 1770 that saw the killing of five colonists.
- After the Boston Massacre, a committee of correspondence formed to encourage resistance to British rule in other colonies.
- In 1773, after Parliament passed the unpopular Tea Act, poorly disguised Bostonians dumped British tea in to the Boston Harbor leading the British to close the Boston Harbor.
- Women belonging to the Daughters of Liberty also played a role in resistance to the British by spinning their own cloth to lighten the effect of boycotting British goods.
- In the back country, Regulators resisted royal authorities, and conflicts with Indians were exacerbated by British policies that hindered expansion.
- Along with the rally cry of "No taxation without representation" the colonists complained that they had no voice in the passage of various acts such as the Quebec Act, Quartering Act, and Intolerable Acts.
- The First Continental Congress formed in 1774 to unite against what they perceived to be British tyranny, and share their grievances against the crown. Although few in this congress were ready for independence, the delegates agreed to meet again in relations with England did not improve.
- As talks of rights and freedom from oppression stirred in the colonies, the issue of slavery brought talks of contradiction and hypocrisy to the forefront of the discussion

WAR FOR INDEPENDENCE

- By 1775, the colonists engaged in warfare with the British army as the seeds of revolution had been planted.
- Sensing the growing rebellion, British troops set out to Concord to seize militia arms but were met at Lexington at what became the first battle of the Revolution.
- The Battle of Lexington, along with the subsequent Battle of Bunker Hill (actually fought at Breed's Hill) outside of Boston solidified the inevitable break with England.
- The fight between Britain and its rebelling colonists brought slaves to both sides of the conflict. Many slaves joined the side of the British, and some even gained their freedom after the war, and some in the northern colonies fought for the Patriots as well.
- In 1775, the Second Continental Congress convened, formed the Continental Army, and placed George Washington in command of this force, but it took the Congress a year to decide if it wanted independence or not.
- Thomas Paine's *Common Sense* became an influencing factor in 1776 that swayed many in the colonies to lean towards independence.

- By the summer of 1776, Congress appointed a committee to draft a declaration for the independence of the colonies, with Thomas Jefferson writing the first draft. After revisions, Congress adopted Jefferson's revision Declaration of Independence on July 4, 1776. A year later, Congress adopted the Articles of Confederation as the nation's first national government.
- Initially, the war seemed to be a clear mismatch between Washington's Continental Army which appeared much weaker than the British army. Yet Washington's effectiveness as a military commander proved to overcome many of the extreme obstacles that the Patriots faced. His knowledge of the British troops led him to lead his forces with an effective but non-traditional tactic of fighting that would eventually wear down the British army.
- Despite forcing the British to evacuate from Boston, Washington suffered a devastating defeat in New York and had to eventually retreat to Philadelphia, but not without gaining an impressive victory at Trenton, New Jersey.
- The Battle of Saratoga in New York proved to be a turning point in the war in that it brought the assistance of both France and Spain to the Patriot cause.
- Despite suffering from hunger and the cold at Valley Forge, Washington's troops received valuable training and eventually more supplies.
- By 1778, the English decided to attack the south to split it from the rest of the colonies.
- No doubt assistance from France and Spain proved to be vital but these countries needed some convincing that the colonists were serious and capable of gaining independence. Ultimately both of these countries declared war on England and turned this event into a world war.
- During the course of the war, whereas the Iroquois sided with the British and clashed with Washington's forces, thousands of Loyalists fought for the British and faced the wrath of their Patriot counterparts.
- In providing assistance to Washington's troops the Ladies Associations sewed thousands of shirts for the soldiers and other women helped to harvest farms of Patriots who were off and fighting.
- Towards the latter part of the war, the British made significant gains in the south, until the Patriots won an impressive battle at Cowpens, South Carolina. Thereafter, in 1781, Lord Cornwallis lost the decisive Battle of Yorktown in Virginia which led many in England to believe that the war would end in favor of the Patriots.
- Two years later, under the Treaty of Paris, England recognized the independence of the United States.

MULTIPLE CHOICE QUESTIONS

1. The French and Indian War resulted in
   A. French dominance in the Ohio Valley.
   B. extinction of the Iroquois tribe.
   C. England's loss of the southern colonies.
   D. deep and severe English debt.

2. Pontiac's goal was
   A. to eliminate the colonists from the frontier of Massachusetts.
   B. to eliminate white people from the Ohio Valley.
   C. to create better trade relations with the English.
   D. to follow the British call for assimilation.

3. All of the following experienced major revolutions after the French and Indian War EXCEPT
   A. the British North American colonies.
   B. France.
   C. Latin American countries in Central and South America.
   D. England.

4. The difference between the British taxes imposed on the colonists in the 1760s and taxes of earlier periods was
   A. The taxes of the 1760s aimed to deter trade with foreign nations.
   B. The latter taxes aimed to provide the colonists with more services for the general welfare.
   C. The taxes of the 1760s aimed to generate revenue for the British government.
   D. Earlier taxes aimed to generate money for an indebted England.

5. Which of the following act(s) would make a lawyer in colonial America the most resentful?
   A. The Quartering Act
   B. The Stamp Act
   C. The Revenue Act
   D. The Tea Act

6. The Daughters of Liberty assisted in the revolution by
   A. harassing British Redcoats.
   B. preparing the tar and feathers for tax collectors.
   C. weaving homespun cloth to assist in colonial boycotts.
   D. cooking for the soldiers.

7. John Adams believed revolution was possible if
   A. the Loyalists switched sides.
   B. the British supported the freedom of the slaves.
   C. farmers agreed with mob action in cities such as Boston.
   D. the right declaration was formed.

8. During the War for Independence, slaves
   A. fought for both the English and the Patriots.
   B. gained the trust of George Washington from the beginning of the war.
   C. were emancipated by the Second Continental Congress.
   D. stayed with their masters throughout the entire war.

9. In fighting the British, Washington
    A. fought a conventional-style war against the British.
    B. confront the British forces head-on at every opportunity.
    C. wore down British forces with non-traditional tactics.
    D. led a large standing professional army.

10. In his pamphlet, *Common Sense*, Thomas Paine argued
    A. that the colonists must stay loyal to England.
    B. the sensibility of living under British protection.
    C. that the colonists enjoyed the trading partnership with England.
    D. that the colonies must separate from England.

Questions 11-12 refer to the following visual.

11. The members of what body signed the Declaration of Independence?
    A. First Continental Congress
    B. Second Continental Congress
    C. Committee of Correspondence
    D. Sons of Liberty

12. The final draft of the Declaration of Independence did not include
    A. the abolition of slavery.
    B. a list of complaints against King George III.
    C. the influence of John Locke.
    D. a formal statement of separation from England.

Questions 13-15 refer to the following excerpt.

Most Excellent Governor:

Permit us, in behalf of ourselves, and many others of His Majesty's most dutiful and loyal subjects within the County of Anson, to take the earliest opportunity of addressing your Excellency, and expressing our abomination of the many outrageous attempts now forming on this side of the Atlantick...It is with the deepest concern...that we see in all public places and papers disagreeable votes, speeches and resolutions, said to be entered into by our sister Colonies, in the highest contempt...of the legislative authority of Great Britain. . . We are truly invigorated with the warmest zeal and attachment in favour of the British Parliament, Constitution and Laws, which our forefathers gloriously struggled to establish...We are truly sensible that those invaluable blessings which we have hitherto enjoyed under His Majesty's auspicious Government, can only be secured to us by the stability of his Throne...And we do assure your Excellency that we are determined, by the assistance of Almighty God, in our respective stations, steadfastly to continue His Majesty's loyal Subjects, and to contribute all in our power for the preservation of the publick peace... And may the Almighty God be pleased to direct his Councils, his Parliament, and all those in authority under him, that their endeavors may be for the advancement of piety, and the safety, honour and welfare of our Sovereign and his Kingdoms, that the malice of his enemies may be assuaged, and their evil designs confounded and defeated; so that all the world may be convinced that his sacred person, his Royal family, his Parliament, and our Country, are the special objects of Divine dispensation and Providence.

--Letter to Governor Josiah Martin from Inhabitants of Anson County (North Carolina)

13. The Loyalist author of this letter more than likely supported the British government because
    A. colonial dissenters had less experience in government matters.
    B. Loyalist inhabitants probably enjoyed economic stability under British rule.
    C. independence did not appeal to the Loyalists.
    D. the dissenters were too strict in the application of constitutional law.

14. The use of the words "God-Almighty" indicates that the author of this letter was not influenced by
    A. Divine Right.
    B. the Enlightenment.
    C. the Tories.
    D. Parliament.

15. According to the author of this letter
    A. England is an overbearing country aimed at destroying the colonies.
    B. England cannot effectively rule the colonies.
    C. all rights of the Loyalists in Anson County will be lost if the rebels are victorious.
    D. the Loyalists will be accepted by the rebels after the conflict is over.

Questions 16-18 refer to the following excerpt.

. . . On the evening of Monday, being the fifth current, several soldiers of the 29th Regiment were seen parading the streets with their drawn cutlasses and bayonets, abusing and wounding numbers of the inhabitants.

A few minutes after nine o'clock four youths, named Edward Archbald, William Merchant, Francis Archbald, and John Leech, jun., came down Cornhill together...the two former were passing the narrow alley leading to Murray's barrack in which was a soldier brandishing a broad sword of an uncommon size...A person of mean countenance armed with a large cudgel bore him company. Edward Archbald admonished Mr. Merchant to take care of the sword, on which the soldier turned round and struck Archbald on the arm, then pushed at Merchant and pierced through his clothes inside the arm close to the armpit and grazed the skin. Merchant then struck the soldier with a short stick he had; and the other person ran to the barrack and brought with him two soldiers, one armed with a pair of tongs, the other with a shovel. He with the tongs pursued Archbald back through the alley, collared and laid him over the head with the tongs. The noise brought people together; and John Hicks, a young lad, coming up, knocked the soldier down but let him get up again; and more lads gathering, drove them back to the barrack where the boys stood some time as it were to keep them in. In less than a minute ten or twelve of them came out with drawn cutlasses, clubs, and bayonets and set upon the unarmed boys and young folk who stood them a little while but, finding the inequality of their equipment, dispersed. On hearing the noise, one Samuel Atwood came up to see what was the matter...and when the boys had dispersed he met the ten or twelve soldiers aforesaid rushing down the alley towards the square and asked them if they intended to murder people? They answered Yes, by G-d, root and branch! With that one of them struck Mr. Atwood with a club which was repeated by another.. Retreating a few steps, Mr. Atwood met two officers and said, gentlemen, what is the matter? They answered, you'll see by and by. Immediately after, those heroes appeared in the square, asking where were the boogers? where were the cowards? But notwithstanding their fierceness to naked men, one of them advanced towards a youth who had a split of a raw stave in his hand and said, damn them, here is one of them. But the young man seeing a person near him with a drawn sword and good cane ready to support him, held up his stave in defiance; and they quietly passed by him up the little alley by Mr. Silsby's to King Street where they attacked single and unarmed persons till they raised much clamour, and then turned down Cornhill Street, insulting all they met in like manner and pursuing some to their very doors. Thirty or forty persons, mostly lads, being by this means gathered in King Street, Capt. Preston with a party of men with charged bayonets, came from the main guard to the commissioner's house, the soldiers pushing their bayonets, crying, make way! They took place by the custom house and, continuing to push to drive the people off, pricked some in several places, on which they were clamorous and, it is said, threw snow balls. On this, the Captain commanded them to fire; and more snow balls coming, he again said, damn you, fire, be the consequence what it will! One soldier then fired, and a townsman with a cudgel struck him over the hands with such force that he dropped his firelock; and, rushing forward, aimed a blow at the Captain's head which grazed his hat and fell pretty heavy upon his arm. However, the soldiers continued the fire successively till seven or eight or, as some say, eleven guns were discharged.

--Description of the Boston Massacre from the *Boston Gazette*

16. Who did the British soldiers clash with prior to using their bayonets?
    A. revolutionary leaders angered by their presence
    B. angry store merchants who were bitter at the Townshend Acts
    C. the Sons of Italy who were organizing a massive protest
    D. Boston youth who were irritated by the soldiers presence

17. What context surrounded the occupation of British Redcoats in Boston?
    A. anger sparked by the Stamp Act
    B. anger and resentment against the Townshend Acts
    C. clashing between Redcoats and Patriots at Lexington
    D. the infamous Boston Tea Party

18. What proved to be the final act of provocation that led the soldiers to fire their weapons after Captain Preston commanded "Damn you, fire, be the consequence what it will!"?
    A. The presence of minutemen rushing to the scene
    B. Snowballs being thrown at the soldiers
    C. Angry Bostonians firing at the soldiers with bayonets
    D. A slew of insulting curses directed at the soldiers

Questions 19-21 refer to the following excerpt.

There is [a] late act of Parliament, which seems to me to be . . . destructive to the liberty of these colonies, . . . that is the act for granting duties on paper, glass, etc. It appears to me to be unconstitutional. ...The Parliament unquestionably possesses a legal authority to regulate the trade of Great Britain and all its colonies. Such an authority is essential to the relation between a mother country and its colonies and necessary for the common good of all. He who considers these provinces as states distinct from the British Empire has very slender notions of justice or of their interests. We are but parts of a whole; and therefore there must exist a power somewhere to preside, and preserve the connection in due order. This power is lodged in the Parliament, and we are as much dependent on Great Britain as a perfectly free people can be on another. ..have looked over every statute relating to these colonies, from their first settlement to this time; and I find every one of them founded on this principle till the Stamp Act administration. All before are calculated to preserve or promote a mutually beneficial intercourse between the several constituent parts of the Empire. And though many of them imposed duties on trade, yet those duties were always imposed with design to restrain the commerce of one part that was injurious to another, and thus to promote the general welfare. . . . Never did the British Parliament, till the period abovementioned, think of imposing duties in American for the purpose of raising a revenue. . . . This I call an innovation, and a most dangerous innovation...That we may be legally bound to pay any general duties on these commodities, relative to the regulation of trade, is granted. But we being obliged by her laws to take them from Great Britain, any special duties imposed on their exportation to us only, with intention to raise a revenue from us only, are as much taxes upon us as those imposed by the Stamp Act. . . . It is nothing but the edition of a former book with a new title page, . . . and will be attended with the very same consequences to American liberty...Sorry I am to learn that there are some few persons, [who] shake their heads with solemn motion, and pretend to wonder what can be the meaning of these letters. . . . I will now tell the gentlemen. . . . The meaning of them is to convince the people of these colonies that they are at this moment exposed to the most imminent dangers, and persuade them immediately, vigorously, and unanimously to exert themselves, in the most firm, but most peaceable manner for obtaining relief. The cause of liberty is a cause of too much dignity to be sullied by turbulence and tumult. It ought to be maintained in a manner suitable to her nature. . . . I hope, my dear countrymen, that you will in every colony be upon your guard against those who may at any time endeavour to stir you up, under pretences of patriotism, to any measures disrespectful to our sovereign and our mother country. Hot, rash, disorderly proceedings injure the reputation of a people as to wisdom, valour and virtue, without procuring them the least benefit. . . .Every government, at some time or other, falls into wrong measures. They may proceed from mistake or passion. But every such measure does not dissolve the obligation between the governors and the governed. The mistake may be corrected, the passion may pass over. It is the duty of the governed to endeavour to rectify the mistake and appease the passion. They have not at first any other right than to represent their grievances and to pray for redress. . .

--John Dickinson, from *Letters from a Farmer in Pennsylvania* (1768)

19. According to Dickinson, the colonies in 1768
    A. were still bound to the Mother Country of England.
    B. were not obligated to follow the instruction of England.
    C. were no longer subjects of England.
    D. were ripe for independence.

20. The tone of Dickinson's letter indicates
    A. that the damage England inflicted on the colonies was irreparable.
    B. cautious protest of the Stamp Act was in order.
    C. that furious protest and revolt must be enacted against England.
    D. England was completely justified in passing the Stamp Act.

21. In his letter, Dickinson indicated that
    A. the Stamp Act was constitutional because Parliament passed it.
    B. the Stamp Act was the same as any other law that Parliament imposed on the colonies.
    C. the purpose of the Stamp Act was to raise revenue and not regulate trade.
    D. the Stamp Act was to deter trade with foreign countries.

SHORT ANSWER QUESTIONS

The Treaty of Paris established the official formation of the United States.

    a. Choose ONE of the following and explain why your choice represents the event that most significantly impacted this establishment.

- The French and Indian War
- The Stamp Act Crisis
- Battle of Lexington

    b. Contrast your choice against ONE of the other options, demonstrating why that option is not as significant as your choice.

LONG ESSAY QUESTION

What enabled Washington's ragtag army to defeat the British during the War for Independence?

ANSWERS AND EXPLANATIONS

Multiple Choice Questions

1. D Although England won this war, they found themselves in deep debt afterward.
2. B Like many other Indians, Pontiac wanted to revisit a time when the white man did not exist in his territory.
3. D England did not experience major upheaval as seen in other parts of the world.
4. C In order to raise pay for war debt, England needed to raise revenue.
5. B Lawyers relied on documents for their practice and documents were subject to the Stamp tax.
6. C As part of the boycott of British goods, protesters would buy homespun material.
7. C After the passage of the Intolerable Acts, farmers began to worry that like the Boston Harbor, the British could shut their business as well.
8. A Although slaves most notable fought for the British, they did serve the ranks of the Patriots as well.
9. C Knowing that the Patriots couldn't fight a traditional style of war, Washington looked to make the British military grow weary of the war.
10. D Paine's call for independence influenced many to push for separation with England.

11. B The Second Continental Congress pushed for independence after the clash at Lexington.
12. A The signers of the Declaration of Independence were leery of turning the American Revolution into a radical upheaval of society.
13. B Many inhabitants of the English colonies benefited economically under the rule of England.
14. B The reasoning of the Enlightenment tended to undermine religious doctrine.
15. C Many feared that the rebels would turn lawless and not respect established property rights if independence was gained.
16. D Youth gangs in Boston often harassed British Redcoats.
17. B Bostonians were especially hard hit by the effects of the Townshend Acts.
18. B After previous skirmishes, the throwing of snowball proved to be the last straw of provocation for the British Redcoats.

19. A In being more conservative than his revolutionary counterparts, Dickinson pleaded caution and feared a break with England.

20. B In not wanting to damage relations with England, Dickinson urged protesting of the Stamp Act to be civil.
21. C Dickinson agreed that the Stamp Act differed from other taxes in that it looked to raise money instead of regulating trade.

Long Essay Question

What enabled Washington's ragtag army to defeat the British during the War for Independence?

(Key topics to focus and elaborate on)
- Leadership and commitment of Washington
- Support from France and Spain
- England's logistical and commitment difficulties

Chapter 6
CREATING A NATION, 1783-1789

- The American Revolution resulted in different endings for people of different circumstances.

THE STATE OF THE NATION AT WAR'S END

- Though inequality still existed after independence, acceptance of it proved to be less common after the American Revolution.

FOR THE REVOLUTIONARY ARMY OFFICERS: THE NEWBURGH CONSPIRACY

- The immediate years after Yorktown led to frustration for soldiers who had no money. The army at Newburgh petitioned a new government that could not raise revenue. A rift in Congress formed between those who wanted a strong central government to raise taxes, and those who opposed this idea.
- Officers demanded a quicker response and the Newburgh Addresses threatened more aggressive action that alarmed Washington.
- Through Washington's influence, the threat of a *coup d'etat* was averted and funds eventually made their way to the officers.

FOR POOR WHITE FARMERS: SHAYS'S REBELLION

- After the war, many former soldiers, as well as other residents in Massachusetts faced tremendous economic hardship and demanded economic relief from the state legislature. When the legislature refused, armed farmers led by Daniel Shays shut down the courts to stop the processing of foreclosures in 1786.
- The rebellion then aimed to overthrow the state government but was suppressed by the state militia.
- The rebellion terrified the elite of the nation and led to the call for a stronger national government that could prevent any similar actions from occurring.

FOR WHITE SETTLERS IN OHIO AND THE NORTHWEST TERRITORY

- England's loss of the Ohio Valley to the new nation opened the doors for extensive white settlement.
- As part of settlement towards the west, Congress (under the Articles of Confederation) passed ordinances to systematically settle the Northwest, thus leading to the creation of several states in this territory.
- Further south the states of Kentucky, Tennessee, Alabama, and Mississippi were established as slave states.

FOR AMERICAN INDIANS

- Just as disaster followed the fate of the Indians after the French and Indian War, so too was disaster the fate of Indians after the Revolution.
- The new government did not recognize England's treaty with the Iroquois and fighting between this tribe and other tribes against white settlers persisted well into the 1790s. This was especially the case after Iroquois leader, Joseph Brant, organized a confederation of tribes to lead violent resistance against white settlement.

FOR SLAVES, FORMER SLAVES, AND THOSE WHO CLAIMED OWNERSHIP OF THEM

- In the spirit of revolution and independence, Benjamin Banneker, a free African American in a letter to Jefferson pointed to the contradiction the Declaration of Independence which did not include the freedom from slavery.
- Even in the North, the disappearance of slavery moved at a painstakingly slow pace.
- Nevertheless, a free black population began to emerge in even in states such as Maryland, Virginia, and North Carolina.
- Slaves began to perform different tasks and slave owners encouraged reproduction for the purpose of selling adolescent slaves to needed markets.
- In the lower south, slaveholders strictly denied the language of freedom while the slave population of Georgia and South Carolina exploded.

FOR WOMEN: THE RISE OF REPUBLICAN MOTHERHOOD

- During the American Revolution, women of all walks of life faced challenges, especially Loyalists who supported the British. At the same time, new expectations and behavior arose from women.
- An ideology known as Republican Motherhood suggested that with a special type of education, mothers could influence their husbands and sons to be active citizens.

CREATING A GOVERNMENT: WRITING THE U.S. CONSTITUTION

- With a growing sense of unhappiness in the new nation, revolutionary leaders looked to create "a more perfect union."

THE CRISIS OF THE 1780S: THE FAILURE OF THE ARTICLES OF CONFEDERATION

- The real power that governed the nation under the Articles rested with the states. Yet this loose confederation found itself in debt without a means to tax, and its credit was dangerously on shaky grounds.
- As a catalyst to a nation-changing government, the Annapolis Convention assembled leaders to discuss the nation's problems and to establish a meeting for another convention at Philadelphia in 1787.

- The purpose of the convention was to revise the Articles of Confederation, but the gathering produced a much more radical government than what most delegates expected.

THE CONSTITUTIONAL CONVENTION

- The delegates to the convention represented all of the states except Rhode Island. Revolutionaries such as Thomas Jefferson, John Adams, Samuel Adams, and Patrick Henry were also notably absent from the proceedings.
- The final product of these delegates would be a lasting constitution that still survives today.

DECISIONS ON THE STRUCTURE OF A UNIFIED GOVERNMENT

- The Virginia Plan proved to be the first plan introduced at the convention which called for a two house legislature whose membership would be proportional to the population of the states.
- The countering New Jersey Plan called for a legislature that would have the same number of representatives from each state.
- To appease both plans, the Great Compromise (or Connecticut Plan) called for a House of Representatives whose membership would be based proportionally on the states' population, and a Senate in which each state would have two members.
- To ensure that the "wisest and best" citizens selected the president, an Electoral College was formed, and a four year term was set for the presidency.
- The president also gained strong executive powers, but Congress gained the power to override any veto by the president.

THE EFFECTS OF SLAVERY ON A UNIFIED GOVERNMENT

- Although many of the Framers of the Constitution despised slavery, the document they created firmly solidified its position in the states where it already existed. Southern slaveholders considered slaves to be property, and the right to protect one's property was critical in order for the Constitution to be valid.
- The argument as to whether slaves should be counted as part of the population for representation in the House of Representatives led to a compromise known as the three-fifths clause.
- Moreover, the Constitution allowed for the importation of slaves to continue without taxation until 1808, and protected the slaveholder's right to reclaim fugitive slaves.

DEBATING AND ADOPTING THE CONSTITUTION

- By September of 1787, the delegates of the Constitution signed the document and sent it to the states for ratification.
- James Madison, Alexander Hamilton, and John Jay wrote *The Federalist Papers* to persuade the nation to support the ratification of the Constitution. Essentially, supporters

of the Constitution, known as the Federalists, highlighted the benefits of a strong national government.

- The Antifederalists argued that a strong national government would take away the power of the states and the rights of individual citizens.
- During ratification, many states had reservations with the Constitution because it did not include a Bill of Rights.
- By 1788, the Constitution had been ratified, and became the official framework of the national government in the United States.

MULTIPLE CHOICE QUESTIONS

1. The danger of the Newburgh Conspiracy was that
   A. many dissatisfied Americans threatened to rejoin the side of England.
   B. Native Americans threatened a huge revolt against the eastern states.
   C. the threat of a military *coup d'etat* became a real possibility.
   D. the individual states threatened to form their own nations.

2. The source of tension that led to Shays's Rebellion stemmed from
   A. threats of Indian raids on white settlers.
   B. British harassment from their still occupied forts.
   C. financial difficulties and the threat of foreclosures.
   D. ratification of the Constitution.

3. The Northwest Ordinance that the Articles of Confederation created
   A. allowed for the organized settlement of the Northwest Territory.
   B. allowed for slavery to exist in the Northwest Territory.
   C. led to the creation of New Hampshire and Vermont.
   D. led to a disorderly settlement of the Northwest Territory.

4. The exploration of Daniel Boone eventually led to the settlement of
   A. Ohio.
   B. Michigan.
   C. Kentucky.
   D. Indiana.

5. Without the presence of the British, American relations with Native Americans
   A. often times became violent with white settlers.
   B. improved without the meddling of a foreign nation.
   C. improved since new boundaries of settlement were recognized.
   D. became non-existent as the Indians were pushed to Oklahoma.

6. Benjamin Banneker's letter to Thomas Jefferson
    A. praised him for the equality the Declaration of Independence offered.
    B. criticized the hypocrisy of the Declaration of Independence and the existence of slavery.
    C. threatened the possibility of a slave revolt.
    D. complimented Jefferson's Declaration of Independence as a flawless document.

7. As a result of the American Revolution, women
    A. gained the right to suffrage.
    B. gained full rights to inheritance.
    C. were respected for the values of Republican Motherhood.
    D. embraced the same form of education as males.

8. The result of the Great Compromise was that
    A. representation in the House of Representatives became equal.
    B. representation in the Senate would be apportioned according to population.
    C. representation in both the House and Senate became equal.
    D. the Senate would consist of two members from each state.

9. All of the following proved to recognize the existence of slavery in the Constitution EXCEPT
    A. Three Fifths clause.
    B. acceptance of slave trade until 1808.
    C. the Connecticut Compromise.
    D. reclaiming of fugitives.

10. Many Anti-Federalists objected to the Constitution on the grounds that
    A. it gave the states too much power.
    B. it did not allow for a standing army.
    C. it did not give the national government the power to tax.
    D. it did not contain a Bill of Rights.

Questions 11-12 refer to the following visual.

James Madison

11. Why is Madison important to understanding the history of the Constitutional Convention?
   A. He wrote a book entitled, *History of the Constitution.*
   B. He wrote newspaper articles regarding the Convention.
   C. He spoke extensively to contemporaries about the Convention.
   D. He took notes during the Constitutional Convention.

12. Along with Alexander Hamilton and John Jay, what did Madison write to encourage the passage of the Constitution?
   A. *Poor Richard's Almanac*
   B. *The Federalist Papers*
   C. *The Bill of Rights*
   D. *Common Sense*

Questions 13-15 refer to the following excerpt.

In order to lay a due foundation for that separate and distinct exercise of the different powers of government, which to a certain extent is admitted on all hands to be essential to the preservation of liberty, it is evident that each department should have a will of its own; and consequently should be so constituted that the members of each should have as little agency as possible in the appointment of the members of the others. Were this principle rigorously adhered to, it would require that all the appointments for the supreme executive, legislative, and judiciary magistracies should be drawn from the same fountain of authority, the people, through channels having no communication whatever with one another....But the great security against a gradual concentration of the several powers in the same department, consists in giving to those who administer each department the necessary constitutional means and personal motives to resist encroachments of the others. The provision for defense must in this, as in all other cases, be made commensurate to the danger of attack. Ambition must be made to counteract ambition. The interest of the man must be connected with the constitutional rights of the place. It may be a reflection on human nature, that such devices should be necessary to control the abuses of government. But what is government itself, but the greatest of all reflections on human nature? If men were angels, no government would be necessary. If angels were to govern men, neither external nor internal controls on government would be necessary. In framing a government which is to be administered by men over men, the great difficulty lies in this: you must first enable the government to control the governed; and in the next place oblige it to control itself. A dependence on the people is, no doubt, the primary control on the government; but experience has taught mankind the necessity of auxiliary precautions.

--James Madison Federalist No. 51

13. According to Madison, the branches of government derive their power from
   A. from the branches themselves.
   B. from an electoral college.
   C. from the people.
   D. from the Framers of the Constitution.

14. "...but experience has taught mankind the necessity of auxiliary precautions" reflects the notion
    A. That governments can be controlled exclusively by the people.
    B. That government must be controlled by a system of governmental checks and balances.
    C. That a supreme court must have superior power than all other branches.
    D. That an executive leader must dominate over all other governmental powers.

15. "If men were angels, no government would be necessary" implies that
    A. government power does not need to separated.
    B. government power does not need a system of checks and balances.
    C. governments consist of men with self-interests.
    D. governments should not exist.

Questions 16-18 refer to the following excerpt.

...I hope it will not be conceived from these observations, that it is my wish to hold the unhappy people, who are the subject of this letter, in slavery. I can only say that there is not a man living who wishes more sincerely than I do, to see a plan adopted for the abolition of it; but there is only one proper and effectual mode by which it can be accomplished, and that is by Legislative authority; and this, as far as my suffrage will go, shall never be wanting. But when slaves who are happy and contented with their present masters, are tampered with and seduced to leave them; when masters are taken unawares by these practices; when a conduct of this sort begets discontent on one side and resentment on the other, and when it happens to fall on a man, whose purse will not measure with that of the Society, and he looses his property for want of means to defend it; it is oppression in the latter case, and not humanity in any; because it introduces more evils than it can cure.

--George Washington's letter to Robert Morris

16. Washington believed that the only way to abolish slavery was
    A. to have a civil war.
    B. through slavery insurrection.
    C. through a legislative process.
    D. through voluntary emancipation by masters.

17. According to Washington, if he could have his way
    A. He would abolish slavery.
    B. He would perpetually maintain the existence of slavery.
    C. He would lead an army to destroy the institution of slavery.
    D. He would free his slaves but encourage the existence of slavery elsewhere.

18. In the letter, Washington is irritated with
    A. outsiders trying to tamper with slaves with abolitionist ideas.
    B. the existence of slavery.

C. a lack of legislative authority to abolish slavery.

D. Morris's indifference to the matter of slavery.

Questions 19-21 refer to the following excerpt.

Paris, January 30th, 1787

Dear Sir,

My last to you was the 16th of December; since which, I have received yours of November 25 and December 4, which afforded me…a treat on matters public, individual, and economical. I am impatient to learn your sentiments on the late troubles in the Eastern states. So far as I have yet seen, they do not appear to threaten serious consequences. Those states have suffered by the stoppage of the channels of their commerce, which have not yet found other issues. This must render money scarce and make the people uneasy. This uneasiness has produced acts absolutely unjustifiable; but I hope they will provoke no severities from their governments. A consciousness of those in power that their administration of the public affairs has been honest may, perhaps, produce too great a degree of indignation; and those characters, wherein fear predominates over hope, may apprehend too much from these instances of irregularity. They may conclude too hastily that nature has formed man insusceptible of any other government than that of force, a conclusion not founded in truth or experience…I hold it that a little rebellion now and then is a good thing, and as necessary in the political world as storms in the physical. Unsuccessful rebellions, indeed, generally establish the encroachments on the rights of the people which have produced them. An observation of this truth should render honest republican governors so mild in their punishment of rebellions as not to discourage them too much. It is a medicine necessary for the sound health of government…

Yours affectionately,

Th. Jefferson

--Letter from Jefferson to Madison

19. According to Jefferson's letter to James Madison, Shays's Rebellion
    A. was a deplorable act that had to be dealt with a crushing punishment.
    B. was an understandable rebellion caused by financial hardship.
    C. proved that a strong central government had to be formed.
    D. deserved to provoke severe consequences from the Massachusetts government.

20. In the opinion of Jefferson, little rebellions
    A. had to be seriously punished.
    B. actually can lead to positive outcomes.
    C. never led to anything constructive in society.
    D. were unnecessary in the political world.

21. One can infer from Jefferson's letter that
    A. he supported just uprisings.
    B. he was ultra conservative.
    C. he supported strong central governments.
    D. he supported oppressive governments.

SHORT ANSWER QUESTIONS

Framers at the Constitutional Convention create a new national government in 1787.

   a. Choose ONE of the following and explain why your choice represents the event that led to the Constitutional Convention.

   - Treaty of Paris
   - Shays's Rebellion
   - Anapolis Convention

   b. Contrast your choice against ONE of the other options, demonstrating why that option in not as significant as your choice.

LONG ESSAY QUESTION

   What debates arose during and after the Constitutional Convention in 1787?

ANSWERS AND EXPLANATIONS

Multiple Choice Questions

1.   C   Financially stressed soldiers had thoughts of taking over the government.
2.   C   Taxes and a depressed economy threatened the financial livelihood of farmers in Massachusetts.
3. A Settlement of the Northwest Territory proved to be one of the Articles of Confederation's few achievements.
4. C Boone's exploring adventure led to the settlement of this frontier state.
5. A England's promise to provide the Indians with land after the French and Indian War was expunged by settlers of the new country.
6. B The daring letter by Banneker pointed to the slave hypocrisy that haunted many of the Founding Fathers.
7. C The revolution allowed for women to be respected for their efforts in the home.
8. D The Great Compromise called for a mix of both equal and proportional representation in Congress.
9. C The Connecticut Compromise dealt with issues of proportional and equal representation and not with slavery.
10. D The Anti-Federalists demanded that the civil liberties of citizens be spelled out in the Constitution.
11. D Madison's notes gives valuable insight into the proceedings of the Constitutional Convention.

12. B *The Federalist Papers* urged for the passage of the Constitution and a strong central government it created.
13. C The Constitution created a republic where final governmental authority rested with the people.
14. B Madison believed that a system of checks and balances was needed to keep the branches of the national government in line.
15. C Madison knew that self-interest in man is part of nature and a system was needed to check this natural inclination.
16. C Although Washington personally had a distaste for slavery, he believed that the only through a legal process could it be eliminated.
17. A Washington despised a system that he hesitated to abolish.
18. A Despite his objection to slavery, Washington objected to efforts of abolitionist agitators.
19. B Jefferson understood the circumstance that led to this rebellion
20. B Jefferson believed that rebellions can serve as "medicine for the sound health of government."
21. A Jefferson did not shy away from radical activity that was rooted in just causes.

Long Essay Question

What debates arose during and after the Constitutional Convention in 1787?

(Key topics to focus and elaborate on)
- Small states vs. Large states
- Southern population/slaves
- Office of the presidency

Chapter 7
PRACTICING DEMOCRACY, 1789-1800

CONVENING A CONGRESS; INAUGURATING A PRESIDENT, ADOPTING A BILL OF RIGHTS

- In 1789, elections for the House of Representatives, the Senate, and the President were held and the leaders of the new government were chosen. Of course, George Washington was elected as the unanimous choice to become the president; he preferred to be called "Mr. President."
- Thereafter, Washington selected the nation's first presidential cabinet which included two fierce political rivals, Alexander Hamilton and Thomas Jefferson.
- That same year, James Madison drafted a Bill of Rights he promised would be added to the Constitution. Ultimately Congress adopted ten amendments that protected the basic civil liberties of Americans and protected the powers of the states as well.

CREATING AN ECONOMY: ALEXANDER HAMILTON AND THE U.S. ECONOMIC SYSTEM

- In the midst of Washington's inauguration, the nation faced a deep financial crisis stemming from the enormous Revolutionary debt. To Hamilton, the only viable option would be for the federal government to assume all debt owed by the states and to finance this plan through taxes.
- To entice the South's compliance with this debt assumption, the nation's capital moved from New York to land wedged between Virginia and Maryland.
- In order to promote Hamilton's vision of establishing a nation of manufacturing and self-sufficiency based on England's economy, the Secretary of the Treasury pushed for a national bank. The bank would manage the economy, fund a national government, provide loans to encourage industry, and ultimately attach the wealthy to the new government.
- Hamilton's proposed bank met fierce opposition, in particular by Jefferson who believed the bank would empower cities such as Boston and New York and undermine the honest nature of agrarianism.
- Furthermore, Jefferson believed the federal government did not have the power to establish a bank because the Constitution did not permit it. Hamilton disagreed and argued that through the elastic clause, the federal government had the implied power to establish a bank.
- In the end, Washington signed the bank bill and the Bank of the United States was born.
- During the course of Washington's presidency, the philosophical views of Jefferson and Hamilton clearly came in to view: Jefferson promoted a nation of farms and strict adherence to the Constitution, and Hamilton favored urbanism/commercialism and a loose interpretation of the Constitution.

SETTING THE PACE: THE WASHINGTON ADMINISTRATION

- Upon stepping into the presidency, George Washington toured the nation to gain support for the new government and the constitution that created it.
- As he became familiar with the nation, a familiar dilemma erupted in the Ohio Valley...Indian resistance to white settlement. Though attempts were made to negotiate peace in this region, treaties such as those established by territorial governor Arthur St. Clair proved to be a failure.
- Indeed, natives led by Mohawk Joseph Brant vowed to their people that no white settlement would enter west of the Ohio Valley. Through the military leadership of General Anthony Wayne, US troops soundly defeated Indian forces at the Battle of Fallen Timbers in 1794. The subsequent Treaty of Grenville permanently ended Indian resistance in the region.
- While Native Americans resisted white settlement out west, in western Pennsylvania, farmers resisted Hamilton's tax on whiskey. As a means to generate extra revenue to fund debt assumption, Hamilton believed that a tax on whiskey would be unpopular, but not to the whole nation.
- Given the dependence on whiskey as a source of revenue for these Pennsylvania farmers, the tax was simply unbearable. Visions of the 1760s reappeared as protestors tarred and feathered tax collectors, and protestors even organized a Committee of Public Safety in detestation of the tax.
- George Washington led 12,000 troops into Pennsylvania to crush the rebellion, although once the troops arrived, the rebels dispersed without a fight. Undoubtedly, this action proved that the federal government would reign supreme.
- Although Washington proved willing to use force to end domestic insurrection, he did not follow the same policy when it came to foreign affairs. Thus when the French Revolution broke out, followed by war in Europe largely between France and England, Washington declared an official stance of neutrality for the United States.
- Steering the course of neutrality would be a difficult task given the trading nature of the US. In effect, the 1790s featured provocation by both the British and French in regards to American shipping neutrality bringing much tension, fury, and frustration to both the Washington and Adams Administration.

THE BIRTH OF POLITICAL PARTIES: ADAMS AND JEFFERSON

- The stances regarding French Revolution in the United States signified the permanent split between the Federalists and Anti-Federalists, and the latter would claim the name of the Democratic-Republicans.
- In embracing the ideals of Hamilton and Jefferson, the Federalists and Democratic-Republicans essentially formed the origins of the nation's first political parties.
- Whereas Hamilton's Federalists favored a strong central government, promoted manufacturing and industry, and admired the British, Jefferson's Democratic-Republicans favored the power of the states, promoted agrarianism, and

sympathized with the French. This factional political system would be a key factor in the Election of 1796 which saw John Adams, a Federalist, defeat Thomas Jefferson, a Democratic-Republican.

- Oddly enough, these two rivals would be part of the same administration when Adams was elected as the president and Jefferson elected as the vice president.
- The Adams Administration immediately dealt with foreign struggles when the French seized 300 American ships in 1797. When Adams sent diplomats to France to negotiate with its foreign minister, French officials identified as X,Y,Z, demanded a bribe. Outraged, the US refused and Adams prepared for a possible confrontation with France by beefing up US naval forces.
- Preparation for war immediately provoked the ire of the Democratic-Republicans who began to question power of the Adams Administration. Consequently, the Federalists pushed through Congress the Alien and Sedition Acts in an effort to weaken the support of the Democratic-Republicans and to silence the criticism against the Adams Administration.
- In response to these acts, Jefferson and Madison created the Kentucky and Virginia Resolutions to effectively nullify the Alien and Sedition Acts. Meanwhile, as the US and France fought a quasi-war, the Federalist Party pushed for an official declaration of war against France.
- Surprisingly, Adams opted for peace with France and by 1899 the quasi-war came to an end. Unfortunately, the presidency of Adams also came to an end since he went against his party's demand for war.
- With Adams losing his support to be reelected by the Federalists, the Election of 1800 seemed to heavily favor the Democratic-Republican candidate, Thomas Jefferson. However, Aaron Burr, received the same number of electoral votes as Jefferson.
- In not trusting the ambition and morality of Burr, Hamilton lent his support to Jefferson enabling the Virginian to win the tiebreaker in the House of Representatives. Hence, a new faction had taken over the government without a drop of blood being spilled.

MULTIPLE CHOICE QUESTIONS

1. Citizen Edmund Genet provoke the fury of George Washington in 1794 because
   A. he criticized the contentious nature of Washington's cabinet.
   B. he endorsed the stipulations of Jay's Treaty.
   C. he encouraged Americans vessels to attack British shipping
   D. he openly endorsed the policies of Thomas Jefferson.

2. The following was NOT a characteristic of the Federalist Party.
   A. It favored building roads and canals and favored the Bank of the U.S.
   B. It was generally pro-British and wanted the US to model British institutions.
   C. It favored a strong central government and sponsored the Alien and Sedition Acts.
   D. It sponsored the Alien and Sedition Acts and was generally supportive of the French Revolution.

3. Hamilton believed in the necessity of the federal government to assume all Revolutionary War debt in order
   A. to establish the credit of the newly formed federal government.
   B. to tie the regions of the North and South into a more unified entity.
   C. to gain the support of common citizens such as farmers and shopkeepers.
   D. to preserve the location of the nation's capital in New York.

4. James Madison wrote the Bill of Rights to add to the Constitution
   A. to appease the Federalists who believed the Constitution didn't address civil liberties.
   B. because he promised the Anti-Federalists these rights would be added to the Constitution during the process of ratification.
   C. because George Washington refused to be inaugurated unless a Bill of Rights was included in the Constitution.
   D. because the US Supreme Court mandated that a list of expressly written guarantees of civil liberties be included in the Constitution in order for the government to convene.

5. John Adams signed the Alien and Sedition Acts in 1798
   A. to curb the power and to quiet the criticism of the Democratic-Republicans.
   B. to halt the French immigration into the United States.
   C. to provoke treasonous acts by political rivals such as Thomas Jefferson and James Madison.
   D. to prepare for a possible invasion by British forces.

6. Hamilton's tax on whiskey in western Pennsylvania was controversial because
   A. Pennsylvania was not represented in the decision to establish this excise tax.
   B. Anti-Federalist leaders such as Patrick Henry were heavily involved in the production of corn whiskey.
   C. Washington's government needed extra revenue to prepare for war with England.
   D. the production of whiskey was not seen as harmful.

7. The purpose of Washington touring the nation was
   A. to show the military strength of the United States.
   B. to deter the threat of uprisings in places such as the South and Northwest.
   C. to show support for religious freedom and to personalize a distant government.
   D. to build support for a national road.

8. The effect of the Battle of Fallen Timbers would be
   A. Indian resistance to white settlement in the Ohio Valley came to an end.
   B. decades of Indian retaliation in the Ohio Valley.
   C. the U.S. gained full navigation rights to the Mississippi River.
   D. the British evacuated their posts in the Northwest Territory.

9. The irony of the Democratic Republicans and their political philosophy was
   A. they fully supported Thomas Jefferson despite the revolutionary support he had from radicals in France.
   B. they embraced the ideals of states' rights.
   C. their advocacy of liberty and equality was underlined by their sympathy towards slavery.
   D. they embraced the ideals and virtues of agrarianism.

10. Hamilton justified establishing a national bank because it intended
   A. to serve as a means for foreign investors to stabilize the new government.
   B. to encourage the wealthy to invest in the bank and become attached to the national government.
   C. to provide loans that would strengthen the agrarian nature of the United States.
   D. to gain support from southern cities such as Charleston, Savannah, and Baltimore.

11. Adam Smith's *Wealth of Nations* influenced Alexander Hamilton in that
   A. the book encouraged Hamilton to emulate England's economic system in the United States.
   B. the book convinced Hamilton that the nation's wealth was in the ability to own land and gold.
   C. the book discouraged Hamilton from creating an economic system in the United States that was based on competition.
   D. the book encouraged Hamilton to create a system of mercantilism to enrich the United States.

12. The Election of 1800 initially resulted in a tie between Thomas Jefferson and Aaron Burr since
   A. John Adams did not have enough electoral votes to win the election outright.
   B. Hamilton's support of Burr catapulted him to a tie with Jefferson.
   C. Burr actually received the same number of electoral votes as Jefferson.
   D. the Federalists equally supported both candidates more so than their own party leader John Adams.

Questions 13-14 refer to the following illustration.

13. The above political cartoon is propaganda belonging to which of the following groups
    A. the Federalists.
    B. the Democratic-Republicans.
    C. the Jacobins.
    D. the Anti-Federalists.

14. The five-headed monster in the political cartoon represents
    A. the Federalists.
    B. Agents of Talleyrand.
    C. King George III.
    D. King Louis XVI.

15. Based on this political cartoon, the French Revolution is depicted as
    A. lawless and deceitful anarchy.
    B. righteous overthrow of monarchy.
    C. a respectable movement with cordial diplomacy.
    D. a movement that respected the democracy of the United States.

Questions 16-18 refer to the following excerpt.

That the General Assembly doth particularly protest against the palpable and alarming infractions of the Constitution, in the two late cases of the Alien and Sedition Acts" passed at the last session of Congress…That the several states who formed (the Constitution), being sovereign and independent, have the unquestionable right to judge of its infraction; and that a nullification, by those sovereignties, of all unauthorized acts done under the colour of that instrument, is the rightful remedy...

--Excerpt from the Virginia and Kentucky Resolutions

16. The following men supported this statement except
    A. Alexander Hamilton.
    B. John Adams.
    C. George Washington.
    D. Thomas Jefferson.

17. The authors of these resolutions clearly supported the notion of
    A. power of the central government.
    B. power of the state governments.
    C. power of the U.S. Supreme Court.
    D. power of Congress to establish enforceable laws.

18. The term *nullification* in the excerpt refers to
    A. obedience to federal laws.
    B. right to judicial review by the U.S. Supreme Court.
    C. right to appeal questionable laws to the U.S. Supreme Court.
    D. the right of states to ignore laws they deem as unconstitutional.

Questions 19-21 refer to the following excerpt.

But the four western counties of Pennsylvania undertake to rejudge and reverse your decrees. You have said, 'The Congress shall have power to lay excises.' They say, 'The Congress shall not have this power,' or-what is equivalent-'they shall not exercise it': for a power that may not be exercised is a nullity. Your representatives have said, and four times repeated it, 'An excise on distilled spirits shall be collected.' They say, 'It shall not be collected. We will punish, expel, and banish the officers who shall attempt the collection. We will do the same by every other person who shall dare to comply with your decrees expressed in the constitutional charter, and with that of your representatives expressed in the laws. The sovereignty shall not reside with you, but with us. If you presume to dispute the point by force, we are ready to measure swords with you, and if unequal ourselves to the contest, we will call in the aid of a foreign nation. We will league ourselves with a foreign power."

--Alexander Hamilton 1794

19. In the excerpt, Hamilton attacked
    A. the Federalist Party.
    B. Congress.
    C. the British.
    D. Western Pennsylvania.

20. Within the excerpt, the complaint of Alexander Hamilton was about
    A. the high taxes of whiskey.
    B. the power of Congress to pass excise tax laws.

94

C. the non-compliance and refusal to pay the whiskey tax.

D. the alliance between western Pennsylvania and England.

21. The justification Hamilton used for the passage of the excise tax on whiskey was

A. the necessity of the tax to generate revenue for his debt assumption plan.

B. that the tax would align the states with the federal government.

C. that the tax was created by the state of Pennsylvania itself.

D. that essentially the American people passed it through their representatives.

Questions 22-24 refer to the following excerpt.

The excise tax is an infernal one. The first error was to admit it by the Constitution; the second, to act on that admission; the third and last will be, to make it the instrument of dismembering the Union, and setting us afloat to choose what part of it we will adhere toe. The information of our militia, returned from the westward, is uniform, that though the people there let them pass quietly, they were objects of their laughter, not of their fear: that one thousand men could have cut off their whole force in a thousand places of the Allegheny; that their detestation of the excise tax is universal, and has now associated to it a detestation of the government; and that a separation which perhaps was *a very distant and problematic event, is now near and certain, and determined in the mind of every man.*

--Thomas Jefferson, 1794

22. In response to the Whiskey Rebellion, Jefferson believed all of the following EXCEPT

A. excise taxes are evil.

B. excise taxes should not have been included in the Constitution in the first place.

C. the federal government had the right enforce the collection of excise taxes.

D. Pennsylvanians did not approve of the excise tax.

23. What sense of mockery is presented by Jefferson in the excerpt?

A. The national government is foolish for passing an excise tax.

B. Western Pennsylvania chose not to follow the excise tax law.

C. The federal government acted on its power to enforce the excise tax.

D. The militia sent to enforce the excise tax was not as powerful as first believed.

24. What political philosophy does Jefferson indicate in the excerpt?

A. Federal law reigns supreme.

B. States have ultimate authority in determining the legitimacy of laws.

C. The federal government is justified in enforcing laws.

D. States may secede from a distrusted Union.

SHORT ESSAY QUESTIONS

The newly formed nation remained financially solvent through first decade of its existence (1790s)

a. Choose ONE of the following and explain why your choice represents the event that most significantly impacted this financial solvency.

- Adoption of Hamilton's debt assumption plan
- Establishment of a national bank
- Issuance of Hamilton's Report on Manufactures

b. Contrast your choice against ONE of the other options, demonstrating why that option is not as significant as your choice.

LONG ESSAY QUESTION

Who were the Federalists and the Republicans, and how did they differ over the meaning of liberty and the power of the national government?

ANSWERS AND EXPLANATIONS

Multiple Choice Questions

1. C   By encouraging American vessels to attack British shipping, Genet directly violated Washington's official stance of neutrality.
2. D   Although the Federalists sponsored the Alien and Sedition Acts, they generally favored the British and were not supportive of the French Revolution.
3. A   Hamilton believed that only by a debt assumption plan could the nation build financial credibility.
4. B   The Anti-Federalists demanded that an explicit and expressed Bill of Rights be added to the Constitution in order to ensure the guarantee of civil liberties.
5. A   The Alien and Sedition Acts crippled the political support of French immigrant and made criticism of the national government illegal.
6. D   Producing and transferring whiskey in western Pennsylvania was far more profitable than transferring corn or grain in eastern markets.
7. C   Despite enduring occasional subpar accommodations, Washington wanted to build rapport and gain support from states throughout the Union.
8. A   General Anthony Wayne's crushing victory over Indian forces and the subsequent Treaty of Grenville permanently ended Indian resistance in the Ohio Valley.
9. C   Many of the Democratic Republicans were slaveholders in the South.
10. B   Hamilton believed the national government needed the investments of the wealthy to stabilize it and give it financial credibility.
11. A   Hamilton believed that real wealth was generated through manufacturing, commerce, and competition such as that seen in England.
12. C   Since there were no official vice presidential candidates until the passage of the twelfth amendment, Jefferson and Burr each received 73 votes in the Electoral College.
13. A   The political cartoon does not depict the French Revolution in good terms and the Federalists were not advocates of the French.

14. B The five-headed monster represents the agents who tried to gain a bribe from American diplomats.

15. A With the beheadings in the background, a dagger held by the monster, and stealing at the table, the French Revolution is not depicted as a righteous event.

16. D In response to the Alien and Sedition Acts, Jefferson was actually an author of the Kentucky and Virginia Resolutions.

17. B The Kentucky and Virginia Resolutions directly supported the right of states to interpret the Constitutionality of laws and nullify them if necessary.

18. D The Kentucky and Virginia Resolutions argued that any federal law that did not serve the best interest of a state did not have to be followed.

19. D Hamilton attacked farmers of western Pennsylvania for not complying with the whiskey tax.

20. C Hamilton complained that despite Constitutional powers of Congress to levy excise taxes, farmers in western Pennsylvania still did comply with them.

21. D Unlike the hated taxes of the British during the American Revolution, the whiskey tax was passed by representatives of the American people.

22. C Jefferson questioned the use of military force that were used to end the Whiskey Rebellion.

23. D Jefferson argued that Washington's troops could have been cut off in a thousand places along the Allegheny River.

24. D Jefferson argued that states who feel abused by the federal government may seek to break from the Union.

Long Essay Question

Who were the Federalists and the Republicans, and how did they differ over the meaning of liberty and the power of the national government?

(Key topics to focus and elaborate on)
- Federalists as supporters of Hamilton's policies
- Republicans formed by Jefferson and Madison
- Market economy vs agrarian society

Chapter 8
Creating a New People, Expanding the Country, 1801-1823

JEFFERSON AND THE REPUBLICAN IDEAL

- Jefferson's ideals of limited government seemed to mirror much of the country's desire for limited government.
- Jefferson represented the ideals of American republicanism which manifested itself in various ways, from state dinners to independent decision-making. Jefferson's success also represented many ironies that existed throughout his presidency.
- During his presidency, Jefferson reduced the size of the federal government so that the states could be the center of American life.
- The case of *Marbury v. Madison* involved a judge who outgoing president John Adams had appointed at midnight in 1801. The significance of the decision in this case is that the US Supreme Court (led by Chief Justice John Marshall at that time) asserted it power of judicial review. Essentially, this power gave the court the authority to declare an act of Congress unconstitutional.
- Jefferson presided over a nation that consisted mostly of farmers.
- As the nation's white male electorate grew, so too did the expectations of equality amongst this group.
- Violence, through fighting and dueling, was a feature of the country that became very common throughout the early 1800s. In fact, two of the most prominent men in American history, Alexander Hamilton and Andrew Jackson, had been involved in separate duels.
- Many suffered from this aura of violence including Indians, slaves, and families.
- Jefferson's public life and private life proved to be extreme opposites, as the simplicity of his public persona gave way to an extremely lavish and extravagant personal lifestyle.
- Jefferson's relationship with one of his slaves, Sally Hemings, became a national story in 1802.

THE IDEALS OF RELIGIOUS FREEDOM

- Jefferson reflected a republican ideal in 1802 when, in a letter, he declared that a "wall of separation between church and state" should exist. Americans who wanted to live an individualistic life without government intrusion believed that religion also fell into this equation.
- During the Jefferson Administration, Connecticut, New Hampshire, Massachusetts, and Maryland still had state-sponsored religions.
- Connecticut proved to be a strong supporter of state-sponsored religion, but lost this distinction when Oliver Wolcott became governor. Massachusetts soon thereafter followed suit.
- Jefferson's presidency witnessed the beginnings of the Second Great Awakening.

- A revival in Kentucky in 1799 led to more religious gatherings that featured the utilization of outdoor campgrounds. One of the largest of these gatherings occurred in Cane Ridge, Kentucky in 1801.
- The Methodists and Baptists became the largest Protestant denominations at this time. Although both denominations brought higher levels of emotion into their faith, they differed in their structure and organization.
- Religion also became prominent in the slave quarters of the South, although masters and slaves had different agendas with their messages. Whereas the master message embraced obedience, the slave message promoted freedom (in the next life or current one).
- Masters feared that slave religion would lead to revolt.
- Free blacks formed congregations in the north such as those seen in Philadelphia and Baltimore.
- Catholics and Jews embraced the ideals of Jeffersonian America. Catholics would see the appointment of the first Catholic bishop in America and also the founding of the Catholic university of Georgetown. The Jewish faith would spread beyond the traditional cities such as New York City and into cities such as New Orleans and Cincinnati.

BEYOND THE MISSISSIPPI: THE LOUISIANA PURCHASE AND THE EXPEDITION OF LEWIS AND CLARK

- American access to the Mississippi River and use of the city of New Orleans seemed to be firmly in place until Spain ceded New Orleans and the Louisiana Territory to France. Jefferson moved quickly to purchase New Orleans from the French.
- The offer came at a good time since France needed money and was on the verge of losing Haiti. Thus Napoleon offered the whole Louisiana Territory for $15 million.
- Constitutional issues arose with the Louisiana Purchase in 1803, but the offer proved to be too good to pass up.
- In essence, the Louisiana Purchase doubled the size of the United States.
- In many aspects, New Orleans proved to be completely different than the new country that it belonged to. From language, to religion, to slave culture, to music, to inter-racial mixing, New Orleans became a unique addition to the United States.
- In 1804, Jefferson sent Meriwether Lewis and William Clark to explore the Louisiana Territory and beyond. Along this journey, a Shoshone woman named Sacagawea, became a valuable guide. By 1805, the Lewis/Clark expedition reached the Pacific and returned to Saint Louis in 1806.

THE WAR OF 1812

- The conflict between France and England proved to be the source of tension between the US and England that eventually led to war in 1812.
- The British practice of impressment had long infuriated the United States as it was seen as a direct threat to American liberty and freedom.
- In 1807, Jefferson passed the Embargo Act to deter the threat of impressment but it only served to devastate the economy in the North.

- Another threat from within came from Indians who had long been displeased with the Treaty of Grenville. Tenskwatawa and Tecumseh looked to create an Ohio territory that was void of European contact and influence.
- When war broke out between England and the United States, a tribal confederation, with British support, also fought an all-our-war with the United States.
- The advocates that pushed James Madison to go to war with England became known as the War Hawks. The Federalists rejected this notion of war and deemed it as commercially foolish.
- War began in 1812 and proved to be an immediate disaster for the United States as its military suffered one embarrassment after another. Yet, U.S. forces gained important victories at Thames, in Canada and at Lake Erie.
- In 1814, the British raided Washington D.C. and burned it and the White House to the ground. However, the British failed to capture Ft. McHenry which inspired Francis Scott Key to write the "Star Spangled Banner".
- The death of Tecumseh weakened the Indian alliances that fought against the US allowing Andrew Jackson to crush the Creeks and Cherokees in 1814.
- In December of 1814, the US and England ended the war by agreeing to the Treaty of Ghent.
- At the same time, Federalists at the Hartford Convention spoke of peace (even though it was unknown to them it was already being negotiated), nullification, and secession if peace with England could not be achieved.
- The Battle of New Orleans was fought in January of 1815 before the participants knew of the peace treaty. The battle solidified the terms of the treaty and made Andrew Jackson a war hero.
- Despite losing more battles than it won, the United States still celebrated the Treaty of Ghent and the Battle of New Orleans, and peace between the U.S. and England would be permanent.
- The war also encouraged industrialization in the northeast and instilled a sense of pride amongst Americans.

EXPANDING AMERICAN TERRITORY AND INFLUENCE

- As Daniel Boone resettled from Kentucky to Missouri, other Americans moved to various frontier territories as well.
- The U.S. saw Spanish Florida as a threat to shipping in the Gulf of Mexico, a safe haven for escaped slaves, and as a launching point for Spanish-incited Indian attacks by tribes such as the Seminoles.
- In 1817, Andrew Jackson led an excursion into Florida to attack marauding Seminoles and upon arriving, executed European enticers and Seminoles as well. Upon discovering the vulnerability of Spanish control over Florida, Spain agreed to cede Florida to the U.S. with the assurance that the U.S. would not pursue Texas or assist in independence revolutions in Latin America.
- Further out west, other nations were making their presence felt as both England and Russia began to establish settlements on the west coast.

- The Adams-Onis Treaty allowed the U.S. to obtain Florida and Spanish claims to the Oregon Territory. At the same time the U.S. negotiated with England to jointly occupy the Oregon Territory.
- Having witnessed the independence of several Latin American countries from Spain, the U.S. issued the Monroe Doctrine. This doctrine forbade any European intervention or acquisition of any new territory in both North and South America. In essence, the U.S. opposed any new colonization in the Americas, and the Monroe Doctrine became the foundation for future U.S. foreign policy in this region.

MULTIPLE CHOICE QUESTIONS

1. In holding true to his political virtues, Jefferson
   A. expanded the size of the federal government.
   B. decreased the size of the federal government.
   C. poured money into the build-up of the military.
   D. held extremely formal dinners at the White House.

2. John Marshall's decision in the case of *Marbury v. Madison*
   A. was a crushing blow to the Federalist Party.
   B. allowed for William Marbury to be a justice of peace.
   C. asserted the U.S. Supreme Court's power of judicial review.
   D. ruled the Judiciary Act of 1801 to be unconstitutional.

3. A controversial aspect of Jefferson's presidency proved to be
   A. his duel with Aaron Burr
   B. a relationship with a slave named Sally Hemings.
   C. his warning to European countries not to colonize in Latin America.
   D. his decision to go to war with England.

4. A main religious topic that masters taught their slaves was
   A. deliverance.
   B. the achievement of Moses.
   C. obedience and submission.
   D. rhe Book of Exodus.

5. The city that Jefferson believed to be vital to the economic well-being of the United States was
   A. Charleston.
   B. Philadelphia.
   C. Baltimore.
   D. New Orleans.

6. All of the following could be said about New Orleans EXCEPT
   A. it was without a Catholic presence.

B. there were inter-racial relationships.

C. there was a strong French presence.

D. farmers stored their goods there.

7. Americans viewed the British practice of impressment as
   A. necessary to retrieve their sailors.
   B. a violation of the rights of a sovereign nation.
   C. not much of a nuisance.
   D. a justifiable act.

8. The Hartford Convention proved to be unnecessary since
   A. Andrew Jackson was victorious at New Orleans.
   B. the British were close to winning the war.
   C. Madison was not going to run for the presidency again.
   D. the Treaty of Ghent was being signed by the U.S. and England.

9. The War of 1812 resulted in all of the following EXCEPT:
   A. decades of conflict between the U.S. and England came to an end.
   B. the power of the Federalists grew stronger.
   C. a spirit of pride emerged.
   D. Native Americans no longer had any foreign allies.

10. The Monroe Doctrine came in response to
    A. Spain's attempt to regain Mexico.
    B. Russia's settlement activity in the west coast.
    C. England's plan to colonize in South America.
    D. Greece's takeover of Spain.

Questions 11-12 refer to the following.

The Fall of Washington or Maddy in Full Flight

11. The fire burning in the background in this political cartoon is
    A. a British fort.
    B. the White House.
    C. Ft. McHenry.
    D. a U.S. vessel.

12. One of the men fleeing the scene is
    A. Oliver Perry.
    B. Thomas Jefferson.
    C. Lord North.
    D. James Madison.

Questions 13-15 refer to the following excerpt.

In December, 1800, a few days after Congress had for the first time met in our new Metropolis, I was one morning sitting alone in the parlour, when the servant opened the door and showed in a gentleman who wished to see my husband. The usual frankness and care with which I met strangers, were somewhat checked by the dignified and reserved air of the present visitor; but the chilled feeling was only momentary, for after taking the chair I offered him in a free and easy manner, and carelessly throwing his arm on the table near which he sat, he turned towards me a countenance beaming with an expression of benevolence and with a manner and voice almost femininely soft and gentle, entered into conversation on the commonplace topics of the day, from which, before I was conscious of it, he had drawn me into observations of a more personal and interesting nature... in truth so kind and conciliating were his looks and manners that I forgot he was not a friend of my own, until on the opening of the door, Mr. Smith entered and introduced the stranger to me as Mr. Jefferson....I felt my cheeks burn and my heart throb, and not a word more could I speak while he remained. Nay, such was my embarrassment I could scarcely listen to the conversation carried on between him and my husband. For several years he had been to me an object of peculiar interest. In fact my destiny, for on his success in the pending presidential election, or rather the success of the democratic party, (their interests were identical) my condition in life, my union with the man I loved, depended. In addition to this personal interest, I had long participated in my husband's political sentiments and anxieties, and looked upon Mr. Jefferson as the corner stone on which the edifice of republican liberty was to rest, looked upon him as the champion of human rights, the reformer of abuses, the head of the republican party, which must rise or fall with him, and on the triumph of the republican party I devoutly believed the security and welfare of my country depended. Notwithstanding those exalted views of Mr. Jefferson as a political character; and ardently eager as I was for his success, I retained my previously conceived ideas of the coarseness and vulgarity of his appearance and manners and was therefore equally awed and surprised, on discovering the stranger whose deportment was so dignified and gentlemanly, whose language was so refined, whose voice was so gentle, whose countenance was so benignant, to be no other than Thomas Jefferson. How instantaneously were all these preconceived prejudices dissipated, and in proportion to their strength, was the reaction that took place in my opinions and sentiments. I felt that I had been the victim of prejudice, that I had been unjust. The revolution of feeling was complete and from that moment my heart warmed to him with the most affectionate interest and I implicitly believed all that his friends and my husband believed and which the after experience of many years confirmed. Yes, not only was he great, but a truly good man!

--Margaret Mayard Smith, "Reminiscences," 1800

13. Upon entering her and her husband's home, how did Jefferson put Margaret Smith's apprehensions about him at ease?
    A. He brought several gifts.
    B. He engaged in a warm and friendly conversation.
    C. He told Mrs. Smith that he was Thomas Jefferson.
    D. He engaged in prayer.

14. Based on her husband's friendship and connection with Jefferson, one can conclude that her husband supported
    A. the Federalists.
    B. the Democratic-Republicans.
    C. no party affiliation.
    D. the Whigs.

15. Based on hearsay, Margaret Smith viewed Jefferson to be all of the following EXCEPT
    A. vulgar.
    B. coarse.
    C. refined.
    D. unrefined.

Questions 16-18 refer to the following excerpt.

This treaty must of course be laid before both Houses, because both have important functions to exercise respecting it. They, I presume, will see their duty to their country in ratifying & paying for it, so as to secure a good which would otherwise probably be never again in their power. But I suppose they must then appeal to the nation for an additional article to the Constitution, approving & confirming an act which the nation had not previously authorized. The constitution has made no provision for our holding foreign territory, still less for incorporating foreign nations into our Union. The Executive in seizing the fugitive occurrence which so much advances the good of their country, have done an act beyond the Constitution. The Legislature in casting behind them metaphysical subtleties, and risking themselves like faithful servants, must ratify & pay for it, and throw themselves on their country for doing for them unauthorized what we know they would have done for themselves had they been in a situation to do it. It is the case of a guardian, investing the money of his ward in purchasing an important adjacent territory; & saying to him when of age, I did this for your good; I pretend to no right to bind you: you may disavow me, and I must get out of the scrape as I can: I thought it my duty to risk myself for you. But we shall not be disavowed by the nation, and their act of indemnity will confirm & not weaken the Constitution, by more strongly marking out its lines.

--Letter from Thomas Jefferson to John Breckinridge 1803

16. Jefferson's letter that dealt with the issue of obtaining the Louisiana Territory revealed his concerns regarding
    A. having the funds to pay for this territory.
    B. whether the Constitution would permit the acquisition of this territory.
    C. being able to maintain such a vast territory.
    D. inheriting land occupied by a vast number of Indians.

17. Jefferson's concern is especially highlighted by
    A. the looming threat of conflict between the North and South.
    B. Jefferson's earlier objection to Hamilton's views of the Constitution.
    C. the sincerity of France's offer.
    D. the slave culture inherent in New Orleans.

18. Jefferson believed the body that would have to consider a treaty to purchase the Louisiana Territory was
    A. the U.S. Supreme Court.
    B. the collective voice of the state legislatures.
    C. the U.S. Congress.
    D. the president's cabinet.

Questions 19-21 refer to the following excerpt.

To cherish peace and friendly intercourse with all nations having correspondent dispositions; to maintain sincere neutrality toward belligerent nations; to prefer in all cases amicable discussion and reasonable accommodation of differences to a decision of them by an appeal to arms; to exclude foreign intrigues and foreign partialities, so degrading to all countries and so baneful to free ones; to foster a spirit of independence too just to invade the rights of others, too proud to surrender our own, too liberal to indulge unworthy prejudices ourselves and too elevated not to look down upon them in others; to hold the union of the States as the basis of their peace and happiness; to support the Constitution, which is the cement of the Union, as well in its limitations as in its authorities; to respect the rights and authorities reserved to the States and to the people as equally incorporated with and essential to the success of the general system; to avoid the slightest interference with the right of conscience or the functions of religion, so wisely exempted from civil jurisdiction; to preserve in their full energy the other salutary provisions in behalf of private and personal rights, and of the freedom of the press; to observe economy in public expenditures; to liberate the public resources by an honorable discharge of the public debts; to keep within the requisite limits a standing military force, always remembering that an armed and trained militia is the firmest bulwark of republics -- that without standing armies their liberty can never be in danger, nor with large ones safe; to promote by authorized means improvements friendly to agriculture, to manufactures, and to external as well as internal commerce; to favor in like manner the advancement of science and the diffusion of information as the best aliment to true liberty; to carry on the benevolent plans which have been so meritoriously applied to the conversion of our aboriginal neighbors from the degradation and wretchedness of savage life to a participation of the improvements of which the human mind and manners are susceptible in a civilized state -- as far as sentiments and intentions such as these can aid the fulfillment of my duty, they will be a resource which cannot fail me.

19. Based on his Inaugural Address, Madison encouraged
    A. war with England
    B. war with France
    C. peace and discussion with nations at war
    D. total isolation from foreign affairs

20. Madison reveals in his desire"*… to avoid the slightest interference with the right of conscience or the functions of religion, so wisely exempted from civil jurisdiction…*"
    A. that church and state should be closely intertwined.
    B. that church and state should be separate.
    C. that his office should be used to religiously guide the moral direction of the nation.
    D. that religious interest in the nation was fading.

21. All of the following are true of Madison's address EXCEPT
    A. he looked to preserve the powers of the states.
    B. he respected the authority of the Constitution.
    C. he looked to convert the Indians into farmers.
    D. he preferred war over peaceful negotiation.

SHORT ESSAY QUESTIONS

The United States purchased the Louisiana Territory from France in 1803.

a. Choose ONE of the following and explain why your choice represents the event that led to the Louisiana Purchase.

   • U.S. and Spain sign Pinckney's Treaty in 1795
   • France and Spain sign the secret Treaty of Ildefonso in 1800
   • Toussaint Louverture leads a rebellion against the French in Santo Domingo

b. Contrast your choice against ONE of the other options, demonstrating why that option in not as significant as your choice.

LONG ESSAY QUESTION

Explain the road that led to war between the United States and England in 1812.

Answers and Explanations

Multiple Choice Questions

1. B As a Republican, Jefferson believed in limited government.
2. C The Supreme Court gained the power to review the Constitutionality of acts and laws.
3. B Jefferson had children with Sally Hemings.
4. C Masters used religion to try to control their slaves.
5. D New Orleans was a hub center for farmers along the Mississippi River.
6. A The French brought Catholicism to New Orleans.
7. B The U.S. saw impressment as a direct violation to freedom of the seas.
8. D Peace between England and the U.S. was being negotiated as the Hartford Convention convened.
9. B The Hartford Convention during the war alienated the Federalist Party.
10. B The Russians had settlements as far south as California.
11. B The British burned the capital, including the White House, during the War of 1812.
12. D James Madison had to flee from the White House during the British invasion.
13. B Jefferson could be a sociable person.
14. B Margaret Smith's husband was the editor of a Republican newspaper.
15. C Contrary to her preconceived ideas of Jefferson, she found him to be refined.
16. B Being a strict constructionist, Jefferson had reservations about acquiring Louisiana.
17. B Jefferson had clashed with Hamilton over the Bank of the United States and whether the Constitution permitted it.
18. C Jefferson believed that both Houses of Congress had to approve and ratify the treaty.
19. C Madison didn't want war but was pressured into it by the War Hawks.
20. B Like Jefferson, Madison advocated the separation of church and state.
21. D Madison preferred peaceful negotiation before war.

Long Essay Question

Explain the road that led to war between the United States and England in 1812.

(Key topics to focus and elaborate on)
- Renewed war between England and France
- Impressment leads to Embargo Act
- Pressure by War Hawks

Chapter 9
New Industries, New Politics, 1815-1828

- Cotton transformed the nation economically, politically, and socially.

CREATING THE COTTON ECONOMY

- Both as a preference for comfort and through a series of technological innovations, including Eli Whitney's cotton gin, the production of cotton would vastly increase.
- The cotton gin dramatically changed the nation both in the production of cotton in the South, and in the production of textiles in the North.
- The advent of cotton brought many growers into newly acquired regions such as Alabama and Mississippi where the land proved to be more fertile than in states such as South Carolina.
- The cotton-growing lands of Georgia, Alabama, Mississippi, and Louisiana saw over a million slaves migrate to these states to engage in cotton production. This in turn led to the break-up of many slave families.
- Growing cotton was back-breaking work requiring labor from sunrise to sunset.
- Much of the cotton was grown on small farms where the master often worked alongside the slaves.
- In these new cotton-producing regions, new slave communities formed where family, community, faith, and hope became priorities.
- Mills in the North and in England purchased the cotton produced in the South for textile production. Francis Lowell created his mill from memory in his time in England and also introduced the concept of creating a corporation to manufacture cloth on a large scale.
- The creation of the company town, Lowell, Massachusetts began a new era in the north in which the American Industrial Revolution was born.
- The Lowell mill hired single young women (known as factory girls) who lived in boarding houses and were given opportunities for religious instruction and educational activities.
- The benevolence of this treatment would wear off as reduced wages provoked strikes and the grind of factory life would not be much better than those seen in England.
- Southerners shipped most of their cotton to England after the War of 1812.
- New York City, with its deep harbor and miles of docks proved became the center of shipment of cotton across the Atlantic to England. Agents from New York would buy cotton from the south to place on larger transatlantic ships headed to England. In return, English goods would be sent back to New York for distribution.
- The Black Ball Line established a fixed schedule of departures from New York and Liverpool and the packet ships of this line delivered U.S. mail.
- The New York Stock Exchange and a number of banks were formed in the early 1800s to fund this trading and commercial enterprise.

- Conditions in Europe led to less demand for American farm products which resulted in an economic disaster known as the Panic of 1819. The interconnection between the north and south and the policies of the Bank of the United States led this crisis to be a national affair.

COMMERCE, TECHNOLOGY, AND TRANSPORTATION

- The diversity of the economy that spread to different parts of the country led to the need for internal transportation.
- Canals became vital for the transportation of goods, and the Erie Canal essentially opened up New York City to the whole Ohio Valley, thereby transforming the city into the commercial capital of the nation. The canal dramatically reduced shipping costs and connected isolated farmers.
- The development of the steamboat, largely credited to Robert Fulton, increased the speed of shipping goods and allowed for shipping to move in more than one direction.
- Roads also played an important role in establishing a national economy. The National Road connected Maryland to eventually Illinois with a route of crushed rock, yet the Republican presidents didn't show much enthusiasm for these projects.
- Improved transportation allowed for news to travel more quickly and extensively throughout the nation as newspapers became more accessible to more Americans.
- The rise of large commercial ventures led to a need for corporations to lessen the risks and liability of investors and to perpetuate the life of the business long after the original investors pass away.
- The story of *Rip Van Winkle* encompasses the changes made to the economy and society decades after the American Revolution and the life of Ichabod Washburn displayed the impact the rise of an internationally connected economy can have on a simple businessman.
- Inherent in these changes was the switch from a barter economy to a cash economy whereby even the most isolated of farmers often purchased luxury goods from distant places.

FROM THE ERA OF GOOD FEELINGS TO THE POLITICS OF DIVISION

- The disappearance of the Federalists after the War of 1812 allowed President James Monroe to enjoy an Era of Good Feelings in which the Republicans had no opposing political party to contend with. Yet political tensions still existed.
- As the Chief Justice of the U.S. Supreme Court, John Marshall expanded the power and role of the federal government. In *Dartmouth College v. Woodward, McCulloch v. Maryland, and Gibbons v. Ogden,* Marshall's decisions regarding these cases essentially took power away from the states and placed it in the hands of the federal government.
- The issue of admitting Missouri into the Union sparked a heated debate between the North and South over the issue of slavery.
- The rise in value of slaves, an abolitionist movement arising, and the political edge the South would have attained if Missouri was admitted as a slave state, all led to the makings of a heated debate over Missouri's admittance.

- The Missouri Compromise that solved this conflict saw Missouri enter the Union as a slave state, and Maine as a free state.
- The Election of 1824 featured five candidates who all belonged to the Democratic-Republican Party: William Crawford, John Quincy Adams, John C. Calhoun, and Andrew Jackson. Convinced that he could not win, Calhoun dropped out before the election leaving Crawford, Adams, Calhoun, and Jackson to vie for the presidency.
- Jackson won the popular vote but did not have a majority of electoral votes to win the presidency. Thus the election shifted to a run off in the House of Representatives between Jackson and Adams (Crawford had a stroke and therefore was not assumed to be fit for the presidency).
- In the House, with Clay presiding as the Speaker, Adams won the presidency. Shortly thereafter, Adams named Clay to be his Secretary of State. This appointment sparked the ire of Jackson who proclaimed this action to be a "corrupt bargain" and consequently spent the next four years preparing for the next election.
- Adams was determined to unify the nation by investing in federal projects that would connect the nation more efficiently.
- Henry Clay, with his American System, shared this belief and pushed for investment in internal improvements and the implementation of high protective tariffs.
- New England states praised the high tariff that protected their infant industries but southern cotton states that relied heavily on imports did not.
- The Election of 1828 featured a determined Andrew Jackson who sought vindication for his loss four years earlier. At this time, the Democratic-Republicans would splinter into the National Republicans led by Adams and the Democratic Party led by Jackson.
- The election featured intense mudslinging with both sides highlighting the imperfections of the opposition. In the end, Jackson won the election convincingly.

MULTIPLE CHOICE QUESTIONS

1. The rise of cotton in the 1800s developed prominently in the so-called black belt states that all of the following states except
   A. Georgia.
   B. Louisiana.
   C. Alabama.
   D. Virginia.

2. Francis Lowell developed a textile mill industrial city in Massachusetts that initially featured the hiring of
   A. free blacks.
   B. German and Irish immigrants.
   C. young ladies.
   D. troubled young men.

3. During the antebellum period, New York City flourished into a cotton commercial center due to all of the following factors EXCEPT
   A. it had a deep harbor necessary for large-scale shipping.
   B. it had miles of docks.
   C. it already had a large crew of experienced dock workers.
   D. farmers in western New York cultivated massive harvests of cotton.

4. New York's Erie Canal was
   A. funded entirely through loans from the Bank of the United States.
   B. a transportation route that dramatically lowered shipping costs.
   C. highly inefficient since lock systems had not been invented yet.
   D. a water route that utilized the Mohawk River, Lake Ontario, and Lake Erie.

5. Better transportation in the form of roads and canals resulted in
   A. a decrease in the distribution of newspapers.
   B. a increase in the transportation of goods.
   C. the development of a national market.
   D. the perpetuation of isolated and subsistence farming.

6. Washington Irving's *Rip Van Winkle* is a story that
   A. reflects how little changed after twenty years had passed in the early 1800s
   B. shows how people had reflected on their lives and slowed down their daily activity.
   C. shows how the little village he lived in became isolated.
   D. shows how the population had grown and how busy people's lives were.

7. In the case of *McCulloch v. Maryland*, John Marshall declared the "power to tax is the power to destroy" which implied that
   A. Congress could destroy the states through taxation.
   B. high tariffs would destroy the south.
   C. states could drive out a federal institution through taxation.
   D. taxes on cotton would destroy the southern economy.

8. Missouri's application for statehood led to tension between the North and South because
   A. it applied as a free state.
   B. Missouri's statehood threatened to tilt the balance power in the Senate to the South.
   C. Missouri stood as a fountain for abolitionism.
   D. the location of Missouri was above the 36 30 line.

9. Andrew Jackson accused John Quincy Adams of a "corrupt bargain" since
   A. Adams named Henry Clay to be his secretary of state just days after the election.
   B. Adams used funds from the national bank for his campaign.
   C. Adams pushed for internal improvements by taxing the south.
   D. Adams received campaign funds from those seeking federal offices.

10. Henry Clay's American System consisted of all of the following EXCEPT
   A. high protective tariffs.
   B. using federal funds to build canals.
   C. using federal funds to build roads.
   D. elimination of the national bank.

Questions 11-12 refer to the following image.

11. Robert Fulton's steamboat, *The Clermont*, represented in America
   A. the commitment to subsistence farming.
   B. the emergence of a national economy.
   C. the end of canal transportation.
   D. one-way only travelling and shipping.

12. Before the introduction of the steamboat, boats on the Mississippi River
   A. relied on sails.
   B. had to sold for lumber in New Orleans.
   C. went both directions with strong horses.
   D. were actually faster than the heavier steamboats.

Questions 13-15 refer to the following excerpt.

Among the enumerated powers, we do not find that of establishing a bank or creating a corporation. But there is no phrase in the instrument which, like the articles of confederation, exclude incidental or implied powers; and which requires that everything granted shall be expressly and minutely described...A constitution, to contain an accurate detail of all the subdivisions of which its great powers will admit...would partake of the prolixity of the legal code, and could scarcely be embraced by the human mind. It would probably never be understood by the public. Its nature, therefore, requires, that only its great outlines should be marked...After the most deliberate consideration, it is the unanimous and decided opinion of this Court, that the act to incorporate the Bank of the United States is a law made in pursuance of the constitution, and is a part of the supreme law of the land...We proceed to inquire-...whether the State of Maryland may, without violating the constitution, tax that branch?...the constitution and the laws made in pursuance thereof are supreme; that they control the constitution and laws of the respective States, and cannot be controlled by them...The Court has bestowed on this subject its most deliberate consideration. The result is a conviction that the States have no power, by taxation or otherwise, to retard, impede, burden, or in any manner control the operations of the constitutional laws enacted by Congress....We are unanimously of opinion, that the law passed by the legislature of Maryland, imposing a tax on the Bank of the United States, is unconstitutional and void...

--Chief Justice John Marshall/Opinion of the Court-*McCulloch v. Maryland*

13. In order to justify the constitutional existence of the Bank of the United States, Chief Justice John Marshall cites
    A. the existence of expressed powers.
    B. the existence of implied powers.
    C. the principles of strict constructionism.
    D. the doctrine of the Kentucky and Virginia Resolutions.

14. According to John Marshall, the Bank of the United States
    A. is a part of the states that allow it to exist.
    B. is an institution that that should be destroyed.
    C. is a part of the supreme law of the land.
    D. is a private entity that is subject to taxation.

15. According to John Marshall, constitutional laws
    A. control the states.
    B. control only federal actions.
    C. exist to exclusively check the power of the national government.
    D. can be nullified by the states.

Questions 16-18 refer to the following excerpt.

When gentlemen have succeeded in their design of an immediate or gradual destruction of the American System, what is their substitute? Free trade? Free trade! The call for free trade is as unavailing as the cry of a spoiled child, in its nurse's arms, for the moon, or the stars that glitter in the firmament of heaven. It never has existed, it never will exist. Trade implies, at least two parties. To be free, it should be fair, equal and reciprocal. But if we throw our ports wide open to the admission of foreign productions, free of all duty, what ports of any other foreign nation shall we find open to the free admission of our surplus produce? We may break down all barriers to free trade on our part, but the work will not be complete until foreign powers shall have removed theirs. There would be freedom on one side, and restrictions, prohibitions and exclusions on the other. The bolts, and the bars, and the chains of all other nations will remain undisturbed. It is, indeed, possible, that our industry and commerce would accommodate themselves to this unequal and unjust, state of things; for, such is the flexibility of our nature, that it bends itself to all circumstances. The wretched prisoner incarcerated in a jail, after a long time becomes reconciled to his solitude, and regularly notches down the passing days of his confinement...Gentlemen deceive themselves. It is not free trade that they are recommending to our acceptance. It is in effect, the British colonial system that we are invited to adopt; and, if their policy prevail, it will lead substantially to the re-colonization of these States, under the commercial dominion of Great Britain. . . .

--Henry Clay Defense of the American System

16. The free trade that Henry Clay speaks of comes in direct opposition to
    A. an embargo established by John Quincy Adams.
    B. a restriction of enumerated goods that could be sent of England.
    C. a tariff inherent in the American System.
    D. a restriction of goods imported by England.

17. According to Clay, free trade cannot exist because
    A. the U.S. would be an unwilling participant.
    B. a foreign country would not reciprocate.
    C. duties are unnatural to countries.
    D. England was at war with the U.S. at that time.

18. According to Clay, opponents of his system didn't really want free trade, they wanted
    A. higher tariffs than those that existed.
    B. higher export duties than those that existed.
    C. a British colonial system reemerging in the U.S.
    D. higher internal taxes on manufactured goods.

Questions 19-21 refer to the following excerpt.

The last two days have presented in this village, a scene of the liveliest interest; and I consider it among the privileges of my life to have been present to witness it. On Friday afternoon I walked to the head of the Grand Canal, the eastern extremity of which reaches within a very short distance of the village, and from one of the slight and airy bridges which crossed it, I had a sight that could not but exhilarate and elevate the mind. The waters were rushing in from the westward, and coming down their untried channel towards the sea. Their course, owing to the absorption of the new banks of the canal, and the distance they had to run from where the stream entered it, was much slower than I had anticipated; they continued gradually to steal along from bridge to bridge, and at first only spreading over the bed of the canal, imperceptibly rose and washed its sides with a gentle wave. It was dark before they reached the eastern extremity; but at sunrise next morning, they were on a level, two feet and a half deep throughout the whole distance of thirteen miles. The interest manifested by the whole country, as this new internal river rolled its first waves through the state, cannot be described. You might see the people running across the fields, climbing on trees and fences, and crowding the bank of the canal to gaze upon the welcome sight. A boat had been prepared at Rome, and as the waters came down the canal, you might mark their progress by that of this new Argo, which floated triumphantly along the Hellespont of the west, accompanied by the shouts of the peasantry, and having on her deck a military band. At nine the next morning, the bells began a merry peal, and the commissioners in carriages, proceeded from Bagg's hotel, to the place of embarkation.

The governor, accompanied by Gen. Van Rensselaer, Rev. Mr. Stansbury, of Albany, Rev. Dr. Blatchford, of Lansingburgh, Judge Miller, of Utica, Mr. Holly, Mr. Seymour, Judge Wright, Col. Lansing, Mr. Childs, Mr. Clark, Mr. Bunner, and a large company of their friends, embarked, at a quarter past nine, and were received with the roll of the drum, and the shouts of a large multitude of spectators ..A military band played patriotic airs. From bridge to bridge, from village to village, the procession was saluted with cannon, and every bell whose sound could reach the canal, swung, as with instinctive life, as it passed by.

--Extract from the *Albany Daily Advertiser*, 1819

19. The description of the Erie Canal's beginnings
    A. showed the anticipation of a significant connection.
    B. marked the beginning of similar federal projects.
    C. gave praise to the efforts of James Monroe.
    D. marked the beginning of the railroad industry.

20. The Erie Canal was funded by
    A. the federal government.
    B. investors from England.
    C. the state of New York.
    D. cotton investors from the South.

21. The celebration of the Erie Canal at each village indicated
    A. the growth of the canal system throughout the United States.
    B. prosperity the canal would bring to each canal-side village.
    C. the willingness of the federal government to fund internal improvements.
    D. the re-election of Governor Clinton.

SHORT ESSAY QUESTIONS

New Orleans becomes the largest slave trading center in the United States by the 1820s.

    a.   Choose ONE of the following and explain why your choice represents the event that led New Orleans to be such a prominent slave trading center.

- Eli Whitney invented the cotton gin
- Samuel Slater built a textile mill in New England
- Great Britain imported 81% of its cotton from the US

    b.   Contrast your choice against ONE of the other options, demonstrating why that option in not as significant as your choice.

LONG ESSAY QUESTION

How did Alexander Hamilton's vision of a commercial society begin to take root in the United States by the early 1800s?

ANSWERS AND EXPLANATIONS

Multiple Choice Questions

1. D   Virginia was primarily a tobacco producing state.
2. C   Young ladies were hired until replaced by immigrants.
3. D   Farmers in western New York did not grow cotton.
4. B   The use of the canal lowered shipping costs dramatically.
5. C   Once-isolated areas now had access to distant markets.
6. D   The story describes the far-reaching changes that occurred in the early 1800s.
7. C   Marshall believed that Maryland could drive the Bank or any federal institution from its state through taxation.
8. B   Missouri would enter as a slave state thereby giving the South more political power.
9. A   This appointment haunted Adams throughout his presidency.
10.   D Clay needed the Bank to provide loans for commercial investment.
11.   B The steamboat contributed to expanded markets.
12.   B Since boats could not go upstream, they were broken apart for lumber.
13.   C Marshall reasserts Hamilton's elastic clause to defend the Bank.
14.   C The Bank was made in pursuance of the constitution and therefore supreme.
15.   A Constitutional laws control the states and cannot be controlled by the states.
16.   C Clay advocated tariffs to protect America's infant industries.
17.   B Clay believed that free trade was never reciprocal.
18.   C Clay believed that free trade would turn the US once again into a British colony.
19.   A Residents who lived near the canal knew the impact such a form of transportation would have.
20.   C The Erie Canal would be funded exclusively by the state of New York.
21.   B Each canal-side village would benefit greatly by the commerce of the canal,

Long Essay Question
How did Alexander Hamilton's vision of a commercial society begin to take root in the United States by the early 1800s?

(Key topics to focus and elaborate on)
- Canals and steamboats are developed
- Roads connecting distant places are established
- Commercial corporations begin to emerge

Chapter 10
DEMOCRACY IN THE AGE OF ANDREW JACKSON, 1828-1844

- After Jackson's raucous inauguration, his presidency would be unlike any others that preceded him.
- Jackson's agenda included destroying the national bank, forcing Indians out of lands desired by whites, and leading a modest government; the period he presided as the president came to be known as the Age of Jackson.

JACKSONIAN DEMOCRACY, JACKSONIAN GOVERNMENT

- Jackson introduced the spoils system to reward supporters of his campaign with government jobs, relied on his own "Kitchen Cabinet" to implement his policies and agendas, and was determined to show both Congress and those who opposed federal policies that he was a force to be reckoned with.
- Members of the Five Civilized Tribes in the Old Southwest stood in the way of white settlement expansion, and the Cherokees proved to be the most difficult to remove due to their sophistication and adoption of white farming techniques.
- In 1830, Congress passed the Indian Removal Act which severely restricted the rights of the Cherokees in Georgia, and forced Indians in this region to resettle to land that is today present-day Oklahoma.
- The Cherokees challenged this removal, and Chief Justice John Marshall supported this challenge, but Jackson ignored the Supreme Court. The result of Jackson's approach towards these Indians was their tragic removal to land they had no familiarity with.
- The last wave of removal for the Cherokees came in 1837 when federal troops forced 12,000 of them to Oklahoma on a journey that came to be known as the Trail of Tears.
- The Cherokees proved to be resilient in their new home and today are the largest federally recognized tribe today.
- After the Second Bank of the United States formed in 1816, the bank faced much opposition and was seen as an institution aimed to benefit only the nation's commercial elite and this perception continued through Jackson's presidency.
- During the Election of 1832, Nicholas Biddle attempted to obtain a renewal of the bank, but Jackson vetoed it and transferred the federal revenue into the state banks instead of the national bank.
- The Nullification Crisis, in part, stemmed from a rivalry that pitted Andrew Jackson against his own vice president, John C. Calhoun.
- By 1828, Calhoun had become a staunch supporter of states' rights and his home state of South Carolina took a stance against the federal union in fear that the union targeted the abolishment of slavery.
- Calhoun argued that states had the right to decide the constitutionality of a law and thus could nullify any law that they deemed to be detrimental. Nullification was tested when Congress passed a high tariff in 1828 that southerners called the Tariff of Abominations;

a tariff that threatened to devastate the economic livelihood of southern states, including South Carolina.

- After an unforgettable debate between proponents of states' rights and federal rights, Jackson declared "the union, it must be preserved". However, South Carolina still voted to nullify the tariffs of 1828 and 1832.
- In response, Jackson was appalled and threatened to use force against this state. In essence, he set a precedent in not allowing a state to nullify a federal law and threatening to use force to make a rebellious state comply with federal policy.

DEMOCRATIZED RELIGION: THE SECOND GREAT AWAKENING

- Whereas Charles G. Finney used logic and wit to influence thousands to embrace religion by joining churches and reform movements especially in New York, Lyman Beecher supported revivals and moral reform in New England.
- In addition, Beecher helped to form interdenominational organizations that contributed in distributing Bibles and providing curriculum materials for Sunday schools.
- Beecher's goal was to build a Protestant culture that would reinforce common Protestant beliefs and practices.
- The new generation of revivalists encouraged more women to be involved in church affairs.
- Inherent in both Finney and Theodore Dwight Weld's revivalism was a staunch support for abolitionism and this movement influenced northerners to embrace the fight to end slavery.
- Reformers also looked to improve prisons so that the incarcerated could re-enter society as productive citizens by teaching them new ways of behavior and restructuring the living and communal arrangements of prisons.
- Dorothea Dix fought for more humane treatment of the mentally ill and through her efforts, institutions of state hospitals began to emerge in the 1840s.
- Whereas members of the religious group known as the Shakers advocated a life of celibacy, members of the Oneida community viewed sex as a gift that should be shared with several companions.
- Joseph Smith founded an American-born religion that many argued represented a rebirth of true Christianity.
- The religion came to be known as Mormonism that for a short time centered in Illinois and then moved to the Mexican territory of Utah under the leadership of Brigham Young. The controversy of the Mormons was that the religion allowed polygamy until 1890.
- Through the efforts of Ralph Waldo Emerson and George Ripley, the Transcendentalist movement formed to search for a direct experience with the divine.

DEMOCRATIZED EDUCATION: THE BIRTH OF THE COMMON SCHOOL

- Educational reformers sought to counter Jackson's brand of individualism, and pushed for women to become teachers as seen with the forming of Mouth Holyoke College.
- Schools also underwent major restructuring largely through the efforts of Horace Mann who was instrumental in establishing a state board of education and pushing for school standards in Massachusetts.

- Mann had many supporters but also met opposition from Jackson supporters and Catholics.
- *McGuffey's Reader* became a handbook in citizenry that focused on speaking skills, hard work, patriotism and morality.

MULTIPLE CHOICE QUESTIONS

1. The introduction of Jackson's spoils system
   A. led to efficiency in the postal service that lasted until the 1880s.
   B. maintained government jobs held by the staff of previous administrations.
   C. saw the supporters of Jackson's campaign receive government jobs.
   D. came in response to a well-known accusation that corruption had existed amongst previous government officials

2. The federal government had a difficult time removing the Cherokees from Georgia because
   A. Jackson was intent on blocking Indian removal.
   B. they were settled farmers that even had their own newspaper.
   C. they were fierce nomadic warriors.
   D. they were too elusive to capture.

3. Andrew Jackson destroyed the Second Bank of the United States by
   A. using the national bank to pay government bills and not depositing revenue in it.
   B. transferring the banks funds to the state banks.
   C. ordering its immediate closing.
   D. signing a renewal for only four years.

4. Jackson responded to South Carolina's decision to nullify the tariffs of 1828 and 1832
   A. by supporting the measure since he was a southerner himself.
   B. by supporting the measure due to his views on states' rights.
   C. by threatening to use federal force in South Carolina to uphold the tariffs.
   D. by challenging John C. Calhoun to a debate over the controversy.

5. During the Second Great Awakening, Charles G. Finney
   A. called on people to accept specific creeds within the Christian faith.
   B. sought an emotional catharsis from his congregants.
   C. preached in a manner that gave way to a more egalitarian spirit.
   D. focused most of his preaching efforts in the South.

6. As a preacher during the Second Great Awakening, Lyman Beecher
   A. argued that people relied too much on Bibles to receive their religious instruction.
   B. became convinced that the key to transforming the nation lay in New York.
   C. argued against the formation of interdenominational organizations.
   D. became instrumental in the preparation of ministers especially in the Midwest

7. The prisons that emerged in the 1830s and 1840s saw
   A. prisoners who had access to dining quarters, workshops, and a chapel.
   B. solitary confinement leading to obedience rather than insanity.
   C. punishment becoming more cruel and inhumane.
   D. the reformers giving up their efforts to rehabilitate prisoners.

8. Dorothea Dix is most noted for her efforts to
   A. improve the prison system and its use of solitary confinement.
   B. advocate the use of common ground areas for prisoners.
   C. create a system of state hospitals for the insane.
   D. push for a stronger form of discipline and punishment in the asylums.

9. The Shakers believed that the only way to live a godly life
   A. was to have monogamous marital relationships that produced children.
   B. was to live a life of celibacy.
   C. was to live in communes that contained polygamous relationships.
   D. was to live in isolation from all people.

10. Due to the persecution of the Mormons, their final destination of settlement
   A. ended in Utah.
   B. ended in New York.
   C. ended in Illinois.
   D. ended in California.

Questions 11-12 refer to the following visual:

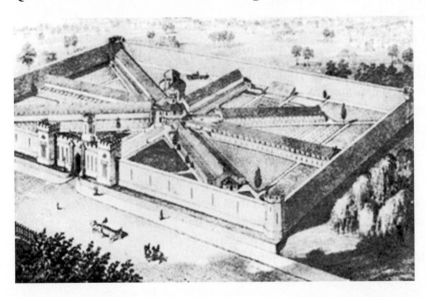

11. The reforms in the prison system during the Age of Reform
   A. saw solitary cells where prisoners had no contact with each other.
   B. saw cells that were shared by 2-3 cellmates.
   C. saw solitary cells with common areas for prisoner interaction.
   D. saw no cells but large holding rooms.

12. Prisons during the Age of Reform
   A. aimed at harsh punishment.
   B. looked to change the behavior of the prisoner.
   C. looked to use prisoners as slave labor.
   D. aimed to scare potential prisoners away.

Questions 13-15 refer to the following excerpt.

And whereas, the said Congress, exceeding its just power to impose taxes and collect revenue for the purpose of effecting and accomplishing the specific objects and purposes which the Constitution of the United States authorizes it to effect and accomplish, hath raised and collected unnecessary revenue, for objects unauthorized by the Constitution—

We, therefore, the People of the State of South Carolina, in Convention assembled, do Declare and Ordain, and it is hereby Declared and Ordained, That the several acts and parts of acts of the Congress of the United States, purporting to be laws for the imposing of duties and imposts on the importation of foreign commodities, and now having actual operation and effect within the United States, and more especially an act entitled "an act in alteration of the several acts imposing duties on imports," approved on the nineteenth day of May, on thousand eight hundred and twenty-eight, and also, an act entitled "an act to alter and amend the several acts imposing duties on imports," approved on the fourteenth day of July, one thousand eight hundred and thirty-two, are unauthorized by the Constitution of the United States, and violate the true meaning and intent thereof, and are null, void, and no law, nor binding upon this State, its officers or citizens; and all promises, contracts and obligations, made or entered into, or to be made or entered into, with purpose to secure the duties imposed by said acts, and all judicial proceedings which shall be hereafter had in affirmance thereof, are, and shall be held, utterly null and void.

--Excerpt from South Carolina's Ordinance of Nullification, 1832

13. The acts that the state of South Carolina protested dealt with
   A. the expansion of slavery.
   B. tariffs on manufactured goods.
   C. fugitive slave laws.
   D. internal taxes.

14. The act that South Carolina committed came to be known as
   A. the South Carolina Resolutions.
   B. secession.
   C. Nullification.
   D. the Force Bill.

15. *Null and void* refers to
   A. the imposing of duties on imports that South Carolina refused to implement.
   B. the imposing of duties on exports that South Carolina refused to implement.

C. the acts that South Carolina deemed to be Constitutional and thus obeyed.

D. the necessary revenue that Congress could obtain from South Carolina.

Questions 16-18 refer to the following excerpt.

According to the European theory, men are divided into classes-some to toil and earn, others to seize and enjoy. According to the Massachusetts theory, all are to have an equal chance for earning, and equal security in the enjoyment of what they earn. A republican form of government, without intelligence in the people, must be, on a vast scale, what a mad-house without superintendent or keepers would be on a small one. . . . However elevated the moral character of a constituency may be, however, well-informed in matters of general science or history, yet they must, if citizens of a republic, understand something of the true nature and functions of the government under which they live. . . . The establishment of a republican government, without well-appointed and efficient means for the universal education of the people, is the most rash and foolhardy experiment ever tried by man. . . . It may be an easy thing to make a republic, but it a very laborious thing to make republicans; and woe to the republic that rests upon no better foundations than ignorance, selfishness, and passion! . . . Such, then, . . . is the Massachusetts system of common schools. Reverently it recognizes and affirms the sovereign rights of the Creator, sedulously and sacredly it guards the religious rights of the creature. . . . In a social and political sense, it is a free school system. It knows no distinction of rich and poor, of bond and free, or between those, who, in the imperfect light of this world, are seeking, through different avenues, to reach the gate of heaven. Without money and without price, it throws open its doors, and spreads the table of its bounty, for all the children of the State. Like the sun, it shines not only upon the good, but upon the evil, that they may become good; and, like the rain, its blessings descend not only upon the just, but upon the unjust, that their injustice may depart from them, and be know no more.

--Horace Mann, excerpt from *Report of the Massachusetts Board of Education*, 1848

16. According to Horace Mann, the most effective republics are those that
    A. have strong leaders with the support of the people.
    B. have an educated constituency that understand the functions of government.
    C. have an educated leadership.
    D. have strong leaders with an obedient uneducated constituency.

17. Through his support of public education Mann implies that
    A. a knowledgeable but dangerous society can be formed.
    B. an ungovernable constituency will be formed.
    C. a righteous and law-abiding society can develop.
    D. there will still be inevitable evil and deceit in society.

18. According to Mann, the difference between European theory and Massachusetts theory was
    A. that Europe had more social mobility.

B. that Europe had a better public school system.

C. that Massachusetts bred social inequity.

D. that Massachusetts offered a better chance at equality.

Questions 19-21 refer to the following excerpt.

As the weather precludes all possibility of ploughing, hoeing, sowing and other such operations, I bethink me that you may have no objection to hear something of my whereabout and whatabout. You are to know then, that I took up my abode here on the 12th ultimo, in the midst of a snowstorm, which kept us all idle for a day or two. At the first glimpse of fair weather, Mr. Ripley summoned us into the cowyard and introduced me to an instrument with four prongs, commonly called a dung-fork. With this tool, I have already assisted to load twenty or thirty carts of manure, and shall take part in loading nearly three hundred more. Besides, I have planted potatoes and peas, cut straw and hay for the cattle, and done various other mighty works. This very morning, I milked three cows; and I milk two or three every night and morning. The weather has been so unfavorable, that we have worked comparatively little in the fields; but, nevertheless, I have gained strength wonderfully-grown quite a giant, in fact-and can do a day's work without the slightest inconvenience. In short, I am transformed into a complete farmer.

This is one of the most beautiful places I ever saw in my life, and as secluded as if it were a hundred miles from any city or village. There are woods, in which we can ramble all day, without meeting anybody, or scarcely seeing a house. Our house stands apart from the main road; so that we are not troubled even with passengers looking at us. Once in a while, we have a transcendental visitor, such as Mr. [Bronson] Alcott; but, generally, we pass whole days without seeing a single face, save those of the brethren. At this present time, our effective force consists of Mr. Ripley, Mr. Farley (a farmer from the far west), Rev. Warren Burton (author of various celebrated works), three young men and boys, who are under Mr. Ripley's care, and William Allen, his hired man, who has the chief direction of our agricultural labors. In the female part of the establishment there is Mrs. Ripley and two women folks. The whole fraternity eat together; and such a delectable way of life has never been seen on earth, since the days of the early Christians. We get up at half-past four, breakfast at half-past six, dine at half-past twelve, and go to bed at nine.

We shall be very much occupied during most of this month, ploughing and planting; so that I doubt whether you will see me for two or three weeks...I would write more; but William Allen is going to the village, and must have this letter; so good-bye.

Nath Hawthorne

Ploughman

> --Nathaniel Hawthorne, A Letter from Brook Farm, 1841

19. Hawthorne's letter to his fiancé describes
    A. a pure idle life on an isolated farm.

B. a life of pure leisure.
C. a busy life of farm work when weather permits.
D. a life conducive to only to writing.

20. Hawthorne describes Brook Farm as being
    A. a farm with clear signs of intruding urbanism.
    B. very secluded with many trees.
    C. secluded but crowded.
    D. polluted with lumbering activities.

21. Hawthorne described the occupants of Brook Farm as
    A. inhabitants who never interacted with each other.
    B. brainwashed transcendentalists.
    C. as a whole fraternity.
    D. lazy, idle, and isolated.

SHORT ANSWER QUESTIONS

In 1837, federal troops force the Cherokees to embark on the Trail of Tears from Georgia to Oklahoma.

a. Choose ONE of the following and explain why your choice represents the event that led the Cherokees to embark on a forced Trail of Tears.

- Seqoyah devises a Cherokee alphabet
- Congress passes the Indian Removal Act in 1830
- Jackson refuses to uphold Marshall's decision regarding the Cherokees

b. Contrast your choice against ONE of the other options, demonstrating why that option in not as significant as your choice.

LONG ESSAY QUESTION

In what way did Andrew Jackson become one of the first presidents to use fully utilize the power of the presidency?

ANSWERS AND EXPLANATIONS

Multiple Choice Questions

1. C Jackson began a long tradition of "rotation in office" with his spoils system.

2. B The Cherokees essentially lived like the white settlers who would replace them.
3. A Without a stream of revenue, the Bank could not maintain its operations.
4. C Jackson offered to lead troops into South Carolina to enforce the law.
5. C Finney went away from the rigid orthodox religion of the day to embrace a more egalitarian spirit.
6. D Beecher prepared ministers in the Midwest and also contributed to the public school system.
7. A Prisons began to move away from being places of just punishment.
8. C Dix looked to separate the mentally ill from hardened criminals.
9. B The Shakers believed that abstinence from sex prevented sin.
10. A Led by Brigham Young, the Mormons migrated to Utah in the 1840s.
11. C Prisons had common areas but solitary cells.
12. B Reformers stressed the importance of rehabilitation of the prisoner.
13. B Tariffs hurt Southerners because they relied on imported manufactured goods.
14. C South Carolina regarded the Tariff of Abominations as null and void.
15. A South Carolina refused to implement taxes on manufactured imports.
16. B According to Mann, an educated public is the key to a successful government.
17. C According to Mann, education can create a law-abiding society.
18. D Class division was more pronounced in Europe than in Massachusetts.
19. C Hawthorne found farm life to be a lot of work.
20. B Hawthorne described the farm as beautiful, secluded and miles from any city or village.
21. C The people at Brook Farm are described as a whole fraternity that eats together.

Long Essay Question

In what way did Andrew Jackson become one of the first presidents to use fully utilize the power of the presidency?

(Key topics to focus and elaborate on)
- Jackson enacts the spoils system
- Jackson pushes through Congress the Force Bill
- Jackson vetoes a bill the renew the Second Bank of the United States

Chapter 11
Manifest Destiny: Expanding the Nation, 1830-1853

- The idea of spreading west and expanding the nation had been an ongoing trend of the United States since its inception, and this trend continued in the 1830s/40s.

MANIFEST DESTINY-THE IMPORTANCE OF AN IDEA

- Editor John L. O'Sullivan created the term "manifest destiny" to describe how the United States had a mission to spread across the continent of North America and bring democracy and the Protestant faith to the inhabitants it conquered. Inherent in this belief was the notion that God had blessed this mission.
- From religion to land speculation to farming, many Americans had different reasons to support the ideals of Manifest Destiny. However, many Americans feared the consequences of acquiring new territory, especially from Mexico.
- In 1823, the Mexican government granted Stephen Austin the title of empresario, thereby allowing him to establish a colony of Americans in the sparsely settled region of Texas, a northern province in Mexico.
- The forbiddance of slavery and the requirement of becoming Catholic was ignored by the American settlers.
- By 1830, Mexico ended American migration into Texas and sent troops to enforce more restrictive guidelines. In effect this ultimately led to a call for independence for the Americans in Texas which provoked the Mexican government to crush this insurrection in 1836.
- Seemingly, the rebellion appeared to be crushed after the fall and execution of American forces at the Alamo and Goliad, until a Texas commander captured Mexico's president, Santa Anna at the Battle of San Jacinto. This capture led to the independence of Texas in 1836.
- The U.S. government was hesitant to annex Texas because of the political ramifications of adding a slave state, and thus, Texas remained an independent republic for nine years.
- Further west, California remained dormant from thoughts of independence until the 1840s. The Spanish ignored California until the 1700s when Franciscan friars began to build a series of missions along its coastline.
- The independence of Mexico in 1821 saw the transfer of mission land in California to powerful Mexican landowners who specialized in cattle ranching. Meanwhile, by the 1840s, many Americans had their eye on the possible acquisition of California.
- As the spirit of Manifest Destiny fomented, so too did the spirit of party politics with a fierce rivalry between Jackson's Democrats and a newly formed party called the Whigs.
- Jackson's successor, Martin Van Buren contended with many issues including the remnants of nullification the rising voice of abolitionism, and an economic disaster known as the Panic of 1837.

126

- The economic crisis that lasted until 1843 saw numerous banks failing, the value of cotton land and slaves plummeting, and thousands of northern factory workers losing their jobs.
- The strong-handed policies of Jackson combined with the inability of Van Buren to resolve the nation's economic policies opened the doors for the Whigs to win the presidency in 1840 under the ticket of William Henry Harrison and John Tyler.
- A month into his presidency, Harrison died of pneumonia leaving Tyler to assume the presidency in 1841.
- Tyler did not share the same ideals as the rest of the Whigs and was ousted from his own political party.
- One of Tyler's main goals was to annex Texas and an initial attempt to acquire Texas in 1844 failed due to the presence of slavery in Texas.
- Thus the chances of reelection for Tyler were doomed, and the Election of 1844 would feature the well-known Whig, Henry Clay, versus a true "dark-horse" candidate, James Polk.
- Polk's campaign focused on the essence of Manifest Destiny with Oregon and Texas as definite priorities to be addressed.
- This in turn led outgoing president, John Tyler to support Polk's campaign and, as a last act of his presidency (in March of 1845), Tyler signed a resolution allowing Texas to be admitted as a state instead of being acquired as a territory.
- A decade before the annexing of Texas, interest in Oregon began to grow largely through the glowing descriptions of this region by missionaries, Marcus and Narcissa Williams.
- Through earlier treaties, both England and the U.S. jointly occupied this territory, but by the 1840s looked to end this joint ownership.
- Polk's campaign featured an ambitious claim for the U.S. to acquire all of the Oregon territory up to the 54 40 parallel.
- With a possible war looming against Mexico due to the annexation of Texas, in 1846 the U.S. and Britain agreed to a compromise allowing the U.S. to acquire the Oregon territory up to the 49th parallel instead of the 54 40 parallel.

THE U.S. WAR WITH MEXICO, 1846-1848

- Immediately following the annexation of Texas, Mexico severed diplomatic relations, but soon after negotiations would resume in 1846.
- However, a breakdown of these negotiations proved to be a dispute as to what constituted the border between Texas and Mexico.
- As these negotiations began to crumble, Polk sent General Zachary Taylor to the Rio Grande thereby provoking an attack launched by Mexican forces.
- The attack proved to be just what Polk needed to begin a war with Mexico and ultimately gather the fruits of victory with the acquisition of the southwest.
- Not all Americans embraced the war, among them notable figures such as Abraham Lincoln and Henry David Thoreau.
- During the war, Taylor succeeded in controlling much of northern Mexico, including the city of Monterey.

- To capture Mexico City, Polk turned to Winfield Scott who landed a large amphibious force at Veracruz before marching on to the capital. By September of 1847, Mexico City surrendered.
- As U.S. forces gained important victories in the heartland of Mexico, California and New Mexico also saw fighting. Through the efforts of Stephen Kearney, American forces captured New Mexico in 1846.
- At the same time, an uprising against Mexican authorities in northern California erupted in what organizers of this rebellion called the Bear Flag Revolt. Shortly after, the U.S. Navy captured Monterey Bay near San Francisco.
- Despite some opposition to U.S. forces, such as that seen by Andres Pico near Los Angeles, California experienced limited warfare.
- This war culminated in the signing of the Treaty of Guadalupe Hidalgo which yielded to the United States most of the present-day southwestern portion of the country including California.
- In 1853, the U.S. purchased the lowermost portions of present-day Arizona and New Mexico in preparations for a southern transcontinental railroad.
- The acquisition of this new territory led to the creation of the Free Soilers who opposed the expansion of slavery. Thus the Election of 1848 featured three parties; the Whig, Zachary Taylor, won.

WEST INTO THE PACIFIC

- As the U.S. and Mexico negotiated the Treaty of Guadalupe Hidalgo, gold was discovered in California sparking a gold rush that would forever change the would-be state.
- In addition, California and Oregon proved to be vital components in establishing the United States as a major player in the Pacific Ocean.
- After James Marshall discovered gold near Sutter's Fort in 1848, gold rushers from near and distant places arrived in California to seek their riches.
- The rush of settlers established gold camps that featured rowdiness and lawless behavior, much of which was directed at Chinese, *Californio*, and Indian gold rushers.
- The acquisition of the west enhanced an already successful whaling industry that flourished until the Civil War.
- Whale oil had many uses and the crews of whale ships proved to be dominated by men of old New England English stock, though there were other types of crewmen as well.
- The acquisition of California meant that San Francisco would serve as a vital port and that the United States would secure American interests in Hawaii throughout the 1800s until the nation eventually annexed it in 1898.
- Hawaii and San Francisco also served as stepping stones of trade with China as the United States gained access to some of China's lucrative ports in 1844. Likewise, in 1853, the United States opened the doors to trade with Japan under the negotiations of Commodore Mathew Perry.

MULTIPLE CHOICE QUESTIONS

1. John L. O'Sullivan's term "Manifest Destiny" referred to
   A. an urging for the United States to build from within.
   B. a mindset that fueled territorial expansion.
   C. a prediction of war between the North and South.
   D. the tragic fate of the Plains Indians.

2. All of the following opposed Manifest Destiny to some degree EXCEPT
   A. Henry Clay.
   B. John C. Calhoun.
   C. Antonio Maria Osio.
   D. James Polk.

3. Santa Anna's forces killed all of the following at the Alamo EXCEPT
   A. Davy Crockett.
   B. Jim Bowie.
   C. Sam Houston.
   D. William B. Travis.

4. The core of the Whig Party was
   A. to destroy the Bank of the United States.
   B. to establish a smaller federal government.
   C. to oppose Andrew Jackson.
   D. to discourage federal funding for internal improvements.

5. The focus of Polk's campaign in the Election of 1844 was
   A. the growing tensions between the North and South.
   B. the struggle for power between the federal government and state governments.
   C. the influence of Manifest Destiny.
   D. restoring the Bank of the United States.

6. Polk did not pursue his desire to acquire the Oregon Territory up to the 54 40 parallel because
   A. the amount of resources needed to maintain all of this territory.
   B. he genuinely feared the power of the British military.
   C. the U.S. did not have the funds to purchase it from England.
   D. he needed military troops for a possible war with Mexico.

7. The principle reason the U.S. went to war with Mexico was
   A. to overthrow the dictatorship of Antonio Lopez de Santa Anna.
   B. because of disputed territory in Texas claimed by both the U.S. and Mexico.
   C. to overthrow slavery in Mexico.
   D. to gain access to raw materials for northeastern factories.

8. Polk helped to provoke war with Mexico by
   A. giving impassioned speeches that glorified Manifest Destiny.
   B. convincing Americans that the gold in California was worth going to war.
   C. sending General Zachary Taylor to the northern edge of the Rio Grande.
   D. sending Winfield Scott to capture Veracruz.

9. The completion of the U.S. conquest of California came
   A. during the Bear Flag Revolt.
   B. when General Mariano Vallejo was arrested.
   C. when the U.S. Navy sailed into Monterey Bay.
   D. when *Californio* defender, Andres Pico, negotiated for an honorable surrender.

10. The most common route used by gold rushers to get to California was
   A. traveling by ship around South America to San Francisco.
   B. hiking across Nicaragua and then traveling by ship to San Francisco.
   C. by traveling overland across the continent.
   D. utilizing the nation's first transcontinental railroad to Sacramento.

Questions 11-12 refer to the following

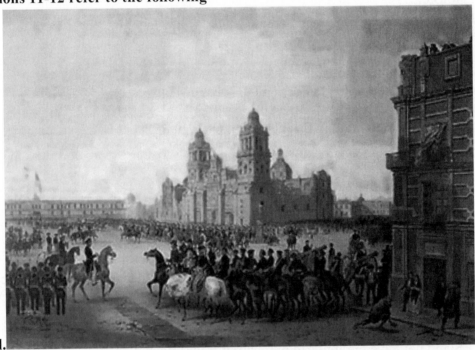

visual.

11. What was the significance of Scott's capturing of Mexico City?
   A. It led to permanent U.S. occupancy.
   B. The U.S. controlled its customs duties for decades.
   C. It essentially ended the war between the U.S. and Mexico.
   D. It proved to be the catalyst for another war between the countries.

130

12. Why was Scott relieved of his commanding duties not long after this impressive victory?
    A. Scott led unnecessary executions of Mexican leaders.
    B. Scott threatened a *coup d'etat*.
    C. Polk feared the potential political ambition of Scott.
    D. Too many American lives were lost with this victory

Questions 13-15 refer to the following excerpt:

The Californians are an idle, thriftless people, and can make nothing for themselves. The country abounds in grapes, yet they buy bad wine made in Boston and brought round by us, at an immense price, and retail it among themselves at a real [a Spanish coin then worth 12 1/2 cents] by the small wine-glass. Their hides, too, which they value at two dollars in money, they give for something which costs seventy-five cents in Boston; and buy shoes (as like as not, made of their own hides, which have been carried twice round Cape Horn) at three and four dollars, and "chicken-skin" boots at fifteen dollars apiece. Things sell, on an average, at an advance of nearly three hundred per cent upon the Boston prices . . . .Their complexions are various, depending-- as well as their dress and manner--upon their rank; or, in other words, upon the amount of Spanish blood they can lay claim to. Those who are of pure Spanish blood, having never intermarried with the aborigines, have clear brunette complexions, and sometimes, even as fair as those of English women. There are but few of these families in California . . . . These form the aristocracy; intermarrying, and keeping up an exclusive system in every respect. They can be told by their complexions, dress, manner, and also by their speech . . . . From this upper class, they go down by regular shades, growing more and more dark and muddy, until you come to the pure Indian, who runs about with nothing upon him but a small piece of cloth, kept up by a wide leather strap drawn round his waist. Generally speaking, each person's caste is decided by the quality of the blood, which shows itself, too plainly to be concealed, at first sight. Yet the least drop of Spanish blood . . . is sufficient to raise them from the rank of slaves, and entitle them to a suit of clothes--boots, hat, cloak, spurs, long knife, and all complete, though coarse and dirty as may be--and to call themselves Espanolos, and to hold property, if they can get any . . . .No Protestant has any civil rights, nor can he hold any property, or, indeed, remain more than a few weeks on shore, unless he belongs to some vessel. Consequently, the Americans and English who intend to reside here become Catholics, to a man; the current phrase among them being--"A man must leave his conscience at Cape Horn." . . . .

--Richard Henry Dana, Jr., Assesses California in *Two Years before the Mast*, 1840

13. Based on Dana's description of the Californians, why would Americans from Boston want to journey thousands of miles to trade in this region?
    A. to vacation in this sunny region
    B. to profit greatly by trading manufactured goods
    C. to witness an egalitarian society
    D. to bring back to Boston finished leather products

14. Why did Americans who moved to California convert to Catholicism?
    A. They were influenced by the Second Great Awakening to embrace a new religion.

B. They grew tired of Protestantism.
C. They wanted to experience the rituals of the Catholic Church.
D. Spain was a Catholic nation.

15. According to Dana, the most fortunate in California were
    A. those who had struck gold.
    B. the innocent aborigines.
    C. those with the most Spanish blood.
    D. those that had a mixture of Spanish and Indian blood.

Questions 16-18 refer to the following excerpt.

A scene occurred about this time that exhibits in a striking light, the summary manner in which "justice" is dispensed in a community where there are no legal tribunals. We received a report on the afternoon of January 20th, that five men had been arrested at the dry diggings, and were under trial for a robbery. The circumstances were these:-A Mexican gambler, named Lopez, having in his possession a large amount of money, retired to his room at night, and was surprised about midnight by five men rushing into his apartment, one of whom applied a pistol to his head, while the others barred the door and proceeded to rifle his trunk. An alarm being given, some of the citizens rushed in, and arrested the whole party. Next day they were tried by a jury chosen from among the citizens, and sentenced to receive thirty-nine lashes each, on the following morning. Never having witnessed a punishment inflicted by Lynch-law, I went over to the dry diggings on a clear Sunday morning, and on my arrival, found a large crowd collected around an oak tree, to which was lashed a man with a bared back, while another was applying a raw cowhide to his already gored flesh. A guard of a dozen men, with loaded rifles pointed at the prisoners, stood ready to fire in case of an attempt being made to escape. After the whole had been flogged, some fresh charges were preferred against three of the men-two Frenchmen, named Garcia and Bissi, and a Chileno, named Manuel. These were charged with a robbery and attempt to murder, on the Stanislaus River, during the previous fall. The unhappy men were removed to a neighbouring house, and being so weak from their punishment as to be unable to stand, were laid stretched upon the floor. As it was not possible for them to attend, they were tried in the open air, in their absence, by a crowd of some two hundred men, who had organized themselves into a jury, and appointed a pro tempore judge. The charges against them were well substantiated, but amounted to nothing more than an attempt at robbery and murder; no overt act being even alleged. They were known to be bad men, however, and a general sentiment seemed to prevail in the crowd that they ought to be got rid of. At the close of the trial, which lasted some thirty minutes, the Judge put to vote the question whether they had been proved guilty. A universal affirmative was the response; and then the question "What punishment shall be inflicted?" was asked. A brutal-looking fellow in the crowd, cried out, "Hang them." The proposition was seconded, and met with almost universal approbation. I mounted a stump, and in the name of God, humanity, and law, protested against such a course of proceeding; but the crowd, by this time excited by frequent and deep potations of liquor from a neighbouring groggery, would listen to nothing contrary to their brutal desires, and even threatened to hang me if I did not immediately desist from any further remarks. Somewhat fearful that such might be my fate, and seeing the utter uselessness of further argument with them, I ceased, and prepared to witness the horrible tragedy. Thirty minutes only were allowed the unhappy victims to prepare themselves to enter on the scenes of eternity. Three ropes were procured, and attached to the limb of a tree. The prisoners were marched out, placed upon a wagon, and the ropes put round their necks. No time was given them for explanation. They vainly tried to speak, but none of them understanding English, there were obliged to employ their native tongues, which but few of those assembled understood. Vainly they called for an interpreter, for their cries were drowned by the yells of a now infuriated mob. A black handkerchief was bound around the eyes of each; their arms were pinioned, and at a given signal, without priest or prayer-book, the wagon was drawn from under them, and they were launched into eternity. Their graves were dug ready to receive them, and when life was entirely extinct, they were cut down and buried in their blankets. This was the first execution I ever witnessed.-God grant that it may be the last!

--Edward Gould Buffum, Six Months in the Gold Mines, 1850

16. Since this town had no official court system or police force, how can one term the punishment process as described by Edward Gould Buffem?
    A. a legal process.
    B. a lawful process.
    C. a process of vigilantism.
    D. a process guided by logic.

17. Based on the fact that the accusers were foreign and couldn't speak English, what can one infer about the executioners?
    A. They were motivated by racism.
    B. They were fair and just.
    C. They were concerned with constitutional law.
    D. They were unbiased and impartial.

18. The lack of due process in these executions indicated that
    A. boomtowns were stable.
    B. boomtowns were unstable and violent.
    C. boomtowns promoted the 6th Amendment.
    D. boomtowns were benevolent.

Questions 19-21 refer to the following excerpt.

What is the territory, Mr. President, which you propose to wrest from Mexico? It is consecrated to the heart of the Mexican by many a well-fought battle with his old Castilian master. His Bunker Hills, and Saratogas, and Yorktowns are there! The Mexican can say, "There I bled for liberty! and shall I surrender that consecrated home of my affections to the Anglo-Saxon invaders? What do they want with it? They have Texas already.

There is one topic connected with this subject which I tremble when I approach, and yet I cannot forbear to notice it. It meets you in every step you take; it threatens you which way soever you go in the prosecution of this war. I allude to the question of slavery. Opposition to its further extension, it must be obvious to everyone, is a deeply rooted determination with men of all parties in what we call the non-slaveholding states. New York, Pennsylvania, and Ohio, three of the most powerful, have already sent their legislative instructions here. So it will be, I doubt not, in all the rest. It is vain now to speculate about the reasons for this. Gentlemen of the South may call it prejudice, passion, hypocrisy, fanaticism. I shall not dispute with them now on that point. You and I cannot alter or change this opinion, if we would. These people only say we will not, cannot consent that you shall carry slavery where it does not already exist. They do not seek to disturb you in that institution as it exists in your states. Enjoy it if you will and as you will. This is their language; this their determination. How is it in the South? Can it be expected that they should expend in common their blood and their treasure in the acquisition of immense territory, and then willingly forgo the right to carry thither their slaves, and inhabit the conquered country if they please to do so? Sir, I know the feelings and opinions of the South too well to calculate on this. Nay, I believe they would even contend to any extremity for the mere right, had they no wish to exert it. I believe (and I confess I tremble when the conviction presses upon me) that there is equal obstinacy on both sides of this fearful question.

If, then, we persist in war, which, if it terminates in anything short of a mere wanton waste of blood as well as money, must end (as this bill proposes) in the acquisition of territory, to which at once this controversy must attach-this bill would seem to be nothing less than a bill to produce internal commotion. Should we prosecute this war another moment, or expend one dollar in the purchase or conquest of a single acre of Mexican land, the North and the South are brought into collision on a point where neither will yield. Who can foresee or foretell the result! Who so bold or reckless as to look such a conflict in the face unmoved! I do not envy the heart of him who can realize the possibility of such a conflict without emotions too painful to be endured. Why, then, shall we, the representatives of the sovereign states of the Union-the chosen guardians of this confederated Republic, why should we precipitate this fearful struggle, by continuing a war the result of which must be to force us at once upon a civil conflict? Sir, rightly considered, this is treason, treason to the Union, treason to the dearest interests, the loftiest aspirations, the most cherished hopes of our constituents. It is a crime to risk the possibility of such a contest. It is a crime of such infernal hue that every other in the catalogue of iniquity, when compared with it, whitens into virtue. . . .

--Thomas Corwin, "Against the Mexican War," 1847

19. The reference that Corwin makes to the "Bunker Hills, Saratogas, and Yorktowns" indicates

    A. that Mexico fought bravely for its independence and the U.S. should respect its sovereignty.

    B. Mexico had been oppressive to the people of Texas.

    C. the Americans in Texas fought bravely for their independence.

    D. the United States is obligated to spread the virtues of independence.

20. What did Corwin correctly predict would occur if the U.S. went to war with Mexico?

    A. that the U.S. would become a world empire.

    B. that the economic prosperity of the U.S. would flourish.

C. that the virtues of democratic government would spread to Mexico.

D. that a war between the North and South would erupt.

21. According to Corwin, war with Mexico would amount to

A. economic prosperity.

B. treason against the United States.

C. the ideals of Manifest Destiny coming into fruition.

D. new territories for peaceful American settlement.

SHORT ANSWER QUESTIONS

As part of the Treaty of Guadalupe, California became a territory of the United States in 1848.

   a. Choose ONE of the following and explain why your choice represents the event that led to the acquisition of California.

   - The Republic of Texas is formed
   - James Polk is elected
   - The Bear Flag Revolt begins

   b. Contrast your choice against ONE of the other options, demonstrating why that option in not as significant as your choice.

LONG ESSAY QUESTION

Why did the United States go to war with Mexico in 1848?

ANSWERS AND EXPLANATIONS

Multiple Choice Questions

1. B Manifest Destiny reflected the expansive mood of Americans in the 1830s/1840s.
2. D Polk fully embraced the ideals of Manifest Destiny.
3. C Sam Houston eventually captured Santa Anna.
4. C The Whig Party formed to challenge Andrew Jackson, especially after he vetoed a bill to renew the Second Bank of the United States.
5. C Polk wanted to annex Texas and acquire the Oregon Territory.
6. D Conflict over Texas eventually led to war with Mexico.
7. B After the U.S. annexed Texas, both the U.S. and Mexico immediately clashed over a land dispute.

8. C By approaching the Rio Grande, Mexican forces believed that Taylor had invaded their territory.
9. D Pico's surrender in Los Angeles completed the U.S. conquest of California.
10. C Despite the treacherous journey, most gold rushers travelled overland to California.
11. C With the Mexican capital being captured, the war was essentially over.
12. C Polk believed that a popular war hero would seek political office.
13. B Dana explains that Californians were willing to pay high prices for manufactured goods.
14. D California was controlled by the Catholic country of Spain.
15. C Those with the most Spanish blood received the most favoritism in California society.
16. C Townspeople often took the law into their own hands.
17. A Racism was high in the gold rush camps.
18. B Boomtowns were very volatile and lawless.
19. A Corwin points out that Mexico had fought Spain for its independence.
20. D The acquisition of Mexican territory served as a catalyst to North-South conflict.
21. B War with Mexico would lead the U.S. to fight a war with itself.

Long Essay Question

Why did the United States go to war with Mexico in 1848?

(Key topics to focus and elaborate on)
- Manifest Destiny inspired Americans
- Texas becomes the 28th state of the U.S.
- Polk secretly attempts to negotiate for California

Chapter 12
LIVING IN A NATION OF CHANGING LANDS, CHANGING FACES, CHANGING EXPECTATIONS, 1831-1854

- The period between the 1830s and 1850s featured many changes with a new wave of immigration, a growing push to end slavery, and the demand of women to attain equality.

THE CHANGING FACE OF THE AMERICAN PEOPLE IN THE 1840S AND 1850S

- Between the 1830s and 1850s, the nation's population would grow due to the healthy birthrate of native-born Americans and immigration from Ireland, Germany, and China. Due to this growth, the nation would become more diverse both ethnically and religiously
- As instability ravaged China in the early 1800s, the lure of work and opportunity presented itself to the Chinese in the United States, in particular California., and most of this immigrant population were males
- Resistance against the Chinese grew in the 1850s, but the necessity of their labor provided an impetus for them to work in the building of the nation's first transcontinental railroad
- The Irish that arrived in America during the 1840s were overwhelmingly poor Catholics unlike their predecessors who were largely Presbyterian Protestants. Due to a fungus that devastated potato crops, over 2 million Irish migrated to the United States to escape the famine
- In the United States, work was available for both men and women, and these Irish immigrants found most of this employment in the urban communities of the nation such as New York and Boston. The rise of Irish immigration resulted in the growth of the Catholic Church in the U.S.
- German immigrants also arrived in the U.S. in the mid-1800s but with more financial resources than the Irish, and because of this, their destination proved to be in the farms of the Midwest. Although German immigrants lived primarily isolated from the rest of the community, they did introduce many traditions that are still practiced today.
- The rise of immigration into the United States led to anti-immigrant groups such as the Know-Nothing Party which was anti-Catholic and anti-immigrant
- The transition from Mexican citizenship to U.S. citizenship proved to be difficult after the signing of the Treaty of Guadalupe Hidalgo as the dreams of becoming equal to their American counterparts never happened. On the contrary, many Mexicans in the U.S. who had land could not prove their ownership and thus lost it.
- In California, white hostility often resulted in violence against Mexicans, especially in the form of vigilante justice.

- The cotton industry exploded after the War of 1812 thereby making slavery an all-important institution in the South.
- As this importance grew, so too did the voices against it from northern abolitionists that undoubtedly terrified southern slaveholders.
- The new defenders of slavery began to justify their institution in creative ways and at the same time increased their criticism of the northern industrial wage-labor system.
- Ultimately, southerners saw slavery no longer as necessary evil, but a result of black inferiority.
- The rising importance of slavery influenced masters to take better care of their slaves and regard them as valuable investments.
- To be sure, improved living conditions, dietary rations, and working hours became the norm for slaves during the antebellum period.
- Despite improved conditions, the cruelty of slavery remained intact until its dissolution. Unfortunately for slave women, this cruelty included the constant threat of rape.
- The social conditions in which a slave lived depended on whether the slave lived on a large plantation or a small farm, and whether the master was cruel or not.
- Whether on a small farm or large plantation, family (nuclear or extended) was vital as a means for a slave's emotional well-being.
- Slaves resisted in both passive and serious manners. Slaves found various ways to escape along the Underground Railroad and "conductors" assisted in their journey to the north.
- The more notable runaways that later inspired the abolitionist movement included Henry Highland Garnet and Frederick Douglass, and Harriet Tubman became the most famous conductor of the Underground Railroad.
- The fear of revolt always permeated the minds of slaveholders. No doubt, the revolts of Gabriel Prosser, Denmark Vesey, and Nat Turner only confirmed this fear, and the call by free northern blacks for slaves to revolt heightened this fear even more.
- The call for freedom also came from abolitionists such as William Lloyd Garrison who published an abolitionist newspaper known as *The Liberator.*
- As Garrison worked alone with his abolitionism, "Oberlin abolitionism" promoted an evangelical anti-slavery movement beginning in the 1830s.

NEW STRENGTH FOR AMERICAN WOMEN

- With the opening statement, "We hold these truths to be self-evident; that all men and women are created equal…" the Seneca Falls Convention began what would be the start of the women's right movement in the United States.
- Yet other women such as Sarah Grimke laid the foundations for such a movement to begin through their writing that stressed the equality of men and women.
- In sharing their frustration with their limited role as female abolitionists, Elizabeth Cady Stanton and Lucretia Mott called for the Seneca Falls Convention to address the numerous inequities women faced in 1848.

- The women's rights movement of this era focused on a number of issues including higher education for women, the right of women to control property, and the right to obtain divorces.
- Even with the women's movement, black women were reluctant to join various integrated societies since white women tended to dominate them.

MULTIPLE CHOICE QUESTIONS

1. In 1852, the population of the United States stood at
   A. 13 million.
   B. 17 million.
   C. 23 million.
   D. 34 million.

2. After the California gold rush, Chinese immigrants found themselves
   A. returning back to China.
   B. laying the tracks of the Union Pacific Railroad.
   C. laying the tracks of the Central Pacific Railroad.
   D. joining Irish workers to form a labor union.

3. The Irish workers of the 1840s tended to be
   A. of the Protestant Presbyterian faith.
   B. of the Catholic faith.
   C. farmers in the Midwest.
   D. financially stable.

4. Many Mexicans who became U.S. citizens as a result of the Treaty of Guadalupe Hidalgo
   A. sold their land to American settlers.
   B. lost their land because they couldn't provide documents that proved their ownership.
   C. were forced to live in large reservations.
   D. never were in jeopardy of losing any of their land.

5. After 1830, slaveholders began to describe slavery as
   A. a necessary evil.
   B. an institution that was at best unfortunate.
   C. a positive good that benefited the slaves.
   D. an unprofitable institution on the verge of extinction.

6. The opportunity to create a slave community and cultural identity of their own was
   A. on a small farm that had only 1-2 slaves.
   B. on a large plantation.
   C. at the master's church service.
   D. when a meeting with free blacks took place.

7. The ultimate and realistic place where runaway slaves could escape without the fear of being recaptured proved to be
   A. in Canada.
   B. in Massachusetts.
   C. in Africa.
   D. in Spanish Florida.

8. Harriet Tubman found success in freeing slaves because
   A. she was very wealthy and could afford the costs of escape.
   B. she was a white abolitionist who nobody suspected of freeing slaves.
   C. she received the support of northern abolitionists.
   D. she paid off slave owners to let their slaves go.

9. As an abolitionist, William Lloyd Garrison burned a copy of the U.S. Constitution since
   A. it limited the power of the states.
   B. the inherent Bill of Rights didn't protect individual civil liberties.
   C. it gave the executive branch too much power.
   D. it protected slavery.

10. The Seneca Falls Convention focused on
    A. women's rights.
    B. issues and concerns of the Iroquois.
    C. abolitionism.
    D. secession from the Union.

Questions 11-12 refer to the following image.

11.   The African Americans in the picture represented
    A. runaway slaves.
    B. free blacks.
    C. abolitionists.
    D. revolting slaves.

12.   The whites in the picture represented
    A. conductors on the Underground Railroad.
    B. slave owners.
    C. professional slave catchers.
    D. southern church members.

Questions 13-15 refer to the following excerpt.

Very soon after I went to live with Mr. and Mrs. Auld, she very kindly commenced to teach me the A, B, C. After I had learned this, she assisted me in learning to spell words of three or four letters. Just at this point of my progress, Mr. Auld found out what was going on, and at once forbade Mrs. Auld to instruct me further, telling her, among other things, that it was unlawful, as well as unsafe, to teach a slave to read. To use his own words, further, he said, "If you give a nigger an inch, he will take an ell. A nigger should know nothing but to obey his master—to do as he is told to do. Learning would spoil the best nigger in the world. Now," said he, "if you teach that nigger (speaking of myself) how to read, there would be no keeping him. It would forever unfit him to be a slave. He would at once become unmanageable, and of no value to his master. As to himself, it could do him no good, but a great deal of harm. It would make him discontented and unhappy." These words sank deep into my heart, stirred up sentiments within that lay slumbering, and called into existence an entirely new train of thought. It was a new and special revelation, explaining dark and mysterious things, with which my youthful understanding had struggled, but struggled in vain. I now understood what had been to me a most perplexing difficulty—to wit, the white man's power to enslave the black man. It was a grand achievement, and I prized it highly. From that moment, I understood the pathway from slavery to freedom. It was just what I wanted, and I got it at a time when I the least expected it. Whilst I was saddened by the thought of losing the aid of my kind mistress, I was gladdened by the invaluable instruction which, by the merest accident, I had gained from my master. Though conscious of the difficulty of learning without a teacher, I set out with high hope, and a fixed purpose, at whatever cost of trouble, to learn how to read.

--Frederick Douglass Excerpt from *The Narrative of the Life of Frederick Douglass*

13. Mr. Auld didn't want Frederick Douglass to learn how to read for all of the following reasons EXCEPT
    A. he would be unmanageable.
    B. he would learn how to become a better slave.
    C. he would become discontented and unhappy.
    D. he would be unfit to be a slave.

14. Douglass implied that white man's power to enslave the black man lay in
    A. the use of brute force.
    B. establishing an elaborate patrol system.
    C. keeping the slaves ignorant.
    D. teaching the concept of biblical obedience.

15. With no teacher, how might a slave such as Douglass learn how to read?
    A. from other illiterate slaves
    B. by sneaking into the schoolhouse
    C. from other white children
    D. from the master's Sunday church service

Questions 16-18 refer to the following excerpt.

The negro slaves of the South are the happiest, and in some sense, the freest people in the world. The children and the aged and infirm work not at all, and yet have all the comforts and necessaries of life provided for them. They enjoy liberty, because they are oppressed neither by care or labor. The women do little hard work, and are protected from the despotism of their husbands by their masters. The negro men and stout boys work, on the average, in good weather, no more than nine hours a day. The balance of their time is spent in perfect abandon. Besides, they have their Sabbaths and holidays. White men, with som muh of license and abandon, would die of ennui; but negroes luxuriate in corporeal and mental repose. With their faces upturned to the sun, they can sleep at any hour; and quiet sleep is the greatest of human enjoyments. "Blessed be the man who invented sleep." 'Tis happiness in itself--and results from contentment in the present, and confident assurance of the future. We do not know whether free laborers ever sleep. They are fools to do so; for, whilst they sleep, the wily and watchful capitalist is devising means to ensnare and exploit them. The free laborer must work or starve. He is more of a slave than the negro, because he works longer and harder for less allowance than the slave, and has no holiday, because the cares of life with him begin when its labors end. He has no liberty and not a single right. . . . The world at large looks on negro slavery as much the worst form of slavery; because it is only acquainted with West India slavery. But our Southern slavery has become a benign and protective institution, and our negroes are confessedly better off than any free laboring population in the world. How can we contend that white slavery is wrong, whilst all the great body of free laborers are starving; and slaves, white or black, throughout the world, are enjoying comfort? . . . Whilst, as a general and abstract question, negro slavery has no other claims over other forms of slavery, except that from inferiority, or rather peculiarity, of race, almost all negroes require masters, whilst only the children, the women, and the very weak, poor, and ignorant, &c., among the whites, need some protective and governing relation of this kind; yet as a subject of temporary, but worldwide importance, negro slavery has become the most necessary of all human institutions.

--George Fitzhugh, The Blessings of Slavery, 1857

16. Slaveholders portrayed the institution of slavery to be benevolent
    A. in order to counter the criticism of the abolitionists.
    B. to suppress the guilt of two centuries of southern slavery.
    C. to convince their slaves that freedom was not beneficial for them.
    D. to quiet the voices of free southern blacks.

17. According to Fitzhugh, northern industrialists were cruel in that they didn't
    a. offer immigrant workers any wages for their labor.
    b. provide steady work.
    c. take care of the children and elderly parents of the workers.
    d. feed their workers an adequate lunch.

18. According to Fitzhugh, like children and women, negroes require
    a. an education to be responsible.
    b. role models to learn from.
    c. biblical guidance for leadership.
    d. masters to protect and govern.

Questions 19-21 refer to the following excerpt.

We hold these truths to be self-evident: that all men and women are created equal; that they are endowed by their Creator with certain inalienable rights; that among these are life, liberty, and the pursuit of happiness; that to secure these rights governments are instituted, deriving their just powers from the consent of the governed…The history of mankind is a history of repeated injuries and usurpations on the part of man toward woman, having in direct object the establishment of an absolute tyranny over her. To prove this, let facts be submitted to a candid word…He has never permitted her to exercise her inalienable right to the elective franchise…He has compelled her to submit to laws, in the formation of which she had no voice…He has withheld from her rights which are given to the most ignorant and degraded men-both natives and foreigners… Having deprived her of this first right of a citizen, the elective franchise, thereby leaving her without representation in the halls of legislation, he has oppressed her on all sides…He has made her, if married, in the eye of the law, civilly dead…He has taken from her all right in property, even to the wages she earns… In the covenant of marriage, she is compelled to promise obedience to her husband, he becoming, to all intents and purposes, her master, the law giving him power to deprive her of her liberty, and to administer chastisement …After depriving her of all rights as a married woman, if single, and the owner of property, he has taxed her to support a government which recognizes her only when her property can be made profitable to it…He has monopolized nearly all the profitable employments, and from those she is permitted to follow, she receives but a scanty remuneration. He closes against her all the avenues to wealth and distinction which he considers most honorable to himself. As a teacher of theology, medicine, or law, she is not known…He has denied her the facilities for obtaining a thorough education, all colleges being closed against her…

--Elizabeth Cady Stanton, *Declaration of Sentiments,* 1848

19. A central deprivation that women faced when the Seneca Falls Convention was held proved to be
    A. a lack of moral influence within the family home.
    B. the lack of enfranchisement.
    C. a lack of religious inspiration.
    D. a lack of any type of employment.

20. *The Declaration of Sentiments and Resolutions* argued that women did not have professions in theology, medicine, and law because
    A. they lacked the motivation.
    B. they lacked the interest.
    C. they lacked the educational opportunity.
    D. they simply chose not to enter those fields.

21. According to the declaration, a woman becomes civilly dead when
    A. she remains single.
    B. she gets married.
    C. she inherits property.
    D. she is born.

SHORT ANSWER QUESTIONS

In 1848, the Seneca Falls Convention opens with the Declaration of Sentiments and Resolutions which stated, "We hold these truths to be self-evident that all men and women are created equal…"

a. Choose ONE of the following and explain why your choice represents the event that led to this declaration.

  • Abigail Adams reminds her husband John Adams to "remember the ladies"
  • Sarah Grimke publishes *Letters on the Equality of the Sexes*
  • Lucretia Mott and Elizabeth Cady Stanton meet to discuss their frustrations with the abolitionist movement

b. Contrast your choice against ONE of the other options, demonstrating why that option in not as significant as your choice.

LONG ESSAY QUESTION

Compare and contrast the immigration of the Germans, Irish, and Chinese in the early to mid 1800s.

ANSWERS AND EXPLANATIONS

Multiple Choice Questions

1. C The population had grown tremendously between the 1830s and 1850s.
2. C The Central Pacific found the Chinese workers to be excellent workers.
3. B Unlike their predecessors who were Protestant, the Irish immigrants of the 1840s tended to be Catholic.
4. B Despite obtaining U.S. citizenship, many Mexicans lost their lands because they couldn't prove ownership.
5. C The attacks of abolitionists made slave owners become creative with their justifications of slavery.
6. B Large plantations meant the slaves were further away from the masters and within the company of their own kind.
7. A Canada was out of the jurisdiction of slave-catchers.
8. C Tubman received assistance from those who wanted to rid America of slavery.
9. D The Constitution acknowledged the existence of slavery and had no mandate to abolish it.
10. A The Seneca Falls Convention would be the beginning of the women's civil rights movement.
11. A Thousands of African Americans escaped to the North via the Underground Railroad.
12. A Those who assisted runaway slaves travelling along the Underground Railroad came to be known as conductors.
13. B Reading knowledge would not produce obedient slaves.
14. C Ignorance was the key to keeping slaves from questioning their position in life.
15. C Douglass gave food he stole from his master to white children in return for reading lessons.
16. A Slaveholders felt the pressure to answer the attacks on slavery by abolitionists.
17. C Fitzhugh pointed out that Northern industrialist had no concern for their workers or their families.
18. D Fitzhugh uses the notion of paternalism to justify slavery.
19. B The right to female suffrage became a main issue of the convention.
20. C Higher education for professional careers was exclusively for males at this time.
21. B Getting married would forfeit rights such as inheritance for women.

Long Essay Question

Compare and contrast the immigration of the Germans, Irish, and Chinese in the early to mid 1800s.

(Key topics to focus and elaborate on)

- All provided valuable labor and faced nativism
- They had different religions
- They migrated to different parts of the country

Chapter 13
THE POLITICS OF SEPARATION, 1850-1861

- In the 1850s, tensions between the North and South led southerners to believe that they could no longer remain in the Union.

FROM UNION TO DISUNION

- The debate over admitting California into the Union was a contentious one. The presence of abolitionism along with previous discussions laid out by the Wilmot Proviso served to aggravate this dispute between Northern and Southern senators.
- The Compromise of 1850 allowed for California to enter the Union as a free state, New Mexico and Utah became territories, and a Fugitive Slave Act was attached to intensify efforts to retrieve runaway slaves.
- Not surprisingly, the compromise was met with opposition between both northern and southern interests.
- The Fugitive Slave Act created uproar in the north as the law established a force of agents that worked with slave-catchers to pursue fugitive slaves. Many northerners often flouted this law by continuing to assist runaway slaves.
- Harriet Beecher Stowe's *Uncle Tom's Cabin* brought images of slavery to readers that were praised in the North and scorned in the South.
- In order to build a transcontinental railroad through Nebraska, Senator Stephen Douglas proposed that popular sovereignty, the power for settlers to decide the fate of this territory, would be applied.
- In essence, this proposal threatened to dissolve the boundary between free and slave territories that the Missouri Compromise established in 1820.
- Despite northern opposition, the proposal became a reality with the passage of the Kansas-Nebraska Act in 1854.
- The controversy of the Kansas-Nebraska Act fueled the creation of a new political party, the Republican Party, to replace the Whigs in 1854.
- At this time, Abraham Lincoln, still as a Whig, entered the political scene by challenging popular sovereignty and opposing the threat of slavery expanding.
- After 1854, political candidates carried the label pro-slavery or anti-slavery, and the Republican Party represented those opposed to the expansion of slavery. Thus, the Republicans had no southern members.
- Kansas quickly became a hostile quagmire as both pro- and anti-slavery settlers poured into this territory, and hence had their own elections and established their own governments, that is, pro-slavery and anti-slavery governments, by 1856.
- Complications further arose when a subsequent election in 1857 established a free legislature, but the pro-slavery Lecompton Constitution essentially legalized slavery in Kansas.

- Meanwhile, violence erupted in Kansas between pro-slavery and anti-slavery settlers, leading many to label the territory as Bleeding Kansas.
- The Senate also witnessed violence as southern Senator Preston Brooks attacked northern Senator Charles Sumner for his anti-slavery "Crimes Against Kansas" speech.
- In an attempt to gain his freedom, Missouri slave, Dred Scott, sued for his freedom on the basis that he lived in a free territory.
- After series of appeals, the U.S. Supreme Court denied Scott his freedom based on the notion that blacks had no rights that white men were bound to respect, and that as property of slave holders, slaves were still under the subjection of their masters.
- Thus the court ruled the stipulations of the Missouri Compromise to be unconstitutional. Undoubtedly, the Dred Scott decision galvanized the rift between the North and South even further.
- In addition to their disagreement over slavery, the North and South also differed over their views regarding internal improvements, and high tariffs. The Panic of 1857 highlighted these differences between these two regions.
- Lincoln's "house divided against itself" speech set forth the strong position the Republicans had in halting the spread of slavery to the new territories. The Senate race in Illinois against Stephen Douglas featured Douglas attacking Lincoln as a radical abolitionist and Lincoln defending himself as a candidate who only wanted to ban slavery in the new territories.
- Although Lincoln lost this race, he put himself in a good position to win a much bigger prize with the presidential election looming in 1860.
- As an attempt to lead a slave insurrection in Virginia, extreme abolitionist John Brown led an assault on Harper's Ferry in 1859. Although the attack was quickly suppressed, Brown became a martyr for the cause of ending slavery.
- In fact, some northerners even believed that violence would be necessary to eliminate slavery from the United States.
- From a southern perspective, the raid only served to prove that most northerners were in league with radical abolitionists and looked to eradicate slavery from everywhere in the US, including the South.

THE ELECTION OF 1860 AND THE SECESSION OF THE SOUTH

- After receiving the nomination for the Republican Party, Lincoln faced a tough campaign against a pro-slavery Democrat, John Breckinridge, the popular sovereignty candidate, Stephen Douglas, and Constitutional Union Party candidate, John Bell.
- Lincoln's name wasn't on southern ballots, but despite this exclusion, he won a solid majority in the Electoral College with an impressive victory in the north.
- Lincoln's election victory led several southern states to secede from the Union, beginning with South Carolina in December of 1860, and several others followed in January of 1861 to form the Confederate States of America.
- The Crittenden Compromise called for the Missouri Compromise line to extend to the Pacific Ocean, but Lincoln refused to budge, thus holding true to his conviction to stop the spread of slavery.
- Some northerners argued that the seceding states should just be left alone, whereas others were vehemently against it.

- On inauguration day in March of 1861, Lincoln held steadfast on his promise not to attack slavery where it already existed but not to let it spread beyond the South. He also didn't share the South's' right to secession and regarded them as being in a state of rebellion.
- After the bombardment of the Union's Fort Sumter in April of 1861, other southern states such as Virginia joined the Confederacy.
- After Fort Sumter, several border states became key in the strategic defense and positioning of Union military forces. In particular, because of their proximity to the capital, Delaware and Maryland came under quick Union control.
- Both sides were wrong in thinking that the war--or conflict as many saw it—would be sort. It would last four years and claim the lives of over 600,000 Americans.

MULTIPLE CHOICE QUESTIONS

1. Under the Compromise of 1850, all of the following stipulations applied except:
   A.   California became a free state.
   B.   New Mexico became a territory.
   C.   a strict Fugitive Slave Act was enacted.
   D.   Texas became a free state.

2. The Supreme Court denied Dred Scott his freedom because
   A. his citizenship was not finalized.
   B. he didn't live in a free territory long enough.
   C. they considered slaves property.
   D. he didn't fill out the proper paperwork to sue.

3. The Kansas/Nebraska Act featured a system of settlement in which
   A. congressional hearings determined the status of these territories.
   B. executive orders determined the status of these territories.
   C. court decisions determined the status of these territories.
   D. popular sovereignty determined the status of these territories.

4. During the Lincoln-Douglas Debates, Lincoln displayed the flaws of
   A. the Wilmot Proviso.
   B. the Compromise of 1850.
   C. the Fugitive Slave Act.
   D. Popular Sovereignty.

5. The caning of William Sumner by Preston Brooks was precipitated by
   A. the raid on Harper's Ferry.
   B. Sumner's comments regarding Bleeding Kansas.
   C. the Supreme Court's Dred Scott decision.
   D. Sumner's open support of the Fugitive Slave Act.
6. The political party that vowed to stop the expansion of slavery in the new territories was
   A. the Whig Party.

B. the Democratic Party.

C. the Republican Party.

D. the Constitution Party.

7. In the Dred Scott case, the Supreme Court ruled
   A. that Dred Scott would be free.
   B. Scott had lived in a free territory.
   C. the Missouri Compromise to be unconstitutional.
   D. slaves were not considered to be property.

8. In terms of the economy, Republicans and Democrats differed over
   A. internal taxes.
   B. taxes on personal incomes.
   C. export duties.
   D. protective tariffs.

9. Whereas the Democrats were divided during the Election of 1860, the Republicans ran
   A. Stephen Douglas.
   B. Jefferson Davis.
   C. James Buchanan.
   D. Abraham Lincoln.

10. The Crittenden Compromise called for
    a. California to be a free state
    b. Extending the Missouri Compromise to the Pacific Ocean
    c. Annexing Cuba to make it a slave state
    d. Popular sovereignty in New Mexico and Utah

Questions 11-12 refer to the following visual.

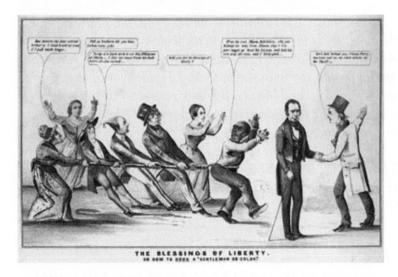

11. The runaway slave is being held back by southerners. To deal with runaway slaves, the Fugitive Slave Act established all of the following EXCEPT

A. a federal force of agents to capture fugitive slaves.

B. heavy fines for those assisting fugitives.

C. prison time for those assisting fugitives.

D. assurance that free blacks would not be harassed.

12. In the political cartoon, the author of the Fugitive Slave Act, Henry Clay (with cane) appears

A. concerned about the plight of the runaway slave.

B. regretful that he created the Fugitive Slave Act.

C. indifferent to the struggles of the fugitive slaves.

D. to be making a deal to end slavery.

Questions 13-15 refer to the following excerpt at.

I have, may it please the Court, a few words to say.

In the first place, I deny everything but what I have already admitted, of a design on my part to free Slaves. I intended, certainly, to have made a clean thing of that matter, as I did last winter, when I went into Missouri, and there took Slaves, without the snapping of a gun on either side, moving them through the country, and finally leaving them in Canada. I desired to have done the same thing again, on a much larger scale. That was all I intended. I never did intend murder, or treason, or the destruction of property, or to excite or incite Slaves to rebellion, or to make insurrection.

I have another objection, and that is, that it is unjust that I should suffer such a penalty. Had I interfered in the manner, and which I admit has been fairly proved,--for I admire the truthfulness and candor of the greater portion of the witnesses who have testified in this case,-- had I so interfered in behalf of the Rich, the Powerful, the Intelligent, the so-called Great, or in behalf of any of their friends, either father, mother, brother, sister, wife, or children, or any of that class, and suffered and sacrificed what I have in this interference, it would have been all right. Every man in this Court would have deemed it an act worthy a reward, rather than a punishment.

This Court acknowledges too, as I suppose, the validity of the Law of God. I saw a book kissed, which I suppose to be the Bible, or at least the New Testament, which teaches me that, "All things whatsoever I would that men should do to me, I should do even so to them." It teaches me further, to "Remember them that are in bonds, as bound with them." I endeavored to act up to that instruction. I say I am yet too young to understand that God is any respecter of persons. I believe that to have interfered as I have done, as I have always freely admitted I have done, in behalf of his despised poor, I have done no wrong, but RIGHT.

Now, if it is deemed necessary that I should forfeit my life, for the furtherance of the ends of justice, and MINGLE MY BLOOD FURTHER WITH THE BLOOD OF MY CHILDREN, and with the blood of millions in this Slave country, whose rights are disregarded by wicked, cruel, and unjust enactments,--I say, LET IT BE DONE.

John Brown

--John Brown's Address before Sentencing, 1859

13. According to John Brown in his letter, the Bible justified his actions since

A. he felt instructed to treat slave holders with an eye for an eye.

B. he believed the notion of obey your master was wrongfully used by slave holders.

C. he felt instructed to bound with the slaves.

D. he wasn't working for men but for the Lord.

14. Brown's willingness to forfeit his life to end slavery
    A. terrified slaveholders throughout the South.
    B. was mocked by people in the North.
    C. had no effect in either the North or South.
    D. did not make him a martyr.

15. Brown's contention that he didn't want to start an insurrection can be refuted in that
    A. his whole goal in life was to end slavery.
    B. he went to several plantations in Virginia to free slaves.
    C. he had no intentions of taking arms at Harper's Ferry.
    D. he was falsely accused of murdering slaveholders in Kansas.

Questions 16-18 refer to the following excerpt.

"And now," said Legree, "come here, you Tom. You see, I telled ye I didn't buy ye jest for the common work. I mean to promote ye, and make a driver of ye; and tonight ye may jest as well begin to get ye hand in. Now, ye jest take this yer gal and flog her; ye've seen enough on't [of it] to know how." "I beg Mas'r' pardon," said Tom; "hopes Mas'r won't set me at that. It's what I an't used to-never did-and can't do, no way possible."

"Ye'll larn a pretty smart chance of things ye never did know, before I've done with ye!" said Legree, taking up a cowhide and striking Tom a heavy blow across the cheek, and following up the infliction by a shower of blows.

"There!" he said, as he stopped to rest; "now, will ye tell me ye can't do it?"

"Yes, Mas'r," said Tom, putting up his hand, to wipe the blood that trickled down his face. "I'm willin' to work, night and day, and work while there's life and breath in me. But this yer thing I can't feel it right to do; and, Mas'r, I never shall do it-never!"

Tom had a remarkably smooth, soft voice, and a habitually respectful manner that had given Legree an idea that he would be cowardly and easily subdued. When he spoke these last words, a thrill of amazement went through everyone. The poor woman clasped her hands and said, "O Lord!" and everyone involuntarily looked at each other and drew in their breath, as if to prepare for the storm that was about to burst.

Legree looked stupefied and confounded; but at last burst forth: "What! Ye blasted black beast! Tell me ye don't think it right to do what I tell ye! What have any of you cussed cattle to do with thinking what's right? I'll put a stop to it! Why, what do ye think ye are? May be ye think ye're a gentleman, master Tom, to be a telling your master what's right, and what an't! So you pretend it's wrong to flog the gal!"

"I think so, Mas'r," said Tom; "the poor crittur's sick and feeble; 'twould be downright cruel, and it's what I never will do, nor begin to. Mas'r, if you mean to kill me, kill me; but, as to my raising my hand again any one here, I never shall-I'll die first!"

Tom spoke in a mild voice, but with a decision that could not be mistaken. Legree shook with anger; his greenish eyes glared fiercely, and his very whiskers seemed to curl with passion. But, like some ferocious beast, that plays with its victim before he devours it, he kept back his strong impulse to proceed to immediate violence, and broke out into bitterly raillery.

"Well, here's a pious dog, at last, let down among us sinners-a saint, a gentleman, and no less, to talk to us sinners about our sins! Powerful holy crittur, he must be! Here, you rascal, you make believe to be so pious-didn't you never hear, out of yer Bible, 'Servants, obey yer masters'? An't I yer master? Didn't I pay down twelve hundred dollars, cash, for all there is inside yer old cussed black shell? An't yer mine, now, body and soul?" he said, giving Tom a violent kick with his heavy boot; "tell me!"

In the very depth of physical suffering, bowed by brutal oppression, this question shot a gleam of joy an triumph through Tom's soul. He suddenly stretched himself up, and, looking earnestly to heaven, while the tears and blood that flowed down his face mingled, he exclaimed, " No! no! no! my soul an't yours, Mas'r! You haven't bought it-ye can't buy it! It's been bought and paid for by One that is able to keep it. No matter, no matter, you can't harm me!"

"I can't!" said Legree, with a sneer; "we'll see-we'll see! Here Sambo, Quimbo, give this dog such a breakin' in as he won't get over this month!"

The two gigantic Negroes that now laid hold of Tom, with fiendish exultation in their faces, might have formed no unapt personification of powers of darkness. The poor woman screamed with apprehension, and all rose, as by a general impulse, while they dragged him unresisting from the place.

--Harriet Beecher Stowe, from *Uncle Tom's Cabin*, 1852

16. Why did Tom's owner, Legree, believe that Tom should flog the slave girl?
    A. She did something terrible.
    B. She committed a sin.
    C. Because Tom was his slave.
    D. As a demotion, Tom had to engage in this act.

17. Despite being mauled by his master, why was Tom still joyful?
    A. He knew was running away.
    B. He knew he would get his revenge on his master.
    C. He knew that he was too valuable to kill.
    D. He knew his master couldn't take his soul.

18. An anguishing feature of slavery that Stowe points out in the passage was that
    A. Slaves were often whipped.
    B. Slave drivers had to inflict punishment on fellow slaves.
    C. Slaves had no control over their spiritual fate.
    D. Some slaves were freed but family members were not.

Questions 19-21 refer to the following excerpt.

If we could first know where we are, and whither we are tending, we could better judge what to do and how to do it. We are now far into the fifth year since a policy was initiated with the avowed object, and confident promise, of putting an end to slavery agitation. Under the operation of that policy, that agitation has not only not ceased but has constantly augmented. In my opinion, it will not cease until a crisis shall have been reached and passed. "A house divided against itself cannot stand." I believe this government cannot endure permanently half-slave and half-free. I do not expect the Union to be dissolved--I do not expect the house to fall--but I do expect it will cease to be divided. It will become all one thing or all the other. Either the opponents of slavery will arrest the further spread of it and place it where the public mind shall rest in the belief that it is in the course of ultimate extinction or its advocates will push it forward, till it shall become alike lawful in all the states, old as well as new--North as well as South.

--Abraham Lincoln, "A House Divided," 1858

19. In preparing his speech, Lincoln
    A. was determined to stop slavery from spreading.
    B. was determined to eradicate slavery in the South.
    C. conceded that slavery would spread to the new territories.
    D. conceded that slavery would bleed into other surrounding countries.

20. Lincoln thought that slavery would
    A. live forever.
    B. die out.
    C. be mixed with immigrant labor in the south.
    D. mix with immigrant labor in the new territories.

21. In regards to the United States, Lincoln
    a. saw a great Civil War on the horizon
    b. saw the breakup of the nation
    c. saw the nation remaining intact
    d. saw a division in the nation's structure

SHORT ANSWER QUESTIONS

Between December of 1860 and March of 1861, several southern states secede from the Union and form the Confederate States of America.

    a. Choose ONE of the following and explain why your choice represents the event that led to secession.

- The Dred Scott Decision
- John Brown's raid on Harper's Ferry
- Lincoln's Election victory

b. Contrast your choice against ONE of the other options, demonstrating why that option in not as significant as your choice.

LONG ESSAY QUESTION

How did Manifest Destiny affect the issue of slavery in the 1840s and 1850s?

ANSWERS AND EXPLANATIONS

Multiple Choice Questions

1. D Texas remained a slave state and was not part of the compromise.
2. C Masters had the right to maintain their property wherever they were.
3. D Under popular sovereignty, the settlers were to decide the fate of Kansas and Nebraska.
4. D With the Dred Scott decision, popular sovereignty no longer seemed an option for determining the status of a territory that applied for statehood.
5. B Sumner blamed slaveholders and southern views for the violence in Kansas.
6. C Borrowing from the ideals of the Free Soil Party, the Republicans aimed to stop the spread of slavery into the new territories.
7. C Because of the 5th Amendment, the Supreme Court argued that the 36 30 line of the Missouri Compromise could not deprive a slaveholder from owning their property.
8. D The North benefited from protective tariffs; the South did not.
9. D Lincoln had a solid Republican base behind him.
10. B The Crittenden Compromise attempted to reestablish the 36 30 line but all the way to the West.
11. D Free blacks were sometimes captured and sold into slavery.
12. C The admission of the Fugitive Slave Act within the Compromise of 1850 turned the compromise into a slave-hunting expedition.
13. C Brown cites "Remember them that are in bonds, as bound with them."
14. A Slaveholders were convinced that there were other radical abolitionists ready to attack the South.
15. A Brown's obvious goal was to rid the South of slavery.
16. C Legree believed that Tom should do anything he demanded, even flog a slave girl.
17. D Tom's soul was his to keep and he knew it.
18. B Drivers had the unbearable dilemma of flogging fellow slaves.
19. A Lincoln utilized the Republican platform in writing his speech.
20. B Lincoln believed that within the south, eventually slavery would become extinct.
21. C Lincoln didn't expect the nation to split into two nations.

LONG ESSAY QUESTION

How did Manifest Destiny affect the issue of slavery in the 1840s and 1850s?

(Key topics to focus and elaborate on)
- Wilmot Proviso
- Compromise of 1850
- Kansas-Nebraska Act

Chapter 14
AND THE WAR CAME: THE CIVIL WAR, 1861-1865

- Most Americans didn't believe that war between the states would be a long and bloody conflict and few could have imagined the impact it would have in the course of the history of the United States.

FORT SUMTER TO ANTIETAM, 1861-1862

- General Winfield Scott's Anaconda Plan, a plan to squeeze the South into submission, became the initial strategy of the Union at the outset of the war.
- After the First Battle of Bull Run, many in the Union realized that the war would not be an easy one, and many Southerners looked to attack Washington D.C.
- Jefferson Davis, the president of the Confederacy, pushed for a strategy of survival and possible partnership with England.
- To Lincoln, his generals were too cautious and slow and this would be the case until the latter part of the war.
- The Union had a stronger navy and blocked most southern commerce. The Civil War also featured the first ironclad ships, the *Virginia* and the *Merrimac.*
- River warfare also featured important Union victories in early 1862.
- On land, Union General Ulysses S. Grant won the bloody Battle of Shiloh in 1862, a battle that convinced many that the war would be dreadful and long.
- Yet General George McClellan failed to capture Richmond that same year and had to retreat after unsuccessful engagements with Confederate troops led by Robert E. Lee and Stonewall Jackson.
- In September of 1862, Lee tried to encircle Washington D.C. at Antietam Creek, but failed to advance after clashing against McClellan. After Lee retreated from the bloodiest battle of the war, the Battle of Antietam, Lincoln relieved McClellan for not pursuing Lee.

THE ROAD TO EMANCIPATION

- At the start of the war, Lincoln had no intention of attacking the institution of slavery in the states it already existed in. Instead, his main goal was to bring the Union back together again.
- During the course of the war, slaves who had escaped and fled to the Union army came to be known as contraband.
- As the war progressed even further, the Union military saw the value of the slaves, and soldiers even began to sympathize with their plight.
- Even the northern public began to shift its position regarding slavery, especially since it became obvious that slaves who had escaped their masters assisted in the Union cause.

- Moved by this growing public support, Lincoln issued the Emancipation Proclamation after the Battle of Antietam to free the slaves in states that were in rebellion as a "military necessity."
- After the Emancipation Proclamation went into effect in January of 1863, blacks (free and slave) joined the Union military by the thousands.
- Many of these black soldiers earned the distinction of being some of the war's bravest soldiers, including those in the 54th Massachusetts.

THE HOME FRONT-SHORTAGES, OPPOSITION, RIOTS, AND BATTLES

- From the outset of the war, the financial stability of the South was shaky and worsened as the war progressed. Inflation ran rampant in the south; some areas literally went starving due to lack of transportation.
- Women played a vital role in maintaining the home front in the south since most men were off fighting in the war. The difficulties of war often led to riots for food in places such as Richmond.
- In the north (as well as the south) the federal government sold war bonds, imposed taxes, and issued "greenbacks". Like the south, the north also saw a depopulation of many of its towns.
- The north also saw its share of dissenters, from those who spoke out against Lincoln's Emancipation Proclamation, to Copperheads who promoted peace.
- The draft that was enacted after Emancipation even sparked a race riot against blacks in 1863.
- Although war centered in the east, fighting and clashing occurred throughout the Midwest and West.
- Fighting also occurred amongst Indians as tribes would take sides according to what seemed advantageous and beneficial to them.

From Gettysburg to Appomattox and Beyond
- From 1863 to the end of the war, the Union followed the lead of Lee and turned its focus to fighting a large-scale offensive war.
- Lee had already been fighting more aggressively, but after Lincoln chose Ulysses S. Grant to lead the Army of the Potomac, the Union fought more aggressively as well. Consequently, massive bloodshed resulted from this aggression on both sides.
- After a major victory at Chancellorsville, Lee looked to attack the North and cut off Washington D.C. from the rest of the Union. Pennsylvania became the target of this attack, and on July 1, 1863, Confederate and Union forces met in a fierce battle.
- After three days of fighting, and massive losses on both sides, Lee retreated but Union general, George Meade, did not pursue him. Nevertheless, Lee's forces would never be the same.
- At the same time, the Union also gained another significant victory at the Battle of Vicksburg led by Grant. With the capturing of Vicksburg, the Union gained control of the Mississippi River thereby cutting the south in half.
- After the vicious battles of Wilderness and Cold Harbor in Virginia, Union forces suffered terribly, but Grant did not retreat. He then laid siege to the city of Petersburg.

- With Grant and Lee in charge of their respective armies, the war shifted from being a limited war to a war of attrition. The introduction of more advanced weapons such as the rifle and canister turned the battlefields into slaughterhouses.
- The lack of knowledge in regards to germs and infection also contributed to the high death toll of the war.
- During the war, women played a huge role as nurses, and Elizabeth Blackwell's Sanitary Commission helped to organize the treatment of the wounded in the North. In the South, women also served as nurses and established military hospitals to tend to the wounded.
- In 1864, Lincoln's bid for reelection was in serious jeopardy until General William Tecumseh Sherman of the Union took Atlanta, and Union Naval Commander, David Farragut, captured Mobile Bay, Alabama.
- As a direct result of these victories, Lincoln defeated his former general, George McClellan to earn a second presidential term.
- Meanwhile, from Atlanta, Sherman began his famous "march to the sea" campaign and presented Savannah to Lincoln as a Christmas present in December of 1864.
- From Georgia, Sherman left a burning path of destruction through South Carolina and completed the destruction through North Carolina.
- Sherman's victories, along with Lee's inability to hold on to Petersburg, left the Confederate capitol of Richmond wide open for a Union invasion.
- By April of 1865, Union forces marched into Richmond and took the city that had earlier been evacuated by Confederate leaders.
- On April 9, 1865, Lee surrendered to Grant in Appomattox, Virginia which essentially ended the war. Just months prior to this surrender, the Thirteenth Amendment was passed which abolished slavery throughout the United States.
- Many questions arose immediately following Lee's surrender including the fate of the former slaves and the seceded states.
- On his last day alive, Lincoln had ordered the southern states to be under the control of military districts until the whole issue of "reconstruction" could be sorted out.
- On April 14, 1865 Lincoln was shot by John Wilkes Booth and died early the next morning. Thus, the nation would be in mourning and wondering what lie ahead for the future.

MULTIPLE CHOICE QUESTIONS

1. The First Battle of Bull Run proved to the Union that
   A. the war would not be an easy one.
   B. the military of the south was vastly inferior.
   C. Richmond would be easily accessible.
   D. the Confederacy was unbeatable.

2. Lincoln's biggest complaint concerning his generals early in the war was
   A. they were too reckless.
   B. their men suffered too many casualties.
   C. they were too cautious and hesitant.
   D. they were too willing to sacrifice their men for victory.

3. The city on the Mississippi River that the Confederacy desperately clung to (until 1863) in order to keep the South fully intact was
   A. Vicksburg.
   B. Gettysburg.
   C. New Orleans.
   D. St. Louis.

4. Lincoln's *Emancipation Proclamation* applied to slaves
   A. only in the border states.
   B. in states rebelling against the Union.
   C. throughout the whole Confederacy.
   D. only the territories.

5. Republicans often referred to Peace Democrats as
   A. Scalawags.
   B. Anacondas.
   C. Copperheads.
   D. Loyalists.

6. Managing the home front in the South largely fell to the responsibility of
   A. overseers.
   B. women.
   C. teenage sons.
   D. senior slaves.

7. The New York Draft Riot was largely directed at
   A. anti-abolitionists looking to end the war.
   B. Irish-Catholics eager to join the war.
   C. free blacks who became scapegoats.
   D. Peace Democrats against the war.

8. Upon being captured by Lee's forces in Pennsylvania, free blacks were
   A. immediately set free.
   B. sold into slavery in the South.
   C. all executed.
   D. taken as hostages with a high ransom.

9. During the latter part of the Civil War, Lee and Grant's tactics shifted to
   A. a limited war.
   B. guerrilla warfare.
   C. exclusive sieges.
   D. a war of attrition.

10. Lincoln's chances of reelection were greatly boosted by
    A. success of Sherman and Farragut.
    B. the quieting voices of the Peace Democrats.
    C. the lack of opposing candidates with name recognition.
    D. his fiery militant speeches.

Questions 11-12 refer to the following visual.

11. Picket's Charge proved to be a turning point in the Civil War because
    A. Lee's troops demoralized the northern outlook.
    B. the North would be irreversibly demoralized for not attacking Lee's retreating troops.
    C. Lee's fighting force would never be the same.
    D. the charge produced a major Confederate victory on Northern soil.

12. Pickett's Charge occurred during the
    A. Battle of Vicksburg.
    B. Battle of Gettysburg.
    C. Battle of Chancellorsville.
    D. Battle of Cold Harbor.

Questions 13-15 refer to the following excerpt.

At 10 0'clock Sunday (August 31) our train drew up at Fairfax Station. The ground, for acres, was a thinly wooded slope—and among the trees on the leaves and grass, were laid the wounded who pouring in by scores of wagon loads, as picked up on the field the flag of truce. All day they came and the whole hillside was red. Bales of hay were broken open and scattered over the ground littering of cattle, and the sore, famishing men were laid upon it...And when the night shut in, in the midst and darkness about us, we knew that standing apart from the world of anxious hearts, throbbing over the whole country, we were a little band of almost empty handed workers literally by ourselves in the wild woods of Virginia, with 3,000 suffering men crowded upon the few acres within our reach...After gathering up every available implement or convenience for our work, our domestic inventory stood 2 water buckets, 5 tin cups, 1 camp kettle, 1 stew pan, 2 lanterns, 4 bread knives, 3 plates, and a 2-quart tin dish, and 3,000 guest to serve...You will perceive by this, that I had not yet learned to equip myself, for I was no Pallas, ready armed, but grew into my work by hard thinking and sad experience. It may serve to relieve your apprehension for the future of my labors if I assure you that I was never caught so again...But the most fearful scene was reserved for the night. I have said that the ground was littered with dry hay and that we had only two lanterns, but there were plenty of candles. The wounded were laid so close that it was impossible to move about in the dark. The slightest misstep brought a torrent of groans from some poor mangled fellow in your path...Consequently here were seen persons of all grades from the careful man of God who walked with a prayer upon his lips to the careless driver hunting for his lost whip—each wandering about among this hay with an open flaming candle in his hands...The slightest accident, the mere dropping of a light could have enveloped in flames this whole mass of helpless men...How we watched and pleaded and cautioned as we worked and wept that night! How we put socks and slippers upon their cold feet, wrapped your blankets and quilts about them, and when we no longer these to give, how we covered them in the hay and left them to their rest! ...About three o'clock in the morning I observed a surgeon with a little flickering candle in hand approaching me with cautious step up in the wood. "Lady," he said as he drew near, "will you go with me? Out on the hills is a poor distressed lad, mortally wounded, and dying. His piteous cries for his sister have touched all our hearts none of us can relieve him but rather seem to distress him by presence."...By this time I was following him back over the bloody track, with great beseeching eyes of anguish on every side looking up into our faces, saying so plainly "Don't step on us."

--Clara Barton, Passage from Her Memoirs about Medical Life at the Battlefield, 1862

13. Barton's description of a battle's aftermath displays all of the following EXCEPT
    A. the primitive nature of battlefield medical care.
    B. the lack of medical resources.
    C. the suffering of wounded soldiers.
    D. the spacious layout for wounded soldiers.

14. The scene that Barton described actually was considered to be
    A. a cemetery.
    B. a hospital.
    C. a prison.
    D. an asylum.

15. The night proved to be especially precarious for an immobile wounded soldier in that
    A. it was cold and misty.
    B. darkness provoked fear.

C. they could get stepped on.
D. the enemy could reappear.

Questions 16-18 refer to the following excerpt.

MY DEAR AMELIA:

I have been in two fights, and am unhurt. I am about to go in another I believe to-night. Our men fought well on both occasions. The last was desperate we charged that terrible battery on Morris Island known as Fort Wagoner, and were repulsed with a loss of 3 killed and wounded. I escaped unhurt from amidst that perfect hail of shot and shell. It was terrible. I need not particularize the papers will give a better than I have time to give. My thoughts are with you often, you are as dear as ever, be good enough to remember it as I no doubt you will. As I said before we are on the eve of another fight and I am very busy and have just snatched a moment to write you. I must necessarily be brief. Should I fall in the next fight killed or wounded I hope to fall with my face to the foe.

If I survive I shall write you a long letter. DeForrest of your city is wounded George Washington is missing, Jacob Carter is missing, Chas Reason wounded Chas Whiting, Chas Creamer all wounded. The above are in hospital.

This regiment has established its reputation as a fighting regiment not a man flinched, though it was a trying time. Men fell all around me. A shell would explode and clear a space of twenty feet, our men would close up again, but it was no use we had to retreat, which was a very hazardous undertaking. How I got out of that fight alive I cannot tell, but I am here. My Dear girl I hope again to see you. I must bid you farewell should I be killed. Remember if I die I die in a good cause. I wish we had a hundred thousand colored troops we would put an end to this war.

Good Bye to all Write soon Your own loving LEWIS.

--Lewis Douglass, Morris Island, S.C.

16. In the attack against Fort Wagner in South Carolina, Lewis Douglass fought for
    A. *Corps de Afrique.*
    B. 29th Connecticut.
    C. 54th Massachusetts.
    D. Company E, 4th US Colored Troops.

17. Why did Douglass believe that falling "face to the foe" was particularly important?
    A. It increased the chance of surviving.
    B. It proved the bravery of black soldiers.
    C. Dying soldiers wouldn't have to look at enemy with face to the ground.
    D. The tactic made identification easier.

18. Lincoln authorized the creation of black regiments
    A. at the outset of the war.
    B. the last year of the war.

162

C. when the Emancipation Proclamation went into effect.

D. after the First Battle of Bull Run.

Questions 19-21 refer to the following excerpt.

. . . The skill and success of the men in collecting forage was one of the features of this march. Each brigade commander had authority to detail a company of foragers, usually about fifty men, with one or two commissioned officers selected for their boldness and enterprise. This party would be dispatched before` daylight with a knowledge of the intended day's march and camp; would proceed on foot five or six miles from the route traveled by their brigade, and then visit every plantation and farm within range. They would usually procure a wagon or family carriage, load it with bacon, corn-meal, turkeys, chickens, ducks, and every thing that could be used as food or forage, and would then regain the main road, usually in advance of their train. When this came up, they would deliver to the brigade commissary the supplies thus gathered by the way.

. . . No doubt, many acts of pillage, robbery, and violence, were committed by these parties of foragers, usually called "bummers"; for I have since heard of jewelry taken from women, and the plunder of articles that never reached the commissary; but these acts were exceptional and incidental. I never heard of any cases of murder or rape; and no army could have carried along sufficient food and forage for a march of three hundred miles; so that foraging in some shape was necessary. The country was sparsely settled, with no magistrates or civil authorities who could respond to requisitions, as is done in all the wars of Europe; so that this system of foraging was simply indispensable to our success. . . .

--William T. Sherman, The March Through Georgia, 1875

19. What led Sherman's march to rely on foraging?
    A. an insatiable quest to extract goods from the enemy.
    B. decision to sever supply lines in Atlanta.
    C. the inherent robbing nature of Union troops.
    D. curiosity to explore the southern countryside.

20. According to Sherman, the act of foraging as conducted by his army
    A. was done in an haphazard manner.
    B. was skillful and systematic.
    C. always featured violence and pillage, and robbery.
    D. frequently featured murder and rape.

21. Ultimately, Sherman viewed foraging as
    A. indispensable to the success of his campaign.
    B. despicable and unnecessary.
    C. solely as a way to entertain his troops.
    D. conduct unbecoming of soldiers.

SHORT ANSWER QUESTIONS

On April 9, 1865 General Robert E. Lee surrendered to General Ulysses S. Grant at Appomattox, Virginia.

   a. Choose ONE of the following and explain why your choice represents the event that led to Lee's surrendering

   - The Battle of Gettysburg
   - The Battle of Vicksburg
   - Lincoln's issuing of the Emancipation Proclamation

   b. Contrast your choice against ONE of the other options, demonstrating why that option in not as significant as your choice.

LONG ESSAY QUESTION

What impact did women and blacks have on the Civil War?

ANSWERS AND EXPLANATIONS

Multiple Choice Questions

   1. A People in the North expected a quick end to the war but the First Battle of Bull Run proved otherwise.
   2. C Lincoln was often frustrated that his generals had a case of the "slows."
   3. A Vicksburg was heavily fortified to keep the South as one entity.
   4. B *Emancipation Proclamation* applied only to areas that were in the state of rebellion.
   5. C Copperheads were considered to be venomous to the cause of the Union.
   6. B Women took the place of their husbands during the war.
   7. C Over 100 blacks were killed during this riot.
   8. B Terror reigned over the Pennsylvania countryside as many tried to hide blacks from Confederate troops.
   9. D The war became bloody especially with Grant in charge of the Army of the Potomac.
   10. A Victories in the lower south and at Mobile Bay boosted Lincoln's reelection chances.
   11. B Lee lost too many of his soldiers to launch further offensives.
   12. B Pickett's failure to break through enemy lines at Gettysburg proved to be a fatal blow for the Confederacy.

13. D Wounded soldiers on the battlefield were packed closely together.
14. B A medical scene to assist the soldiers was considered a hospital no matter what the circumstance.
15. C Tending to the ill in the dark could lead doctors and nurses to step on the wounded.
16. C The 54th Massachusetts was one of the first free black regiments formed in the north.
17. B Many blacks wanted to prove themselves during the Civil War.
18. C The *Emancipation Proclamation* did more than free the slaves in rebelling areas, it also served as a catalyst to create black regiments.
19. B With supply lines intentionally cut at Atlanta, Sherman's troops needed supplies.
20. B Sherman's foragers had a system in taking supplies and transferring them.
21. A Sherman relied on foraging to feed his army.

Long Essay Question

What impact did women and blacks have on the Civil War?

(Key topics to focus and elaborate on)
- Women served as nurses and assisted in organizing commissions to tend to the wounded
- Women took care of the farms while their husbands were off fighting
- Blacks formed regiments to fight against the Confederacy

Chapter 15
RECONSTRUCTION, 1865-1877

- Emancipation for the slaves came as a result of the Civil War and a future that seemed endless with possibilities fell well short of this potential.

FEDERAL RECONSTRUCTION POLICY

- Toward the end of the war, prominent figures debated whether former slaves should have the right to vote.
- The Radical Republicans pushed to give former slaves land and the right to vote.
- A debate ensued about how to deal with the Southern states and whether they had left the Union or merely engaged in rebellion against the federal government.
- Lincoln established the Freedmen's Bureau to assist the former slaves in various ways.
- Essentially, the post-Civil War was divided into three distinct time periods: Presidential Reconstruction, Congressional Reconstruction, and Redemption.
- When Andrew Johnson succeeded Lincoln, many Radical Republicans expected to work closely with him given his loyalty to the Union and his hatred towards the master class. Yet, Johnson cared little for the equality of the former slaves and issued many pardons to ex-Confederates.
- As the new state governments in the South formed, they had a distinct Confederate flavor and they developed Black Codes to severely limit the power and freedoms of the former slaves. The conditions of the codes essentially equated to slavery with a different name in the South.
- The Radical Republicans who opposed Andrew Jackson were led by Charles Sumner and Thaddeus Stevens, and even though many of the Republicans weren't radical, they did share the Radicals' disappointment in Johnson's amnesty policy towards the old Confederate leaders.
- In 1865, the Republican-dominated Congress refused to seat the newly elected Congressional delegates from the South because of their strong ties to the Confederacy.
- Lyman Trumbull proposed the Civil Rights Bill of 1866 to give all persons born in the US (except Indians) citizenship, and thereby enjoy all the rights of citizens. President Johnson not only vetoed this bill, he also vetoed the extension of the Freedmen's Bureau.
- Yet Congress would override Johnson's vetoes. To add permanency to the Civil Rights Act, Congress pushed to insert it into the Constitution as an amendment. Consequently, the Fourteenth Amendment guaranteed rights of citizenship to former slaves and others born or naturalized in the U.S..
- The Reconstruction Act of 1867 divided the former Confederate states into five military districts to ensure that each state would ratify the Fourteenth Amendment to order to have its representatives admitted to Congress.
- Although weakened, Johnson still had considerable power as president and aimed to block any Reconstruction plans that benefitted the former slaves. Thus, his opponents sought to remove him from office by passing the Tenure of Office Act; an act that the Radicals know Johnson would violate.

- The resulting impeachment trial saw Johnson fall just one Senate vote of being impeached.
- The Election of 1868 featured a victory for the Republican candidate and war hero, Ulysses S. Grant.
- Shortly after, the Republicans pushed the Fifteenth Amendment through Congress and the states. It guaranteed all males (but not women) the right to vote.
- Many women were disappointed that they too did not receive the right to vote with the passage of the Fifteenth Amendment.

THE IMPACT OF RECONSTRUCTION

- Initially, ex-Confederates held positions in government offices until Radical Reconstruction took over. As a result, former slaves, as well as abolitionists and northerners took over the South's leadership positions.
- Hiram Revels became the nation's first African American senator in 1870 and Blanch K. Bruce became the second in 1874.
- During Reconstruction 22 blacks served in Congress.
- Following the Civil War, African Americans had an unquenchable thirst for knowledge and education. The Freedmen's Bureau played a critical role in providing teachers, many of which came from the north, to the freedmen. Both black and white teachers taught freedmen.
- An obvious goal for the freedmen after the war was to acquire land and Sherman was the first to institute the "40 Acres and a Mule" program. However President Johnson quickly put an end to this policy.
- Many freedmen found themselves working on the very same plantations where they had served as slaves, but now they earned wages.
- Sharecropping became the new southern economic arrangement in which the landowner provided supplies to the land tenant and in return the tenant gave the landowner a share of the tenant's crop.
- The landowners eventually developed a manipulative system whereby they created a system of debt that entangled sharecroppers could never get out of.

TERROR, APATHY, AND THE CREATION OF THE SEGREGATED SOUTH

- The advancements made during Reconstruction failed to last due to numerous factors.
- Despite the initial gains made by the freedmen, white opposition in the South had always been prevalent. No doubt, they despised the newly empowered freedmen, scalawags, and carpetbaggers.
- Whereas the scalawags consisted of southerners who supported the Union, carpetbaggers migrated from the north (many of them were veterans of the Union army).
- The Democratic Party mobilized to crush the gains and advancements of the freedmen and became a powerful force in the south as opposition to Radical Reconstruction.
- The Ku Klux Klan rose to cripple and terrorize the freedmen and those who assisted them, including white Republicans and the teachers that educated freedmen. Even

before the rise of the KKK, violence against Republicans and freedmen in the south existed.

- The transition from slavery to freedom met violent opposition in numerous places such as Colfax, Louisiana, Lamar, Mississippi, Yazoo City, Mississippi, and Vicksburg, Mississippi.
- To counter the violence directed at Reconstruction in the South, Congress passed the Enforcement Acts which protected African Americans in the South in numerous ways.
- Grant sent federal troops to places such as South Carolina to enforce this legislation.
- As time passed, Democrats gained power in Congress and people in the North began to lose interest in Southern affairs.
- The fact that corruption existed in the coalition Reconstruction governments meant that support from the North would waver. Grant's administration was also riddled with corruption and scandal.
- The Election of 1876 displayed the interest the nation had towards Reconstruction. The confusion of the election led the Democrats to offer the presidency to the Republican Rutherford B. Hayes. In return, Hayes would end Reconstruction and remove all federal troops from the South.
- Slowly but surely, the presence of African Americans in the Senate would disappear.
- Jim Crow laws passed in the South to segregate whites from blacks, and the Supreme Court solidified this segregation with the passage of *Plessy v. Ferguson.*

MULTIPLE CHOICE QUESTIONS

1. In regard to giving blacks the right to vote, Lincoln believed
   A. an amendment should be passed guaranteeing black suffrage.
   B. Congress should mandate black suffrage.
   C. states should determine who could vote.
   D. an executive order should allow for black suffrage.

2. The most vocal advocates of black suffrage proved to be
   A. Northern Democrats.
   B. Radical Republicans.
   C. Modest Republicans.
   D. Abolitionists.

3. During the phase of presidential reconstruction, Andrew Johnson
   A. severely punished those involved in the Confederate government.
   B. did not allow former Confederate leaders to be part of the new state governments.
   C. gave numerous pardons to those who participated in the Confederate government.
   D. pushed for black suffrage.

4. The Freedmen's Bureau did all of the following EXCEPT
   A. provide assistance to the former slaves in understanding their contracts.
   B. provide medical assistance to the former slaves.

C. provide education to the former slaves.

D. provide support for the passage of Black Codes.

5. During the impeachment trial of Andrew Johnson, he came just
   A. one vote short of being removed from office.
   B. five votes short of being removed from office.
   C. ten votes short of being removed from office.
   D. twenty votes short of being removed from office.

6. *The right of citizens of the United States to vote shall not be denied or abridged by the United States or by any State on account of race, color, or previous condition of servitude* is inherent in
   A. Thirteenth Amendment.
   B. Fourteenth Amendment.
   C. Fifteenth Amendment.
   D. Civil Rights Act of 1866.

7. The amendment that guaranteed the rights of citizenship to former slaves and others born or naturalized in the Unites States was the
   A. Thirteenth Amendment.
   B. Fourteenth Amendment.
   C. Fifteenth Amendment.
   D. Sixteenth Amendment.

8. The nation's first African American ever elected to the Senate was
   A. Hiram R. Revels.
   B. Blanche K. Bruce.
   C. Lucius Q. C. Lamar.
   D. Frederick Douglass.

9. Under the system of sharecropping, most southern blacks
   A. owned the land on which they farmed.
   B. had plantation stores to provide supplies to other blacks.
   C. fell into a hopeless cycle of debt to landowners.
   D. made huge profits.

10. To counter the terror of the Ku Klux Klan
    A. Congress threatened renewed war with the South.
    B. the Freedmen's Bureau adopted self-defense tactics.
    C. The Knights of the White Camellia formed to combat the KKK.
    D. Congress passed the Enforcement Acts.

Questions 11-12 refer to the following image.

11. The "First Vote" occurred during the
    A. period of the Civil War.
    B. period of Presidential Reconstruction.
    C. period of Radical Reconstruction.
    D. period of Redemption.

12. The voters in the image more than likely voted
    A. in favor of northern Democrats.
    B. in favor of southern Democrats.
    C. in favor of Republicans.
    D. in favor of the Black Codes.

Questions 13-15 refer to the following selection.

Some of the Outrages

Greensboro, N.C. May 24, 1870.
Gen. Jos. C. Abbott

My Dear General:

It is my mournful duty to inform you that our friend John W. Stephens, State Senator from Caswell, is dead. He was foully murdered by the Ku-Klux in the Grand Jury room of the Court House on Saturday or Saturday night last... Another brave, honest Republican citizen has met his fate at the hands of these fiends...Against the advice of his friends, against the entreaties of his family, he constantly refused to leave those who had stood by him in the day of his disgrace and peril...He was accustomed to say that 3,000 poor, ignorant, colored Republican voters in that county had stood by him and elected him, at the risk of persecution and starvation, and that he had no idea of abandoning them to the Ku-Klux....The uselessness, the utter futility of complaint from the lack of ability in the laws to punish is fully known to all. The danger of making such complaint is also well understood. It is therefore not unfrequently by accident that the outrage is found out, and unquestionably it is frequently absolutely concealed.

...Men and women come scarred, mangled, and bruised, and say: "The Ku-Klux came to my house last night and beat me almost to death, and my old woman right smart, and shot into the house, Ôbust' the door down, and told me they would kill me if I made complaint;" and the bloody mangled forms attest the truth of their declarations. On being asked if any one knew any of the party it will be ascertained that there was no recognition, or only the most uncertain and doubtful one. In such cases as these nothing can be done by the court...These crimes have been of every character imaginable. Perhaps the most usual has been the dragging of men and women from their beds, and beating their naked bodies with hickory switches, or as witnesses in an examination the other day said, "sticks" between a "switch" and a "club." From 50 to 100 blows is the usual allowance, sometimes 200 and 300 blows are administered. Occasionally an instrument of torture is owned. Thus in one case two women, one 74 years old, were taken out, stripped naked, and beaten with a paddle, with several holes bored through it. The paddle was about 30 inches long, 3 or 4 inches wide, and 1/4 of an inch thick, of oak. Their bodies were so bruised and beaten that they were sickening to behold. They were white women and of good character until the younger was seduced, and swore her child to its father. Previous to that and so far as others were concerned her character was good...

I could give other incidents of cruelty, such as hanging up a boy of nine years old until he was nearly dead, to make him tell where his father was hidden, and beating an old negress of 103 years old with garden pallings because she would not own that she was afraid of the Ku-Klux. But it is unnecessary to go into further detail...

And yet the Government sleeps...I am ashamed of the nation that will let its citizens be slain by scores, and scourged by thousands, and offer no remedy or protection...How much more worthy of detestation is a Government which in time of peace will permit such wholesale slaughter of its citizens? It is simple cowardice, inertness, and wholesale demoralization. The wholesale slaughter of the war has dulled our Nation's sense of horror at the shedding of blood, and the habit of regarding the South as simply a laboratory, where every demagogue may carry on his reconstructionary experiments at will, and not as an integral party of the Nation itself, has led our Government to shut its eyes to the atrocities of these times. Unless these evils are speedily remedied, I tell you, General, the Republican party has signed its death warrant. It is a party of cowards or idiots - I don't care which alternative is chosen. The remedy is in our hands, and we are afraid or too dull to bestir ourselves and use it...

And yet this same Congress has the control of the militia and can organize its own force in every county in the United States, and arm more or less of it. This same Congress has the undoubted right to guarantee and provide a republican government, and protect every citizen in "life, liberty, and the pursuit of happiness," as well as the power conferred by the XVth Amendment. ..What then is the remedy? First: Let Congress give to the U. S. Courts, or to Courts of the States under its own laws, cognizance of this class of crimes, as crimes against the nation, and let it provide that this legislation be enforced. Why not, for instance, make going armed and masked or disguised, or masked or disguised in the night time, an act of insurrection or sedition? Second: Organize militia, National-State militia is a nuisance - and arm as many as may be necessary in each county to enforce its laws. Third: Put detectives at work to get hold of this whole organization. Its ultimate aim is unquestionably to revolutionize the Government. If we have not pluck enough for this, why then let us just offer our throats to the knife, emasculate ourselves, and be a nation of self-subjugated slaves at once.

...I say to you plainly that any member of Congress who, especially if from the South, does not support, advocate, and urge immediate, active, and thorough measures to put an end to these outrages, and make citizenship a privilege, is a coward, a traitor, or a fool. The time for action has come, and the man who has now only speeches to make over some Constitutional scarecrow, deserves to be damned.

--Letter from Judge Tourgee to Senator Abbott

13. According to Judge Tourgee, in most cases why did the court system fail to prosecute Klan members for the violence they inflicted in the South?
    A. The victims couldn't identify their attackers.
    B. The judges and jury members were Klansmen.
    C. The Klan was known only as a social fraternity.
    D. The victims feared the consequences of identifying attackers.

14. Judge Tourgee identifies the Klan's victims as all of the following EXCEPT
    A. Republicans.
    B. African-Americans.
    C. White women.
    D. Democrats/

15. President Grant and Congress finally responded to the violence of the Ku Klux Klan by
    A. creating a constitutional amendment that outlawed Klan activity.
    B. placing, once again, the South into military districts.
    C. passing the Enforcement Acts.
    D. declaring that the South was under martial law.

Questions 16-18 refer to the following excerpt.

AN ACT TO ESTABLISH A BUREAU FOR THE RELIEF OF FREEDMEN AND REFUGEES

Be it enacted, That there is hereby established in the War Department, to continue during the present war of rebellion, and for one year thereafter, a bureau of refugees, freedmen, and abandoned lands, to which shall be committed, as hereinafter provided, the supervision and management of all abandoned lands, and the control of all subjects relating to refugees and freedmen from rebel states, or from any district of country within the territory embraced in the operations of the army, under such rules and regulations as may be prescribed by the head of the bureau and approved by the President. The said bureau shall be under the management and control of a commissioner to be appointed by the President, by and with the advice and consent of the Senate...

Sec. 2. . That the Secretary of War may direct such issues of provisions, clothing, and fuel, as he may deem needful for the immediate and temporary shelter and supply of destitute and suffering refugees and freedmen and their wives and children, under such rules and regulations as he may direct.

Sec. 3. That the President may, by and with the advice and consent of the Senate, appoint an assistant commissioner for each of the states declared to be in insurrection, not exceeding ten in number, who shall, under the direction of the commissioner, aid in the execution of the provisions of this act;... And any military officer may be detailed and assigned to duty under this act without increase of pay or allowances...

Sec. 4. That the commissioner, under the direction of the President, shall have authority to set apart, for the use of loyal refugees and freedmen, such tracts of land within the insurrectionary states as shall have been abandoned, or to which the United States shall have acquired title by confiscation or sale, or otherwise, and to every male citizen, whether refugee or freedman, as aforesaid, there shall be assigned not more than forty acres of such land, and the person to whom it was so assigned shall be protected in the use and enjoyment of the land for the term of three years at an annual rent not exceeding six per centum upon the value of such land, as it was appraised by the state authorities in the year eighteen hundred and sixty, for the purpose of taxation, and in case no such appraisal can be found, then the rental shall be based upon the estimated value of the land in said year, to be ascertained in such manner as the commissioner may by regulation prescribe. At the end of said term, or at any time during said term, the occupants of any parcels so assigned may purchase the land and receive such title thereto as the United States can convey, upon paying therefor the value of the land, as ascertained and fixed for the purpose of determining the annual rent aforesaid

16. According to the act, the Freedmen's Bureau provided refugees, freedmen, and their families with all of the following EXCEPT

   A. provisions.
   B. temporary shelter.

C. clothing.
D. labor contracts.

17. Under the direction of the Freedmen's Bureau, loyal refugees and freedmen would havethe opportunity to

A. vote for their own officials.
B. own land.
C. become generals in the U.S. Army.
D. return to their masters.

18. According to the act, the commissioner to lead the Freedmen's Bureau was chosen by

A. the U.S. Senate.
B. the Supreme Court.
C. the U.S. Army.
D. the president.

Questions 19-21 refer to the following excerpt.

After freedom, we worked on shares a while. Then we rented. When we worked on shares, we couldn't make nothing, just overalls and something to eat. Half went to the other man and you would destroy your half if you weren't careful. A man that didn't know how to count would always lose. He might lose anyhow. They didn't give no itemized statement. No, you just had to take their word. They never give you no details. They just say you owe so much. No matter how good account you kept, you had to go by their account and now, Brother, I'm tellin' you the truth about this. It's been that way for a long time. You had to take the white man's work on note, and everything. Anything you wanted, you could git if you were a good hand. You could git anything you wanted as long as you worked. If you didn't make no money, that's all right; they would advance you more. But you better not leave him, you better not try to leave and get caught. They'd keep you in debt. They were sharp. Christmas come, you could take up twenty dollar, in somethin' to eat and much as you wanted in whiskey. You could buy a gallon of whiskey. Anything that kept you a slave because he was always right and you were always wrong it there was difference. If there was an argument, he would get mad and there would be a shooting take place.

And you know how Negroes is. Long as they could git somethin', they didn't care. You see, if the white man came out behind, he would feed you, let you have what you wanted. He'd just keep you on, help you get on your feet, that is, if you were a good hand. But if you weren't a good hand, he'd just let you have enough to keep you alive. A good hand could take care of forty or fifty acres of land and would have a large family. A good hand could git clothes, food, whiskey, whenever be wanted it.

--Henry Blake Talks about Sharecropping after the Civil War

19. Why did landowners allow and even provide sharecroppers with whiskey?
    A. It kept their spirits up.
    B. It was cheaper than water.
    C. It made for a good gift.
    D. It kept them like slaves.

20. Why didn't the landowners give sharecroppers itemized statements of their harvests?
    A. The sharecroppers already trusted the landowners.
    B. The process of creating statements was too lengthy.
    C. The landowners would take more than they deserved.
    D. Paper was at a premium and thus limited.

21. Landowners always kept sharecroppers in debt to
    A. keep them on their land like slaves.
    B. provide them with extravagant provisions.
    C. establish the credit of the freedmen.
    D. serve as benevolent creditors.

SHORT ANSWER QUESTIONS

African Americans in the South endured decades of social, economic, and political hardship.

  a. Choose ONE of the following and explain why your choice represents the event that led to these decades of hardships.

  - The birth of the Ku Klux Klan
  - The death of Charles Sumner
  - Compromise of 1877

  b. Contrast your choice against ONE of the other options, demonstrating why that option in not as significant as your choice.

LONG ESSAY QUESTION

How did the Radical Republicans try to better the lives of the freedmen during Reconstruction?

ANSWERS AND EXPLANATIONS

Multiple Choice Questions

1. C Lincoln thought that suffrage was a state matter.
2. B The Radical Republicans sought to revolutionize the South by giving freedmen the right to suffrage.

3. C Despite his verbal opposition to Confederacy, he gave pardons to many of them.
4. D The Radical Republicans found the Black Codes to be despicable.
5. A Johnson was one vote shy of being the first president to ever be removed from office.
6. C The Fifteenth Amendment solidified black suffrage by inserting its guarantee in the Constitution.
7. B The Fourteenth Amendment guaranteed citizenship to the former slaves.
8. A Hiram Revels became the first African American U.S. senator in U.S. history.
9. C Hopeless debt became a normal fact of life for the black sharecropper.
10. D Congress passed the Enforcement Acts to halt the violence of the Ku Klux Klan.
11. C The Radical Republicans pushed to give the freedmen the right to vote.
12. C Since the Republicans pushed for black suffrage, blacks voted exclusively for Republicans.
13. D The Ku Klux Klan successfully intimidated blacks and all those who supported them.
14. D The Democrats were the party of the Old South and advocates of white redemption.
15. C The Enforcement Acts would see the military force used to restore order and halt the violence of the Klan.
16. D The Freedmen's Bureau oversaw labor contracts but did not issue them.
17. B For a short time, under the direction of the Freedmen's Bureau, former slaves had the opportunity to farm and own confiscated land.
18. D The commissioner of the Freedmen's Bureau was under the direction of the president.
19. D Whiskey was used to impair the sharecropper's judgment and concern for fair Contracts.
20. C By not itemizing harvest statements, the landowners could cheat the sharecroppers by taking more than their fair share.
21. A Keeping sharecroppers in debt ensured that they could never leave the land they farmed on.

Long Essay Question

How did the Radical Republicans try to better the lives of the freedmen during Reconstruction?

(Key topics to focus and elaborate on)
- Freedmen's Bureau
- 14th Amendment
- 15th Amendment

Chapter 16
CONFLICT IN THE WEST, 1865-1912

- Immediately following the Civil War, war against Indians erupted in the Great Plains which led to the destruction of their way of life.
- Replacing this way of life would first be the cattle ranches and subsequently smaller farms that produced beef and wheat.

THE TRIBES OF THE WEST

- After the Civil War, whites and blacks looked to gain land that was occupied by the Plains Indians.
- The Comanche had built themselves into a powerful force in the Southwest prior to the 1850s. They were fierce warriors and relied on buffalo hunting for their livelihood.
- During the Civil War and Reconstruction, the Comanche developed a rich cattle trade with New Mexicans who came to be known as Comancheros.
- In 1867, the Comanche met with General William Tecumseh Sherman and were told that they were longer to remain sovereign and had to adopt farming techniques on reservations.
- The Medicine Lodge Creek Treaty called for a Comanche reservation with occasional open plains hunting, but both the federal government and the Comanche had different interpretations of the treaty.
- This lack of communication led to fighting between the U.S. Army and the Comanches and resulted in devastation for the Comanche way of life by 1873. Despite the initial fighting, the Comanches eventually settled on reservations and a way of life highlighted by the life of Quannah Parker.
- The Navajo and Apache also came under attack by the U.S. Army in New Mexico in 1863 where they were forced to live in a reservation known as Bosque Redondo.
- The result was a disaster since the Navajos and Apaches were natural enemies. Consequently a new reservation was created for the Navajos in their natural homeland and they experienced a large population growth between 1864 and 1900.
- The gold rush proved to be devastating for the Indians of California as their reservation boundaries were essentially ignored by gold seekers.
- The Modocs tried to survive in the Lost River region of California, but eventually succumbed to the U.S. Army.
- The Nez Perce divided over whether they should live on a reservation in Idaho or not, and some chose to live independently along the Salmon and Snake Rivers in Idaho and Oregon.
- The U.S. Army chased the Nez Perce (led by Chief Joseph) living along the Snake River on a tragic journey that made its way to the Canadian border. They eventually were forced to live in Indian Territory in 1877.
- The largest of the Indian tribes in the Great Plains were the Sioux with the Lakota Sioux being the most powerful by the 1860s-1870s. In an attempt to avoid war, the Lakota Sioux led by Red Cloud signed the Treaty of Fort Laramie in 1868, but the treaty met opposition by Sitting Bull.

- The discovery of gold led to the Great Sioux War in the Black Hills region where General George Custer lost his life at the Battle of Little Bighorn in 1876. Subsequent battles crippled the Sioux.
- In desiring to bring a return to their former way of life that featured the roaming buffalo and land without whites, the Sioux engaged in the Ghost Dance. Fearful of this ritual, the U.S. Army fueled a gunfight in which approximately 200 Sioux were killed at the Wounded Knee Massacre.
- Expansion after the Civil War led to rapid settlement of the Great Plains despite agreements such as the Treaty of Fort Laramie (1851). The end of the war allowed for more soldiers to be transferred to the west, thereby allowing the U.S. government to become more aggressive with the settlement of the west.
- The Homestead Act provided 160 acres of federal land to each family that would settle on that land and maintain it for five years.
- The settlement of whites on the Great Plains was protected by larger forces of the U.S. Army.
- The Reconstruction Congress created the Indian Peace Commission which believed that large tracts of land or reservations would protect the Indians and pave the way for assimilation. This idea naturally was met with much resentment among the Indians.
- Grant's Peace Policy aimed at assimilation and placing Indians on reservations where they were not to be harassed and to be managed by missionaries instead of the military. Initially the policy frustrated the military, but eventually they ignored it and continued to clash with the Indians.
- By the 1870s, government officials believed that assimilation would only occur if reservations were transferred into smaller tracts of individual plots.
- The Dawes Act allotted 160 acres of reservation land to a family that could be sold in 25 years. Yet individual plots went against the communal nature of the Indians.
- Schooling was seen as another way to assimilate the Indians into the American culture. For example, the Carlisle School taught Indian students religion and western customs.

THE IMPACT OF THE TRANSCONTINENTAL RAILROAD, 1869

- The Pacific Railway Act authorized the construction of a transcontinental railroad with the Central Pacific building from Sacramento and the Union Pacific building from Omaha.
- The line officially connected when the last spike was hammered at Promontory Point, Utah in 1869. Other major lines would follow. Better technology made travelling by rail across the country cheaper and quicker than ever before. The rapidity of the connections led to standardized clocks to synchronize with railroad schedules.
- Railroads increased international trade due to the ease in transferring goods to docks.

- By the late 1800s, the American West had been transformed into a region of farms and ranches. Yet not all of the inhabitants got along.
- Texas Longhorn cattle was resilient to the conditions of the Great Plains
- After the war, veterans came home to round up the cattle in Texas.
- Unlike on the King Ranch, most cattle herding occurred openly on federal land with the use of branding
- Joseph McCoy founded the nation's first cattle town in Abilene, Kansas to facilitate the loading of cattle onto the transcontinental trains. The Chisolm Trail from Texas would be used to drive cattle to towns such as Abilene.
- The end of the trail saw celebrating cowboys visiting saloons in places such as Dodge City where less than reputable women would frequent.
- Refrigerated cars would transfer the beef to packing towns such as Chicago which quickly became the hub of the nation's meatpacking industry.
- The cowboys who handled the herding had varied backgrounds from former slaves to ex-Confederate veterans to American Indians to those of Mexican descent.
- Charles Goodnight and his "Chuck Wagons" provided food and bedding for the roundups and trail drives.
- By the 1880s, cattle owners began to use barbed wire fencing to keep their herds in one area. The 1880s also proved to be a tough time for the cattle industry with harsh weather and a declining market for beef.
- The end of the open ranges, round ups, and cattle drives came when the industry switched to smaller scale ranches that were maintained largely by families.
- The West featured a battle between those who wanted open grazing versus those who wanted to fence the land with cheap barbed wire. In particular, Mexicanos in New Mexico favored open grazing but Anglo Americas wanted to create their own fenced cattle ranches.
- Tensions rose between Mexicans and Anglos in places such as Texas and New Mexico in various forms such as that caused by fence-cutting and Spanish-language newspapers that supported Mexican Americans to run for office.
- In the late 1800s, more people arrived on the Great Plains to farm from various parts of the United States and the world. Land became available from the government through the Homestead Act of 1862 and from the railroads who owned large tracts of land.
- Wheat became a staple of the Great Plains because it was more durable than corn.
- Settlers were also lured by the discovery of minerals such as Henry Comstock's find of silver in Nevada. Gold was also discovered in the Dakotas and Colorado.
- Mining towns were dominated by males and they became ghost towns soon after miners extracted all the minerals of a location.
- Ranch owners hired gunfighters to drive out people they deemed as troublemakers.
- Wyatt Earp and his brothers helped to establish order in Tombstone, Arizona after a gunfight at the O.K. Corral in 1881.
- Jesse and Frank James went on a train robbing rampage in 1886 in Missouri, and Billy the Kid wreaked havoc in Lincoln County until Pat Garret shot him dead.

- William Cody created Buffalo Bill's Wild West Show that became highly popular and featured Sitting Bull and Annie Oakley. Although popular, the show did not embody a true representation of the West.
- Several territories emerged from the oversight of the federal government and became states in the late 1800s. Among these states, Wyoming and Colorado granted women the right to vote.
- After deciding to drop the acceptance of plural marriage, Utah was admitted as a state in 1896.
- Oklahoma was admitted as a single state in 1907 despite objections from Indians who wanted to be admitted as a separate Indian state, and New Mexico and Arizona became states in 1912.

MULTIPLE CHOICE QUESTIONS

1. Grant's Peace Policy called for all of the following EXCEPT
   A. reservations for Indians to maintain their traditional ways.
   B. peace with ex-Confederates.
   C. administering by religious groups.
   D. administering by the military.

2. In 1887, Congress passed the Dawes Act to
   A. create more reservations for the Indians of the Great Plains.
   B. transform the reservations into individual plots of land.
   C. create schools for Indians.
   D. provide for farm education to the Indians.

3. The transcontinental railroad became
   A. the first railroad to connect all of the states of the eastern seaboard.
   B. a source of labor for Italian immigrants.
   C. the first railroad to connect the nation from coast to coast.
   D. an important route to Mexico.

4. The Homestead Act offered
   A. 160 Acres of land to each family who agreed to settle and maintain it.
   B. the extension of reservation land throughout the West.
   C. free land exclusively in Oklahoma.
   D. to divide land in the east.

5. The Comanche Empire was located primarily in
   A. the northeast.
   B. the southwest.
   C. the southeast.
   D. the northwest.

6. The comancheros traded goods from the northeast to the Comanches in exchange for
   A. furs.
   B. corn.
   C. cattle.
   D. gold.

7. The Sioux's Ghost Dance called for
   A. a migration to Canada.
   B. a return of the buffalo and disappearance of whites.
   C. the destruction of enemy tribes.
   D. the transformation to white culture.

8. By the 1880s federal reformers came to believe that the Indians
   A. could only assimilate if the reservations were gone.
   B. Indians could never be assimilated.
   C. had to leave the nation altogether.
   D. should be educated in their own ways.

9. In the late 1800s, Abilene, Kansas became
   A. one of the largest reservations in U.S. history.
   B. one of the nation's first cattle towns.
   C. the starting point for cattle drives.
   D. the largest meatpacking city in the country.

10. *Buffalo Bill's Wild West Show* featured all of the following EXCEPT
    A. scenes of Indian battles.
    B. scenes of Indian dancing.
    C. stagecoach robberies.
    D. minority cowboys.

Questions 11-12 refer to the following visual.

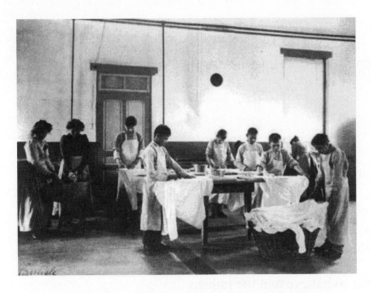

11. The Carlisle Indian School was created to
    A. help Indians learn about their own culture.
    B. teach them nomadic survival skills.
    C. help Indian youths to assimilate to white culture.
    D. teach whites about Indian culture.

12. The Carlisle Indian School held the notion that
    A. confidence can be gained through pride in your culture.
    B. the Indian culture had invaluable transitional traits.
    C. the European culture was inferior to the Indian culture.
    D. Indians could be successful if they immersed themselves in Euro-American culture.

Questions 13-15 refer to the following excerpt.

I will tell you the reason for the trouble. When we first made treaties with the Government, our old life and our old customs were about to end; the game on which we lived was disappearing; the whites were closing around us, and nothing remained for us but to adopt their ways,-the Government promised us all the means necessary to make our living out of the land, and to instruct us how to do it, and with abundant food to support us until we could take care of ourselves. We looked forward with hope to the time we could be as independent as the whites, and have a voice in the Government...The army officers could have helped better than anyone else but we were not left to them. An Indian Department was made with a large number of agents and other officials drawing large salaries-then came the beginning of trouble; these men took care of themselves but not of us. It was very hard to deal with the government through them-they could make more for themselves by keeping us back than by helping us forward...We did not get the means for working our lands; the few things they gave us did little good...Our rations began to be reduced; they said we were lazy. That is false. How does any man of sense suppose that so great a number of people could get work at once unless they were at once supplied with the means to work and instructors enough to teach them?...Our ponies were taken away from us under the promise that they would be replaced by oxen and large horses; it was long before we saw any, and then we got very few. We tried with the means we had, but on one pretext or another, we were shifted from one place to another, or were told that such a transfer was coming. Great efforts were made to break up our customs, but nothing was done to introduce us to customs of the whites. Everything was done to break up the power of the real chiefs...The men who counted (census) told all around that we were feasting and wasting food. Where did he see it? How could we waste what we did not have? We felt we were mocked in our misery; we had no newspaper and no one to speak for us. Our rations were again reduced...You who eat three times a day and see your children well and happy around you cannot understand what a starving Indian feels! We were faint with hunger and maddened by despair. We held our dying children and felt their little bodies tremble as their soul went out and left only a dead weight in our hands. They were not very heavy but we were faint and the dead weighed us down. There was no hope on earth. God seemed to have forgotten.

--Chief Red Cloud's Speech

13. In his speech, Chief Red Cloud admitted that his people
    A. were not ready to assimilate to the dominant white culture.
    B. defiant at the government's attempt to assimilate them.
    C. were willing to adopt the way of white farmers.
    D. would maintain their nomadic lifestyle.

14. Chief Red Cloud's major complaint is that the federal government
    A. didn't follow through on its promise to provide the means to change their lifestyle.
    B. made his people adopt a non-nomadic lifestyle.
    C. provided more supplies than his people knew what to do with.
    D. taught farming skills that his people could never get used to.

15. Chief Red Cloud's description of the tragedy his people faced is highlighted by
    A. the end of the buffalo hunts.
    B. the starvation of their children.
    C. the reservations his people had to live in.
    D. the government's assimilations policy.

Questions 16-18 refer to the following excerpt.

The only time I ever had serious trouble was at an even more primitive little hotel than the one in question. It was also on an occasion when I was out after lost horses. Below the hotel had merely a bar-room, a dining-room, and a lean-to kitchen; above was a loft with fifteen or twenty beds in it. It was late in the evening when I reached the place. I heard one or two shots in the bar-room as I came up, and I disliked going in. But there was nowhere else to go, and it was a cold night. Inside the room were several men, who, including the bartender, were wearing the kind of smile worn by men who are making believe to like what they don't like. A shabby individual in a broad hat with a cocked gun in each hand was walking up and down the floor talking with strident profanity. He had evidently been shooting at the clock, which had two or three holes in it face...He was not a "bad man" of the really dangerous type, the true man-killer type, but he was an objectionable creature, a would-be bad man, a bully who for the moment was having things all his own way. As soon as he saw me he hailed me as "Four eyes," in reference to my spectacles, and said, "Four eyes is going to treat." I joined in the laugh and got behind the stove and sat down, thinking to escape notice. He followed me, however, and though I tried to pass it off as a jest this merely made him more offensive, and he stood leaning over me, a gun in each hand, using very foul language. He was foolish to stand so near, and moreover, his heels were close together, so that his position was unstable. Accordingly, in response to his reiterated command that I should set up the drinks, I said, "Well, if I've got to, I've got to," and rose, looking past him...As I rose, I struck quick and hard with my right just to one side of the point of his jaw, hitting with my self as I straightened out, and then again with my right. He fired the guns, but I do not know whether this was merely a convulsive action of his hands or whether he was trying to shoot at me. When he went down he struck the corner of the bar with his head. It was not a case in which one could afford to take chances, and if he had moved I was about to drop on his ribs with my knees; but he was senseless. I took away his guns, and the other people in the room, who were now loud in their denunciation of him, hustled him out and put him in a shed. I got dinner as soon as possible, sitting in a corner of the dining-room away from the windows, and then went upstairs to bed where it was dark so that there would be no chance of any one shooting at me from the outside. However, nothing happened.

--Teddy Roosevelt, Cowboy, 1884

16. Roosevelt's description of his nemesis indicates that even the rowdiest of cowboys
    A. didn't like to drink.
    B. objected to foul language.
    C. were not the dangerous or killer type.
    D. treated strangers with courtesy.

17. Most historians agree that cowboys tended to be rowdy because
    A. they came from broken homes.
    B. they were genetically predisposed to rebellion.
    C. they were blowing off steam from a long cattle drive.
    D. they had to fight to survive the barren plains.

18. Roosevelt's description of his encounter indicates that the common meeting ground of the cowboys could be found
    A. on the range.
    B. at the general store.
    C. at a bar or saloon.
    D. at the ranch.

Questions 19-21 refer to the following excerpt.

We heard that Big Foot was coming down from the Badlands with nearly four hundred people. Some of these were from Sitting Bull's band. They had run away when Sitting Bull was killed, and joined Big Foot on Good River. There were only about a hundred warriors in this band, and all the others were women and children and some old men. They were all starving and freezing, and Big Foot was so sick that they had to bring him along in a pony drag. They had all run away to hide in the Badlands, and they were coming in now because they were starving and freezing. Soldiers were over there looking for them. The soldiers had everything and were not freezing and starving. Near Porcupine Butte the soldiers came up to the Big Foots, and they surrendered and went along with the soldiers to Wounded Knee Creek....It was in the evening when we heard that the Big Foots were camped over there with the soldiers, about fifteen miles by the old road from where we were. It was the next morning that something terrible happened. ...In the morning I went out after my horses, and while I was out I heard shooting off toward the east, and I knew from the sound that it must be wagon-guns [cannon] going off. The sounds went right through my body, and I felt that something terrible would happen.... In a little while we had come to the top of the ridge where, looking to the east, you can see for the first time the monument and the burying ground on the little hill where the church is. That is where the terrible thing started...There was much shooting down yonder, and there were many cries, and we could see cavalrymen scattered over the hills ahead of us. Cavalrymen were riding along the gulch and shooting into it, where the women and children were running away and trying to hide in the gullies and the stunted pines....We followed down along the dry gulch, and what we saw was terrible. Dead and wounded women and children and little babies were scattered all along there where they had been trying to run away. The soldiers had followed along the gulch, as they ran, and murdered them in there. Sometimes they were in heaps because they had huddled together, and some were scattering all along. Sometimes bunches of them had been killed and torn to pieces where the wagon guns hit them. I saw a little baby trying to suck its mother, but she was bloody and dead....When we drove the soldiers back, they dug themselves in, and we were not enough people to drive them out from there. In the evening they marched off up Wounded Knee Creek, and then we saw all that they had done there....Men and women and children were heaped and scattered all over the flat at the bottom of the little hill where the soldiers had their wagon-guns, and westward up the dry gulch all the way to the high ridge, the dead women and children and babies were scattered....When I saw this I wished that I had died too, but I was not sorry for the women and children. It was better for them to be happy in the other world, and I wanted to be there too. But before I went there I wanted to have revenge. I thought there might be a day, and we should have revenge....In the morning the soldiers began to take all the guns away from the Big Foots, who were camped in the flat below the little hill where the monument and burying ground are now. The people had stacked most of their guns, and even their knives, by the teepee where Big Foot was lying sick. Soldiers were on the little hill and all around, and there were soldiers across the dry gulch to the south and over east along Wounded Knee Creek too. The people were nearly surrounded, and the wagon-guns were pointed at them....It was a good winter day when all this happened. The sun was shining. But after the soldiers marched away from their dirty work, a heavy snow began to fall. The wind came up in the night. There was a big blizzard, and it grew very cold. The snow drifted deep in the crooked gulch, and it was one long grave of butchered women and children and babies, who had never done any harm and were only trying to run away.

19. The ultimate outcome of the Indian Wars was determined by the numbers of the U.S. military and its advanced weapons. What proof does the writer give of this advanced weaponry in this excerpt?
    A. mention of muskets
    B. mention of cannons
    C. mention of machine guns
    D. mention of long range rifles
20. The initial spark of the Wounded Knee Massacre was

A. the killing of Red Cloud.
B. the killing of Crazy Horse.
C. the killing Sitting Bull.
D. the killing of Bigfoot.

21. The "dirty work" that the soldiers engaged in was
   A. the stealing from Bigfoot's camp.
   B. the attempted arrest of Sitting Bull.
   C. leaving Bigfoot's people to starve.
   D. the brutal murdering of men, women, and children.

SHORT ANSWER QUESTIONS

The Indian Wars that featured Indians in the West versus the U.S. Army came to an end by 1890.

   a. Choose ONE of the following and explain why your choice represents the event that led to the end of these wars.

      • Wounded Knee Massacre
      • Congress passes the Dawes Act
      • The first transcontinental railroad is completed

   b. Contrast your choice against ONE of the other options, demonstrating why that option in not as significant as your choice.

LONG ESSAY QUESTION

What did the transformation of the West feature in the late 1800s?

ANSWERS AND EXPLANATIONS

Multiple Choice Questions

1. A Grant's experience during the Civil War led him to seek a peaceful solution for Indian settlement.
2. B The Dawes Act aimed to break up the reservations.
3. C The lines that connected at Promontory Point in 1869 essentially connected the nation by rail.
4. A Federal land was offered to Homesteaders beginning in 1862.
5. B The Comanche Empire could be seen in eastern Texas and New Mexico.
6. C The comancheros often received stolen cattle from the Comanche.

7. B   The ritual to bring back the pre-white settlement past frightened the U.S. military.
8. A   Reformers believed that reservations deterred Indians from settling and farming.
9. B   Joseph McCoy established this cow town to as a means to load cattle on rail lines.
10. D   A good portion of the cowboys, especially African Americans, were minorities.
11. C   The school was one of several boarding schools that tried to change the Indian mindset of its students.
12. C   Reformers believed that if given the chance to be immersed into a dominant culture, Indian youths could be more successful in America.
13. C   Red Cloud concedes and accepts the required changes of his people.
14. A   Red Cloud complains that the agents the government sent are only out for themselves and not for the benefit of his people.
15. B   The lack of provisions resulted in starving children.
16. C   The dangerous and/or killer type were the rare exceptions to cowboy society.

17. C   After months of isolation, the cowboys celebrated when they got to the end of their trail.
18. C   The saloon stood as the social center of the cowboy world once the drive was completed.
19. B   The writer refers to cannons as wagon guns.
20. C   The attempt to arrest Sitting Bull led to his killing and the subsequent massacre at Wounded Knee.
21. D   The horrific slaughter of the Sioux at the hands of the US military marked the end of the Indian Wars.

Long Essay Question

What did the transformation of the West feature in the late 1800s?

(Key topics to focus and elaborate on)
- End to buffalo hunting for the Indians
- Cattle herding and driving
- Farming in the Great Plains

Chapter 17

THE GILDED AGE: BUILDING A TECHNOLOGICAL AND INDUSTRIAL GIANT AND A NEW SOCIAL ORDER, 1876-1910

- A new era emerged between 1876-1910, and the impact of business, manufacturing, and technology would be dramatic in America's economic, social, and political scene.

TECHNOLOGY CHANGES THE NATION

- Alexander Graham Bell revolutionized communication and quickly replaced the telegraph.with his development of the telephone.
- Thomas Edison became the most productive American inventor of all time by introducing the stock printer, the phonograph, and the electric light bulb.
- George Westinghouse and Nikola Tesla created alternating current to transmit electricity over great distances.
- The makings of the automobile also emerged in the late 1800s/early 1900s, and its production was revolutionized by Henry Ford's utilization of the assembly line. Ford made the automobile affordable to Americans and helped to change the landscape of America as it adapted to this new form of transportation.
- Orville and Wilbur Wright invented the airplane in 1903 to introduce a new form of travelling that would later become safer and more efficient.

CORPORATIONS AND MONOPOLIES

- The new industries that rose in the late 1800s required the oversight of large corporations and the financing of powerful banks.
- Mark Twain's "Gilded Age" referred to enormous discrepancy between the wealthy and the poor in the late 1800s.
- The bankruptcy of Jay Cooke launched the Panic of 1873 that saw the U.S. tailspin into an economic crisis. Essentially, the panic displayed the boom and bust cycle of the new era.
- Having amassed fortunes in the steamship industry, Cornelius Vanderbilt became even richer with railroads and began a managerial revolution that featured new bureaucracies of central business control.
- Taking advantage of the oil that drillers extracted, John D. Rockefeller built an oil refinery in Cleveland. In 1870, Rockefeller became a founder of Standard Oil, bought out his competition or drove them out of business, and used horizontal integration to create a powerful monopoly.

- Standard Oil used every tactic imaginable to drive out competition, from buying its own train cars to building its own refineries.
- After migrating from Scotland, Andrew Carnegie worked his way up from textiles to railroads, to eventually his own business in the steel industry. Using meticulous and obsessive methods to cuts costs, Carnegie Steel grew to dominate the steel industry.
- With the implementation of vertical integration, Carnegie created a steel monopoly in the U.S.
- Eventually the free market economy of the U.S. became dominated by a series of trusts in which single corporations reigned supreme over each industry.
- JP Morgan became a banking juggernaut who guided the U.S. through the Panic of 1893 by offering the federal government gold in return for 30-year bonds. He later went on to purchase Carnegie Steel and turned it into U.S. Steel.

LIVES OF THE MIDDLE CLASS IN THE GILDED AGE

- The rise of the middle class could be seen with the elaborate celebration of Christmas, the emergence of department stores, and the beautification of public places such as parks. In fact, the designers of these parks and buildings all aimed to illustrate the permanence and prosperity of this new era.
- Urban developers also improved the water systems of the cities to promote a healthier environment and to eliminate diseases such as cholera.
- With better forms of transportation and shorter railroad lines, suburbs began to form, and the concept of commuting to work every day became a reality for the middle class.
- As the industrial age developed, the Protestant faith became more prevalent in the United States. Dwight L. Moody reflected this prevalence with his tireless efforts to reach out to many groups and in his words to "save all you can."
- During the Gilded Age, the Republicans and Democrats reflected the interests of the American middle class.
- In 1881, just three months after his inauguration, President James A. Garfield was shot by an angry office-seeker and died a few months later. Subsequently, the Election of 1884 featured a mudslinging campaign between James G. Blaine and Grover Cleveland, in which Cleveland eventually won.
- Cleveland lost the next election, but won again in 1892 and became the first president in U.S. history to serve in non-consecutive terms.
- The late 1800s would see a number of American religious missions established in foreign countries such as China and India. Thereafter, business interests followed to establish foreign markets and to invest in Cuba and Mexico.

IMMIGRATION

- Push-pull factors brought in new immigrants after 1890 who did not fit in the typical northern European and Protestant mold.
- The push of these immigrants reflected either extreme poverty or persecution in their homeland.
- Pogroms and the Pale of Settlement in Russia resulted in a large number of Jews escaping this persecution by moving to the United States.

- Between 1880 and 1914, some four million Italian immigrants came to the U.S. to escape poverty and violence.
- Despite the passage of the Chinese Exclusion Act in 1882, some Chinese were still allowed to migrate to the United States. Meanwhile, Japanese immigration would make its way into the United States by the 1880s.
- In addition, French-Canadian and Mexican migrants also made their way to the United States in the late 1800s.
- The pull factor that drew immigrants into the Unites States was undoubtedly economic in nature.
- The processing of immigrants at Ellis Island proved to be both intrusive and in many cases Americanizing. To be sure, names of immigrants were often changed to sound more American.
- On the West Coast, Angel Island became the processing center for Asians arriving in San Francisco. For the Chinese, processing at Angel Island proved to be a difficult process given that they had to prove that they were returning immigrants or had relatives who were already in the United States.
- The notion that America became a "melting pot" during this period of intense immigration is somewhat of a misnomer in that the newcomers tended to reside in their own communities, continue to speak their native tongue, and practice their same cultural customs that they did in their homelands.
- The Lower East Side of Manhattan featured a very strong Jewish presence, and many from this community worked in the garment industry.
- Italians also created their own ethnic communities in cities such as New York, Chicago, Boston, and Milwaukee.
- French Canadians migrated largely from Quebec to New England to find a more prosperous life; Mexican migrants also arrived in the U.S. during the Industrial Revolution.
- Mexican communities in the United States came to be known as barrios where Mexican traditions, food, and the Catholic religion were prominent.
- The Catholic religion practically doubled in size from the time of the Civil War to 1900 as it served both native and foreign born Americans.
- The Chinese began a tradition in America that featured the establishment of laundries; the Japanese worked in the sugarcane plantations of Hawaii.

MULTIPLE CHOICE QUESTIONS

1. The inventions and innovations of Alexander Graham Bell, Thomas Edison, and George Westinghouse did all of the following EXCEPT
   A. contributed to the rise of the Industrial Revolution.
   B. made life easier for the masses.
   C. increased business activity.
   D. merely served as only gadgets/

2. Through his railroad empire, Cornelius Vanderbilt introduced
   A. vertical integration.

B. managerial bureaucracy.

C. intense competition.

D. small and local business entities.

3. To eliminate what Rockefeller believed to be wasteful competition in the oil industry, he engaged in the practice of
   A. vertical integration.
   B. horizontal integration.
   C. trust busting.
   D. price raising.

4. To cut costs in the manufacturing of steel, Carnegie utilized the practice of
   A. vertical integration.
   B. horizontal integration.
   C. labor arbitration.
   D. price gouging.

5. All of the following dominated an industry EXCEPT
   A. Gustavus Swift.
   B. Charles Pillbury.
   C. James G. Blaine.
   D. Frederick Weyerhauser.

6. J.P. Morgan saved Grover Cleveland's fiscal nightmare by
   A. selling the federal government his bonds and buying government gold.
   B. offering the government $65 million in gold in return for 30-year bonds.
   C. offering the government huge supplies of silver.
   D. buying government bonds.

7. As industrialism progressed in the United States, business leaders
   A. raised the wages of its workers so they could buy more.
   B. lowered the prices of goods.
   C. looked overseas to expand their markets.
   D. went on an full-on advertising assault.

8. Immigrants after the 1890s were predominantly
   A. Northern European.
   B. Protestant.
   C. Catholic and Jewish.
   D. highly skilled.

9. With the pressure of anti-immigrant sentiment, the Chinese became the only named group in U.S. history to
   A. be excluded from migrating into the U.S.
   B. join Russian Jews in being expulsed from the country.
   C. face migration quotas.
   D. be placed in permanent camps.

10. All of the following applied to immigration into the United States EXCEPT
    A. immigrants moved into their own ethnic neighborhoods.
    B. immigrants continued to speak their native language.
    C. immigrants continued to follow their cultural practices.
    D. native born Americans embraced their cultural and language differences.

Questions 11-12 refer to the following visual.

THE AMERICAN NATIONAL GAME OF BASE BALL.

11. The people watching the baseball game represent a new trend that developed during the Industrial Revolution and they came to be known as
    A. mugwamps.
    B. pogroms.
    C. spectators.
    D. vaudevilles.

12. Baseball became popular in cities such as New York, Boston, and Pittsburg because
    A. immigrants brought in this tradition from the Old World.
    B. Little League prospered in these cities.
    C. the game had existed in these cities since the colonial days.
    D. industrial workers could find leisure in attending baseball games.

Questions 13-15 refer to the following excerpt.

The problem of our age is the proper administration of wealth, so that the ties of brotherhood may still bind together the rich and poor in harmonious relationship. The conditions of human life have not only been changed, but revolutionized, within the past few hundred years. In former days there was little difference between the swelling, dress, food, and environment of the chief and those of his retainers. The Indians are today where civilized man then was. When visiting the Sioux, I was led to the wigwam of the chief. It was just like the others in external appearance, and even within the difference was trifling between it and those of the poorest of his braves. The contrast between the palace of the millionaire and the cottage of the laborer with us today measures the change which has come with civilization.

This change, however, is not to be deplored, but welcomed as highly beneficial. It is well, nay, essential for the progress of the race, that the houses of some should be homes for all that is highest and best in literature and the arts, and for all the refinements of civilization, rather than that none should be so. Much better this great irregularity than universal squalor. Without wealth there can be no Maecenas. The "good old times" were not good old times. Neither master nor servant was as well situated then as to-day. A relapse to old conditions would be disastrous to both -- not the least so to him who serves -- and would sweep away civilization with it. But whether the change be for good or ill, it is upon us, beyond our power to alter, and therefore to be accepted and made the best of. It is waste of time to criticize the inevitable...

The price which society pays for the law of competition, like the price it pays for cheap comforts and luxuries, is also great; but the advantages of this law are also greater still, for it is to this law that we owe our wonderful material development, which brings improved conditions in its train.

...This, then, is held to be the duty of the man of Wealth: First, to set an example of modest, unostentatious living, shunning display or extravagance; to provide moderately for the legitimate wants of those dependent upon him; and after doing so to consider all surplus revenues which come to him simply as trust funds, which he is called upon to administer, and strictly bound as a matter of duty to administer in the manner which, in his judgment, is best calculated to produce the most beneficial results for the community -- the man of wealth thus becoming the mere agent and trustee for his poorer brethren, bringing to their service his superior wisdom, experience, and ability to administer, doing for them better than they would or could do for themselves.

--Andrew Carnegie, "Wealth," 1889

12. Andrew Carnegie viewed the gap between the rich and poor as all of the following EXCEPT
   A. deplorable and unjust.
   B. inevitable and not worth criticizing.
   C. a sign of progress.
   D. more civilized than the Sioux.

14. "Without wealth, there can be no Maecenas" refers to
    A. Carnegie's control over his workers.
    B. Carnegie's use of vertical integration.
    C. Carnegie's patronage of literature and the arts.
    D. Carnegie's rags to riches story.

15. According to Carnegie, surplus revenues are
    A. to be amassed into endless fortune.
    B. to be redistributed to his workers.
    C. to be reinvested back into business.
    D. to be used to benefit the community.

Questions 16-18 refer to the following excerpt.

The light is designed to serve precisely the same purposes in domestic use as gaslights. It requires no shade, no screen of ground glass, to modify its intensity, but can be gazed at without dazzling the eyes. The amount of light is equal to that given by the gas-jets in common use; but the light is steadier, and consequently less trying to the eyes. It is also a purer light than gas, being white, while gaslight is yellow. Further, the electric lamp does not vitiate the surrounding atmosphere by consuming its oxygen, as gaslights do, and discharging into it the products of combustion. The heat emitted by the lamp is found to be only one fifteenth of that emitted by a gaslight of equal illuminating power: the glass bulb remains cool enough to be handled. Of course, there are here no poisonous or inflammable gases to escape, and the danger of fire is reduced to nil with a consequent reduction of the rate of insurance. Again, this light, unlike gas, is always of uniform quality. A sort of meter registers exactly the amount of electricity consumed in each house. Finally, not to enumerate all the advantages which this system possesses over gas-lighting, the lamp -can be manipulated even by the most inexperienced domestic servant; nor can the most careless person do injury to himself, to others, or to property, through not understanding its mechanism.

16. Before the use of Edison's incandescent light bulb all of the following applied EXCEPT
    A. the common household used kerosene lamps.
    B. candles were used.
    C. gas lamps were seen in city streets.
    D. fluorescent lights were used.

17. To operate his light bulb, Edison would rely on
    A. gas.
    B. kerosene.
    C. electricity.
    D. Coal.

18. The invention of the light bulb by Edison reduced the risk of
    A. being electrocuted.
    B. being shocked.
    C. being injured through overtime exhaustion.
    D. fire breaking out.

Questions 19-21 refer to the following excerpt.

The Chinese laundryman does not learn his trade in China; there are no laundries in China....

All the Chinese laundrymen here were taught in the first place by American women just as I was taught. When I went to work for that American family I could not speak a word of English, and I did not know anything about housework. The family consisted of husband, wife and two children. They were very good to me and paid me $3.50 a week, of which I could save $3....

When I first opened a laundry it was in company with a partner, who had been in the business for some years. We went to a town about 500 miles inland, where a railroad was building. We got a board shanty and worked for the men employed by the railroads....

We were three years with the railroad, and then went to the mines, where we made plenty of money in gold dust, but had a hard time, for many of the miners were wild men who carried revolvers and after drinking would come into our place to shoot and steal shirts, for which we had to pay. One of these men hit his head hard against a flat iron and all the miners came and broke our laundry, chasing us out of town. They were going to hang us. We lost all our property and $365 in money, which a member of the mob must have found. Luckily most of our money was in the hands of the Chinese bankers in San Francisco. I drew $500 and went east to Chicago, where I had a laundry for three years, during which I increased my capital to $2500. After that I was four years in Detroit. I went home to China in 1897, but returned in 1898, and began a laundry business in Buffalo. The ordinary laundry shop is generally divided into three rooms. In front is the room where the customers are received, behind that a bedroom and in the back the work shop, which is also the dining room and kitchen. The stove and cooking utensils are the same as those of the Americans....

I have found out, during my residence in this country, that much of the Chinese prejudice against Americans is unfounded, and I no longer put faith in the wild tales that were told about them in our village, tho some of the Chinese, who have been there twenty tears and who are learned men, still believe that there is no marriage in this country, that the land is infested with demons and that all the people are given over to general wickedness. I know better. Americans are not all bad, nor are they wicked wizards. Still, they have their faults, and their treatment of us is outrageous....

The reason why so many Chinese go into the laundry business in this country is because it requires little capital and is one of the few opportunities that are open....

There is no reason for the prejudice against the Chinese. The cheap labor cry was always a falsehood. Their labor was never cheap, and is not cheap now. It has always commanded and highest market price. But the trouble is that the Chinese are such excellent and faithful workers that bosses will have no others when they can get them. If you look at men working on the street you will find an overseer for every four or five of them. That watching is not necessary for Chinese. They work as well when left to themselves as they do when some one is looking at them....

--Lee Chew, "Life of a Chinese Immigrant," 1903

19. According to Chew, the Chinese laundrymen founded their craft
    A. in small Chinese villages.
    B. in Hong Kong.
    C. in America.
    D. on the steerage passage.

20. From Chew's story about the gold rush, one could infer that
    A. the Chinese made fortunes in gold.
    B. the Chinese made more money servicing gold miners.
    C. gold miners treated the Chinese with kindness.
    D. the Chinese made no money during this period.

21. Lee's statement,"Their labor was never cheap…" was in reference to
    A. Chinese workers.
    B. Japanese workers.
    C. Irish workers.
    D. Mexican workers.

SHORT ANSWER QUESTIONS

Andrew Carnegie becomes one of the nation's first billionaires.

a. Choose ONE of the following and explain why your choice represents the event that led to Carnegie's wealth.

- The connection of the transcontinental railroad begins a flurry of railroad construction
- Carnegie utilizes a system of vertical integration
- The Great Railroad Strike gives unions a negative image

b. Contrast your choice against ONE of the other options, demonstrating why that option in not as significant as your choice.

LONG ESSAY QUESTION

Can industrial giants such as Rockefeller and Carnegie be considered captains of industry or robber barons?

ANSWERS AND EXPLANATIONS

Multiple Choice Questions

1. D The inventions and innovations of Bell, Edison, and Westinghouse revolutionized society in more ways than gadgets ever could.
2. B Vanderbilt's management style served as a model for future corporations.
3. B Through horizontal integration, Rockefeller bought out his competition.
4. A Through vertical integration, Carnegie owned all phases in the production of steel.
5. B Blaine was more of a politician than a captain of industry.
6. B Morgan replenished the gold reserve during Cleveland's presidency.
7. C Industrialists looked to gain new markets during the Age of Imperialism.
8. C The new immigrants of this age were not of the old traditional Protestant stock.
9. A The Chinese Exclusion Act of 1882 effectively barred the immigration of the U.S. until after World War II.
10. D Native-born Americans tried to assimilate immigrants rather than embrace their diversities.
11. C Baseball would be one of the nation's first spectator sports.
12. D Baseball became a popular sport amongst both the wealthy and industrial workers.
13. C Carnegie argued that uncivilized societies contained no wealthy individuals.
14. C Maecenas was a patron of art and literature.
15. D Carnegie donated to various causes including the establishment of libraries.
16. D Fluorescent lights had not been invented yet.
17. C Edison built an electricity power plant in New York to operate his light bulbs.
18. D Fires would frequently break out as a result of tipped-over kerosene lamps.
19. C Chinese laundrymen learned their craft not in China but in the United States.
20. B Having been discriminated in the gold fields, many Chinese men provided laundry services to the miners.
21. C Irish workers and unions argued that Chinese laborers undermined wages and were key figures in having the Chinese excluded from immigrating into the U.S.

Long Essay Question

Can industrial giants such as Rockefeller and Carnegie be considered captains of industry or robber barons?

(Key topics to focus and elaborate on)
- Industrial giants paid their workers extremely low wages
- Industrial giants used ruthless tactics to eliminate competition
- Industrial giants provided jobs and products to America
- Industrial giants often became million dollar philanthropists

Chapter 18
RESPONSES TO INDUSTRIALISM, RESPONSES TO CHANGE, 1877-1914

- As massive changes occurred with industrialism and technological advancements, the working class struggled for a better life within this modern economic system.

CONFLICT IN THE NEW SOUTH

- Leaders of the New South did not apologize for the Civil War but instead boasted of the region's railroads and industrialization. As the South began to rebuild, both optimism and misery would prevail.
- The new railroads brought a host of new jobs to the South and established a network of connections to the North and isolated regions.
- New industries such as those seen in lumber, turpentine, tobacco cigarettes, and soda emerged in the South to diversify its economy.
- "The Lost Cause" became nostalgic homage for the Confederate struggle to win the Civil War and the days of slavery. Authors glorified the Old South as orderly and romantic.
- Religion thrived in the post-Reconstruction South, and black and white churches sprung up with millions of members. Sam Jones became one of the most prominent preachers of the South and had audiences of both black and white listeners.
- The railroads became a symbol of segregation with first angry mobs attacking blacks who rode first class, to the law stepping in and enforcing separation of the races. In the case of *Plessy v. Ferguson,* the Supreme Court ruled that "separate but equal" facilities were constitutional and did not violate the 14th Amendment.
- Exclusion of African Americans in politics occurred over a course of two stages between the 1870s and 1900. To end the violence of the Klan that had emerged to keep blacks from voting, white legislators created literacy tests and poll taxes as a means to keep blacks from going to the polls. Grandfather clauses were passed to include poor whites in the voting process.
- By 1900, the South became the "solid South" in which white voters and white elected officials dominated the political landscape. Any challenge to this system could be met by a lynching which became prevalent throughout the South to maintain segregation.
- Whereas Booker T. Washington advocated African Americans to accept the system of segregation in the South and instead build themselves up economically, W.E.B. Dubois urged for an end to segregation and discrimination throughout the South and became active in the Niagara Movement and the NAACP to combat these injustices.

THE POLITICS OF CONFLICT-FROM POPULIST MOVEMENT TO POPULIST PARTY

- Having struggled with the rates of the railroads, farmers began to unite into certain groups such as the Grange and the Farmer's Alliance.

- The Farmer's Alliance began in Texas and quickly spread to other agricultural states. The goal of the alliance was to negotiate with the businesses that farmers had to deal with to improve their economic conditions.
- Although the Colored Farmers' National Alliance and Cooperative Union also formed to improve their conditions, they never had the same clout as the white alliance.
- Both alliances welcomed women, and Mary Lease became one of the Farmers Alliance's most famous speakers.
- To ease the burden of the farming, the Alliance advocated for lower interest rates on loans and for government ownership of the railroads.
- Farmers also wanted access to more currency and thus pushed for silver to be added along with the existing gold standard. Essentially this would cause inflation thereby making it easier to pay back loans.
- In the 1890s, the Populist Party was formed in an attempt to give farmers a voice through government participation. The platform of Populists included the expansion of currency.
- The Election of 1896 featured Democratic candidate William Jennings Bryan adopting the Populist demand for the unlimited coinage of silver. Consequently, the Populists joined forces with the Democrats but lost to the Gold Bug, William McKinley. The loss of this election effectively ended any political power the Populists had.

WORKERS PROTEST AND THE RISE OF ORGANIZED LABOR

- The Great Railroad Strike of 1877 began in Maryland and West Virginia simultaneously and quickly spread through many parts of the nation. The strike was marred with violence that featured rioting and death.
- President Rutherford B. Hayes sent federal troops to end the strike, and the event led to the formation of the National Guard and the rise of labor unions.
- The Knights of Labor formed in 1869 and accepted virtually any kind of member. Under Terrence Powderly, the Knights led a number of strikes, most of which resulted in peaceful negotiations.
- The American Federation of Labor became a more elite union that only accepted skilled laborers. The goals of this union focused on more immediate aims such as wage increases and eight-hour workdays.
- The Haymarket Riot in Chicago began as a protest for an eight-hour workday and involved many groups including socialists and anarchists. At a rally in Haymarket Square, an unidentified suspect threw a bomb into the ranks of a police force killing several. The strike displayed to many that unions would not be looked upon very favorably during the Gilded Age.
- The Homestead Strike featured a strike against Carnegie Steel in Pennsylvania, through the shrewd leadership of Henry Fricke, the strikers were replaced and the Pinkerton Agency was hire to protect the replacement workers. An ensuing gun battle erupted killing several, yet no one was ever convicted. The strike ended in failure as Carnegie never reinstated the striking union.
- In an attempt to get the unemployed back to work by building roads, Jacob Coxey led a march to Washington D.C. Though the plan failed, it did serve as a model for the New Deal of the 1930s.

- In 1894, the American Railway Union went on strike against the Pullman Palace Car Company. Layoffs, wage cuts, and high rents sparked the strike which erupted into violence when federal troops arrived to end the strike. The strike led union leader, Eugene Debs, to establish the Socialist Party.
- The dangers of working in a coal mine were not rewarded with wage increases. Since a strike in 1875 proved to be unsuccessful, a group known as the Molly Maguires lashed out at the leadership of the coal mines. Subsequently, a new union known as the United Mine Workers had greater success in getting better pay and better working conditions in the 1890s.
- In 1905, the Industrial Workers of the World formed to create one unified union of all types of workers and for fifteen years served as solid force for labor organization.
- Women in the garment industry faced long hours of hard work with low wages and struck a number of times in the early 1900s. In 1911, a fire at the Triangle Shirtwaist Factory killed 146 workers, most of which were women.
- In 1912, workers in Lawrence, Massachusetts an estimated 14,000 workers went on strike against mill companies. With the slogan, "We Want Bread and Roses, Too," the strike ended successfully with higher wages.
- Rockefeller's coal mines in southern Colorado saw strikes in which workers pushed for higher wages and fewer hours among other things. The strike was long and bloody as violence culminated in the Ludlow Massacre.

MULTIPLE CHOICE QUESTIONS

1. The New South featured all of the following EXCEPT
   A. pride in Confederacy.
   B. support for blacks.
   C. forms of industrialization.
   D. emergence of the railroads.

2. As religion grew in the South, blacks tended to become
   A. Baptists.
   B. Catholics.
   C. Episcopalians.
   D. Presbyterians.

3. In the case of *Plessy v. Ferguson,* the Supreme Court
   A. struck down segregation on trains.
   B. introduced the "separate but equal" doctrine.
   C. ruled segregation in urban transit to be unconstitutional.
   D. struck down segregation in public schools.

4. Booker T. Washington's view on segregation was that
   A. African Americans had to adjust to the reality of segregation.
   B. African Americans had to immediately stand up to segregation.
   C. African Americans had to use the courts to fight segregation.
   D. African Americans had to form groups like the NAACP.

5. The nation's earliest nationwide farmer organization was
   A. the Populist Party.
   B. the Grange.
   C. the Alliance.
   D. the Agricultural Wheel.

6. The Populists promoted all of the following EXCEPT
   A. government ownership of the railroads.
   B. lower interest rates loans for bankers.
   C. continuing the gold standard.
   D. a bimetallic standard of gold and silver.

7. The Haymarket Square riot featured
   A. clashing between the Pinkerton Agency and workers.
   B. a strike against the Pullman Palace Car Company.
   C. Rutherford B. Hayes sending federal troops.
   D. a bomb that killed several policemen.

8. Irish immigrant coal miners who attacked the administrators of the coal mines in Pennsylvania came to be known as
   A. Wobblies.
   B. Populists.
   C. Scabs.
   D. Molly Maguires.

9. Most of the victims of the Triangle Shirtwaist Company fire were
   A. German immigrants.
   B. Jewish and Italian women.
   C. Irish children.
   D. Russian men.

10. The Ludlow Massacre in 1914 featured
    A. the killing of policemen in Colorado.
    B. over thirty killed during a coal mine strike.
    C. miners killed at the Homestead plant.
    D. strikers killed during the Great Railroad Strike of 1877.

Questions 11-12 refer to the following visual.

11. The Molly Maguires as seen in the photo were of
    A. Irish descent.
    B. German descent.
    C. Italian descent.
    D. Russian descent.

12. The main purpose of the Molly Maguires was to
    A. improve conditions for miners in Pennsylvania through terror.
    B. serve as spies for the Pinkerton Private Detective Agency.
    C. organize skilled and unskilled workers for the IWW.
    D. promote the ideals of socialism and anarchy.

Questions 13-16 refer to the following excerpt.

My friends, we declare that this nation is able to legislate for its own people on every question, without waiting for the aid or consent of any other nation on earth; and upon that issue we expect to carry every State in the Union. I shall not slander the inhabitants of the fair State of Massachusetts nor the inhabitants of the State of New York by saying that, when they are confronted with the proposition, they will declare that this nation is not able to attend to its own business. It is the issue of 1776 over again. Our ancestors, when but three millions in number, had the courage to declare their political independence of every other nation; shall we, their descendants, when we have grown to seventy millions, declare that we are less independent than our forefathers? No, my friends, that will never be the verdict of our people. Therefore, we care not upon what lines the battle is fought. If they say bimetallism is good, but that we cannot have it until other nations help us, we reply that, instead of having a gold standard because England has, we will restore bimetallism, and then let England have bimetallism because the United States has it. If they dare to come out in the open field and defend the gold standard as a good thing, we will fight them to the uttermost. Having behind us the producing masses of this nation and the world, supported by the commercial interests, the laboring interests, and the toilers everywhere, we will answer their demand for a gold standard by saying to them: You shall not press down upon the brow of labor this crown of thorns, you shall not crucify mankind upon a cross of gold.

--William Jennings Bryan, *Cross of Gold Speech*, 1896

13. Bryan's speech pits the following regions against each other
    A. North versus South.
    B. East versus West.
    C. South and West versus Northeast.
    D. Northwest vs. Southeast.

14. By promoting bimetallism, Bryan and the Democrats adopted the ideals of
    A. the Gold Bugs.
    B. the Populists.
    C. the Republicans.
    D. the Greenbacks.

15. Bryan's phrase, "…you shall not crucify mankind upon a cross of gold" refers to
    A. the damage the gold standard would do to the farmer.
    B. the struggles of northeast bankers.
    C. J.P. Morgan's supply of gold to the federal government.
    D. the need for England to get off the gold standard.

Questions 16-18 refer to the following except.

This case turns upon the constitutionality of an act of the general assembly of the state of Louisiana, passed in 1890, providing for separate railway carriages for the white and colored races. . . .

The constitutionality of this act is attacked upon the ground that it conflicts both with the 13th Amendment of the Constitution, abolishing slavery, and the 14th Amendment, which prohibits certain restrictive legislation on the part of the states.

1. That it does not conflict with the 13th Amendment, which abolished slavery and involuntary servitude, except as a punishment for crime, is too clear for argument. . . . Indeed, we do not understand that the 13th Amendment is strenuously relied upon by the plaintiff. . . .

The object of the [14th] amendment was undoubtedly to enforce the absolute equality of the two races before the law, but in the nature of things it could not have been intended to abolish distinctions based upon color, or to enforce social, as distinguished from political, equality, or a commingling of the two races upon terms unsatisfactory to either. Laws permitting, and even requiring their separation in places where they are liable to be brought into contact do not necessarily imply the inferiority of either race to the other, and have been generally, if not universally, recognized as within the competency of the state legislatures in the exercise of their police power. . . .

We consider the underlying fallacy of the plaintiff's argument to consist in the assumption that the enforced separation of the two races stamps the colored race with a badge of inferiority. If this be so, it is not by reason of anything found in the act, but solely because the colored race chooses to put that construction upon it. . . .

The argument also assumes that social prejudice may be overcome by legislation, and that equal rights cannot be secured to the Negro except by an enforced commingling of the two races. We cannot accept this proposition. If the two races are to meet on terms of social equality, it must be the result of natural affinities, a mutual appreciation of each other's merits and a voluntary consent of individuals. . . . Legislation is powerless to eradicate racial instincts or abolish distinctions based upon physical differences and the attempt to do so can only result in accentuating the difficulties of the present situation. If the civil and political right of both races be equal, one cannot be inferior to the other civilly or politically. If one race be inferior to the other socially, the Constitution of the United States cannot put them upon the same plane.

--Opinion of the Supreme Court for *Plessy v. Ferguson*, 1896

16. In the case of *Plessy v. Ferguson*, the U.S. Supreme Court found no relevance whatsoever in the plaintiff's interpretation of
    A. the 13th Amendment.
    B. the 14th Amendment.
    C. the 15th Amendment.
    D. the Civil Rights Act of 1866.

17. In terms of society, the Supreme Court ruled
    A. legal means were required to ensure social equality.
    B. the U.S. Constitution had no place to ensure social equality.
    C. blacks and whites would never be equal.
    D. social equality had to be enforced by the federal government.

18. According to the Court, separation of the races
    A. inherently promoted inferiority.
    B. was unconstitutional.
    C. did not promote inferiority.
    D. had to be abolished.

Questions 19-21 refer to the following excerpt.

. . . These ideas have gained such a hold upon public opinion, that they bid fair to cause a complete change in our form of government, as far as its industrial conditions are concerned, during the next quarter of a century. It looks as though, before that period was passed, the government would assume control and ownership of all means of transportation in the form of railroads; that the government would adopt a system of issuing money to the people without the aid of banking institutions, and that a larger volume per capita would be in circulation than ever before in the history of any government in the world; that the local governments of cities and towns would assume control and complete ownership of all street railroads, gas and water works. In fact, it bids fair to be a radical revolution in the industrial affairs of government. It looks as though the days of individualism and corporations were doomed, and that the next step in the line of human advancement would be the adoption of the socialistic state of society.

--N.A. Dunning, Ed., *Alliance's Vision of Community*, 1891

19. Why would Dunning want the government to take ownership of the railroads?
    A. to provide better service
    B. to make the lines safer
    C. to outlaw rebates
    D. to lower rates

20. Why would Dunning want the government to own the banks?
    A. to improve better customer service
    B. to provide low interest loans
    C. to print paper money
    D. to raise interest rates on savings

21. Why did Dunning favor a socialistic state?
    A. so workers would have control of their production
    B. to increase the power of factory workers
    C. capitalist elements exploited farmers
    D. the influence of Eugene Debs was on the rise

SHORT ANSWER QUESTIONS

The Democrats adopt the Populist platform in the Election of 1896.

a. Choose ONE of the following and explain why your choice represents the event that led to these decades of hardships.

   - the Alliance is formed
   - the Ocala Demands are made
   - Populist, James Weaver, earns 10% of vote in the

presediential election of 1892

b. Contrast your choice against ONE of the other options, demonstrating why that option in not as significant as your choice.

LONG ESSAY QUESTION

What were the struggles of the farmers in the late 1800s and what did they propose to solve them?

ANSWERS AND EXPLANATIONS

Multiple Choice Questions

1. B The New South advocated the days of the Old South in which whites had complete control over blacks.
2. A After the Civil War, blacks joined the Baptist Church in significant numbers.
3. B The Court ruled that segregation between blacks and whites was not unconstitutional so long as there were "separate but equal" facilities for both races.
4. A Washington believed that blacks had to accept the reality of segregation and focus on attaining vocational skills to establish themselves economically.
5. B The Grange formed to deal with farmer debt especially in the South.
6. C The Populists advocated for a bimetallic monetary system that would include both gold and silver.
7. D The explosion of a bomb at Haymarket Square brought an aura of suspicion and negativity to the nation's unions
8. D The Molly Maguires wreaked havoc amongst coal mine managers and even on owners.
9. B Women dominated the piecing of cloth at the Triangle Shirtwaist Company.
10. B Over 30 were killed at this coal mine strike including eleven children.
11. A Molly Maguire stems from Irish roots.
12. A The Molly Maguires killed several managers and even murdered a coal mine owner.
13. C Farmers of the South and West clashed with bankers of the Northeast.
14. B The Populists became the first political party to advocate bimetallism.
15. A The gold standard induced deflation which hindered the farmers' ability to pay off their debts.
16. A According to the Court, the abolition of slavery had no relation to segregation and the case of *Plessy v. Ferguson*.
17. B The Court believed that inequality was a natural occurrence.
18. C The Court ruled that blacks chose to construct a sense of inferiority by being segregated.
19. D Because it was the only form of transportation to bring crops to eastern markets, the railroads exploited farmers with high rates.
20. B Lower interest rates would've eased the debt of the farmers.
21. C The system of capitalism, in Dunning's opinion, hurt the farmers in many ways.

Long Essay Question

What were the struggles of the farmers in the late 1800s and what did they propose to solve them?

(Key topics to focus and elaborate on)
- high railroad rates and high interest rates
- lack of inflation
- government ownership of railroads and banks
- bimetallic monetary system

Chapter 19
PROGRESSIVE MOVEMENTS, PROGRESSIVE POLITICS, 1879-1917

- Theodore Roosevelt introduced a new system of politics that utilized the power of the presidency. Although Roosevelt did not harbor radical views, he did not follow the traditions of past presidents in being passive either.
- Together with Roosevelt, William Howard Taft and Woodrow Wilson became presidents during a period that came to be known as the Progressive Era.

The Revolt of the Intellectuals
- The rise of industrialization brought about tremendous changes in American society, and intellectuals devised new ways to deal with these changes.
- Whereas Henry George advocated a single tax movement in his book *Progress and Poverty*, Edward Bellamy described a new perfect society, and Ignatius Donnelly described a country rigidly divided between rich and poor.
- John Dewey and Richard Ely believed that intervention in the economy could take place and that the philosophies of Social Darwinists, William Graham Sumner and Herbert Spencer merely served as justifications for social inequality.
- In magazines such as *McClure's Magazine* and *Cosmopolitan* competing New York journalists featured investigative reporting that gained the term muckraking journalists. Essentially, this journalism exposed the ills of industrial society.
- Ida Tarbell, Lincoln Steffens, and Upton Sinclair all became notable muckraking journalists. In fact, Sinclair's *The Jungle* played a significant influence in the passage of the Meat Inspection Act and the Pure Food and Drug Act.

THE TRANSFORMATION OF THE CITIES

- The population growth of the cities featured a shift from the majority of Americans living in the rural farms of America to the cities.
- Political machines rose as the cities grew, with Tammany Hall being the most famous machine, and William Tweed being the most famous boss of his day. The machines featured corruption at many levels, but maintained their power through the voting base of the poor.
- Boston also featured political machines and set the conditions for the first Catholic to be elected mayor.
- The rise of the political machines eventually led to the rise of the urban reformer, and oftentimes this reformer was an older Protestant and native-born elite trying to reclaim political power.
- Grover Cleveland, Hazen Pingree, and Samuel Jones all became Progressive leaders. Cleveland eventually went on to become the president.
- Progressives also introduced the initiative, referendum, and recall to empower voters by integrating them into government policy.

- Having felt the pressure to act after the Triangle Shirtwaist fire, Tammany Hall actually led an investigation into this incident that led to safety measures in New York City. The members of this investigative commission all went on to have notable political careers.
- Progressive education had many different elements of which some were diabolically opposed to each other, such as the concepts of John Dewey and his critics.
- Jane Addam's Hull House became a model for settlement houses in that it provided services to the poor in Chicago.

RELIGIOUS RESPONSES TO THE GILDED AGE

- Reform during Gilded Age often took an evangelical-like approach, and this could especially be seen with the temperance movement led largely by women. The Women's Christian Temperance Union formed to prevent the abuses of alcohol, and to give women the right to vote so they could eradicate alcohol through the power of suffrage. Carrie Nation simply chose to engage in "hatchetations" to deal with the drinking problem.
- These efforts eventually led to the passage of the Eighteenth and Nineteenth Amendments.
- Advocates of the Social Gospel adhered to the notion that religion could be used to deal with many of the social problems of the day. Others saw religion as a refuge from society.

PROGRESSIVE POLITICS ON THE NATIONAL STAGE

- The assassination of William McKinley launched Theodore Roosevelt into the presidency in 1906. Roosevelt's rise the presidency is a colorful story filled with both triumph and tragedy, and even before he entered the presidency, he already was known a reformer.
- In holding true to Progressivism, Roosevelt filed a lawsuit under the Sherman Antitrust Act to break up the Northern Securities Company, a trust backed by the powerful J.P. Morgan.
- Consequently, Roosevelt became known as a trustbuster. Thereafter, Roosevelt moved to expand the powers of the executive branch to guard against the abuses of trusts, but never filed many cases after the dissolution of Northern Securities.
- Roosevelt's love of nature and the great outdoors guided his efforts in becoming arguably the most conservation-minded president in U.S. history, and as president, Roosevelt preserved well over 100 million acres of land.
- Through the Antiquities Act of 1906, hundreds of thousands of acres of forest trees and monuments would be preserved from the exploitation of private developers.
- Whereas Roosevelt's passion for conservation and preservation was notably evident, his concerns for the plight of African Americans were not, despite his dinner with Booker T. Washington.
- Having become an enormously popular president, Roosevelt hand-picked William Howard Taft to succeed him as president.
- Taft faced controversy among Progressives when he signed the Payne-Aldrich Tariff which kept import duties high on most products. The subsequent firing of Gifford Pinchot led Roosevelt to reenter the realm of presidential politics.

- After Taft wrestled the Republican nomination for the Election of 1912, Roosevelt joined the Progressive Party. The Democrats nominated dark horse, Woodrow Wilson. The split between Roosevelt and Taft allowed Wilson to win the presidency.
- Unlike the Payne-Aldrich Tariff, Wilson pushed through Congress the Underwood-Simmons Tariff which reduced taxes on imports. Wilson and Congress also created the Federal Reserve to serve as the core of the nation's banking system.
- Wilson also became more aggressive in attacking trusts, but exempted labor unions from anti-trust lawsuits. Wilson's reputation with the African American community proved to be dismal in a number of ways, including a poor record with the issue of segregation and the filming of *Birth of a Nation* at the White House.

MULTIPLE CHOICE QUESTIONS

1. In order to rid the progressive Theodore Roosevelt from the New York governorship, Republican party leaders
   A. campaigned against him in 1900.
   B. moved for a recall in New York.
   C. nominated him as the vice-presidential candidate for William McKinley.
   D. looked to replace him with William Howard Taft.

2. Advocates of Social Darwinism claimed that society's unfit
   A. could rise to the top through education.
   B. were destined to be laborers and employees.
   C. deserved financial support from the nation's elite.
   D. could be aided through religious institutions.

3. Tammany Hall became notorious in New York City for
   A. preaching the ideals of Social Darwinism.
   B. controlling the city's government through corruption and graft.
   C. leading a strike against the city's transit lines.
   D. inciting a racial riot during World War One.

4. Ida Tarbell's contribution to muckraking journalism included
   A. a scathing attack on the nation's political machines.
   B. a description of urban poverty and living conditions of the poor.
   C. a grotesque illustration of the nation's meat-packing industry.
   D. a damaging history of Standard Oil.

5. The initiative, referendum, and recall all became progressive devices that aimed to
   A. limit the voice of America's voters.
   B. empower the influence of the state legislators.
   C. empower the influence of the nation's voters.
   D. empower the influence of the railroads and big business.

6. Theodore Roosevelt sought to dissolve the Northern Securities Company on the grounds that
   A. it promoted cutthroat competition among railroad lines.
   B. it monopolized the railroad lines across the northern plains.
   C. it refused to accept his arbitration during a railroad strike.
   D. it secretly secured rebates with Andrew Carnegie.

7. Under his conservation and preservation policies, Theodore Roosevelt did all of the following EXCEPT
   A. preserved thousands of acres of land from private developers.
   B. opened up Yellowstone National Park.
   C. established the Muir Woods National Monument.
   D. nominated conservationist, Gifford Pinchot, as head of the Division of Forestry.

8. Despite less than favorable reviews from supporters of Roosevelt, Taft did manage to
   A. establish the Federal Reserve Board.
   B. push through Congress the Meat Inspection Act.
   C. break up John D. Rockefeller's Standard Oil.
   D. sign the Underwood-Simmons Tariff.

9. The Election of 1912 featured all of the following presidential candidates EXCEPT
   A. William Howard Taft.
   B. Woodrow Wilson.
   C. Robert LaFollette.
   D. Theodore Roosevelt

10. Progressivism would come to an end due to
    A. lack of interest in reform.
    B. lack of charismatic progressive leaders.
    C. lack of a coherent agenda.
    D. World War I.

Questions 11-12 refer to the following visual.

11. For the strength of his political machine, Boss Tweed relied on
    A. Blacks who had migrated to the North.
    B. the votes of the middle class.
    C. newly arrived immigrants.
    D. old guard Protestant voters.

12. To entice urban residents to support Tammany Hall, the machine
    A. provided services to potential voters.
    B. campaigned tirelessly for its candidates.
    C. nominated elite Protestants of New York City.
    D. utilized the Pendleton Civil Service Act.

Questions 13-15 refer to the following excerpt.

Mr. Roosevelt attached to his platform some very splendid suggestions as to noble enterprises which we ought to undertake for the uplift of the human race; ...If you have read the trust plank in that platform as often as I have read it, you have found it very long, but very tolerant. It did not anywhere condemn monopoly, except in words; its essential meaning was that the trusts have been bad and must be made to be good. You know that Mr. Roosevelt long ago classified trusts for us as good and bad, and he said that he was afraid only of the bad ones. Now he does not desire that there should be any more of the bad ones, but proposes that they should all be made good by discipline, directly applied by a commission of executive appointment. All he explicitly complains of is lack of publicity and lack of fairness; not the exercise of power, for throughout that plank the power of the great corporations is accepted as the inevitable consequence of the modern organization of industry. All that it is proposed to do is to take them under control and deregulation.

The fundamental part of such a program is that the trusts shall be recognized as a permanent part of our economic order, and that the government shall try to make trusts the ministers, the instruments, through which the life of this country shall be justly and happily developed on its industrial side…

Shall we try to get the grip of monopoly away from our lives, or shall we not? Shall we withhold our hand and say monopoly is inevitable, that all we can do is to regulate it? Shall we say that all we can do is to put government in competition with monopoly and try its strength against it? Shall we admit that the creature of our own hands is stronger that we are? We have been dreading all along the time when the combined power of high finance would be greater that the power of government.

13. Woodrow Wilson essentially criticizes Theodore Roosevelt for
    A. living up to his name as a trustbuster.
    B. classifying trusts as either good or bad.
    C. dissolving trusts such as Northern Securities.
    D. accepting trusts as inevitable.

14. According to Wilson, Roosevelt believed
    A. that trusts were inherently evil.
    B. that trusts had to be destroyed.
    C. that trusts could be regulated and disciplined.
    D. that monopoly only served to harm society.

15. Wilson ultimately suggests that as president he would
    A. accept trusts as inevitable.
    B. try to manage trusts as Roosevelt suggested.
    C. be more aggressive in attacking trusts.
    D. work closely with the boards of the trusts to regulate them.

Questions 16-18 refer to the following excerpt.

Work in the coal breakers is exceedingly hard and dangerous. Crouched over the chutes, the boys sit hour after hour, picking out the pieces of slate and other refuse from the coal as it rushes past to the washers. From the cramped position they have to assume, most of them become more or less deformed and bent-backed like old men. When a boy has been working for some time and begins to get round-shouldered, his fellows say that "He's got his boy to carry around whenever he goes."

The coal is hard, and accidents to the hands, such as cut, broken, or crushed fingers, are common among the boys. Sometimes there is a worse accident: a terrified shriek is heard, and a boy is mangled and torn in the machinery, or disappears in the chute to be picked out later smothered and dead. Clouds of dust fill the breakers and are inhaled by the boys, laying the foundations for asthma and miners' consumption.

I once stood in a breaker for half an hour and tried to do the work a twelve-year-old boy was doing day after day, for ten hours at a stretch, for sixty cents a day. The gloom of the breaker appalled me. Outside the sun shone brightly, the air was pellucid, and the birds sang in chorus with the trees and the rivers. Within the breaker there was blackness, clouds of deadly dust enfolded everything, the harsh, grinding roar of the machinery and the ceaseless rushing of coal through the chutes filled the ears. I tried to pick out the pieces of slate from the hurrying stream of coal, often missing them; my hands were bruised and cut in a few minutes; I was covered from head to foot with coal dust, and for many hours afterwards I was expectorating some of the small particles of anthracite I had swallowed.

As I stood in that breaker I thought of the reply of the small boy to Robert Owen [British social reformer]. Visiting an English coal mine one day, Owen asked a twelve-year-old if he knew God. The boy stared vacantly at his questioner: "God?" he said, "God? No, I don't. He must work in some other mine." It was hard to realize amid the danger and din and blackness of that Pennsylvania breaker that such a thing as belief in a great All-good God existed.

From the breakers the boys graduate to the mine depths, where they become door tenders, switch boys, or mule drivers. Here, far below the surface, work is still more dangerous. At fourteen and fifteen the boys assume the same risks as the men, and are surrounded by the same perils. Nor is it in Pennsylvania only that these conditions exist. In the bituminous mines of West Virginia, boys of nine or ten are frequently employed. I met one little fellow ten years old in Mt. Carbon, W. Va., last year, who was employed as a "trap boy." Think of what it means to be a trap boy at ten years of age. It means to sit alone in a dark mine passage hour after hour, with no human soul near; to see no living creature except the mules as they pass with their loads, or a rat or two seeking to share one's meal; to stand in water or mud that covers the ankles, chilled to the marrow by the cold draughts that rush in when you open the trap door for the mules to pass through; to work for fourteen hours-waiting-opening and shutting a door-then waiting again-for sixty cents; to reach the surface when all is wrapped in the mantle of night, and to fall to the earth exhausted and have to be carried away to the nearest "shack" to be revived before it is possible to walk to the farther shack called "home." Boys twelve years of age may be legally employed in the mines of West Virginia, by day or by night, and for as many hours as the employers care to make them toil or their bodies will stand the strain. Where the disregard of child life is such that this may be done openly and with legal sanction, it is easy to believe what miners have again and again told me-that there are hundreds of little boys of nine and ten years of age employed in the coal mines of this state.

--John Spargo, from *The Bitter Cry of Children,* 1906

16. These boys probably worked in these mines because
    A. they found camaraderie in the mines.
    B. compulsory education was not mandatory.
    C. they got into trouble with the law.

D. they were overpaid.

17. The descriptive and exposing nature of Spargo's writing was a form of
    A. muckraking journalism.
    B. yellow journalism.
    C. dime novel writing.
    D. nationalistic writing.

18. Spargo invokes God in his description of child labor in order to
    A. inspire a blessing to the coal miners.
    B. encourage Christianity amongst the young workers.
    C. illustrate the oblivious nature of the preoccupied child laborers.
    D. justify the hiring of child laborers in the coal mines.

Questions 19-21 refer to the following questions.

This is no figure of speech. The honest citizens of Philadelphia have no more rights at the polls than the Negroes down South. Nor do they fight very hard for this basic privilege. You can arouse their Republican ire by talking about the black Republican votes lost in the Southern States by white Democratic intimidation, but if you remind the average Philadelphian that he is in the same position, he will look startled then say, "That's so, that's literally true, only I never thought of it in just that way." And it is literally true.

The machine controls the whole process of voting, and practices fraud at every stage. The assessor's list is the voting list, and the assessor is the machine's man.... The assessor pads the list with the names of dead dogs, children, and non-existent persons. One newspaper printed the picture of a dog another that of a little four-year-old Negro boy, down on such a list. A ring orator in a speech resenting sneers at his ward as "low down" reminded his hearers that that was the ward of Independence Hall, and naming over signers of the Declaration of Independence, he closed his highest flight of eloquence with the statement that "these men, the fathers of American liberty, voted down here once. And," he added, with a catching grin, "they vote here yet." Rudolph Blankenburg, a persistent fighter for the right and the use of the right to vote (and, by the way, an immigrant), sent out just before one election a registered letter to each voter on the rolls of a certain selected division. Sixty-three per cent were returned marked "not at," "removed," "deceased," etc. From one four-story house where forty-four voters were addressed, eighteen letters came back undelivered; from another of forty-eight voters, came back forty-one letters; from another sixty-one out of sixty-two; from another, forty-four out of forty-seven. Six houses in one division were assessed at one hundred and seventy-two voters, more than the votes cast in the previous election in any one of two hundred entire divisions.

The repeating is done boldly, for the machine controls the election officers, often choosing them from among the fraudulent names; and when no one appears to serve, assigning the heeler ready for the expected vacancy. The police are forbidden by law to stand within thirty feet of the polls, but they are at the box and they are there to see that the machine's orders are obeyed and that repeaters whom they help to furnish are permitted to vote without "intimidation" on the names they, the police, have supplied....

--Lincoln Steffens, from *The Shame of the Cities*, 1904

19. Steffens compares Philadelphia residents to disenfranchised black voters in the South because
  A. they have to pay poll taxes.
  B. they have to take literacy tests.
  C. the machines control their votes.
  D. they're subject to Klan intimidation.

20. The ring orator sly comment, "…they vote here yet…" refers to
  A. the spirit of democracy in Philadelphia.
  B. the fake voters on the voting list.
  C. the legitimate voters of Philadelphia.
  D. middle class voters in Philadelphia.

21. The police assisted in the machine's voting fraud by doing all of the following EXCEPT
  A. make sure the orders of the machine are upheld during elections.
  B. give names to repeat voters to put in the ballot box.
  C. intimidate voters to follow the orders of the machine.
  D. protect the voters freedom of choice.

SHORT ANSWER QUESTIONS

The monopoly of Standard Oil is dissolved in 1911.

  a. Choose ONE of the following and explain why your choice represents the event that led to the dissolution of Standard Oil.

  - The Sherman Anti-Trust Act is passed
  - Northern Securities is dissolved
  - William Howard Taft is elected

  b. Contrast your choice against ONE of the other options, demonstrating why that option in not as significant as your choice.

LONG ESSAY QUESTION

Explain why the period between 1900 and 1913 is described as the Progressive Era.

ANSWERS AND EXPLANATIONS

Multiple Choice Questions

1. C   The nomination of Theodore Roosevelt as vice president would come back to haunt conservative Republicans.
2. B   Herbert Spencer's "survival of the fittest" placed laborers and employees at the bottom of society.
3. B   Tammany Hall became one of the nation's most notorious political machines.
4. D   Tarbell wrote a history of Standard Oil to vindicate her father whom Rockefeller put out of business.
5. C   All three devices gave voters power to influence the governing process.
6. B   Roosevelt believed Northern Securities was a "bad" trust that exploited railroad users.
7. B   The opening of Yellowstone National Park occurred before Roosevelt's presidency.
8. C   Taft actually filed more anti-trust lawsuits than Roosevelt did.
9. C   LaFollette did not become a presidential candidate.
10. D The focus on war abruptly ended Progressive reform.
11. C Boss Tweed and Tammany Hall provided services to immigrants in return for their voter loyalty.
12. A The machine's methods created an instant voter bloc that reformers would try to dismantle.
13. B Roosevelt wanted to control big business and not destroy it.
14. C Roosevelt believed there were good trusts and bad trusts and believed trusts could still exist if the government regulated them.
15. C Just as Taft dissolved a number of trusts, so too did Wilson.
16. B Mandatory school attendance did more to outlaw child labor than any other law did.
17. A Muckraking journalists such as Spargo exposed the ills of society.
18. C Spargo displayed how the coal mine owners kept their workers ignorant to life outside of the mines.
19. C The machines made voter independence virtually impossible in the cities.
20. B The names of the Founding Fathers would be used as registered voters.
21. D The police only served to protect the votes of the machines and not the voters.

Long Essay Question

Explain why the period between 1900 and 1913 is described as the Progressive Era.

(Key topics to focus and elaborate on)
- A number of trusts are dissolved
- Thousands of acres of forests are preserved
- Acts are passed to protect the health of the consumer

Chapter 20
FOREIGN POLICY AND WAR IN A PROGRESSIVE ERA, 1890-1919

- Theodore Roosevelt and Woodrow Wilson became dominant figures in international relations during their presidencies.

CONTINUING EXPANSION

- Alfred T. Mahan's book, *The Influence of Sea Power Upon History* advocated that the nation build up its navy in order to compete with powerful European countries.
- In 1867, the U.S. purchased Alaska from Russia, but did not make it a territory until 1898.
- Americans became familiar with Hawaii in the early 1800s, and initially through missionary work and later trade, came to dominate the islands. After attempting to regain control of the islands for her native Hawaiians, Queen Liliuokalani was removed from power by American annexationists who pushed the U.S. to annex Hawaii, which it eventually did in 1898.

THE SPLENDID LITTLE WAR…WITH SPAIN-CUBA, PUERTO RICO, AND THE PHILIPPINES, 1898

- Despite Spain's efforts to control the last traces of its colonial empire in Cuba and the Philippines, the United States, through war, would eventually replace Spain's dominance in these regions.
- Before war with Spain, the U.S. held much interest in Cuba at the same time that Cubans rebelled for their independence. In response the Spanish placed the Cubans in concentration camps leading to much criticism from American public opinion. Essentially, yellow journalists stirred the American public with stories of horrid Spanish mistreatment of the Cubans.
- Tension mounted between the U.S. and Spain, but with the explosion of the U.S.S. Maine, Americans blamed the Spanish and declared war on this European country in April of 1898.
- To prevent Spanish naval reinforcements from the Philippines, the U.S. destroyed the Spanish naval fleet at Manila Bay and essentially took over the islands.
- After the U.S. defeated Spain, the subsequent Treaty of Paris yielded to the United States Puerto Rico, Guam and for $20 million the Philippines (through the Teller Amendment, the U.S. choose not to annex Cuba).
- Through the Platt Amendment, the U.S. still essentially controlled Cuba, but American debated over whether to annex the Philippines. After the Senate's approval of annexation, Emilio Aguinaldo led a brutal insurrection against the United States that took three years to suppress.
- Despite opposition, the U.S. remained in control of the Philippines until World War II.

- By the time Theodore Roosevelt became the president, the U.S. had the Philippines under control, leaving him to pursue American dominance in Latin America.
- The Roosevelt Corollary would see U.S. interventions in Venezuela and the Dominican Republic, though Roosevelt's main interest was in Panama where he wanted a canal connecting the Atlantic to the Pacific to be constructed.
- With the assistance of the United States, Panama gained its independence from Colombia thereby freeing it to negotiate with the United States to build a canal. Eventually, the canal opened in 1914 making it a valuable transportation trade route.
- Roosevelt also played a hand in negotiating a peace treaty between warring Russia and Japan. Yet tensions emerged between the U.S. and Japan that Roosevelt helped to ease with the negotiation of the Gentlemen's Agreement in 1907 and 1908.
- William Howard Taft encouraged American investment in foreign countries and this came to be known as dollar diplomacy.
- Wilson's dealings with Asia proved to be secondary when compared to America's dealings with Mexico, especially after it had been taken over by a military dictator, Victoriano Huerta.
- After the U.S. intervened to prevent a shipment of arms to Huerta, the dictator resigned and was replaced by Venustiano Carranza, who, in turn, went to war with the revolutionary leader, Pancho Villa.
- Since Wilson recognized Carranza, Villa lashed out against the United States when he led an attack on the town of Columbus, New Mexico. Consequently, Wilson sent Gen. John Pershing to capture Villa in 1916, but the capturing of Villa proved to be unsuccessful.

THE UNITED STATES AND THE GREAT WAR

- Through the forces of nationalism, militarism, imperialism, the formation of alliances, and the successful assassination of the archduke of Austria, Franz Ferdinand, war broke out in Europe in 1914 and subsequently spread to other parts of the world.
- The war in Europe proved to be a bloody and ghastly affair in which both the Central Powers and Allies stood at a stalemate for much of the war in France. The introduction of new weapons only served to exacerbate the bloodshed.
- Initially, Wilson declared neutrality, but the supplying of food and munitions displayed that the U.S. clearly sided with the Allies. Yet most Americans preferred to stay out of the belligerent affair in Europe.
- The looming threat of German submarines known as U-boats threatened the peace that Wilson desperately tried to maintain, especially after the Germans sank the Lusitania in 1915.
- After campaigning on the motto, "He kept us out of war," Woodrow Wilson was reelected in 1916.
- After Germany announced that it was resuming unrestricted warfare on the seas, and after the interception of the Zimmerman Telegram, Wilson asked Congress for a declaration of war and Congress complied in April of 1917.
- Despite opposition from both Congress and components of the American public, Wilson aimed to crush any signs of disloyalty. On the contrary, Wilson intended to build support for the war by creating the Committee on Public Information. The committee, led by

George Creel, used muckraking tactics to influence Americans to support the Allied war effort against the Central Powers.

- Herbert Hoover led the Food Administration to encourage Americans to ration so food would be available for the troops.
- As American military involvement progressed in the war, so too did the opposition to dissenters of the war, and in some instances, lynching occurred.
- To control opposition to the war effort, Congress passed the Espionage Act and Sedition Act in 1917-1918.
- Despite these acts, opposing voices still continued to be heard, including those of Jane Addams and socialist leader Eugene Debs. In fact, the courts actually sentenced Debs to ten years in prison for violating the Espionage Act of 1917.
- When the U.S. entered the war, Wilson named Gen. John Pershing to lead the American Expeditionary Forces to serve as assistance to the Allies and as a separate American entity on the battlefield.
- The entrance of the U.S. into the war was obviously troubling to Germany, but Germany found some relief when Russia dropped out of the war. Yet the arrival of fresh American troops ultimately led the U.S. to sign an armistice in November of 1918.
- Woodrow Wilson led the U.S. at the Paris Peace Conference along with the leaders of England, France, and Italy. His peace plan became known as the Fourteen Points and within this plan Wilson called for the U.S. to join a League of Nations to preserve peace. Although Wilson brought optimism to the conference, his European partners sought punishment and revenge.
- The result of the Treaty of Versailles included severe punishment for Germany, the creation of several new countries in Europe, and the establishment of a League of Nations.
- The Republican, Henry Cabot Lodge, led the opposition to the treaty and the League in the Senate. On a tour to support the League, Wilson travelled across the country urging audiences to pressure their senators to support the treaty. During his return, Wilson collapsed and then suffered a massive stroke at the White House.
- Wilson's refusal to compromise on the treaty and his League led to its demise as the Senate in two votes rejected it. Thus the League of Nations formed but without the participation of the United States.

MULTIPLE CHOICE QUESTIONS

1. Alfred T. Mahan's *Influence of Sea Power Upon History* argued that
   A. The United States needed to practice the policy of isolationism.
   B. The United States needed to build up its navy to protect distant outposts.
   C. The United States needed to reduce the size of its navy.
   D. The United States needed to build up its navy to protect its major coastal ports within the continent.

2. The United States acquired Hawaii by
   A. purchasing it from Japan.
   B. engaging in years of bloody conflict against the local Hawaiians.
   C. overthrowing Queen Liliuokalani.
   D. holding elections in the islands promoting annexation.

3. The triggering factor that led the U.S. to declare war on Spain in 1898 was
   A. the establishment of concentration camps in Cuba.
   B. the influence of Jose Marti.
   C. the influence of yellow journalism.
   D. the sinking of the U.S.S. Maine.

4. As a result of victory during the Spanish American War, the United States acquired the territories of all of the following EXCEPT
   A. Puerto Rico.
   B. Cuba.
   C. Guam.
   D. The Philippines.

5. The last step in securing a deal to build the Panama Canal proved to be
   A. finalizing a deal with Colombia.
   B. finding the right location.
   C. assisting Panama to gain its independence.
   D. a visit to Panama by Theodore Roosevelt.

6. The Gentlemen's Agreement stipulated that the United States
   A. would allow for Chinese immigration again.
   B. would assist in peace talks between Russia and Japan.
   C. would not limit Japanese immigration.
   D. would ban the segregation of Asian students.

7. Woodrow Wilson did not support Victoriano Huerta as the leader of Mexico because
   A. he sided with Pancho Villa.
   B. Huerta relied on assassination to bolster his control over Mexico.
   C. Huerta nationalized all American assets.
   D. Huerta refused military assistance from the U.S.

8. The initial stance of Wilson when war broke out in Europe was
   A. an immediate call for US participation.
   B. an insistence to remain neutral.
   C. preparation of arms and troops.
   D. a complete halt of American shipping to Europe.

9. The American Expeditionary Forces most impressive victory came at
    A. Somme.
    B. Verdun.
    C. Chateau-Thierry.
    D. Ypres.

10. Wilson's peace plan would result in all of the following EXCEPT
    A. the creation of the League of Nations.
    B. the rejection of the Treaty of Versailles by the U.S. Senate.
    C. opposition led by Henry Cabot Lodge.
    D. the U.S. joining the League of Nations.

Questions 11-12 refer to the following visual.

11. What country was responsible for the sinking of the Lusitania?
    A.   England
    B.   France
    C.   Russia
    D.   Germany

12. According to the U.S., the sinking of the Lusitania violated international law that stipulated
    A. passenger ships could not be destroyed without warning.
    B. armed ships could be destroyed but with warning.
    C. passenger ships with arms could be destroyed without warning.
    D. no ship could be destroyed.

Questions 13-15 refer to the following excerpt.

It is a noble land that God has given us; a land that can feed and clothe the world; a land whose coastlines would enclose half the countries of Europe; a land set like a sentinel between the imperial oceans of the globe, a greater England with a nobler destiny.

Have we no mission to perform, no duty to discharge to our fellowman? Has God endowed us with gifts beyond our deserts and marked us as the people of His peculiar favor, merely to rot in our own selfishness, as men and nations must, who take cowardice for their companion and self for their deity - China has, as India has, as Egypt has?

Shall we be as the man who had one talent and hid it, or as he who had ten talents and use them until they grew to riches? And shall we reap the reward that waits on our discharge of our high duty; shall we occupy new markets for what our farmers raise, our factories make, our merchants sell - aye, and, please God, new markets for what our ships shall carry?

The Opposition tells us that we ought not to govern a people without their consent. I answer, The rule of liberty that all just government derives its authority from the consent of the governed, applies only to those who are capable of self-government. We govern the Indians without their consent, we govern our territories without their consent, we govern our children without their consent. How do they know that our government would be without their consent? Would not the people of the Philippines prefer the just, human, civilizing government of this Republic to the savage, bloody rule of pillage and extortion from which we have rescued them?

And, regardless of this formula of words made only for enlightened, self-governing people, do we owe no duty to the world? Shall we turn these peoples back to the reeking hands from which we have taken them? Shall we abandon them, with Germany, England, Japan, hungering for them? Shall we save them from those nations, to give them a self-rule of tragedy?... Then, like man and not like children, let us on to our tasks, our mission, and our destiny.

--Albert Beveridge, "The March of the Flag"

13. In what way is Beveridge's stance similar to that of John L. O' Sullivan's stance regarding Manifest Destiny?
    a. Both admonished the expansionist spirit.
    b. Both believed that economic gain superseded morals.
    c. Both believed that God supported US expansion.

d. Both believed that expansion was not natural.

14. According to Beveridge, the "reeking" hands that the United States saved the Philippines from belonged to
    A. France.
    B. Japan.
    C. England.
    D. Spain.

15. Beveridge's underlying motive to seize the Philippines is
    A. to spread Christianity.
    B. to increase trade.
    C. to build America's prestige.
    D. to establish coaling stations.

Questions 16-18 refer to the following excerpt.

Whether the ruthless slaughter of the Filipinos shall end next month or next year is but an incident in a contest that must go on until the Declaration of Independence and the Constitution of the United States are rescued from the hands of their betrayers. Those who dispute about standards of value while the foundation of the republic is undermined will be listened to as little as those who would wrangle about the small economies of the household while the house is on fire. The training of a great people for a century, the aspiration for liberty of a vast immigration are forces that will hurl aside those who in the delirium of conquest seek to destroy the character of our institutions.

We deny that the obligation of all citizens to support their government in times of grave national peril applies to the present situation. If an administration may with impunity ignore the issues upon which it was chosen, deliberately create a condition of war anywhere on the face of the globe, debauch the civil service for spoils to promote the adventure, organize a truth-suppressing censorship, and demand of all citizens a suspension of judgement (sic) and their unanimous support while it chooses to continue the fighting, representative government itself is imperiled.

We hold with Abraham Lincoln, that "no man is good enough to govern another man without that other's consent. When the white man governs himself, that is self-government, but when he governs himself and also governs another man, that is more than self-government--that is despotism." "Our reliance is in the love of liberty which God has planted in us. Our defense is in the spirit which prizes liberty as the heritage of all men in all lands. Those who deny freedom to others deserve it not for themselves, and under a just God cannot long retain it."

--Carl Schurz, *Platform of the American Anti-Imperialist League*, 1899

16. What is the League inferring when it accused the U.S. policy towards the Philippines of violating the spirit of 1776?
    A. that the United States had the right to acquire the Philippines.
    B. that the U.S. prevented the right of the Philippines to gain its independence.
    C. that a war for independence with the U.S. was unwarranted.
    D. that the U.S. was responsible for who should gain their independence and who should not.

17. According to Schurz, Abraham Lincoln would probably have regarded America's policy towards the Philippines as
    A. noble.
    B. patriotic.
    C. despotic.
    D. destiny.

18. Schurz's description of Filipino bloodshed is in reference to
    A. their suffering at the hands of the Spanish.
    B. America's attempt to halt their rebellion led by Emilio Aguinaldo.
    C. the suffering that Aguinaldo inflicted on the Filipinos who opposed him.
    D. the suffering that resulted from the Spanish American War.

Questions 19-21 refer to the following excerpt.

The spirit of the country seems unusually good, but there is a growing frenzy of suspicion and hostility toward disloyalty. I am afraid we are going to have a good many instances of people roughly treated on very slight evidence of disloyalty. Already a number of men and some women have been "tarred and feathered," and a portion of the press is urging with great vehemence more strenuous efforts at detection and punishment. This usually takes the form of advocating "drum-head courts-martial" and "being stood up against a wall and shot," which are perhaps none too bad for real traitors, but are very suggestive of summary discipline to arouse mob spirit, which unhappily does not take time to weigh evidence.

In Cleveland a few days ago a foreign-looking man got into a street car and, taking a seat, noticed pasted in the window next to him a Liberty Loan poster, which he immediately tore down, tore into small bits, and stamped under his feet. The people in the car surged around him with the demand that he be lynched, when a Secret Service man showed his badge and placed him under arrest, taking him in a car to the police station, where he was searched and found to have two Liberty Bonds in his pocket and to be a non-English Pole. When an interpreter was procured, it was discovered that the circular which he had destroyed had had on it a picture of the German Emperor, which had so infuriated the fellow that he destroyed the circular to show his vehement hatred of the common enemy. As he was unable to speak a single word of English, he would undoubtedly have been hanged but for the intervention and entirely accidental presence of the Secret Service agent.

I am afraid the grave danger in this sort of thing, apart from its injustice, is that the German Government will adopt retaliatory measures. While the Government of the United States is not only responsible for these things, but very zealously trying to prevent them, the German Government draws no fine distinctions.

--Newton D. Baker, "The Treatment of German-Americans," 1918

19. Widespread anti-German sentiment began in the United States
    A. when war erupted in Europe.
    B. after the sinking of the Lusitania.
    C. after the Battle of Somme.
    D. after the U.S. declared war on Germany.

20. The mere thought of disloyalty could be met with
    A. fines.
    B. mob violence.
    C. civil debate.
    D. usually no consequence.

21. The description of society during the war illustrated
    A. the nonchalance of the American public towards the war.
    B. the spirit of brotherhood that existed to all opinions during the war.
    C. the aura of suspicion that the war provoked amongst Americans.
    D. the negative reaction to the government's liberty bonds.

SHORT ANSWER QUESTIONS

In April of 1917, the United States declared war on Germany

    a. Choose ONE of the following and explain why your choice represents the event that led to the declaration of war against Germany.

       • The Lusitania is torpedoed by a Germany U-boat
       • Germany announces unrestricted warfare on the seas
       • The British intercept the Zimmerman Telegram

    b. Contrast your choice against ONE of the other options, demonstrating why that option in not as significant as your choice.

LONG ESSAY QUESTION

How did the United States become an imperial nation in the late 1800s?

ANSWERS AND EXPLANATIONS

Multiple Choice Questions

1. B   Mahan noted that the great empires of the past all had strong navies.
2. C   In 1893, U.S. forces overthrew Queen Liliuokalani without bloodshed.
3. D   The U.S. blamed Spain for the explosion that sank the U.S.S. Maine.
4. B   The Teller Amendment ensured the independence of Cuba.
5. C   Roosevelt sent battleships to Panama to guarantee its independence.
6. C   After tense moments between the U.S. and Japan, this agreement allowed for the continued migration of Japanese immigrants.
7. B   Huerta led a coup against Francisco Madero and had him assassinated.
8. B   Wilson and most Americans did not want to get involved in the war when it began.
9. C   The Battle of Chateau-Thierry was a significant victory over German forces in that it helped to protect Paris from falling.
10. D The U.S. never signed the Treaty of Versailles or joined the League of Nations.
11. D A German U-boat torpedoed the Lusitania in 1915.
12. A Passenger ships had to be evacuated and inspected before they could be destroyed.
13. C Both Beveridge and O' Sullivan believed that God was on the side of American expansion.
14. D The U.S. helped to free the Philippines from Spanish rule.
15. B Beveridge believed the U.S. was "raising more than it could consume" and therefore needed new markets.
16. B Carl Schurz believed that the U.S. prevented the Philippines from enjoying the independence that the American colonists would eventually enjoy.
17. C Since the Filipinos could not control their fate, just as slaves could not control their fate, despotism would reign in the Philippines.
18. B The efforts to stop Aguinaldo's insurrection led to the loss of thousands of lives.
19. D Once the U.S. declared war on Germany, most Americans despised anything associated with Germany.
20. B Many Americans were caught up in a frenzy of patriotism that endangered those with dissenting voices or those with German backgrounds.
21. C Foreigners and disloyalty became the source of American suspicion during the war.

Long Essay Question

How did the United States become an imperial nation in the late 1800s?

(Key topics to focus and elaborate on)
  - The U.S. annexes Alaska and Hawaii
  - The Treaty of Paris yields territory to the U.S.
  - The U.S. builds its naval forces
  - The U.S. intervenes in Latin American affairs (Key topics to focus and elaborate on)

Chapter 21
A UNIQUE, PROSPEROUS, AND DISCONTENTED TIME, 1919-1929

- The experiences for those who lived in the twenties proved to be mixed; some experiences were positive and some were negative.

THE PRELUDE-THE RED SUMMER OF 1919

- The post-war era began with racial and economic tension as blacks returning from the war no longer wanted to live in a segregated South, and labor disputes led to several strikes.
- At the same time of this labor strife, several bombs were sent to various government officials including the U.S. Attorney General and the mayor of Seattle.
- As these tensions mounted, fear of communism emerged in the United States due to the Bolshevik takeover of Russia.
- In an all-out effort to find and remove communist and anarchist radicals, Attorney General A. Mitchell Palmer conducted what came to known as the Palmer Raids that lasted until 1920.
- Racial tension also unfolded and was highlighted by a vicious race riot between blacks and whites that left close to forty people dead.
- Blacks also faced the danger of lynching; there were seventy-six lynchings in 1919.

The 1920s-The Exuberance of Prosperity

- President Warren G. Harding's "return to normalcy" represented a shift away from the reform measures that had dominated American politics for the previous two decades. Yet, prohibition, the changing roles of women, and technological advances made the decade anything but normal.
- The movement towards Prohibition took place over the course of almost a hundred years and gained momentum in the 1910s with the establishment of the Anti-Saloon League.
- Whereas many Protestants saw bar rooms as dens of sin, others, especially immigrants, saw the saloon as a place for social gatherings.
- In the midst of wartime, Congress and the states passed the Eighteenth Amendment that banned the sale, manufacturing, and distribution of liquor.
- The Volstead Act made beer and wine illegal, with the exception of alcohol used for medicinal and religious purposes, and empowered the Department of Treasury to enforce Prohibition.
- Organized crime across the nation quickly took advantage of Prohibition to supply the thirsty nation with alcohol and make millions in the process. Al Capone became one of the most notorious leaders of organized crime in Chicago. Violence and rival gang warfare were a common feature of this period.

- Criminal activity also took place in the realm of financial investments with a scheme devised by Charles Ponzi. Illegal activity also took place at the White House. Secretary of the Interior, Albert Fall, leased oil fields in Elks Hills, California and Teapot Dome, Wyoming to private developers in return for bribes and a no-interest loan. Other scandals would occur under the presidency of Warren G. Harding.
- Through efforts of past suffrage leaders such as Susan B. Anthony, and in the 1910s, Carrie Chapman Catt, women, with the help of Prohibitionists, successfully lobbied for the passage of the Nineteenth Amendment. This amendment allowed for women's suffrage on a nation-wide level.
- As women gained the right to vote, many of them also developed new styles and attitudes as seen with the flappers. The flappers cut their hair short, wore short skirts, and some cussed, smoked, and drank in hidden bars known as speakeasies.
- Whereas some women ran for national offices, Margaret Sanger organized a national effort to promote birth control.
- The spirit of change during the twenties was also seen with the rise in technology that featured radios, appliances, and automobiles.
- KDKA became one of the nation's first radio stations, featuring news and entertainment.
- With the emergence of the automobile in the 1920s, so too related industries grew, such as steel, paint, textiles, and tires. The rise of the automobile also led to the creation of gas stations, repair shops, roadside restaurants and hotels, and even changes in the market for real estate.
- Whereas automobiles became popular during the 1920s, so too did the movie industry. Although movies had been around since the turn of the century, technology enhanced the production of movies and in 1927 the first movies with sound came out. Stars such as Clara Bow, Rudolph Valentino, and cartoon character Mickey Mouse entered the Hollywood movie-making scene during the 1920s.
- The twenties not only featured movie star heroes, but heroes in other realms as well including baseball hero, Babe Ruth, boxer Jack Dempsey, and pilot adventurer Charles Lindbergh
- As heroes emerged in the 1920s, a criticism of the nation's trends of conformity and prosperity also emerged and featured writers of a group known came to be known as the Lost Generation
- Writers also became a key force in New York movement known as the Harlem Renaissance. The Great Migration created many job opportunities in the North, and Harlem became one of the leading neighborhoods of the African American community.
- The art, poetry, and literature of the Harlem Renaissance, in large part, focused on the racism, discrimination, and segregation that blacks faced in America. At the same time, probably the most notable feature of the Harlem Renaissance was the music of jazz. In fact, jazz dominated the music scene during the 1920s.
- Whereas jazz featured a style that went against the traditional music of the day, Marcus Garvey went against the traditional protest of blacks by proclaiming the only way the African American race could truly gain equality was to move to Africa. He even created the Black Star Line to carry passengers to Africa.

The 1920s-The Conflicts about American Ideals

- The twenties brought prosperity and celebration to many, but at the same time, underlying conflict and tension surrounded this decade
- In 1915, William J. Simmons recreated the Klu Klux Klan that featured support for Prohibition and opposition to anything that went against white native-born Protestantism. Essentially, the Ku Klux Klan of the twenties was anti-black, anti-Catholic, anti-Jewish, and anti-immigration (opposed to immigration from southern and eastern Europe).
- In response, anti-Klan groups fought back with slogans such as "Is Your Neighbor a Kluxer?" Through both exposure of its members and corruption within, the popularity of the Ku Klux Klan fell dramatically by the end of the decade.
- The Eugenics movement became a justification to keep immigrants from southern and eastern Europe, and Asia from coming to the United States, and a justification to maintain racial segregation. IQ tests and predictable results were used as evidence for anti-immigrant legislation and segregation.
- The voices of anti-immigration advocates became strong after World War One and in 1924 a quota was set to limit the number of southern and eastern Europeans arriving in the United States. The quota was based on the 1890 census which was taken just before the massive wave of the new immigrants arrived in the U.S.
- Essentially, immigration from Italy, Russia, and Poland fell dramatically with this legislation. Anti-immigrant legislation also severely limited Japanese immigration as well. However, the immigration of Irish, Mexican, and Canadian immigration was not affected.
- In the midst of this anti-immigrant mood, Italian anarchists, Nicolas Sacco and Bartolomeo Vanzetti were convicted and executed for robbery and murder. Many suspect that their conviction and execution stemmed from their national roots and not on evidence.
- As the number of immigrants from across much of Europe came to a trickle, the number of farm exports from the U.S. to Europe also dramatically declined. During World War One, the demand for U.S. farm products proved to be substantial given that much of the farm fields of Europe became battlefields.
- By the 1920s, this demand fell as Europe recovered from the war, leaving American farmers in a deep and serious financial rut. To make matters worse, farmers overproduced and bad weather contributed to the plight of the farmers.
- A struggle that ensued between science and religion would be brought to a national stage with the Scopes Trial. In this trial the theory of evolution was tested against the religious belief of Christian Fundamentalism. At the center of the trial, teacher John Scopes, who violated a Tennessee law prohibiting the teaching of evolution, was the defendant and ultimately convicted for violating this law.

Harding, Coolidge, and Hoover-National Politics and Policies in the 1920s

- The twenties brought three Republicans to the presidency: Warren G. Harding, Calvin Coolidge, and Herbert Hoover

- Despite the scandals that surrounded Harding's presidency, under his time in office, arms limitation occurred and the debt of World War One was cut in half.
- After Harding's death due to a heart attack, Calvin Coolidge assumed the duties of the presidency and during his terms the nation experienced an economic boom.
- Meanwhile, the Democratic Party was divided between urban Catholics and Jews and rural Klansmen. Inevitably this division hindered their ability to win the presidential elections of the 1920s.
- During the twenties, the United States tried to promote world peace through the Kellog-Briand Pact, and also improve relations with Latin America.
- Despite the similarities of the presidential candidates of 1928, Herbert Hoover (Republican) and Al Smith (Democrat), there were significant differences. Smith was a "wet" who opposed Prohibition and Hoover was "dry" who supported Prohibition. In addition, Smith was a Catholic and Hoover was a Quaker.
- Hoover won the Election of 1928 but could not celebrate for too long given the nation was about to tailspin into an economic depression of epic proportions.

MULTIPLE CHOICE QUESTIONS

1. The Red Scare stemmed from
   A. a conservative takeover of the presidency.
   B. Mexican immigration.
   C. the Bolshevik takeover of Russia.
   D. Southern Democrats.

2. The Volstead Act stipulated all of the following *except*
   A. the Department of Treasury enforced Prohibition.
   B. alcohol could be distributed for medical purposes.
   C. alcohol could be distributed for religious purposes.
   D. beer and wine could still be manufactured and sold.

3. Organized crime rose during Prohibition because
   A. the police had their hands full enforcing Prohibition.
   B. it filled the void left by Prohibition.
   C. the courts were filled with racial conflict cases.
   D. the twenties was more of a care-free decade.

4. The secretary of state who took a bribe and no interest loan for leasing naval oil fields to private developers was
   A. William Howard Taft.
   B. Charles Evans Hughes.
   C. Albert Fall.
   D. Edward Doheny.

5. Carrie Chapman Catt argued that the expansion of democracy relied on
   A. winning World War I.
   B. women's suffrage.
   C. elimination of poll taxes.
   D. blocking Prohibition.

6. The flappers engaged in all of the following behaviors *except*
   A. cussing.
   B. wearing short skirts.
   C. smoking at speakeasies.
   D. sporting long hair.

7. The Harlem Renaissance featured all of the following *except*
   A. poetry and literature.
   B. jazz music.
   C. themes of black hardship.
   D. acceptance of segregation.

8. The Scopes Trial dealt with the issue of
   A. the lynching of blacks in the south.
   B. the teaching of evolution in Tennessee.
   C. scandal in Harding's Administration.
   D. Italian anarchy.

9. The Ku Klux Klan of the twenties stood for all of the following *except*
   A. anti-Catholicism.
   B. anti-Judaism.
   C. anti-black.
   D. anti-Prohibition.

10. The Kellog-Briand Pact outlawed
    A. secret alliances.
    B. trading inside information in the stock market.
    C. War.
    D. Lynching.

Questions 11-12 refer to the following visual.

11. Henry Ford revolutionized the automobile industry by
    A. implementing horizontal integration.
    B. implementing vertical integration.
    C. utilizing the assembly line.
    D. eliminating competition.

12. The rise of the automobile during the twenties did all of the following *except*
    A. led to the construction of paved roads.
    B. led to the creation of new roadside businesses.
    C. boosted the business of other industries.
    D. assisted in maintaining traditional family life and morals.

Questions 13-15 refer to the following document.

The Song that STOPPED!

A child of five skipped down the garden path and laughed because the sky was blue. "Jane," called her mother from the kitchen window, "come here and help me bake your birthday cake." Little feet sped. "Don't fall," her mother warned.

Jane stood in the kitchen door and wrinkled her nose in joy. Her gingham dress was luminous against the sun. What a child! Dr. and Mrs. Wentworth cherished Jane.

"Go down to the cellar and get mother some preserves . . . the kind you like."

"The preserves are in the cellar," she chanted, making a progress twice around the kitchen. "Heigh-ho a-derry-o, the preserves are . . ." her voice grew fainter as she danced off. " . . . in the . . ."

The thread of song snapped. A soft thud-thud. Fear fluttered Mrs. Wentworth's heart. She rushed to the cellar door.

"Mother!" . . . a child screaming in pain. Mrs. Wentworth saw a little morsel of girlhood lying in a heap of gingham and yellow hair at the bottom of the dark stairs.

The sky is still blue. But there will be no birthday party tomorrow. An ambulance clanged up to Dr. Wentworth's house today. Jane's leg is broken.

If a flashlight had been hanging on a hook at the head of the cellar stairs, this little tragedy would have been averted. If Jane had been taught to use a flashlight as carefully as her father, Dr. Wentworth, had taught her to use a tooth-brush, a life need not have been endangered.

An Eveready Flashlight is always a convenience and often a life-saver. Keep one about the house, in the car; and take one with you wherever you go. Keep it supplied with fresh Eveready Batteries-the longest-lasting flashlight batteries made. Eveready Flashlights, $1.00 up.

NATIONAL CARBON CO., INC. EVEREADY FLASHLIGHTS & BATTERIES

A THOUSAND THINGS MAY HAPPEN IN THE DARK

13. The little girl fell down the cellar stairs because
    A. the stairs were broken.
    B. she didn't have a flashlight.
    C. she was naturally clumsy.
    D. there was no rail.

14. Besides the story, how else did the advertisement attract the viewer?
    A. visuals.
    B. slogans.
    C. catchy phrases and warnings.
    D. use of movie stars.

15. Advertising became extremely significant in the twenties because
    A. it served as the only source of entertainment.
    B. the onslaught of consumer products available.
    C. nobody cared for the new products.
    D. credit was not available.

Questions 16-18 refer to the following excerpt.

By the President of the United States of America

A Proclamation

Whereas it is provided in the act of Congress approved May 26, 1924, entitled "An act to limit the immigration of aliens into the United States, and for other purposes" that "The annual quota of any nationality shall be two per centum of the number of foreign-born individuals of such nationality resident in continental Untied States as determined by the United States Census of 1890, but the minimum quota of any nationality shall be 100 (Sec. 11 a). . . .

"Such officials shall, jointly, report annually to the President the quota of each nationality under subdivision (a) of section 11, together with the statements, estimates, and revisions provided for in this section. The President shall proclaim and make known the quotas so reported". (Sec. 12 e).

Now, therefore I, Calvin Coolidge, President of the United States of America acting under and by virtue of the power in me vested by the aforesaid act of Congress, do hereby proclaim and make known that on and after July 1, 1924, and throughout the fiscal year 1924-1925, the quota of each nationality provided in said act shall be as follows:

COUNTRY OR AREA OF BIRTH QUOTA 1924-1925

Afghanistan- 100
Albania- 100
Andorra- 100
Arabian peninsula (1, 2)- 100
Armenia- 124
Australia, including Papua, Tasmania, and all islands appertaining to Australia (3, 4)- 121
Austria- 785
Belgium (5)- 512
Bhutan- 100
Bulgaria- 100
Cameroon (proposed British mandate)- 100
Cameroon (French mandate)- 100
China- 100
Czechoslovakia- 3,073
Danzig, Free City of- 228
Denmark (5, 6)- 2,789
Egypt- 100
Estonia- 124
Ethiopia (Abyssinia)- 100
Finland- 170
France (1, 5, 6)- 3,954

Germany- 51,227
Great Britain and Northern Ireland (1, 3, 5, 6)- 34,007
Greece- 100
Hungary- 473
Iceland- 100
India (3)- 100
Iraq (Mesopotamia)- 100
Irish Free State (3)- 28,567
Italy, including Rhodes, Dodecanesia, and Castellorizzo (5)- 3,845
Japan- 100
Latvia-142
Liberia- 100
Liechtenstein- 100
Lithuania- 344
Luxemburg- 100
Monaco- 100
Morocco (French and Spanish Zones and Tangier)- 100
Muscat (Oman)- 100
Nauru (proposed British mandate) (4)- 100
Nepal- 100
Netherlands (1, 5, 6)- 1648
New Zealand (including appertaining islands (3, 4)- 100
Norway (5)- 6,453
New Guinea, and other Pacific Islands under proposed Australian mandate (4)- 100
Palestine (with Trans-Jordan, proposed British mandate)- 100
Persia (1)- 100
Poland- 5,982
Portugal (1, 5)- 503
Ruanda and Urundi (Belgium mandate)- 100
Rumania- 603
Russia, European and Asiatic (1)- 2,248
Samoa, Western (4) (proposed mandate of New Zealand)- 100
San Marino- 100
Siam- 100
South Africa, Union of (3)- 100
South West Africa (proposed mandate of Union of South Africa)- 100
Spain (5)- 131
Sweden- 9,561
Switzerland- 2,081
Syria and The Lebanon (French mandate)- 100
Tanganyika (proposed British mandate)- 100
Togoland (proposed British mandate)- 100
Togoland (French mandate)- 100
Turkey- 100
Yap and other Pacific islands (under Japanese mandate) (4)- 100
Yugoslavia- 671

GENERAL NOTE. -The immigration quotas assigned to the various countries and quota-areas should not be regarded as having any political significance whatever, or as involving recognition of new governments, or of new boundaries, or of transfers of territory except as the United States Government has already made such recognition in a formal and official manner. . .

Calvin Coolidge.

16. Despite their close proximity to each other in Europe, Great Britain, Germany, and Ireland had a significantly higher quota than Italy, Russia, and Poland due to the fact that
    A. Italy, Russia, and Poland were predominantly Protestant nations.
    B. immigrants from Great Britain, Germany, and Ireland came in large numbers before 1890.
    C. British, German, and Irish immigrants were primarily Jewish.
    D. southern and eastern Europeans were all ultra-conservative capitalists.

17. Who pressured Congress to pass immigrant quota legislation in 1924?
    A. Catholic Democrats
    B. southern blacks
    C. white native-born Protestants
    D. Jewish Democrats

18. A term or phrase that best describes the quota system of 1924 would be
    A. melting pot.
    B. 100% Americanism.
    C. I Want You.
    D. Give me your tired, your poor, your huddled masses.

Questions 19-21 refer to the following excerpt.

Now I should say that I am not only innocent of all these things, not only have I never committed a real crime in my life—

We were tried during a time that has now passed into history. I mean by that, a time when there was a hysteria of resentment and hate against the people of our principle, against the foreigner, against slackers...

This is what I say: I would not wish to a dog or to a snake, to the most low and misfortunate creature of the earth—I would not wish to any of them what I have had to suffer for things that I am not guilty of. But my conviction is that I have suffered for things I am guilty of. I am suffering because I am a radical and indeed I am a radical; I have suffered because I was an Italian, and indeed I am an Italian; I have suffered more for my family and for my beloved that for myself; but I am so convinced to be right that if you could execute me two times, and if I could be reborn two other times, I would live again to do what I have done already.

I have finished. Thank you.

--Statement of Bartolomeo Vanzetti

19. Vanzetti's phrase "We were tried during a time that has now passed into history" refers to
    A. the period that accepted unregulated immigration.
    B. the early 1900s.
    C. the early twenties that were filled with resentment towards immigrants.
    D. the 1890s.

20. Vanzetti believed he was convicted and suffered because
    A. he was an Italian radical.
    B. of credible evidence.
    C. a poor defense.
    D. lack of witnesses.

21. In the end, towards the end of his life, Vanzetti was
    A. remorseful.
    B. resentful.
    C. unapologetic.
    D. apologetic.

SHORT ANSWER QUESTIONS

In 1933, the experiment of Prohibition came to an end.

   a. Choose ONE of the following and explain why your choice represents the event that led to the end of Prohibition.

   - Al Capone becomes the leader of organized crime in Chicago
   - Speakeasies emerge immediately after Prohibition goes into effect
   - The Wickersham Commission reveals that enforcement of Prohibition is a complete failure

   b. Contrast your choice against ONE of the other options, demonstrating why that option in not as significant as your choice.

Long Essay Question

In what ways was the excitement and prosperity of the twenties underlined by intolerance and conflict?

ANSWERS AND EXPLANATIONS

Multiple Choice Questions

1. C   Americans feared that Russian communism would spread to the United States.
2. D   The Volstead Act added beer and wine to the list of Prohibited spirits.
3. B   Organized crime took the place of bars, saloons, and stores that provided alcohol.
4. C   Albert Fall was the key figure in the Teapot Dome Scandal.
5. B   Democracy would not be complete without the inclusion of the female vote.
6. D   The flappers cut their hair short which came to be known as "bobbing" their hair.
7. D   Members of the Harlem Renaissance opposed segregation.
8. B   John Scopes was arrested for teaching evolution in a biology classroom.
9. D   As a strict Protestant movement, the Klan of the twenties supported prohibition.
10. C The pact tried to set the conditions in which war could be averted.
11. C In following the method of meatpackers, Ford utilized the assembly line to make his Model T cars.
12. D The car led many families to take Sunday drives instead of going to church and endangered the morals of teenagers by allowing different dating habits.
13. B Without a flashlight, the little girl couldn't see down the stairway.
14. C Warnings and phrases were printed in capital lettering.
15. B New products created a new demand for marketing.
16. B The law intended to keep people who arrived after 1890 out, such as Italians, Russians, and Polish immigrants.
17. C Native-born Protestants viewed immigration from Southern and Eastern Europe as a threat to their way of life.
18. B 100% Americanism meant no Jews or Catholics.
19. C Vanzetti believed the hateful environment led to his conviction and planned execution.
20. A Vanzetti argued that he was convicted more because of his beliefs and background than because of the evidence against him.
21. C Vanzetti never apologized for his conviction.

Long Essay Question

In what ways was the excitement and prosperity of the twenties underlined by intolerance and conflict?

(Key topics to focus and elaborate on)
- The rise of sports, movies, and jazz
- The rise of automobiles and appliances
- Anti-immigration laws passed and evolution attacked
- Lynching of blacks and the rise of the Ku Klux Klan

Chapter 22
LIVING IN HARD TIMES, 1929-1939

- The Stock Market Crash of 1929 unleashed the underlying forces that led to the Great Depression. The earlier drop in agricultural prices and then the loss of jobs caused an economic disaster that affected virtually everyone in the United States.

THE GREAT DEPRESSION

- The economic prosperity of the twenties led the prices of stocks to rise, and this rise led many investors to buy on the margin.
- Stock prices reached their peak by the summer of 1929, but then fell dramatically on October 29, 1929. The downward trend continued year after year into the 1930s.
- After the Crash, the economy quickly worsened to the point where unemployment and homelessness soared.
- Hoover relied on voluntary solutions to keep wages up and the Reconstruction Finance Corporation to assist banks and railroads with loans to keep them from folding. Yet, none of these measures improved the economy. To make matters worse, the Smoot-Hawley Tariff only served to exacerbate the financial crisis.
- Americans blamed Hoover for the Great Depression and it came as no surprise that he would not be reelected as president in 1932.

THE NEW DEAL

- New York governor, Franklin D. Roosevelt, simply known as FDR won the Election of 1932 in a landslide and promised a New Deal for the American people.
- The Stock Market Crash and the poor economy led to the closure of thousands of banks across the nation. Consequently, states across the nation declared bank holidays.
- Through his "fireside chats", and with the help of his wife, Eleanor, FDR helped to instill a sense of hope to the nation.
- Through the Emergency Banking Act and the Glass-Steagall Act, Americans began to feel confident about keeping their money in banks again.
- The "First Hundred Days" brought a stream of legislation that aimed to cut government costs, bring in revenue, and create jobs for thousands of unemployed workers.
- The CCC hired young men to work on outdoor projects, the AAA called for crops and piglets to be destroyed and slaughtered, the PWA hired the unemployed to work on large scale projects, the TVA created a series of dams across the Southeast, and the NRA attempted to get businesses to volunteer to maintain wages and keep prices uniform. These were but a few of the measures FDR and Congress created to fight the Great Depression.
- The Indian New Deal saw the federal government recognize the legal rights of Indian tribes and the right for tribes to hold reservation lands.
- The Great Depression hit African Americans especially hard and the New Deal attempted to bring them relief. Yet, discrimination prevented African Americans from fully gaining the benefits of the New Deal. At the same time, FDR created the Black Cabinet, and

Eleanor Roosevelt helped Mary McLeod Bethune to hold a number of prominent New Deal positions.

- Farmers in the Midwest fared no better during the Great Depression as they first dealt with low wheat prices, and then intense dust storms struck which created what came to be known as the Dust Bowl. Essentially, this natural disaster forced more than a quarter of a million people to migrate to California.
- As migrant workers in California's Central Valley, the newly arrived farmers came to be known as "Okies" and their plight was described in novels by Carey McWilliams and John Steinbeck.
- In California's farm fields, approximately half the workers were Okies, and half were Mexicans and Filipinos.
- The WPA hired the unemployed to work on various construction projects but also hired artists, writers, and musicians as well.
- Whereas some of the nation's unemployed benefited from the New Deal, workers seeking to organize and engage in collective bargaining would benefit from the Wagner Act. The passage of this act quickly bolstered the growth of union membership and spurred the birth of the CIO.
- During the Great Depression, the method of the "sit-down" strike was first employed bringing a number of successes, including strikes at Firestone and General Motors.
- Like every president, FDR had his critics. Conservatives viewed the New Deal as too socialistic, and others viewed the New Deal as not socialistic enough.
- Dr. Francis Townsend proposed a pension of $200/month to any person over sixty years old. Charles Coughlin, through his radio program attacked the New Deal with an anti-Semitic tone. Governor Huey Long called for a Share Our Wealth program which pushed for a guaranteed income to every family.
- Under FDR's Second New Deal, with the influence of Francis Townsend, Congress enacted the Social Security Act which created a retirement system, unemployment insurance, aid to dependent children, and support for public health.
- FDR's second term accomplished far less than the first. In an effort to get the Supreme Court to back off from attacking his New Deal, FDR threatened to push through Congress a "Court packing bill". With the threat made, the Court stopped its attack on the New Deal.
- The Fair Labor Standards Act marked the end of the New Deal, yet the Great Depression continued. Nevertheless, the New Deal set a precedent for government involvement in the economy which set the stage for other safety net measures.

THE DEEP ROOTS OF WAR--THE UNITED STATES, EUROPE, AND ASIA

- The punishment of Germany after World War I combined with severe effects of a world-wide depression, paved the way for dictators to rise in Europe and Asia. In Italy, Benito Mussolini established the Fascist Party with dreams of creating another Roman Empire.
- In Germany, a country devastated by war debt and the depression, the Nazi Party led by Adolf Hitler sought to establish Lebensraum and to eliminate the Jews and others to accommodate the Aryan master race. The Nazi government, even before war broke out, began to harass the Jews with events such as Kristallnacht.

241

- Meanwhile, without a powerful League of Nations to curb the rise of Adolf Hitler, Germany began to rearm and seized the Rhineland, the Sudetenland, and later Czechoslovakia.
- To ensure a consolidation of power in Europe, Italy and Germany created an alliance which later joined forces with Japan.
- Due to strained relations, Japan would ultimately go to war with the United States, but prior to this, Japan sought to dominate Asia by first seizing Manchuria from China and then capturing Shanghai
- As the Italians and Germans became aggressive, England and France stood and watched, and so did the United States. In fact, during the thirties, the United States followed a strict policy of isolationism. Various reasons existed for the isolationism of the U.S., from the disillusionment of World War One to the troubles of the Great Depression.
- Consequently, between 1935 and 1937, Congress passed the Neutrality Acts in an attempt to prevent the U.S. from entangling itself into future conflicts. Yet, the conflict in Asia drew more and more attention, but not enough to become involved in Japanese-provoked conflict. In fact, the U.S. continued to supply oil to the Japanese through the late 1930s.
- As conflict grew in the east, desperation grew in Europe where Jews wanted to escape Nazi persecution but the United States did not offer any assistance.
- After Germany seized Czechoslovakia, the Nazis made a deal with their enemy, the Soviet Union, which would allow them to seize Poland without Soviet retaliation in 1939. With the German invasion of Poland in September of 1939, France and England declared war on Germany. The U.S. remained neutral, but with grave doubts and reservations.

MULTIPLE CHOICE QUESTIONS

1. The phrase "on the margin" referred to
   A. people that were on the economic fringe of society.
   B. the practice of taking out loans to buy shares of stock.
   C. the state of the economy.
   D. the practice of loaning cash without collateral.

2. The Federal Deposit Insurance Corporation was created to
   A. protect investments in the stock market.
   B. guarantee bank deposits.
   C. prevent banks from investing in stock.
   D. close all insolvent banks.

3. The Tennessee Valley Authority was a New Deal program that
   A. hired writers and artists.
   B. hired young men to work in the national parks.
   C. built dams and provided electricity to rural areas.
   D. paid subsidies to farmers to destroy their crops.

4. The purpose of the Public Works Administration was to
   A. hire minority women.

B. hire the unemployed to build large-scale projects.

C. destroy crops to boost agricultural prices.

D. ensure collective bargaining.

5. During the Great Depression, the voting pattern of African American voters shifted to
   A. the Republican Party.
   B. the Democratic Party.
   C. the Populist Party.
   D. the Communist Party.

6. Arguably the best known description of the plight of the Okies in California was
   A. John Steinbeck's *The Grapes of Wrath*.
   B. Carey McWilliam's *Factories in the Fields*.
   C. F. Scott Fitzgerald's *The Great Gatsby*.
   D. John Steinbeck's *Of Mice and Men*.

7. The sit-down strike saw workers
   A. sit at the gates of industrial plants.
   B. sit next to the machinery they used.
   C. sit at the doors of the factories.
   D. sit at the offices of industrial managers.

8. Dr. Francis Townsend called for the federal government to
   A. nationalize the banks.
   B. guarantee each family an income.
   C. provide $200 to every person at least 60 years old.
   D. provide subsidies for landowners.

9. In order to protect acts and legislation of the New Deal, FDR devised
   A. a court-packing scheme.
   B. a method to control Congress.
   C. a method to gain more public support.
   D. a method to override Supreme Court decisions.

10. When World War One began in Europe, the United States reluctantly
    A. declared war on Germany.
    B. declared war on Japan.
    C. opted for neutrality.
    D. signed the Munich Pact.

Questions 11-12 refer to the following visual.

11. The visual is in reference to
    A. the Townsend Plan.
    B. Share Our Wealth.
    C. Social Security.
    D. Public Works Administration.

12. The "monthly check" applied to all of the following *except*
    A. retirement.
    B. unemployment.
    C. dependent children.
    D. guaranteed income.

Questions 13-15 refers to the following excerpt.

It is impossible for the United States to preserve itself as a republic or as a democracy when 600 families own more of this Nation's wealth--in fact, twice as much--as all the balance of the people put together. Ninety-six percent of our people live below the poverty line, while 4 percent own 87 percent of the wealth. America can have enough for all to live in comfort and still permit millionaires to own more than they can ever spend and to have more than they can ever use; but America cannot allow the multimillionaires and the billionaires, a mere handful of them, to own everything unless we are willing to inflict starvation upon 125,000,000 people. . . .
It took the genius of labor and the lives of all Americans to produce the wealth of this land. If any man, or 100 men, wind up with all that has been produced by 120,000,000 people, that does not mean that those 100 men produced the wealth of the country; it means that those 100 men stole, directly or indirectly, what 125,000,000 people produced. . . .

Here is the whole sum and substance of the share-our-wealth movement:

1. Every family to be furnished by the Government a homestead allowance, free of debt, of not less than one-third the average family wealth of the country, which means, at the lowest, that every family shall have the reasonable comforts of life up to a value of from $5,000 to $6,000. No person to have a fortune of more than 100 to 300 times the average family fortune, which means that the limit to fortunes is between $1,500,000 and $5,000,000, with annual capital levy taxes imposed on all above $1,000,000.
2. The yearly income of every family shall be not less than one-third of the average family income, which means that, according to the estimates of the statisticians of the United States Government and Wall Street, no family's annual income would be less than from $2,000 to $2,500. No yearly income shall be allowed to any person larger than from 100 to 300 times the size of the average family income, which means that no person would be allowed to earn in any year more than from $600,000 to $1,800,000, all to be subject to present income-tax laws.

I now ask those who read this circular to help us at once in this work of giving life and happiness to our people--not a starvation dole upon which someone may live in misery from week to week. Before this miserable system of wreckage has destroyed the life germ of respect and culture in our American people let us save what was here, merely by having none too poor and none too rich. The theory of the Share Our Wealth Society is to have enough for all, but not to have one with so much that less than enough remains for the balance of the people. . . .

--Huey Long, "Share Our Wealth"

13. According to Long, who owned most of the nation's wealth?
    A. the nation's masses.
    B. the middle class.
    C. the upper middle class.
    D. 600 families.

14. According to Long, no family's annual income should be less than
    A. $500 to $1000.
    B. $2,000 to $2,500.
    C. $5000 to $7,500.
    D. $10,000 to $15,000.

15. According to Long, American society should have
    A. total equality.
    B. all wealthy residents.
    C. none too poor and none too rich.
    D. all just above the poverty line.

Questions 16-18 refer to the following .excerpt

An Act to Improve the Navigability and to Provide for the Flood Control of the Tennessee River: To Provide for Reforestation and the Proper Use of Marginal Lands in the Tennessee Valley; to Provide for the Agricultural and Industrial Development of Said Valley; to Provide for the National Defense by the Creation of a Corporation for the Operation of Government Properties at and Near Muscle Shoals in the State of Alabama, and for Other Purposes May 18, 1933.

Be it enacted by the Senate and House of Representatives of the United States of America in Congress assembled, That for the purpose of maintaining and operating the properties now owned by the United States in the vicinity of Muscle Shoals, Alabama, in the interest of the national defense and for agriculture and industrial development, and to improve navigation in the Tennessee River and to control the destructive flood waters in the Tennessee River and Mississippi River Basins, there is hereby created a body corporate by the name of the "Tennessee Valley Authority" (hereinafter referred to as the "Corporation"). The board of directors first appointed shall be deemed the incorporators and the incorporation shall be held to have been effected from the date of the first meeting of the board. This Act may be cited as the "Tennessee Valley Authority Act of 1933."

[...]

All contracts to which the Corporation is a party and which require the employment of laborers and mechanics in the construction, alteration, maintenance or repair of buildings, dams, locks, or other projects shall contain a provision that not less than the prevailing rate of wages for work of a similar nature prevailing in the vicinity shall be paid to such laborers or mechanics.

In the event any dispute arises as to what are the prevailing rates of wages, the question shall be referred to the Secretary of Labor for determination, and his decision shall be final. In the determination of such prevailing rate or rates, due regard shall be given to those rates which have been secured through collective agreement by representatives of employers and employees.

--Tennessee Valley Authority Act

16. According to the act, who would step in if labor disputes regarding wages emerged?
    A. the President
    B. the Secretary of Labor
    C. John L. Lewis
    D. the American Federation of Labor

17. The Tennessee Valley Authority did all of the following EXCEPT
    A. provide dams to prevent flooding.
    B. provide electricity to rural residents.
    C. provide for national defense.
    D. provide for the construction of public buildings.

18. The Tennessee Valley Authority hired
    A. workers already employed by the government.
    B. unemployed laborers.
    C. workers outsourced by private companies.
    D. workers contracted from other countries.

Questions 19-21 refer to the following excerpt.

Typical of the shacktown problem are two such areas near the city limits of Sacramento, one on the east side of B Street, extending from Twelfth Street to the Sacramento city dump and incinerator; and the other so-called Hoovertown, adjacent to the Sacramento River and the city filtration plant. In these two areas there were on September 17, 1939, approximately 650 inhabitants living in structures that, with scarcely a single exception, were rated by the inspectors of this division as "unfit for human occupancy." The majority of the inhabitants were white Americans, with the exception of 50 or 60 Mexican families, a few single Mexican men, and a sprinkling of Negroes. For the most part they are seasonally employed in the canneries, the fruit ranches, and the hop fields of Sacramento County. Most of the occupants are at one time or another upon relief, and there are a large number of occupants in these shacktowns from the Dust Bowl area. Describing the housing, an inspector of this division reports:

"The dwellings are built of brush, rags, sacks, boxboard, odd bits of tin and galvanized iron, pieces of canvas and whatever other material was at hand at the time of construction."

"Entire families, men, women, and children, are crowded into hovels, cooking and eating in the same room. The majority of the shacks have no sinks or cesspools for the disposal of kitchen drainage, and this, together with garbage and other refuse, is thrown on the surface of the ground."

19. How could one describe the conditions of these farmworkers?
    A. standard.
    B. sub-standard.

C. Acceptable.
D. middle class.

20. Conditions such as those described by McWilliams existed because
    A. housing had not developed in California.
    B. a massive influx of desperate workers arrived in California.
    C. there weren't enough workers to justify building new tenements.
    D. the workers preferred temporary living conditions.

21. There is no mention of Asian workers in Sacramento because
    A. the Chinese preferred to work in the railroads.
    B. anti-immigration laws limited their numbers in California.
    C. the Japanese were settled in the coastal regions.
    D. the Japanese were placed in internment camps.

SHORT ANSWER QUESTIONS

By 1932, one quarter of the nation's labor force was unemployed.

a. Choose ONE of the following and explain why your choice represents the event that led to this massive unemployment.

- Farm prices fell during the twenties
- The Stock Market crashed
- Banks and businesses closed

b. Contrast your choice against ONE of the other options, demonstrating why that option in not as significant as your choice.

LONG ESSAY QUESTION

How did Hoover and FDR differ in their approach to fighting the Great Depression?

ANSWERS AND EXPLANATIONS

Multiple Choice Questions

1. B Buying "on the margin" would come back to haunt both investors and brokers.
2. B Banks had to pay deposit insurance in the event that they should close.
3. C Arguably one of the New Deal's finest achievements, the TVA preventing flooding and made it possible for rural residents to have electricity.
4. B The PWA created roads, public buildings, bridges, and a number of other large-scale projects.

5. B African Americans switched from the party of Lincoln to the party of FDR.
6. A Steinbeck's *The Grapes of Wrath* vividly described the struggles of the Okies.
7. B Strikers positioned at their machines made it impossible for scabs to replace them.
8. C Townsend believed the elderly needed financial assistance from the federal government.
9. A After several New Deal programs were declared unconstitutional by the Supreme Court, FDR threatened to add more favorable justices to this court.
10. C Many Americans wanted no part in another conflict such as World War I.
11. C Social Security offers a monthly paycheck.
12. D Social Security did not offer a "guaranteed income" to everyone.
13. D The very few elite owned most of the nation's wealth.
14. B $2000 to $2,500 is the minimum of what a family should have every year.
15. C Long believed that there shouldn't be too many poor or wealthy citizens in the U.S.
16. B The Secretary of Labor would step in to arbitrate labor disputes.
17. D The construction of public buildings fell to other agencies.
18. B As part of a way to stimulate the economy, the TVA hired unemployed workers.
19. B These farm workers definitely lived in terrible conditions.
20. B A housing shortage existed when all these workers arrived at once in California.
21. B Anti-Asian immigration laws severely limited the number of Asian farm workers in California.

Long Essay Question

How did Hoover and FDR differ in their approach to fighting the Great Depression?

(Key topics to focus and elaborate on)
* Hoover relied on volunteerism
* Hoover was more conservative in using government intervention
* FDR was more pragmatic in using government intervention
* FDR created more agencies to fight the Great Depression

Chapter 23
LIVING IN A NEW WORLD AT WAR, 1939-1945

- The Japanese attack of Pearl Harbor brought the United States into World War II, thus affecting all aspects of American society.

PREPAREDNESS AND ISOLATION, 1939-1941

- After Germany defeated Poland, for a time there was a calm before the storm until 1940 when the Nazis unleashed its blitzkrieg across Europe. By June of 1940, Hitler had most of Europe under his control, including France.
- Thereafter, Germany began its bombing of Britain with its Luftwaffe killing thousands of British residents.
- FDR placed supporters of intervention into key positions to counter the isolationists in Congress. "Obsolete" destroyer ships were sent to Britain for its defense.
- The looming prospect of war led the American public to select FDR to serve an unprecedented third presidential term.
- In a winter speech in 1940, FDR proposed a Lend-Lease plan to assist Britain in its defense against Germany and he offered the Four Freedoms America needed to secure. Congress passed the act in 1941, giving Winston Churchill and England much needed supplies for its defense. In effect, along with a military draft, Lend-Lease and future war production would end the Great Depression.
- The implementation of Lend-Lease brought the US into direct contact with German submarines which attacked US ships and even sank the USS Reuben James in October of 1941.
- As Japan moved to conquer China and the rest of Asia, it joined forces with Germany and Italy to form the Axis Powers. Subsequently, Japan moved into French Indochina and saw the nationalistic hard-liner, Hideki Tojo become its Prime Minister and he prepared Japan for war.
- War came in December of 1941, when Japan launched a surprise attack on the US naval base at Pearl Harbor, Hawaii. American public opinion now shifted to full support for war.

MASS MOBILIZATION IN A SOCIETY AT WAR

- Shortly after the attack of Pearl Harbor, Japan unleashed its own brand of "blitzkrieg" across Southeast Asia and captured key positions including the oil-rich Dutch East Indies, Malaysia, and the Philippines.
- In the Philippines, the Japanese forced captured American soldiers on a sixty-six mile Bataan Death March.
- After Japan attack Pearl Harbor, Germany and Italy declared war on the United States.

- In 1942, the US would drive back the Japanese at the Battle of the Coral Sea, and successfully defend Midway Island.
- German submarines proved to be a menace in the Atlantic Ocean as they sunk numerous Allied ships.
- The war brought young men from all walks of life into combat. Some volunteered for action, and some were chosen by the Selective Service System.
- Thousands of conscientious objectors served in the military in various capacities, and others who refused to do any type of service were imprisoned.
- During the war, women served in non-combat units such as the WAACs, WAVES, WASPS, or SPARS. Their diverse duties ranged from being nurses in field operating rooms to becoming domestic pilots.
- The war provided tremendous work opportunities for women, building planes, tanks, battleships and other war material. Collectively, these women became known as "Rosie the Riveter."
- In the early stages of the war, the defense industries discriminated against the hiring of blacks. Yet, with the threat of a massive march in Washington D.C., led by A. Philip Randolph, FDR issued Executive Order 8802 which banned these discriminatory practices.
- The mixing of workers was not without its struggles, as violence between blacks and whites broke out in numerous cities including a race riot in Detroit.
- A race riot also broke out in Los Angeles when white sailors attacked Mexican zoot suiters.
- Nevertheless, minorities played a vital role in the war effort against the Axis Powers.
- After the attack of Pearl Harbor, FDR issued Executive Order 9066 in 1942 which called for the internment of anyone of Japanese descent. In total, ten relocation internment camps were set up, with Manzanar being one of the first.
- Both Issei and Nissei had to evacuate their homes and businesses to relocate to these camps.
- In 1944, the case of *Korematsu v. United States* ruled that the internment of the Japanese was legal.
- The United States had huge advantages when it came to building the war machinery necessary to win the war. In essence, the US was already industrialized, already had the factories, and had a hungry work force eager to get back to work.
- Simple methods of production led to a high volume output of tanks, airplanes, battleships, jeeps, and other war machinery. The production of the Liberty Ship increased dramatically from almost a year to build one to just five days by 1942.
- To maintain the momentum of war production a "no strike pledge" dominated the defense industry.
- Despite food rationing and limited living arrangements, most Americans prospered greatly during the wartime period, especially considering that during the decade before many of them were living in cardboard shacks.
- The importance of winning the war superseded concerns about government taxes to pay for the war. The federal government also sold war bonds and received huge loans to fund the war effort.

- Despite the call for an attack on the western front from Russia's leader, Josef Stalin, the US and England successfully attacked German positions in North Africa.
- When American troops entered Sicily, they were cheered by Italian crowds. Allied forces eventually took control of Rome in June of 1944.
- Meanwhile, Russian troops, having been attacked by the Nazis in 1941, pushed German forces out of Russia and subsequently took control of Poland and moved into Germany. This push from Russia was accompanied by terror bombing of Germany by the US and British air force.
- At the Tehran Conference, Stalin got the assurance from FDR and Churchill that Operation Overlord would take place in 1944. To prepare for this invasion, bombs continued to be dropped on key German positions, yet no bombs were dropped on Nazi rail lines that led to the Nazi death camps.
- General Dwight D. Eisenhower led the Allied forces in their attack against Germany at Normandy, France on June 6, 1944. Having gained control of the Normandy beaches and nearby villages, the Allies went on to liberate Paris.
- The German defeat at the Battle of the Bulge was followed by Allied troops moving into Germany. As US troops entered Germany, they discovered the horrors of the Holocaust which had killed over ten million people altogether.
- With the invasion of Allied forces into Berlin, Hitler committed suicide on April 30m 1945. A week later Germany surrendered and only Japan remained.
- After FDR died in April of 1945, his vice president, Harry S. Truman, became the president. Truman led the nation in the final months of the war.
- Through a system of island-hopping, US forces made their way towards Japan.
- Between 1944 and 1945, fierce fighting ultimately led to a recapturing of the Philippines by the US. Equally fierce fighting took place at Okinawa and Iwo Jima, both of which the US took control of in 1945. After these victories, US forces were extremely close for a land invasion, an invasion that would never happen.
- Having been alerted to the potential of a new weapon that was on the brink of being developed, FDR pushed for action and the Manhattan Project was born in 1942.
- Under the direction of Robert Oppenheimer, American scientists developed the atomic bomb and tested it in July of 1945.
- On August 6 the US dropped the bomb on Hiroshima, and on August 9 dropped the bomb on Nagasaki, killing tens of thousands of civilians in both cities. On August 15, Emperor Hirohito announced that Japan had surrendered. World War II was over.

MULTIPLE CHOICE QUESTIONS

1. Through the policy of Lend-Lease, the United States agreed to
   A. provide France with weapons to free itself from German rule.
   B. loan or lease any war material England needed to defend itself from German attack.
   C. provide metal and oil shipments to Japan.
   D. freeze all shipments to the communist Soviet Union.

2. By late October of 1941, the United States was unofficially at war with
   A. Japan.
   B. Italy.
   C. Germany.
   D. Russia.

3. The Home Front of the United States during World War II featured all of the following EXCEPT
   A. job opportunities for both men and women.
   B. race riots.
   C. internment of the Japanese.
   D. uncontrollable inflation.

4. The West Coast featured all of the following EXCEPT
   A. Japanese internment camps.
   B. production of airplanes made in Southern California.
   C. production of battleships made in the Bay Area.
   D. production of tanks made in Ford factories.

5. Defense industries finally ended their hiring discrimination policies against African Americans after
   A. race riots in Detroit.
   B. A. Philip Randolph's threat of a march.
   C. a huge march of African Americans in Washington D.C.
   D. NAACP members met with FDR.

6. The first action of US/British troops came in
   A. Western France.
   B. Southern Italy.
   C. Northern African.
   D. Belgium.

7. D-Day would see Allied troops attack German forces
   A. on the beaches of Normandy.
   B. in the desert of Morocco.
   C. on the coast of Sicily.

D. in the countryside of Belgium.

8. In order to defeat Japan the United States
   A. immediately attacked Tokyo.
   B. employed a system of "island-hopping."
   C. immediately recaptured the Philippines.
   D. immediately recaptured Hong Kong.

9. Japanese intelligence had trouble breaking through American communication lines due to
   A. bad weather.
   B. Navajo code talkers.
   C. advanced communication networks.
   D. counter spies within the U.S. marines.

10. Emperor Hirohito called for a Japanese surrender after
    A. the fire-bombing of Tokyo.
    B. the losses of Okinawa and Iwo Jima.
    C. the bombing of Hiroshima and Nagasaki.
    D. Germany surrendered.

Questions 11-12 refer to the following visual.

11. The message of the poster is
    A. riding alone will make you ride with Hitler.
    B. riding alone will waste gas.
    C. riding alone will make you wealthier.
    D. car-sharing clubs can help you make friends.

11. The group that would benefit the most if people followed the advice of the poster would be
    A. the Nazis.
    B. Consumers.
    C. the U.S. military.
    D. automobile makers.

Questions 13-15 refer to the following document.

Executive Order No. 9066
The President
Executive Order
Authorizing the Secretary of War to Prescribe Military Areas

Whereas the successful prosecution of the war requires every possible protection against espionage and against sabotage to national-defense material, national-defense premises, and national-defense utilities as defined in Section 4, Act of April 20, 1918, 40 Stat. 533, as amended by the Act of November 30, 1940, 54 Stat. 1220, and the Act of August 21, 1941, 55 Stat. 655 (U.S.C., Title 50, Sec. 104); Now, therefore, by virtue of the authority vested in me as President of the United States, and Commander in Chief of the Army and Navy, I hereby authorize and direct the Secretary of War, and the Military Commanders whom he may from time to time designate, whenever he or any designated Commander deems such action necessary or desirable, to prescribe military areas in such places and of such extent as he or the appropriate Military Commander may determine, from which any or all persons may be excluded, and with respect to which, the right of any person to enter, remain in, or leave shall be subject to whatever restrictions the Secretary of War or the appropriate Military Commander may impose in his discretion. The Secretary of War is hereby authorized to provide for residents of any such area who are excluded therefrom, such transportation, food, shelter, and other accommodations as may be necessary, in the judgment of the Secretary of War or the said Military Commander, and until other arrangements are made, to accomplish the purpose of this order. The designation of military areas in any region or locality shall supersede designations of prohibited and restricted areas by the Attorney General under the Proclamations of December 7 and 8, 1941, and shall supersede the responsibility and authority of the Attorney General under the said Proclamations in respect of such prohibited and restricted areas.

Franklin D. Roosevelt
The White House,
February 19, 1942

13. How times does Roosevelt use the term "Japanese" in the Executive Order?
    A. five
    B. once
    C. several
    D. not once

14. The internment of the Japanese in the United States applied to people of
   A. Nisei descent.
   B. Isei descent.
   C. both Nisei and Isei descent.
   D. Asian descent.

15. The "military areas" from which Japanese residents were removed from referred to
   A. the East Coast.
   B. the West Coast.
   C. all of the United States.
   D. Hawaii.

Questions 16-18 refer to the following document.

MEMORANDUM FOR GENERAL ARNOLD

SUBJECT: Groves Project

1. The following plan and schedule for initial attacks using special bombs have been worked out:
a. The first bomb (gun type) will be ready to drop between August 1 and 10 and plans are to drop it the first day of good weather following readiness.
b. The following targets have been selected: Hiroshima, Kokura, Niigata and Nagasaki.
(1) Hiroshima (population 350,000) is an "Army" city; a major POE; has large QM and supply depots; has considerable industry and several small shipyards.
(2) Nagasaki (population 210,000) is a major shipping and industrial center of Kyushu.
(3) Kokura (population 178,000) has one of the largest army arsenals and ordnance works; has the largest railroad shops on Kyushu: and has large munitions storage to the south.
(4) Niigata (population 150,000) is an important industrial city, building machine tools, diesel engines, etc., and is a key port for shipping to the mainland.
c. All four cities are believed to contain large numbers of key Japanese industrialists and political figures who have sought refuge from major destroyed cities.
d. The attack is planned to be visual to insure accuracy and will await favorable weather. The four targets give a very high probability of one being open even if the weather varies from that forecast, as they are considerably separated.
e. The bomb will be carried in a master airplane accompanied by two other project B-29's with observers and special instruments.
f. The three B-29's will take off from North Field Tinian, and fly via Iwo Jima. The use of fighter escort will be determined by General Spaatz upon consideration of all operational factors.
g. The master plane will attack the selected target from [?] feet plus altitude will immediately upon release of the bomb make a steep diving turn away from the target to achieve maximum slant range distance as quickly as possible. Recording planes and fighters if employed will be kept several miles from the target. The participating planes are believed to be safe from the effects of the bomb.
h. The bomb will be detonated by radar proximiter fuze about 2,000 feet above the ground.
i. Emergency arrangements have been provided at Iwo Jima for handling the bomb if required.

2. Two tested type bombs are expected to be available in August, one about the 6th and another the 24th. General Groves expects to have more information on future availabilities in a few days which will be furnished you when received.

3. The above has been discussed with Generals Spaatz and Eaker who concur.

JOHN N. STONE
Colonel, GSC

16. The "special bombs" that Colonel Stone refers to are
    A. hydrogen bombs.
    B. atomic bombs.
    C. incendiary bombs.
    D. heavy water bombs.

17. Hiroshima and Nagasaki were chosen as designated targets because
    A. of their populations.
    B. of their industry and military importance.
    C. they were homes to high ranking government officials.
    D. they were breeding grounds for Kamikaze pilots.

18. Why was the atomic bomb detonated 2000 feet above the ground?
    A. It would be seen over great distances.
    B. Its impact would be maximized over great distances.
    C. It would serve as a warning.
    D. The pilots were ensured that they exploded.

Questions 19-21 refer to the following excerpt.

When the defense program began and billions of the taxpayers' money were appropriated for guns, ships, tanks and bombs, Negroes presented themselves for work only to be given the cold shoulder. North as well as South, and despite their qualifications, Negroes were denied skilled employment. Not until their wrath and indignation took the form of a proposed protest march on Washington, scheduled for July 1, 1941, did things begin to move in the form of defense jobs for Negroes. The march was postponed by the timely issuance (June 25, 1941) of the famous Executive Order No. 8802 by President Roosevelt. But this order and the President's Committee on Fair Employment Practice, established thereunder, have as yet only scratched the surface by way of eliminating discriminations on account of race or color in war industry. Both management and labor unions in too many places and in too many ways are still drawing the color line.

The March on Washington Movement is essentially a movement of the people. It is all Negro and pro-Negro, but not for that reason anti-white or anti-Semitic, or anti-Catholic, or anti-foreign, or anti-labor. Its major weapon is the non-violent demonstration of Negro mass power. Negro leadership has united back of its drive for jobs and justice. "Whether Negroes should march on Washington, and if so, when?" will be the focus of a forthcoming national conference. For the plan of a protest march has not been abandoned. Its purpose would be to demonstrate that

American Negroes are in deadly earnest, and all out for their full rights. No power on earth can cause them today to abandon their fight to wipe out every vestige of second class citizenship and the dual standards that plague them.

A community is democratic only when the humblest and weakest person can enjoy the highest civil, economic, and social rights that the biggest and most powerful possess. To trample on these rights of both Negroes and poor whites is such a commonplace in the South that it takes readily to anti-social, anti-labor, anti-Semitic and anti-Catholic propaganda. It was because of laxness in enforcing the Weimar constitution in republican Germany that Nazism made headway. Oppression of the Negroes in the United States, like suppression of the Jews in Germany, may open the way for a fascist dictatorship.

By fighting for their rights now, American Negroes are helping to make America a moral and spiritual arsenal of democracy. Their fight against the poll tax, against lynch law, segregation, and Jim Crow, their fight for economic, political, and social equality, thus becomes part of the global war for freedom.

--A. Philip Randolph, "Why Should We March?," 1942

19. What did FDR get in return for issuing Executive Order 8802?
    A. African Americans agreed to work for lower wages.
    B. Randolph cancelled his proposed march in Washington D. C.
    C. Randolph agreed to be silent in regards to racial matters.
    D. Blacks would not compare their treatment in France to that in the United States.

20. What did Randolph compare the oppression of Negroes in the United States to?
    A. Japanese oppression of the Chinese in Manchuria
    B. Spanish treatment of communists
    C. Nazi suppression of the Jews
    D. Soviet suppression of dissenters

21. What did Randolph's actions during World War II pave the way for?
    A. Civil Rights Movement of the fifties and sixties
    B. political appointments in FDR's cabinet
    C. immediate segregation of public places during the 1940s
    D. overtime-like pay for African Americans

SHORT ANSWER QUESTIONS

The United States enters World War II in 1941.

    a. Choose ONE of the following and explain why your choice represents the event that led to the entrance of the US into World War II.

- Japanese attack Pearl Harbor
- US ships fighting undeclared war with Germany
- Germany conquers Europe

    b. Contrast your choice against ONE of the other options, demonstrating why that option in not as significant as your choice.

LONG ESSAY QUESTION

In what way did women and minorities assist in the effort to defeat the Axis Powers?

ANSWERS AND EXPLANATIONS

Multiple Choice Questions

1. B Through Lend-Lease, FDR found a loophole to get around the Neutrality Acts.
2. C By supplying England, US ships found themselves targets of Nazi submarines.
3. D The government established price ceilings during World War II.
4. D Ford factories were located primarily in Michigan.
5. B Not wanting to show major dissent within the nation, FDR ordered for the end of hiring discrimination in the defense industries.
6. C Much to the displeasure of Stalin, the U.S. and England began their assault on German forces in Africa.
7. A D-Day occurred in western France along the beaches of Normandy.
8. B The U.S. would skip over Japanese occupied islands on their quest to reach Japan.
9. B Navajo codes could not be deciphered by the Japanese.
10. C The utter destruction of Hiroshima and Nagasaki led the emperor to surrender
11. B Wasting gas at home would help Hitler abroad.
12. A Not having enough fuel for American forces would definitely help the Nazis.
13. D Surprisingly, Executive Order 9066 does not use the term "Japanese" at all even though it directly affected them.
14. C Whether a person was a citizen or not, if he/she was of Japanese descent, they had to evacuate to internment camps.
15. B The military zone the executive order refers to is essentially the West Coast.
16. B Colonel Stone referred to atomic bombs that would be used against Japan.

17. B These cities were particularly important in helping the Japanese fight the war.
18. A Detonation in the air would spread much further than detonation on the ground.
19. B Randolph called off his march after FDR conceded to end hiring discrimination in the defense industries.
20. C Randolph viewed America's treatment of blacks as just as shameful as the Nazi treatment of the Jews.
21. A Randolph helped to set the stage for a major civil rights movement during the fifties and sixties.

Long Essay Question

In what way did women and minorities assist in the effort to defeat the Axis Powers?

(Key topics to focus and elaborate on)
- Women work in the factories and serve in military
- African Americans and work in the factories and serve in the military
- Mexicans work as braceros and work in the shipyards
- Japanese and Native Americans serve in the military

Chapter 24
THE WORLD THE WAR CREATED, 1945-1952

- The aftermath of World War II brought significant changes to Americans living in this atomic age.

THE UNITED STATES IN 1945--A CHANGED COUNTRY IN A CHANGED WORLD

- During the war penicillin and streptomycin had been invented and many other medicines had been created shortly after the war.
- Consumers found a variety of goods that were unavailable during the war including the automobile. The postwar era also featured the explosion of television sales.
- Underlying the innovations and prosperity of the postwar era was the atomic bomb. The United States lost its monopoly, and thus its security, when the Soviet Union successfully detonated its first atomic bomb in 1949.
- Shortly after, both the U.S. and Soviet Union detonated hydrogen bombs in 1952 and 1953 respectively.
- Many soldiers had a hard time adjusting to civilian life, but the government tried to ease this adjustment with the GI Bill.
- After the war a baby boom era had begun and the growth of suburban neighborhoods skyrocketed as well.
- Levittown served as a model for suburban homes in which construction crews could build thirty houses a day.
- Owning a home became a dream come true for many, and because of suburbs such as Levittown, this dream became not just a reality, but the norm…except for African Americans who were not allowed to live in these types of neighborhoods.
- Many found the conformity of suburbia to be difficult if not unthinkable such as single women or members of the "beat generation."
- The Great Migration would not only continue but accelerate during the wartime and postwar periods, especially with dissipation of the sharecropping system in the South due to the mechanized cotton harvester.
- The fleeing of whites to suburbia opened up urban housing for blacks, but these neighborhoods were without means for home improvement. Consequently, black ghettos emerged in the nation's cash-strapped cities.
- The Great Migration was met with fierce white resistance who maintained a rigid pattern of segregation with blacks in the cities, and whites in the suburbs.
- At the same time, new opportunities in voting and business opened up for blacks who moved to the north.
- Latinos also experienced a life of migration especially for the Puerto Rican and Mexican populations. Puerto Ricans migrated largely to Spanish Harlem in New York City where they faced intense discrimination.

- Mexican braceros migrated to the Southwest during the war. The bracero program continued into the sixties but others simply walked across the border and constantly faced the threat of being deported. California became the state that witnessed Mexican-Americans fighting for their rights to end school segregation, and electing Mexican-American candidates to office.
- The changing social scene in the United States would be accompanied by a changing political and economic scene in world affairs.
- The International Monetary Fund aimed to stabilize exchange rates for buying and selling purposes, provide loans to nations, and to provide technical assistance to banks.
- The World Bank was designed to assist in the economic recovery of Europe and to reduce world poverty in places such as Latin America, Africa, and Asia.
- In 1944, the basic structure of the United Nations was formed with its first meeting convening in San Francisco and that same year the U.S .Senate ratified the UN Charter.

THE COLD WAR BEGINS

- During World War II, the United States and the Soviet Union were Allies, but after the war they became bitter enemies for the duration of four decades.
- Whereas FDR was more diplomatic to the Soviet Union, as least verbally, Truman proved to be blunter and openly stern.
- Yet at the Potsdam Conference in 1945, Truman tried to keep the Soviets assurance that they would assist in the fight against Japan once the war in Europe was over. But in 1946, Stalin called for communism around the world, thus leading the U.S. to practice a policy of containment.
- Churchill's "iron curtain" confirmed the division in Europe between the west and the east.
- The Truman Doctrine became an example of American containment in stopping Soviet communism from spreading.
- Similarly, the Marshall Plan, which gave aid for the recovery of Western Europe, was also design to keep Soviet communism from spreading to this region.
- To cut off supplies from West Berlin, a city that the U.S., France, and England controlled, Stalin ordered a blockade which was followed by the Berlin Airlift.
- As the Berlin crisis came to a close, the U.S. joined the North Atlantic Treaty Organization, a move that was unprecedented for the U.S. since previously it had never joined an alliance during peacetime. The Soviets responded with their own alliance known as the Warsaw Pact.
- The Cold War became even more intense when the Soviet Union exploded its first atomic bomb and Mao Tse-tung enforced communist rule in China by forcing Chiang Kai-shek to flee to Taiwan.
- As the U.S. fought a Cold War abroad, it also fought one at home. In particular, the fifties proved to be a decade of intense fear that there were communist enemies within.
- Alger Hiss, a former State Department official, was accused of spying for the Soviets in the 1930s, Julius and Ethel Rosenberg were executed for providing top-

secret atomic information to the Soviet Union, and Joseph McCarthy accused various officials and government workers of being communists who plotted to overtake the nation.

- Americans were deeply concerned over the Rosenberg incident, but even more concerned and stirred with the accusations that Joseph McCarthy was making. Though McCarthy never revealed a name in his list, he was still immensely popular amongst Americans given the climate of fear that surrounded the nation at that time. Although, he lost most of this popularity after televised Senate hearings in 1954.

- Within this communist fear, the House Committee on Un-American Activities held hearings to investigate whether Hollywood harbored communist sympathizers.

- Anti-communism would see a purge of members of various unions, civil rights groups, school districts, and universities.

- As the fear of communist infiltration began and intensified, a war broke out in Korea. The war featured the communist North Korea attacking the U.S.-backed South Korea in an attempt to overtake the peninsula. Under General Douglass MacArthur, U.S. and UN forces eventually drove back the North Koreans to the 38th parallel, but not before Chinese forces intervened and drove American forces back to South Korea.

- Consequently, MacArthur asked to broaden the scope of the war, but instead was fired by Truman. An armistice was finally signed in 1953.

- On the home front, Truman called for a sweeping agenda of domestic policy, including fair employment, but the Republicans met this agenda with strong opposition. Truman, however, was successful in desegregating the military.

- In addition, Truman supported the creation of Israel as a safe haven for Jews, despite concern for the reaction of Arabs in the Middle East.

- During the Election of 1948, two factions of the Democratic Party broke away to oppose Truman by forming two parties, the Progressive Party, and the Dixiecrats. The Republicans ran Thomas Dewey, who seemed to have won, but lost a close election to Truman.

- Though Truman's Fair Deal had lofty intentions, most of it never passed, and the anti-union Taft-Hartley Act was not repealed as well.

- The Election of 1952 saw war hero, Dwight D. Eisenhower win a sound victory over the Democrat, Adlai Stevenson, to become president.

- Upon entering the presidency, Eisenhower was able to end the Korean War, an achievement that eluded Truman.

- Though a conservative, Eisenhower was too wise to even suggest of eliminating Social Security. In fact, he maintained the internationalism of Truman as well.

MULTIPLE CHOICE QUESTIONS

1. In 1955, a scientists discovered a vaccine for
   A. influenza.
   B. polio.
   C. chicken pox.
   D. Measles.

2. The post-World War II era featured all of the following EXCEPT
   A. a baby boom.
   B. a Cold War.
   C. advances in medicine.
   D. diverse suburban neighborhoods.

3. 1949 proved to be a fearful one in that
   A. Germany began to rearm.
   B. Hideki Tojo regained military power in Japan.
   C. the Soviets detonated their first atomic bomb.
   D. the Rosenbergs were accused of spying.

4. Levittown featured all of the following EXCEPT
   A. curved roads and streets.
   B. twelve-by-sixteen-foot living rooms.
   C. variety of home models.
   D. eventual homes for 82,000 people.

5. A major factor that led to a continued migration of African Americans from the South to the North was
   A. cotton picker machine.
   B. decrease in cotton production.
   C. entertainment opportunities.
   D. low rent costs in the North.

6. In joining the North Atlantic Treaty Organization (NATO), the United States
   A. joined an alliance for the first time when there was no war.
   B. joined the Soviet Union in an arms reduction agreement.
   C. joined forces with Poland.
   D. vowed to free Eastern Europe from Soviet control.

7. Despite the Berlin Blockade, the U.S. continued to supply West Berlin by
   A. breaking through Soviet tank forces.
   B. using a secret underground tunnel.
   C. airlifting supplies.
   D. negotiating with Stalin to end the blockade.

8. The intention of the Marshall Plan was to
   A.   provide aid to Turkey and Greece to deter the threat of communism.
   B.   help Western Europe to recover from war and deter the threat of communism.
   C.   provide machinery to the Soviet Union.
   D.   rebuild Japan with a democratic government.

9. Julius and Ethel Rosenberg were convicted and executed for
   A.   providing atomic information to the Soviet Union.
   B.   establishing the Communist Party.
   C.   stealing information regarding the hydrogen bomb.
   D.   sabotaging nuclear labs.

10. The U.S. military forces were desegregated under the presidency of
    A.   FDR.
    B.   Harry Truman.
    C.   Dwight D. Eisenhower.
    D.   John F. Kennedy.

Questions 11-12 refer to the following visual.

11. The creature in this pamphlet represents
    A.   Father Charles Coughlin.
    B.   Franklin D. Roosevelt.
    C.   Vladimir Lenin.
    D.   Josef Stalin.

12. This pamphlet came out in the 1930s. What does this visual and date suggest?
    A.   that communism had already taken control of the world.
    B.   that a Cold War existed even before World War II ended.
    C.   that containment would not work.
    D.   that communism was inevitable and efforts to stop it were useless.

Questions 13-15 refer to the following document.

Mrs. Gould: As editors and parents we are extremely interested in this whole problem. The welfare of our society depends upon the type of children you young mothers and others like you are able to bring up.

Miss Hickey: And understanding. I think there is a lack of understanding, too. Since it would take all day to tell what a busy woman does all day...how about your high points?

Mrs. Petry: I would say in the morning - breakfast and wash time. I put the breakfast out, leave the children to eat it and run into the bathroom - that is where the washer is - and fill it up. I come back into the kitchen and shove a little in the baby's mouth and try to keep the others eating. Then I go back in the bathroom and put the clothes in the wringer and start the rinse water. That is about the end of the half-hour there. I continue then to finish the wash, and either put them out or let them see one program they like on television, and then I go out and hang the wash up...

Miss Hickey: You work on schedule quite a bit. Why do you do that?

Mrs. Petty: Because I am very forgetful. I have an orange crayon and I write "defrost" on the refrigerator every now and then, or I forget to defrost it. If I think of something while I am washing, I write it on the mirror with an eyebrow pencil. It must sound silly, but that is the only way I can remember every-thing I have to do...

Miss Hickey: How often do you and your husband go out together in the evening?

Mrs. Ehrhardt: Not often. An occasional movie, which might be every couple of months or so, on an anniversary...

Miss Hickey: Let us hear about Mrs. Petry's recreation.

Mrs. Petty: Oh, I went to work in a department store that opened in Levittown. I begged and begged my husband to let me work, and finally he said I could go once or twice a week. I lasted for three weeks, or should I say he lasted for three weeks.

Mrs. Gould: You mean you worked in the daytime?

Mrs. Petry: Three evenings, from six until nine, and on Saturday.

Mrs. Gould: And your husband took care of the children during that time?

Mrs. Petry: Yes, but the third week, he couldn't stand it anymore...My husband was hoping they would fire me, but they didn't. But I could see that it wasn't really fair to him, because I was going out for my own pleasure.

Mrs. Gould: In other words, your working was your recreation.

Mrs. Petry: Yes, and I enjoyed it very much.

Miss Hickey: Why did you feel you wanted to do this?

Mrs. Petry: To see some people and talk to people, just to see what is going on in the world...

Miss Hickey: How about your shopping experiences?

Mrs. McKenzie: Usually all three of the children go shopping with me. At one time I carried two and dragged the other one along behind me in the cart with the groceries.

It is fun to take them all. Once a man stopped me and said, "Lady, did you know your son is eating ham-burger?" He had eaten a half-pound of raw hamburger.

Miss Hickey: You go once a week?

Mrs. McKenzie: Once a week or every ten days now, depending on how often I have the use of the car. That day we usually go to the park, too...

Dr. Montagu: There is one very large question I would like to ask. What in your lives, as they are at present, would you most like to see changed or modified?

Mrs. Petry: I would like more time to enjoy my children. I do take time, but if I do take as much time as I like, the work piles up. When I go back to work I feel crabby, and I don't know whether I'm mad at the children, or mad at the work or just mad at everybody sometimes.

I would also like to have a little more rest and a little more time to spend in relaxation with my husband.

--"Young Mother," *Ladies Home Journal*, 1956

13. The same article may have been different during the World War II era for all of the following reasons *except*
    A. the husband being off to war would've doubled the work.
    B. more women would've been in the military.
    C. more women would've been factory workers instead of housewives.
    D. women would've filled roles left behind.

14. Why did Mrs.Petry view work at the department store as recreation?
    A. the workers played games during break.
    B. the business world featured a less rigid environment than previous decades.
    C. managers had contests to see who could sell more products.
    D. work was a way to escape the home and meet new people.

15. The article in *Ladies Home Journal* suggests that
    A. men were eager to share homemaking duties.
    B. housewives were completely happy with their role in society.
    C. housewives were terrified at the prospect of working outside the home.
    D. women were not completely satisfied with their roles as housewives.

Questions 16-18 refer to the following document.

Two complex sets of factors have now basically altered this historical distribution of power. First, the defeat of Germany and Japan and the decline of the British and French Empires have interacted with the development of the United States and the Soviet Union in such a way that power has increasingly gravitated to these two centers. Second, the Soviet Union, unlike previous aspirants to hegemony, is animated by a new fanatic faith, antithetical to our own, and seeks to impose its absolute authority over the rest of the world. Conflict has, therefore, become endemic and is waged, on the part of the Soviet Union, by violent or non-violent methods in accordance with the dictates of expediency. With the development of increasingly terrifying weapons of mass destruction, every individual faces the ever-present possibility of annihilation should the conflict enter the phase of total war.

It is estimated that, within the next four years, the U.S.S.R. will attain the [atomic] capability of seriously damaging vital centers of the United States, provided it strikes a surprise blow and provided further that the blow is opposed by no more effective opposition than we now have programmed. Such a blow could so seriously damage the United States as to greatly reduce its superiority in economic potential.

Effective opposition to this Soviet capability will require among other measures greatly increased air warning systems, air defenses, and vigorous development and implementation of a civilian defense program which has been thoroughly integrated with the military defense systems.

In the initial phases of an atomic war, the advantages of initiative and surprise would be very great. A police state living behind an iron curtain has an enormous advantage in maintaining the necessary security and centralization of decision required to capitalize on this advantage.

For the moment our atomic retaliatory capability is probably adequate to deter the Kremlin from a deliberate direct military attack against ourselves or other free peoples. However, when it calculates that it has a sufficient atomic capability to make a surprise attack on us, nullifying our atomic superiority and creating a military situation decisively in its favor, the Kremlin might be tempted to strike swiftly and with stealth. The existence of two large atomic capabilities in such a relationship might well act, therefore, not as a deterrent, but as an incitement to war.

A further increase in the number and power of our atomic weapons is necessary in order to assure the effectiveness of any U.S. retaliatory blow, but would not of itself seem to change the basic logic of the above points. Greatly increased general air, ground and sea strength, and increased air defense and civilian defense programs would also be necessary to provide reasonable assurance that the free world could survive an initial surprise atomic attack of the weight which it is estimated the U.S.S.R. will be capable of delivering by 1954 and still permit the free world to go on to the eventual attainment of its objectives. Furthermore, such a build-up of strength could safeguard and increase our retaliatory power, and thus might put off for some time the date when the Soviet Union could calculate that a surprise blow would be advantageous. This would provide additional time for the effects of our policies to produce a modification of the Soviet system.

--National Security Council Memorandum Number 68, 1950

16. What led to the establishment of two opposing superpowers, the United States and the Soviet Union?
    a. Both countries developed advanced industrial systems.
    b. Both countries harbored democratic political systems.
    c. Germany, Japan, England and France lost their power by the end of World War II.
    d. The U.S. and the Soviet Union both had developed nuclear weapons by the end of 1945.

17. According to NSC 68, the Soviet Union had more capability to launch a surprise attack since
    A. its submarines were positioned close to the United States.
    B.   the Soviets had nuclear missiles ready to launch from Cuba.
    C.   the police state of the Soviet Union lent itself to effective secrecy.
    D.   the United States did not have the resolve to launch an attack without warning.

18. According the NSC 68, the United States needed all of the following to effectively retaliate against a surprise attack EXCEPT
    A.   increase in the number of atomic weapons.
    B.   greatly increased air, ground, and sea strength.
    C.   adequate civil defense program.
    D.   a new authoritative political system to match the Soviet Union.

Questions 19-21 refer to the following excerpt

Five years after a world war has been won, men's hearts should anticipate a long peace, and men's minds should be free from the heavy weight that comes from war. But this is not such a period-for this is not a period of peace. This is a time of the "cold war." This is a time when all the world is split into two vast, increasingly hostile armed camps. . . .

The reason why we find ourselves in a position of impotency is not because our only powerful potential enemy has sent men to invade our shores, but rather because of the traitorous actions of those who have been treated so well by this Nation. It has not been the less fortunate or members of minority groups who have been selling this Nation out, but rather those who have had all the benefits that the wealthiest nation on earth has to offer-the finest homes, the finest college education, and the finest jobs in Government.

This is glaringly true in the State Department. There the bright young men who are born with silver spoons in their mouths are the ones who have been the worst.

. . . In my opinion, the State Department, which is one of the most important government departments, is thoroughly infested with Communists.

I have in my hand 57 cases of individuals who would appear to be either card carrying members or certainly loyal to the Communist Party, but who nevertheless are still helping to shape our foreign policy. . . .

--Joseph R. McCarthy, Wheeling, West Virginia Speech, 1950

19. According to Senator McCarthy, which group endangered the security of the United States the most?
    A.   the poor of the nation
    B.   the nation's minority groups
    C.   wealthy members of the State Department
    D.   the President and his closest advisors

20. Senator McCarthy claimed that this department was infested with communists
    A.   State Department
    B.   Department of the Interior
    C.   Treasury Department
    D.   Justice Department

21. McCarthyism featured all of the following EXCEPT
    A.   accusations against various public officials.
    B.   a paranoid American public.
    C.   solid proof and evidence of his accusations.
    D.   accusations directed at the U.S. Army.

SHORT ANSWER QUESTIONS

Julius and Ethel Rosenberg are executed in 1953.

a. Choose ONE of the following and explain why your choice represents the event that led to their execution.

   - Soviet Union detonates its first atomic bomb.
   - Joseph McCarthy begins McCarthyism
   - The U.S. detonates its first hydrogen bomb

b. Contrast your choice against ONE of the other options, demonstrating why that option in not as significant as your choice.

LONG ESSAY QUESTION

In what way did the United States practice a policy of "containment"?

ANSWERS AND EXPLANATIONS

Multiple Choice Questions

1. B A vaccine for polio proved to be a major medical achievement.
2. D Suburbs were predominantly white.
3. C To the surprise of government officials and America in general, the Soviets exploded an atomic bomb.
4. C Levittown homes were all uniform.
5. A The cotton picker machine left many sharecroppers without jobs.
6. A Previous alliances the U.S. had been in were during wartime.
7. C The Berlin Airlift proved to be a success and an embarrassment for Stalin.

8. B The plan was to both help a war-torn Western Europe recover and to deter the spread of Soviet-influenced communism.
9. A The Rosenbergs gave atomic information they obtained while working on the Manhattan Project to the Soviet Union.
10. B Truman would be the president to make this bold and controversial move (as many saw it at the time).
11. D Josef Stalin was viewed as another Hitler aimed at conquering the world.
12. B There was tension between the U.S. and the Soviet Union even before World War II started.
13. A Husbands were clearly not ready to share housekeeping duties before the sixties.
14. D Working outside the home was a chance to get away from the hustle and bustle of housekeeping duties.
15. D Underlying the presumed fulfillment of working in the home, some women longed for a life outside of it.
16. C World War II left the United States and the Soviet Union as the only two major powers standing.
17. C The closed environment of the Soviet Union allowed it to act in a stealthy manner.
18. D The U.S. did not have any consideration of reverting to a police state such as that seen in the Soviet Union.
19. C According to McCarthy, ungrateful wealthy government workers betrayed the country.
20. A He claimed to have a list of 205 State Department members who were communists.
21. C McCarthy never revealed his list nor any evidence of it.

Long Essay Question

In what way did the United States practice a policy of "containment"?

(Key topics to focus and elaborate on)
* Truman Doctrine
* Marshall Plan
* Korean War
* Berlin Airlift

Chapter 25
COMPLACENCY AND CHANGE, 1952-1965

- Eisenhower continued many of the New Deal's core programs and Truman's approach towards communism and the Cold War. At the same time, the 1950s was a time of great change.

EISENHOWER'S AMERICA, AMERICA'S WORLD

- The introduction of nuclear weapons, in particular hydrogen bombs, ultimately shaped and guided foreign policy of both the United States and the Soviet Union.
- The combined threat of the Soviet Union and the economic impact of continuing defense production, influenced the continual build-up of nuclear weapons.
- In an effort to keep costs down but still protect U.S. interests, Eisenhower instituted a program of mass retaliation. In addition, Eisenhower's foreign policy relied on the use of the Central Intelligence Agency to both gather intelligence of enemies such as the Soviet Union and to place into power pro-U.S. governments throughout the world, such as in Iran and Guatemala.
- Yet, the dissipation of French control of Vietnam was not an easy fix that either the CIA or massive retaliation could solve. After French forces fell at Dien Bien Phu, under the Geneva Accords the French agreed to relinquish control of Vietnam with elections to be held to determine its fate. However the elections were never held and Vietnam would be split into two countries until a war determined its permanent fate.
- The U.S. also dealt with the Suez crisis in which the Eisenhower threatened to send troops to allow Egypt control the Suez Canal.
- The launching of Sputnik by the Soviet Union led to a "space race" between the U.S. and the Soviet Union in which the Soviets initially had the upper hand. However, after the creation of NASA, the U.S. achieved numerous successes including the launching of satellites and landing men on the moon.
- Due to the fear of Soviet superiority in technology, Eisenhower pushed through Congress the National Defense Education Act to improve science education.
- At the same time, Eisenhower who had seen much war in his time, wanted to establish an era of peace with the Soviet Union and both he and Soviet leader Nikita Khrushchev agreed to meet in Paris in 1960. Yet just days before this meeting, the Soviets shot down an American U-2 plane thereby ending any chance of this meeting or peace for that matter. Eisenhower thus left the presidency with the Cold War situation as tense as ever.
- The Election of 1960 featured Catholic and Democratic John F. Kennedy versus Eisenhower's vice president, Richard M. Nixon. The campaign featured two opposites with Kennedy being the more young and charismatic candidate and Nixon presenting a more conservative and aloof character.
- In the end, Kennedy won an extremely close election, making him not only the first Catholic to be elected, but also the youngest person to be elected as well.

A Culture on the Move

- In the 1950s, the popularity of television skyrocketed with a variety of news and entertainment programming that captured the interest of America.
- Programming featured comedy, soap operas, music, westerns, detective stories, investigative journalism, game shows, and a host of other types of shows.
- The automobile would also increase in popularity, with more attractive styles and gas efficiency.
- The Interstate Highway Act promoted automobile transportation with the construction of 41,000 miles of federal interstate highways. The construction of these highways led to urban sprawl, shopping malls, and easier access to both markets and sites of entertainment such as Disneyland.
- In addition, the rise of highways and roads led to the emergence of fast food restaurants and the construction of more hotels and gas stations.
- Along with the boom in automobiles and television, religion also experienced a boom in popularity in the fifties. Billy Graham played a major role in this boost of popularity with various programming and revivals. Numerous religious books also inspired thousands of Americans as well.
- Catholics such as Richard Cardinal Cushing and Monsignor Fulton Sheen also found ways to reach out, not only to Catholics, but to non-Catholics as well.
- Jewish leaders such as Rabbi Abraham Joshua Heschel would help to boost the attendance at synagogues.
- The attendance of African American churches also grew both in the North and the South with church leaders such as "Sweet Daddy" Grace leading the way.
- Religion also made its way into the political scene when Congress voted to add the phrase "one nation under God" to the Pledge of Allegiance to the Flag.
- The birth of rock n' roll came in the fifties with Elvis Presley becoming one the nation's most popular stars. Many saw Elvis, his music, and his movements as the epitome of the immorality that had begun to surface in America. This was especially the case with the issuing of Playboy and novels that contained scandalous affairs.
- Beatniks such as Jack Kerouac and Allen Ginsberg also wrote novels that dissented against the norm of society.

Race and Civil Rights

- Segregation had long been the norm for African Americans since the end of Reconstruction, especially in the South. However, the fifties became a decade in which segregation gradually started to disappear.
- Yet, desegregation did not happen overnight. Various court cases would chip away at segregation, including the groundbreaking case of *Brown v. Board of Education of Topeka* which banned segregation in public schools. White resistance to integration was fierce, as seen with the protests at Central High School in Little Rock, Arkansas; an incident that witnessed Eisenhower sending in troops to enforce the court's decision.
- In 1955, Rosa Parks defied a bus segregation law and refused to give up her seat for white passengers. Her arrest sparked a massive bus boycott in Montgomery, Alabama.

The boycott proved to be effective and the Martin Luther King's passive resistance began to take hold of the civil rights movement, and in 1956 the Supreme Court ruled in favor of Rosa Parks and her defiance of bus segregation.

- Protesting against segregation continued when in 1960 four African American students refused to leave their seats at a North Carolina lunch counter. The "sit-in" protest as it became known spread rapidly throughout the South despite harassment and occasional beatings.
- After the Supreme Court ruled that segregation on interstate transportation was unconstitutional, "Freedom Riders" aimed to hasten the integration of buses, and were met with fierce resistance, including resistance from the Ku Klux Klan.
- In an effort to desegregate the heavily segregated city of Birmingham, Alabama, King and several other were arrested, but other protesters continued to march and were attacked by the police with fire hoses and police dogs.
- That same year in 1963, a massive march on the nation's capital occurred during which Martin Luther King Jr. gave his famous, "I Have a Dream" speech.
- In the meantime, Southern college students organized SNCC as a means to assist in the Civil Rights Movement by creating a massive student-led campaign for voter registration.
- The political process in Mississippi was also challenged when the Mississippi Freedom Democratic Party formed to challenge the all-white delegation to the 1963 Democratic Convention. The movement brought national attention to the issue of blacks and their inclusion in the democratic process.
- In the North, the leader that emerged to challenge the inequality between blacks and whites was Malcolm X. After joining the Nation of Islam in 1952, he became one of its leading spokesmen and urged blacks to separate themselves from the "white devils".
- His views changed after a pilgrimage to Mecca and thus became accepting of the white race. In regard to the struggles of the American Negro, he intended to bring his case to the United Nations. More importantly, he harnessed a sense of black pride amongst the African American community, a value that would continue even after his assassination in 1965.

MULTIPLE CHOICE QUESTIONS

1. The U.S. "policy of massive retaliation" referred to
   A. the radical plan to desegregate the south.
   B. the threat of using the hydrogen bomb to deter Soviet expansion.
   C. the threat of Ho Chi Minh to conquer Vietnam.
   D. the Soviet threat of seizing Berlin.

2. The world's first satellite that the Soviets launched in 1957 was called
   A. Vanguard.
   B. Flopnik.
   C. Sputnik.
   D. U-2.

3. The Interstate Highway system came at the urging of
   A. Franklin D. Roosevelt.
   B. Harry S. Truman.
   C. Dwight D. Eisenhower.
   D. John F. Kennedy.

4. The Supreme Court decision that banned segregation in public schools was
   A. *Plessy v. Ferguson.*
   B. *Mendez v. Westminster.*
   C. *Roberts v. City of Boston.*
   D. *Brown v. Board of Education of Topeka.*

5. The main theme of Norman Vincent Peale's *The Power of Positive Thinking* was
   A. positive thinking could make you rich.
   B. believe in yourself.
   C. think and grow rich.
   D. Nonconformity.

6. The case of *Brown v. Board of Education* overturned the "separate but equal" premise of
   A. *Sweat v. Painter.*
   B. *McLaurin v. Oklahoma State Regents.*
   C. *Plessy v. Ferguson.*
   D. *Alston v. School Board of the City of Norfolk.*

7. To uphold the decision of the Supreme Court at Central High School in Little Rock, Arkansas, President Eisenhower
   A. threatened to shut down the school.
   B. sent US troops to ensure the safety of the black students.
   C. relied on the Little Rock Police Department.
   D. threatened to halt federal funding to the school.

8. To deal with the bus boycott that African Americans organized in Montgomery, Alabama, protesters did all of the following *except*
   A. quit their jobs.
   B. walked to work.
   C. car pooled.
   D. rode on taxis.

9. The goal of the Southern Christian Leadership Council was to
   A. use violence to achieve equality.
   B. speak in a militant voice.
   C. use non-violence to achieve equality.
   D. separate from all whites.

10. The March of Washington D. C. was suggested by
    A. Martin Luther King Jr.
    B. A. Philip Randolph.
    C. Malcolm X.
    D. Elijah Muhammad.

Questions 11-12 refer to the following visual.

11. The purpose of the march on Washington D.C. was to
    A. end segregation in public schools.
    B. ban segregation in interstate transportation.
    C. support a civil rights bill.
    D. pass an amendment for black suffrage.

12. A main theme of King's "I Have a Dream" speech was
    A. black pride.
    B. integration of the races.
    C. anti-lynching violence.
    D. affirmative action.

Questions 13-15 refer to the following excerpt.

We regard the decision of the Supreme Court in the school cases as a clear abuse of judicial power. It climaxes a trend in the Federal judiciary undertaking to legislate, in derogation of the authority of Congress, and to encroach upon the reserved rights of the States and the people.

The original Constitution does not mention education. Neither does the 14th amendment nor any other amendment. The debates preceding the submission of the 14th amendment clearly show that there was no intent that it should affect the systems of education maintained by the States.

The very Congress which proposed the amendment subsequently provided for segregated schools in the District of Columbia.

When the amendment was adopted, in 1868, there were 37 States of the Union. Every one of the 26 States that had any substantial racial differences among its people either approved the operation of segregated schools already in existence or subsequently established such schools by action of the same lawmaking body which considered the 14th amendment...

This interpretation, restated time and again... It is founded on elemental humanity and commonsense, for parents should not be deprived by Government of the right to direct the lives and education of their own children.

Though there has been no constitutional amendment or act of Congress changing this established legal principle almost a century old, the Supreme Court of the United States, with no legal basis for such action, undertook to exercise their naked judicial power and substituted their personal political and social ideas for the established law of the land...

Without regard to the consent of the governed, outside agitators are threatening immediate and revolutionary changes in our public-school systems. If done, this is certain to destroy the system of public education in some of the States.

With the gravest concern for the explosive and dangerous condition created by this decision and inflamed by outside meddlers:

We reaffirm our reliance on the Constitution as the fundamental law of the land.

We decry the Supreme Court's encroachments on rights reserved to the States and to the people, contrary to established law and to the Constitution...

Even though we constitute a minority in the present Congress, we have full faith that a majority of the American people believe in the dual system of Government which has enabled us to achieve our greatness and will in time demand that the reserved rights of the State and of the people be made secure against judicial usurpation.

We pledge ourselves to use all lawful means to bring about a reversal of this decision which is contrary to the Constitution and to prevent the use of force in its implementation.

In this trying period, as we all seek to right this wrong, we appeal to our people not to be provoked by the agitators and troublemakers invading our States and to scrupulously refrain from disorders and lawless acts.

Signed by:

[Nineteen] Members of the United States Senate

[Eighty-one] Members of the United States House of Representatives

--The Southern Manifesto, 1956

13. The Southern Manifesto came in response to the court case of
    A. *Plessy v. Ferguson.*
    B. *Mendez v. Westminster.*
    C. *Roberts v. City of Boston.*
    D. *Brown v. Board of Education of Topeka.*

14. What contradiction does the Manifesto point out in regard to the court decision that banned the segregation of schools in 1954 and the schools established immediately after the passage of the 14th Amendment?
    A. The schools established during Reconstruction were desegregated.
    B. No schools for blacks were created during Reconstruction.
    C. The very founders of the 14th Amendment created segregated schools.
    D. The 14th Amendment did not protect peoples' rights.

15. What amendment did the *Southern Manifest* believe the 1955 court decision violated?
    A. 10th Amendment
    B. 14th Amendment
    C. 15th Amendment
    D. 19th Amendment

Questions 16-18 refer to the following excerpt.

We come then to the question presented: Does segregation of children in public schools solely on the basis of race, even though the physical facilities and other "tangible" factors may be equal, deprive the children of the minority group of equal education opportunities? We believe that it does.

In Sweatt v. Painter . . . in finding that a segregated law school for Negroes could not provide them equal education opportunities, the Court relied in large part on "those qualities which are incapable of objective measurement but which make for greatness in a law school." In McLaurin v. Oklahoma State Regents . . . the Court, in requiring that a Negro admitted to a white graduate school be treated like all other students, again resorted to intangible considerations: ". . . his ability to study, to engage in discussions and exchange views with other students, and in general, to learn his profession." Such considerations apply with added force to children in grade and high schools. To separate them from others of similar age and qualifications solely because of their race generates a feeling of inferiority as to their status in the community that may affect their hearts and minds in a way unlikely ever to be undone. The effect of this separation on their educational opportunities was well stated by a finding in the Kansas case by a court which nevertheless felt compelled to rule against the Negro plaintiffs:

Segregation of white and colored children in public schools has a detrimental effect upon the colored children. The impact is greater when it has the sanction of the law; for the policy of separating the races is usually interpreted as denoting the inferiority of the Negro group. A sense of inferiority affects the motivation of a child to learn. Segregation with the sanction of law, therefore, has a tendency to retard the education and mental development of negro children and to deprive them of some of the benefits they would receive in a racial[ly] integrated school system.

Whatever may have been the extent of psychological knowledge at the time of Plessy v. Ferguson, this finding is amply supported by modern authority. Any language in Plessy v. Ferguson contrary to this finding is rejected.

We conclude that in the field of public education the doctrine of "separate but equal" has no place. Separate educational facilities are inherently unequal. Therefore, we hold that the plaintiffs and others similarly situated for whom the actions have been brought are, by reason of the segregation complained of, deprived of the equal protection of the laws guaranteed by the Fourteenth Amendment. This disposition makes unnecessary any discussion whether such segregation also violates the Due Process Clause of the Fourteenth Amendment.

16. According to the Supreme Court, the separation of the races is usually interpreted as
    A. the superiority of the Negro group.
    B. the inferiority of the Negro group.
    C. the equality of the Negro group.
    D. a distinction that has no effect at all.

17. How did the Supreme Court view the separate educational facilities of the nation?
    A. inherently unequal
    B. inherently equal
    C. modern and progressive
    D. separate but equal

18. According to the Supreme Court, segregation in schools violated the 14ᵗʰ Amendment in that
    A. segregation denied the citizenship of southern blacks.
    B. segregation deprived blacks of equal protection of the laws.

C. segregation promoted a sense of uniqueness amongst blacks.

D. segregated schools were always equal but separate.

Questions 19-21 refer to the following excerpt.

Life Magazine Identifies the New Teenage Market, 1959

To some people the vision of a leggy adolescent happily squealing over the latest fancy present from Daddy is just another example of the way teen-agers are spoiled to death these days. But to a growing number of businessmen the picture spells out the profitable fact that the American teen-agers have emerged as a big-time consumer in the U.S. economy. They are multiplying in numbers. They spend more and have more spent on them. And they have minds of their own about what they want. The time is past when a boy's chief possession was his bike and a girl's party wardrobe consisted of a fancy dress worn with a string of dime-store pearls. What Depression-bred parents may still think of as luxuries are looked on as necessities by their offspring. Today teen-agers surround themselves with a fantastic array of garish and often expensive baubles and amusements. They own 10 million phonographs, over a million TV sets, 13 million cameras. Nobody knows how much parents spend on them for actual necessities nor to what extent teen-agers act as hidden persuaders on their parents' other buying habits. Counting only what is spent to satisfy their special teen-age demands, the youngsters and their parents will shell out about $10 billion this year, a billion more than the total sales of GM. Until recently businessmen have largely ignored the teen-age market. But now they are spending millions on advertising and razzle-dazzle promotional stunts. Their efforts so far seem only to have scratched the surface of a rich lode. In 1970, when the teen-age population expands from its present 18 million to 28 million, the market may be worth $20 billion. If parents have any idea of organized revolt, it is already too late. Teenage spending is so important that such action would send quivers through the entire national economy.... At 17 Suzie Slattery of Van Nuys, Calif. fits any businessman's dream of the ideal teen-age consumer. The daughter of a reasonably well-to-do TV announcer, Suzie costs her parents close to $4,000 a year, far more than average for the country but not much more than many of the upper middle income families of her town. In an expanding economy more and more teen-agers will be moving up into Suzie's bracket or be influenced as consumers by her example. Last year $1,500 was spent on Suzie's clothes and $550 for her entertainment. Her annual food bill comes to $900. She pays $4 every two weeks at the beauty parlor. She has her own telephone and even has her own soda fountain in the house. On summer vacation days she loves to wander with her mother through fashionable department stores, picking out frocks or furnishings for her room or silver and expensive crockery for the hope chest she has already started. As a high school graduation present, Suzie was given a holiday cruise to Hawaii and is now in the midst of a new clothes-buying spree for college. Her parents' constant indulgence has not spoiled Suzie. She takes for granted all the luxuries that surround her because she has had them all her life. But she also has a good mind and some serious interests. A top student in her school, she is entering Occidental College this fall and will major in political science....

SOME FASCINATING FACTS ABOUT A BOOMING MARKET

FOOD: Teen-agers eat 20% more than adults. They down 3 1/2 billion quarts of milk every year, *almost four times as much as is drunk by the infant population under 1. Teen-agers are a main prop of the ice cream industry, gobbling 145 million gallons a year. BEAUTY CARE: Teen-agers spent $20 million on lipstick last year, $25 million on deodorants (a fifth of total sold), $9 million on home permanents. Male teenagers own 2 million electric razors. ENTERTAINMENT: Teen-agers lay out more than $1.5 billion a year for entertainment. They spend about $75 million on single pop records. Although they create new musical idols, they are staunchly faithful to the old. Elvis Presley, still their favorite, has sold 25 million copies of single records in four years, an all-time high. HOMEMAKERS: Major items like furniture and silver are moving into the teen-age market because of a growing number of teen-age marriages. One-third of all 18- and 19-year-old girls are already married. More than 600,000 teen-agers will be married this year. Teen-agers are now starting hope chests at 15. CREDIT RISKS: Some 800,000 teen-agers work at full-time jobs and can buy major items on credit.*

--The Teenage Consumer, *Life*, 1959

19. The author of the article blatantly argued that teenagers of the fifties were
    A. frugal and thrifty.
    B. appreciative of everything they received.
    C. fully aware of their expenditures.
    D. spoiled to death.

20. The teenage market described in the article reflected
    A. new advertising techniques.
    B. creative credit plans.
    C. post-war economic prosperity.
    D. conservative spending of the fifties.

21. The fascinating facts about the booming teenage market included all of the following EXCEPT
    A. the new rock 'n roll music of the fifties.
    B. the emergence of fast food restaurants.
    C. the pressure to look beautiful.
    D. an absence of furniture purchases.

SHORT ANSWER QUESTIONS

John F. Kennedy is moved to create a civil rights bill in 1963.

a. Choose ONE of the following and explain why your choice represents the event that led to the creation of this bill.

   • *Brown v. Board of Education of Topeka*
   • Four black students refuse to give up their seat in North Carolina
   • Protesters attacked in Birmingham, Alabama

b. Contrast your choice against ONE of the other options, demonstrating why that option in not as significant as your choice.

LONG ESSAY QUESTION

Why was the decade of the fifties both entertaining and yet contentious?

ANSWERS AND EXPLANATIONS

Multiple Choice Questions

1. B Eisenhower wanted to cut back on Cold War expenses by replacing ground troops with bombs.
2. C The launching of Sputnik gave the Soviet Union a brief period of technological superiority.
3. C Arguably his greatest domestic victory came with the passage of the Interstate Highway Act.
4. A The landmark case of *Brown v. Board of Education of Topeka* set the stage for subsequent desegregation throughout the nation, especially the South.
5. B Believe in yourself through the positive Christian thinking became enormously popular.
6. C The idea of "separate but equal" was nullified in 1954.
7. B Eisenhower was not a big fan of integration but felt compelled to uphold the decision of the Supreme Court by sending troops to Central High School.
8. A Boycotters found different ways to get to work other than using the bus.
9. C Non-violence proved to be a key factor in achieving civil rights objectives in the fifties and sixties.
10. A After calling for a march to the capital in 1941, Randolph called for another one that actually occurred, with over 250,000 in attendance.
11. C With a civil rights bill in the works, a march on the capital gave it support.
12. B King's whole focus was to desegregate the South in order to achieve equality.
13. D The Supreme Court's decision in 1954 drew much criticism from Southern Congressional members.
14. C The Manifest points out that the Radical Republicans pushed through the 14th Amendment while at the same time establishing all-black schools for the freedmen.
15. A The Manifesto claimed that the Supreme Court violated the reserved powers of the states.
16. B The Supreme Court argued that segregation promoted a sense of inferiority amongst African Americans, especially school children.
17. A The Court argued that separate was anything but equal.
18. B The Court argued that blacks were deprived of their right to an equal education with the existence of segregated schools.
19. D Teenagers seemed to get whatever they wanted without earning it.
20. C Without the prosperity of the twenties, this article would not have been written.

21. D Teenagers who married early bought furniture.

Long Essay Question

Why was the decade of the fifties both entertaining and yet contentious?

(Key topics to focus and elaborate on)
- Rise of the television and automobile
- Rise of rock' n roll music
- Reactions to Civil Rights Movement
- Fear of nuclear war

Chapter 26
LIVES CHANGED, 1961-1968

- The sixties featured changing times through a variety of modalities including protest, music, and writing.

NEW VOICES, NEW AUTHORITIES

- Jane Jacobs through her writing helped New York to shift its urban planning.
- Rachel Carson wrote what many people consider to be the bible of the conservation movement.
- Michael Harrington, like Jacob Riis, wrote about poverty in America, but unlike Riis, focused on both urban and rural poverty.
- Betty Friedan argued in her writing that women were not satisfied playing the role of housewives and desired more out of life than staying at home.
- Whereas the writing of the sixties tended to be provocative, so too was the music which included that of Bob Dylan, Joan Baez, Jimi Hendrix, The Doors, and the Grateful Dead.
- Yet, traditional family entertainment would still continue to be immensely popular even during the sixties.
- The Students for a Democratic Society, with Tom Hayden as their leader, looked to challenge many of the ills that surrounded society in the 1960s.
- Civil disobedience would make its way to the campus of U.C. Berkeley after the administration did not allow booths for civil rights causes.
- The protest became a center for the Free Speech Movement during the 1960s.

CAMELOT, THE WHITE HOUSE, AND DALLAS-THE KENNEDY ADMINISTRATION

- John F. Kennedy, or simply JFK, brought the exuberance of youth into the White House and his charisma and charm proved to be contagious to the press.
- Although Kennedy spoke of ending racial discrimination, his achievements in this realm were fairly limited, in part because Congress had many southern members.
- Under JFK's New Frontier, minimum wages rose, mental health programs were improved, and more funds were poured into NASA.
- During Kennedy's term various Supreme Court cases were decided, including *Engel v. Vitale* and *Albington School Board v. Schempp*.
- JKF came into the White House as a Cold Warrior and upon entering the presidency he immediately set into motion a plan devised under Eisenhower to remove the communist dictator, Fidel Castro, from Cuba. This goal became especially urgent after Castro nationalized all of the island's land and formed a partnership with the Soviet Union.
- After sending CIA-trained insurgents to lead an uprising against Castro, the Bay of Pigs invasion became an utter disaster and complete embarrassment for the president.
- Shortly after, the leader of the Soviet Union, Nikita Khrushchev ordered the construction of the Berlin Wall to keep workers from East Berlin from escaping to West Berlin.

- The next year in 1962, the Soviets began to build missile bases in Cuba that they pointed at the United States. Members of the National Security Council gathered and demanded the missiles to be removed. Kennedy then ordered a quarantine of the island using the U.S. Navy.
- Ultimately, the Soviets agreed to remove their missiles if the U.S. promised not to invade the island and to remove its missiles from Turkey.
- Despite being called weak by some members of the military, JFK significantly increased the budget of the military during his term.
- To deal with the Cold War in third world countries, Kennedy began a program known as Flexible Response. Whereas the Green Berets represented the military approach to this plan, the Peace Corps offered an alternative approach to fight communism.
- Given that Texas was deeply divided between Republicans and Democrats, JFK went to the Lone Star state to drum up support for his reelection bid. While visiting Dallas, JFK was shot and killed. Vice President Lyndon Baines Johnson assumed the presidency that same day (Nov. 22, 1963).
- Lee Harvey Oswald was arrested for Kennedy's murder and the Warren Commission determined that Oswald acted alone.

THE COMING OF LYNDON B. JOHNSON

- Unlike Kennedy who grew up wealthy, Johnson (or LBJ) knew what it meant to grow up in poverty. As a member of Congress, LBJ became a skilled politician and crafted his famous "Johnson Treatment."
- Upon taking over the presidency, LBJ vowed to carry out JFK's policies, yet he had a certain skill to carry out his promises that the younger Kennedy did not. In effect, Johnson was able to push the Kennedy's civil rights bill through Congress and he signed it into law in 1964.
- Essentially, the Civil Rights Act of 1964 outlawed segregation in all public places and created a federal commission to enforce it.
- Following the Civil Rights Act, Johnson unfolded his Great Society that featured a host of New Deal-like reforms including: VISTA, Head Start, and grants for college students.
- Having won the election of 1964, LBJ pushed through Congress federal aid to education, Medicare and Medicaid, immigration reform, and-- after violent bloodshed in Mississippi--the Voting Rights Act of 1965.
- Johnson's track record in foreign affairs did not equal the success he achieved in domestic affairs. Essentially the Vietnam War ruined his presidency.
- During Kennedy's presidency, the American presence in Vietnam was small with advisors and a limited number of troops.
- South Vietnam's leader, Ngo Dinh Diem who the U.S. supported was a Catholic in a Buddhist nation and his corruption marred his leadership. Ultimately the U.S. backed a coup to overthrow Diem and his opposition executed him.
- Johnson believed in the domino theory which warned that if South Vietnam fell to communism, the rest of Southeast Asia would fall as well. Thus he vowed to protect South Vietnam, no matter how unpopular this decision was.

- The Gulf of Tonkin Resolution allowed LBJ to use whatever "means necessary" to defend U.S. troops and to engage the enemy in combat. Between the years 1965-1968, Johnson would oversee a dramatic increase in troops to half a million men.
- Morale amongst the soldiers began to disintegrate, and so did public support for the war by the late 1960s. Television brought the war to the living rooms of America and this contributed to the dissension that began to grow.
- The war reached America's campus as some students began to protest and some teachers held teach-ins to inform others about the war. As the war progressed, the teach-ins became angry protests against the war.
- Even civil rights leaders such as Martin Luther King Jr., who were initially hesitant to protest against Johnson, began to speak out against the war.
- To avoid the draft, thousands of young men fled to Canada, while some just stayed in the U.S. and refused to cooperate with the draft on any level.
- As the war dragged on, Johnson agonized at the casualties and used the CIA and FBI in an attempt to silence the criticism.
- The Tet Offensive in 1968 disproved any notion that Johnson or General Westmoreland were correct in their assumption that the U.S. was winning the war.
- To make matters worse for LBJ, Robert Kennedy announced that he would run as a presidential candidate in that year's election.
- With the troubles Johnson faced in early of 1968, he announced that he would not seek reelection.
- Days after Johnson's announcement, an assassin shot and killed Martin Luther King Jr. which led to riots across the nation.
- In addition, the actions of the Black Panthers and protesting students at Columbia University displayed the societal disharmony that resonated throughout the United States.
- At the same time, Robert Kennedy seemed to have been just the candidate to bring some calm to the nation until an Arab nationalist shot and killed him in Los Angeles.
- The 1968 Democratic Party Convention featured demonstrators, division, and overall dissension in the city of Chicago.
- In contrast to the Democrats, the Republicans featured a united front with Richard Nixon as their candidate.
- In the end, Richard Nixon won a close election, with Vietnam remaining as an unresolved issue.

MULTIPLE CHOICE QUESTIONS

1. Students protested at U.C. Berkeley because the university
   A. did not allow blacks to attend the university.
   B. did not use affirmative action.
   C. did not allow booths for civil rights on campus.
   D. was seen as place of racial division.

2. In the case of *Engel v. Vitale,* the Supreme Court declared that
   A. segregation in public schools was unconstitutional.
   B. schools could not open their school day with prayer.
   C. schools could not teach religion even in historical context.
   D. schools could open their school day with just a simple prayer.

3. All of the following events occurred under the presidency John F. Kennedy EXCEPT
   A. Bay of Pigs invasion.
   B. Berlin Wall constructed.
   C. Cuban Missile crisis.
   D. Gulf of Tonkin incident.

4. The Warren Commission that investigated John F. Kennedy's assassination concluded that
   A. Lee Harvey Oswald acted alone in murdering Kennedy.
   B. shots were fired from two directions.
   C. Jack Ruby killed Oswald to hide emerging evidence.
   D. Oswald had assistance from unknown sources.

5. The compromise that ended the Cuban Missile Crisis was
   A. the Soviets removed missiles from Cuba with the promise that the U.S. would evacuate forces from West Berlin.
   B. the Soviets removed missiles from Cuba with the U.S. promising that it would not invade Cuba.
   C. the Soviets removed missiles from Cuba and the U.S. would remove missiles from Turkey.
   D. the Soviets kept the missiles in Cuba with the promise to never use them.

6. The purpose of Flexible Response was to
   A. use nuclear weapons to defeat communists.
   B. use a massive buildup of soldiers to defeat communists.
   C. use the Green Berets and the Peace Corps to fight communism.
   D. use incendiary bombs to destroy communist camps.

7. Lyndon Baines Johnson passed all of the following during his presidency EXCEPT
   A. Medicare and Medicaid.
   B. Head Start.
   C. VISTA.
   D. Social Security.

8. The Vietnam War costs the lives of
   A. 10,000 Americans.
   B. 28,000 Americans.
   C. 58,000 Americans.
   D. 88,000 Americans.

9. The number of U.S. troops that eventually went to Vietnam would be
   A. 10,000.
   B. 100,000.
   C. 250,000.
   D. 500,000.

10. The attack on U.S. forces that convinced LBJ to not seek reelection was
    A. the attack on the USS Maddox.
    B. the attack of U.S. troops at Danang.
    C. the Tet Offensive.
    D. the attack at Dien Bien Phu.

Questions 11-12 refer to the following visual.

11. The anti-Vietnam War poster reflected all of the following EXCEPT
    A. disillusionment with the war.
    B. high death toll.
    C. lack of military direction.
    D. guilt of American public for not supporting the war.

12. The Vietnam War proved to be a war that
    A. the United States lost.
    B. was not met with protest.
    C. the United States won.
    D. was not captured on video.

Questions 13-15 refers to the following excerpt.

From Chapter Two: The Obligation to Endure

The history of life on earth has been a history of interaction between living things and their surroundings. To a large extent, the physical form and the habits of the earth's vegetation and its animal life have been molded by the environment. Considering the whole span of earthly time, the opposite effect, in which life actually modifies its surroundings, has been relatively slight. Only within the moment of time represented by the present century has one species - man - acquired significant power to alter the nature of his world.

During the past quarter century this power has not only increased to one of disturbing magnitude but it has changed in character. The most alarming of all man's assaults upon the environment is contamination of air, earth, rivers, and sea with dangerous and even lethal materials. This pollution is for the most part irrevocable; the chain of evil it initiates not only in the world that must support life but in living tissues is for the most part irreversible. In this now universal contamination of the environment, chemicals are the sinister and little-recognized partners of radiation in changing the very nature of the world - the very nature of its life. Strontium 90, released through nuclear explosions into the air, comes to earth in rain or drifts down as fallout, lodges in the soil, enters into the grass or corn or wheat grown there, and in time takes up its abode in the bones of a human being, there to remain until his death. Similarly, chemicals sprayed on croplands or forests or gardens lie long in soil, entering into living organisms, passing from one to another in a chain of poisoning and death. Or they pass mysteriously by underground streams until they emerge and, through the alchemy of air and sunlight, combine into new forms that kill vegetation, sicken cattle, and work unknown harm on those who drink from once pure wells. As Albert Schweitzer has said, "Man can hardly even recognize the devils of his own creation."

--Rachel Carson, *The Silent Spring*

13. According to Rachel Carson, man's assault on the environment is
    A. for the most part reversible.
    B. for the most part irreversible.
    C. by and large harmless.
    D. non-transferable.

14. According to Rachel Carson, Stontium 90 is
    A. released through aerosol cans.
    B. released through cow belches.
    C. released through nuclear explosions.
    D. released through gas pollution.

15. "Man can hardly even recognize the devils of his own creation" refers to
    A. the mental torment that he holds inside.
    B. the pollution that he creates.
    C. the weapons that he creates.

D. the conditions of war that he creates.

Questions 16-18 refer to the following excerpt.

I have called for a national war on poverty. Our objective: total victory.
There are millions of Americans - one-fifth of our people - who have not shared in the abundance which has been granted to most of us, and on whom the gates of opportunity have been closed.
What does this poverty mean to those who endure it?
It means a daily struggle to secure the necessities for even a meager existence. It means that the abundance, the comforts, the opportunities they see all around them are beyond their grasp.
Worst of all, it means hopelessness for the young.
The young man or woman who grows up without a decent education, in a broken home, in a hostile and squalid environment, in ill health or in the face of racial injustice - that young man or woman is often trapped in a life of poverty.
He does not have the skills demanded by a complex society. He does not know how to acquire those skills. He faces a mounting sense of despair which drains initiative and ambition and energy. . . .
The war on poverty is not a struggle simply to support people, to make them dependent on the generosity of others.
It is a struggle to give people a chance.
It is an effort to allow them to develop and use their capacities, as we have been allowed to develop and use ours, so that they can share, as others share, in the promise of this nation.
We do this, first of all, because it is right that we should.
For the establishment of public education and land grant colleges through agricultural extension and encouragement to industry, we have pursued the goal of a nation with full and increasing opportunities for all its citizens.
The war on poverty is a further step in that pursuit.
We do it also because helping some will increase the prosperity of all.
Our fight against poverty will be an investment in the most valuable of our resources - the skills and strength of our people.
And in the future, as in the past, this investment will return its cost many fold to our entire economy.
If we can raise the annual earnings of 10 million among the poor by only $1,000 we will have added $14 billion a year to our national output. In addition we can make important reductions in public assistance payments which now cost us $4 billion a year, and in the large costs of fighting crime and delinquency, disease and hunger.
This is only part of the story.
Our history has proved that each time we broaden the base of abundance, giving more people the chance to produce and consume, we create new industry, higher production, increased earnings and better income for all.
Giving new opportunity to those who have little will enrich the lives of all the rest.
Because it is right, because it is wise, and because, for the first time in our history, it is possible to conquer poverty, I submit, for the consideration of the Congress and the country, the Economic Opportunity Act of 1964.
The Act does not merely expand old programs or improve what is already being done.

It charts a new course.
It strikes at the causes, not just the consequences of poverty.
It can be a milestone in our one-hundred-eighty-year search for a better life for our people.

--Lyndon Baines Johnson, War on Poverty

16. Johnson empathized with the poor and the impoverished because
    A. he joined the Peace Corps.
    B. he took a tour of the inner cities.
    C. he read several books regarding the impoverished.
    D. he grew up impoverished himself.

17. The fight against poverty, to Johnson, is an investment because
    A. taxpayers will feel good about where their money went.
    B. the impoverished will gain jobs and be removed from public assistance.
    C. the poor will be grateful.
    D. taxpayer money will be used for the poor and not for war.

18. According to Johnson, the war against poverty is all of the following EXCEPT
    a. to support people and make them dependent on the generosity of others.
    b. to give young people hope.
    c. an investment for the future.
    d. a war that strikes against the causes of poverty.

Questions 19-21 refer to the following excerpt.

Throughout the 1960s, SDS became increasingly radical. Although the media found it convenient to portray the SDS the one voice of young Americans, in reality the group lost members because of its increasing radicalism and because students were too diverse to be represented by just one organization. In 1969, the organization splintered and eventually dissolved. The most radical students, who became known as the Weathermen, resorted to terrorist violence to further their cause. Even that activity ceased, however, after three Weathermen were killed while making bombs.

In 1962 Tom Hayden and Robert Alan Haber wrote the "Port Huron Statement," which appears below. The statement was a clarion call to their own generation and a warning to their parents' generation that the status quo was unacceptable.

We are the people of this generation, bred in at least modest comfort, housed now in the universities, looking uncomfortably to the world we inherit.

When we were kids the United States was the wealthiest and strongest country in the world; the only one with the atom bomb, the least scarred by modern war, an initiator of the United Nations that we thought would distribute Western influence throughout the world. Freedom and equality for each individual, government of, by, and for the people-these American values we found good, principles by which we could live as men. Many of us began maturing in complacency.

As we grew, however, our comfort was penetrated by events too troubling to dismiss.

First, the permeating and victimizing fact of human degradation, symbolized by the Southern struggle against racial bigotry, compelled most of us from silence to activism.

Second, the enclosing fact of the Cold War, symbolized by the presence of the Bomb, brought awareness that we ourselves, and our friends, and millions of abstract "others" we knew more directly because of our common peril, might die at any time. We might deliberately ignore, or avoid or fail to feel all other human problems, but not these two, for these were too immediate and crushing in their impact, too challenging in the demand that we as individuals take the responsibility for encounter and resolution.

--Students for a Democratic Society, The Port Huron Statement

19. Why did members of SDS become more aware of racial bigotry when they went to college?
    A. As kids they ignored the exposure they had to it.
    B. College discussion and discourse made them aware of it.
    C. It was by chance that they acknowledge racial bigotry.
    D. Their campus was riddled with racial protest.

20. The SDS became concerned about nuclear weapons because
    A. an arms race was about to begin during their time as college students.
    B. it was concerned that the Soviets were testing their first atomic bomb.
    C. it realized how destructive a nuclear war could be.
    D. hydrogen bombs were on the verge of being discovered.

21. The childhoods of SDS members featured all of the EXCEPT
    A. U.S. monopoly on the atomic bomb.
    B. the United Nations.
    C. freedom and equality.
    D. keen awareness of segregation and discrimination.

SHORT ANSWER QUESTIONS

Lyndon Baines Johnson chooses not to seek reelection in 1968.

a. Choose ONE of the following and explain why your choice represents the event that led Johnson to make this decision.

   - Robert Kennedy chooses to run for president
   - Anti-war protests sweep across the nation
   - The Tet Offensive is unleashed

b. Contrast your choice against ONE of the other options, demonstrating why that option in not as significant as your choice.

LONG ESSAY QUESTION

In what ways was Johnson's *Great Society* an extension of the Roosevelt's *New Deal*?

ANSWERS AND EXPLANATIONS

Multiple Choice Questions

1. C   The university did not allow booths for off-campus causes.
2. B   Schools in New York where the case originated and across the nation could not open the school day with prayer.
3. D   The Gulf of Tonkin Incident occurred under LBJ's presidency.
4. A   The Warren Commission, in a controversial conclusion, declared that Oswald acted alone.
5. B   A second message by the Soviets demanded that the U.S. to remove its missiles from Turkey which the U.S. secretly agreed to.
6. C   The Green Berets and the Peace Corps were alternatives to conventional warfare.
7. D   Social Security was passed under Roosevelt's New Deal.
8. C   The death toll was more than anyone expected.
9. D   Half a million soldiers made their way to Vietnam.
10. C   The Tet Offensive proved that North Vietnam and the Vietcong were nowhere near surrendering.
11. D   Massive protest became a feature of this war.
12. A   Vietnam was one of the first wars the U.S. lost convincingly.
13. B   Carson argued that the damage man caused with pollution was irreparable.
14. C   Remnants of this radiation eventually would settle in human bones.
15. B   Carson argued that man didn't realize just how much pollution he was emitting.
16. D   Johnson grew up poor in Texas and taught briefly in a poor Hispanic community.
17. B   The impoverished will become self-sufficient and productive.
18. A   Johnson did not intend to create a cycle of dependency with his war on poverty.
19. B   College can be a place where new ideas and discussion are introduced.
20. C   Fear of dying at any time because a nuclear fallout became a real possibility.
21. D   SDS members were aware of racial problems until they went to college.

Long Essay Question

In what ways was Johnson's *Great Society* an extension of the Roosevelt's *New Deal*?

(Key topics to focus and elaborate on)
- Medicare and Medicaid
- Head Start
- Food Stamps
- Grants for education

Chapter 27
RIGHTS, REACTION, AND LIMITS, 1968-1980

- The period between 1968 and 1980 featured controversy with the Vietnam war, with Nixon's presidency, and with the demands of groups on the fringe of American society.

THE NEW POLITICS OF THE LATE 1960S

- Many Americans were frustrated and appalled at the topics that were featured in the daily headlines, including the civil rights movement, the Great Society, the protest of the Vietnam War, and the lifestyles of the hippies.
- By the 1960s a clear shift in politics could be seen with the liberals siding with the Democrats and the conservatives siding with the Republicans.
- The Republican camp believed that race relations should be handled by the states and not the federal government and that the nation as a whole needed to become more anti-communist.
- Although he was a self-proclaimed conservative, many liberal programs were maintained or established during Nixon's presidency, including an extension of the Voting Rights Act and Title IX. Nixon also did much to strengthen environmental and animal protection with the creation of the EPA and the passage of the Endangered Species Act. In fact Nixon spent billions on social programs.
- Nixon was secretive in his manner and created both a Freeze List and Enemies List of people he believed should be watched carefully.
- Under Nixon, the Vietnam War continued with renewed bombing of North Vietnam and bombing of Cambodia to destroy North Vietnam enclaves. This in turn led to engagement with the dreadful and terrifying Khmer Rouge in Cambodia.
- At the same time of the bombing, Nixon implemented Vietnamization to gradually withdraw American troops from Vietnam.
- Meanwhile, the military was falling apart at the seams in Vietnam with the "fragging" of officers, racial tension, and heavy drug use.
- Anti-war protests continued and became even more heated as seen with the tragedy at Kent State.
- Finally, in 1973, a cease-fire was called for by the U.S. and North Vietnam and U.S. combat troops would leave Vietnam.
- That same year, Nixon made a surprise visit to China to mend relations with this country that had embraced communism since 1949. Essentially, the trip opened up diplomatic relations between two forces that had been at odds with each other since Mao Zedong had taken control of China.
- Meanwhile, Nixon visited the Soviet Union and along with Leonid Brezhnev, agreed to the Strategic Arms Limitation Treaty and the Anti-Ballistic Missile Treaty to begin the process of limiting nuclear weapons.

- Nixon's administration also witnessed Israel's attacks on Egypt and Syria in the Six Day War, a conflict that would reemerge and bring nightmares to the U.S. economy.

THE MOVEMENTS OF THE 1960S AND 1970S

- The late sixties and early seventies saw other groups besides African Americans push for equality, including women, Latinos, American Indians, and members of the white counter- culture movement.
- Even as late as the 1960s, women were not equal to men in many realms, but they started to make gains, especially in the arena of politics.
- Women began to lash out at society's expectations in various ways, including the mockery of the Miss USA pageant, the filing of lawsuits against university hiring practices, the establishment of the Feminist Press, the honoring of Harriet Tubman, and the launching of Ms. Magazine.
- The case of *Roe v. Wade* ended with the Supreme Court granting women the right to have abortions within the first two trimesters of their pregnancies.
- In 1970, the National Organization for Women (NOW) began to lobby for an Equal Rights Amendment and was successful in it getting through Congress but it was not ratified by a sufficient number of states to become law.
- At the same time women fought for their rights, Hispanics also fought for their rights, especially Mexicans involved in field labor. Cesar Chavez and Dolores Huerta founded the United Farm Workers Union, and along with Filipino leader, Larry Itliong, went on strike against grape growers in Delano, California.
- American Indians also pushed for equality by taking over Alcatraz and forming the American Indian Movement which then led to stand-offs at Wounded Knee and Pine Ridge.
- In 1972, the Indian Education Act provided funds for schools under tribal control.
- The focus of racial issues would shift north with the integration of Boston schools, and a city-wide teachers strike in New York City. In addition, more African American mayors would be elected in some of the nation's largest cities.
- Affirmative Action used by universities as part of its application process came under attack with the Supreme Court case of *Regents of the University of California v. Bakke*.
- The Court also ruled that school districts must make accommodations for students who could not speak English.
- The gay liberation movement began in the 1970s after a raid in Greenwich Village, and that same decade would see the American Psychological Association remove homosexuality from its lists of psychiatric disorders. In addition, gays were starting to openly become involved in politics and winning elected offices.
- Protest in general became the theme of a famous concert at Woodstock in 1969, which almost half a million young Americans attended. In essence, Woodstock became a symbol of the nation's countercultural movement. The movement featured drugs such as LSD and music that was anti-war and psychedelic.
- San Francisco became the capital of this movement with the neighborhood of Haight-Ashbury serving as its White House.

THE CULTURE WARS OF THE 1970S

- Conservatives such as Phyllis Schlafly opposed the ERA and was successful in stopping its passage.
- Pat Robertson founded the Christian Broadcasting Network; Jerry Falwell founded the Moral Majority. Both men became key figures in the Religious Right movement of the 1980s.
- The Moral Majority was "pro-life, pro-family, pro-morality, and pro-American." In addition, it fought for prayers in schools and was very anti-communist as well.

POLITICS, ECONOMICS AND THE IMPACT OF WATERGATE

- Whereas the fifties and sixties featured economic prosperity, the seventies did not. Unemployment and inflation combined to create stagflation, and Americans began to discuss the "misery index."
- Controversy in the Middle East led OPEC to raise the price of oil which made gasoline and heating oil very expensive in the United States. The effect would be devastating to the U.S. economy.
- Japanese imported vehicles such as Toyota and Honda became more prevalent in America.
- As the Rustbelt declined, the Sunbelt became a predominant feature of economic importance.
- The crisis of Watergate began when members of CREEP were caught breaking into the Democratic Headquarters in Washington D.C. in 1972. Nixon ordered the CIA to take over the investigation of this burglary from the hands of the FBI, and the incident went unnoticed until the next year. Watergate burglar, James McCord revealed that he was ordered to keep silent for money. Soon after, a Senate Select Committee formed to further the investigation and learned that Nixon had recorded a tape discussing this break-in.
- After being ordered to release the tapes to the House Committee by the Supreme Court, Nixon refused.
- Thereafter the House Committee began the process of impeaching the president for obstruction of justice.
- Rather than face impeachment and a subsequent senate trial, Richard Nixon resigned in 1974.
- Vice President Gerald Ford assumed the presidency and pardoned Nixon to begin the healing process from the turmoil the nation had gone through with Watergate.
- Ford's short term dealt with continuing economic woes, battles with Congress over tax cuts, and the loss of South Vietnam to the communists.
- The Democrats capitalized on Ford's misery by running Jimmy Carter as their candidate for the Election of 1976. In the election, Carter defeated Ford and entered the presidency in an era of oil shocks and trouble in the Middle East.
- The presidency of Carter was seen as a fresh start to the beleaguered nation, but yet the economy was still very sluggish with high unemployment and high inflation. Meanwhile, the price of fuel continued to soar.
- In the arena of foreign policy, Carter fared somewhat better, especially after he negotiated a peace agreement between Egypt and Israel at the Camp David Accords.

- Despite reaching a SALT II agreement with the Soviets, relations between the two superpowers were marred when the Soviet Union invaded Afghanistan in1979.
- After the U.S. received the ousted leader of Iran for medical treatment, Iranian extremists seized the U.S. embassy and held 58 Americans hostage for over a year.
- The troubles of Carter's presidency made him a one-term president, as he lost in a landslide to former actor and California governor, Ronald Reagan in the Election of 1980.

MULTIPLE CHOICE QUESTIONS

1. Title IX called for equal funding in both male and female activities
   A. in the work force.
   B. in student loans.
   C. in schools.
   D. in unemployment payments.

2. The process of Vietnamization called for
   A. immediate removal of U.S. troops.
   B. increased deployment of U.S. troops in Vietnam.
   C. gradual removal of U.S. troops and increased bombing.
   D. a cease fire with North Vietnam.

2. Protests and clashes with the National Guard over the bombing of Cambodia left four students dead at
   A. Jackson State.
   B. UC Berkeley.
   C. University of Mississippi.
   D. Kent State.

4. During his presidency, Nixon achieved all of the following EXCEPT
   A. opened up diplomatic relations with China.
   B. ended the Vietnam War.
   C. signed an arms agreement with the Soviet Union.
   D. served out his second term.

5. In the case of *Roe v. Wade*, the Supreme Court ruled
   A. segregation in private schools was unconstitutional.
   B. affirmative action was constitutional.
   C. women had the right to abortion in the first two trimesters of their pregnancy.
   D. minimum wage had to be increased.

6. Cesar Chavez and Larry Itliong led a strike for higher wages against grape growers at
   A. Salinas, California.
   B. Delano, California.
   C. Fresno, California.
   D. Yuma, Arizona.

7. The mecca of the counter-culture movement centered in
   A. San Francisco.
   B. Seattle.
   C. New York City.
   D. Hollywood.

8. Oil shocks struck the nation and gasoline prices skyrocketed after
   A. a hurricane destroyed oil refineries in Louisiana.
   B. a snowstorm damaged the Alaska Pipeline.
   C. OPEC raised the price of oil.
   D. workers went on strike at oil refineries in Santa Barbara.

9. As a result of the Watergate scandal, Richard Nixon became the first president to
   A. be impeached by the House of Representatives.
   B. be removed by a Senate Trial.
   C. have Articles of Impeachment charged against him.
   D. resign from office.

10. All of the following negative events occurred under Carter's presidency EXCEPT
    A. Camp David Accords.
    B. rise of stagflation.
    C. American hostages taken in Iran.
    D. Soviet Union invades Afghanistan.

Questions 11-12 refer to the following visual.

11. Attorney General John Mitchell and President Richard Nixon are seated in the lifebuoy, *SS Watergate*. What roles did these two men have in the scandal known as Watergate?
    A. Nixon planned the break-in and Mitchell suggested the use of hush money.
    B. Mitchell planned the break-in and Nixon was part of the cover-up.
    C. Mitchell was caught during the break-in and Nixon ordered the FBI to take over the case.
    D. Mitchell ordered the CIA to back off the investigation and Nixon approved the order.

12. What else would sink along with the *SS Watergate*?
    A. the political career of Gerald Ford
    B. the reporting careers of Carl Bernstein and Robert Woodward
    C. the presidency of Richard Nixon
    D. the legal career of federal district judge John Sirica

Questions 13-15 refer to the following excerpt.

Our conviction is that human life is a very special possession given by God to man and that no one has the right to take it for any reason or for any cause, however just it may be. We are also convinced that nonviolence is more powerful than violence. Nonviolence supports you if you have a just and moral cause. Nonviolence provides the opportunity to stay on the offensive, and that is of crucial importance to win any contest. If we resort to violence, then one of two things will happen: either the violence will be escalated and there will be many injuries and perhaps deaths on both sides, or there will be total demoralization of the workers. Nonviolence has exactly the opposite effect.

If for every violent act committed against us we respond with nonviolence, we attract people's support. We can gather the support of millions who have a conscience and would rather see a nonviolent resolution to problems. We are convinced that when people are faced with a direct appeal from the poor struggling nonviolently against great odds, they will react positively. The American people and people everywhere still yearn for justice. It is to that yearning that we appeal.

But if we are committed to nonviolence only as a strategy or tactic, then if it fails our only alternative is to turn to violence. So we must balance the strategy with a clear understanding of what we are doing. However important the struggle is and however much misery, poverty, and exploitation exist, we know that it cannot be more important than one human life. We work on the theory that men and women who are truly concerned about people are not violent by nature. These people become violent when the deep concern they have for people is frustrated and when they are faced with seemingly insurmountable odds. We advocate militant nonviolence as our means of achieving justice for our people, but we are not blind to the feelings of frustration, impatience, and anger that seethe inside every farmworker. The burden of generations of poverty and powerlessness lies heavy in the fields of America. If we fail, there are those who will see violence as the shortcut to change. [...]

Most likely we are not going to do anything else the rest of our lives except build our union. For us there is nowhere else to go. Although we would like to see victory come soon, we are willing to wait. In this sense time is our ally. We learned many years ago that the rich may have money, but the poor have time.

--César Chávez, From "He Showed Us the Way", April 1978

13. The style of protest that Chavez wanted to emulate from Martin Luther King Jr. was based on
    A. militant speeches and occasional violence.
    B. any means possible including violence.
    C. non-violence to gain people's support.
    D. passive inactivity.

14. According to Chavez, people react favorably to the poor that protest non-violently because
    A. people like the entertainment of protest.
    B. people favor the seeking of justice through non-violence.
    C. people are afraid of violent groups.
    D. people like the unfortunate.

15. Chavez believes that nonviolence provides the opportunity to stay on the offensive since
    A. being violent makes one stop to defend one's actions.
    B. being nonviolent makes one defend one's inactiveness.
    C. violence will lead to more violence.
    D. non-violence conserves more energy than protest.

Questions 16-18 refer to the following excerpt.

As I walked around the school, and felt the mood of the school, I thought, "This school is DEATH. The mood of the school is black."

The troopers were happy, however, I was surprised to see. One said, "This is more like it. It gets the old adrenalin going." My sophomores, a mixed class of black and white students, also wanted to talk about the incidents. They explained how the fight before school had started at the front lobby door. A black girl and a white boy were going through the front lobby-the boy first. He let the door slam on her. She screamed; a black male jumped to her defense, and the fight was on. A trooper pushed a white boy back over a desk and dislocated his shoulder. A black student on the stairs started screaming insults at the white students… Fights broke out everywhere in the lobby. Students rushed down from the classrooms, or out of their homerooms to aid the secretaries when they called for help on the intercom.

There was a faculty meeting after school. Dr. Reid took the toll of casualties and names involved in fights. Unconsciously he wiped his brow with the classic tragic sweep of his hand and said, "I don't know what we can do. We were all at our posts doing our jobs. But if a youngster will insult and another responds with his fists, there's nothing we can do-except encourage them to watch their mouths and language." Dr. Reid announced he would like to have an honor roll assembly for sophomores. The assembly, the first this year, is scheduled for Friday, a day when attendance is the lowest. . . .

The sophomore assembly convened as planned. Classes filed to assigned seats room by room without incident. Troopers lined the auditorium. The mood was ugly. Dr. Reid entered from the rear of the hall. ..

After the pledge of allegiance to the flag, Dr. Reid lectured on the courtesy of standing when a guest comes to one's home. A few students snickered. When he alluded to the troopers, the black boys in the row behind me yelled, "Get them out." Then Dr. Reid outlined the sports plan for the winter and told the assembly, "We will be together for the year. After that I don't know. But we're here, and we had better make the best of it. And let's have a little courtesy toward one another. Let's treat each other with respect and watch what we say to one another-treat each other with a little kindness. A smile goes a long way if someone accidentally bumps you, instead of pushing back."

The students listened respectfully. Then, as both black and white students crossed the stage to accept their honor roll cards from Dr. Reid, the assembly applauded. Students left the auditorium room by room. During the day, girl students traveled the school in roving gangs of blacks and whites, bursting out of classes at any provocation, spreading consternation among the police. "They're in holiday mood," I told the police, dismayed at the prospect of chasing pretty girls back to classrooms. At the end of the day in homeroom, I told Martin, "Dr. Reid has put his life on the line about desegregation because it is the law. His house in South Boston is guarded. Then he asks you to stand in the assembly, and you refuse. He is your friend, the friend of all of us, and you should know that." . . .

The number of troopers in the building was increased instead of decreased, contrary to what the troopers had anticipated Friday when I talked to them. The two black boys-Martin and Jeffrey-and one white girl, Kathryn, were present in my homeroom today. Expecting a boycott, I was surprised to see any white students in school until I learned that a walkout of white students was anticipated at 9:45 A.M...

In class Anne described the walkout. "The white kids said, 'See you Tuesday, niggers.' If the black kids had a walkout, I'd go, too. The white kids have to go, or they'll get beaten up."

--Ione Malloy, Boston Busing 1975

16. The desegregation of Boston schools occurred because
    A. blacks and whites lived in the same neighborhoods but attended different schools.
    B. school officials were influenced by the *Southern Manifesto*.
    C. blacks and whites in Boston wanted to prove they could attend school together in harmony.
    D. busing brought students from different racial neighborhoods into the same schools.

17. The fighting at South Boston High School between blacks and whites proved all of the following EXCEPT

A.   racial mixing would not be easy.

B.   blacks and whites were unfamiliar with each other.

C.   blacks and whites were not initially comfortable with integration.

D.   the lessons of integration at Central High School made the transition to integration smooth and without incident.

18. Despite the fighting, Dr. Reid held an assembly to

A. air out the differences between blacks and whites.

B. recognize the bravery of the troops.

C. give advice on how to get along and reward students who made the honor roll.

D. announce that the students would be segregated due to safety concerns.

Questions 19-21 refer to the following speech.

Good evening.

This is a special night for me. Exactly three years ago, on July 15, 1976, I accepted the nomination of my party to run for President of the United States. I promised you a President who is not isolated from the people, who feels your pain, and who shared your dreams and who draws his strength and his wisdom from you. . . .

I know, of course, being president, that government actions and legislation can be very important. That's why I've worked hard to put my campaign promises into law-and I have to admit, with just mixed success. But after listening to the American people I have been reminded again that all the legislation in the world can't fix what's wrong with America. So, I want to speak to you first tonight about a subject even more serious than energy or inflation. I want to talk to you right now about a fundamental threat to American democracy...

The threat is nearly invisible in ordinary ways. It is a crisis of confidence. It is a crisis that strikes at the very heart and soul and spirit of our national will. We can see this crisis in the growing doubt about the meaning of our own lives and in the loss of a unity of purpose for our Nation.

The erosion of our confidence in the future is threatening to destroy the social and the political fabric of America. . . .

The symptoms of this crisis of the American spirit are all around us. For the first time in the history of our country a majority of our people believe that the next five years will be worse than the past five years. Two-thirds of our people do not even vote. The productivity of American workers is actually dropping, and the willingness of Americans to save for the future has fallen below that of all other people in the Western world. . . .

Often you see paralysis and stagnation and drift. You don't like it, and neither do I. What can we do?

First of all, we must face the truth, and then we can change our course. We simply must have faith in each other, faith in our course. We simply must have faith in each other, faith in our ability to govern ourselves, and faith in the future of this Nation. Restoring that faith and that confidence to America is now the most important task we face. It is a true challenge of this generation of Americans. . . .

We are at a turning point in our history. There are two paths to choose. One is a path I've warned about tonight, the path that leads to fragmentation and self-interest. Down that road lies a mistaken idea of freedom, the right to grasp for ourselves some advantage over others. That path would be one of constant conflict between narrow interests ending in chaos and immobility. It is a certain route to failure.

All the traditions of our past, all the lessons of our heritage, all the promises of our future point to another path, the path of common purpose and the restoration of American values. That path leads to true freedom for our Nation and ourselves. We can take the first steps down that path as we begin to solve our energy problems. . . .

--Jimmy Carter, 1979

19. The energy crisis that Jimmy Carter spoke of referred to a shortage of
    A. coal.
    B. hydropower.
    C. thermonuclear power.
    D. oil.

20. Carter's "Crisis in Confidence" speech is most reminiscent of
    A. Theodore Roosevelt's "New Nationalism" speech.
    B. Franklin D. Roosevelt's "Fear" speech.
    C. Abraham Lincoln's "Gettysburg Address."
    D. George Washington's "Farewell Address."

21. Carter points out that the symptoms of America's crisis include all of the following EXCEPT
    A. saving for the future.
    B. decreased voting patterns.
    C. lower productivity.
    D. negative outlook for the future.

SHORT ANSWER QUESTIONS

In the 1970s, the nation went through a period of *détente* with communist nations.

    a. Choose ONE of the following and explain why your choice represents the event that led Johnson to make this decision.

       - Nixon visits China and opens up diplomatic relations
       - Nixon signs SALT I agreement with the Soviet Union
       - The U.S. and North Vietnam agree to a cease-fire

    b. Contrast your choice against ONE of the other options, demonstrating why that option is not as significant as your choice.

LONG ESSAY QUESTION

In what ways did women and minorities fight for equality during the sixties and seventies?

ANSWERS AND EXPLANATIONS

Multiple Choice Questions

1. C Title IX made possible the introduction of more female sports through federal funding.
2. C With the gradual withdrawal of U.S. troops, more responsibility was placed on the soldiers of South Vietnam.
3. D Bringing the war into Cambodia left many furious including students at Kent State.
4. D Nixon resigned during his second term as president.
5. C *Roe v. Wade* opened up the doors for legalized abortions.
6. B Delano would be the scene of a major strike in 1965.
7. A San Francisco was the scene of hippies and the counter-culture movement, especially the neighborhood of Haight-Ashbury.
8. C As a protest to the October War, OPEC strikes back at the U.S.
9. D Two presidents have been impeached; Nixon was the first to resign.
10. A The Camp David Accords were seen as a victory for peace in the Middle East
11. B Mitchell was part of CREEP and Nixon played a role in an attempt to conceal the break-in of Watergate.
12. C Watergate destroyed Nixon's credibility and thus his presidency.
13. C Chavez used the examples of King for his protests.
14. B Chavez believed that non-violent protest ultimately would gain the sympathies of Americans.
15. A Being violent forces protesters to come up with excuses that defend their actions
16. D A system of busing was used to integrate schools in cities such as Boston
17. D South Boston High School did not have a smooth transition with their integration program.
18. C Dr. Reid tried to instill pride and stability by holding the assembly.
19. D The oil shocks bled into his presidency.
20. B Carter, like FDR, tried to instill confidence in the American people.
21. A Americans weren't saving for the future.

Long Essay Question

In what ways did women and minorities fight for equality during the sixties and seventies?

(Key topics to focus and elaborate on)
- Equal Rights Amendment/Roe v. Wade
- Strikes and boycotts against grape and lettuce growers
- American Indian Movement/Indian Education Act

Chapter 28
THE REAGAN REVOLUTION, 1980-1989

- A diverse group of Democrats, anti-tax advocates, and social conservatives catapulted Ronald Reagan into the presidency with a resounding election victory in 1980.

A RAPIDLY CHANGING U.S. GOVERNMENT

- The Reagan Revolution would bring in an era of conservatism that the nation hadn't seen for decades.
- In the midst of this revolution, the Cold War came to an end.
- Reagan had a colorful career as both an actor and GE spokesman before he entered politics as a Republican and became the governor of California in 1966.
- Reagan's economic theory that he applied as president became known as supply-side economics in which the government cut taxes to stimulate the economy and produce more jobs.
- At the same time Reagan made a number of social spending cuts while dramatically increasing the defense budget, and he proved to be no friend of organized labor.
- By 1983, the economy began to improve and Reagan became more and more popular.
- The Election of 1984 saw Reagan versus Walter Mondale. Despite the support of unions, Mondale could not garner the votes to defeat Reagan, and at age seventy three, Reagan was reelected.
- Reagan spent much of his second term focusing on foreign policy, in particular the Soviet Union. Despite not having any experience in foreign affairs, Reagan had a clear vision of what he wanted to accomplish.
- Reagan had fierce anti-communist sentiments that had developed over the course of decades and referred to the Soviet Union as "the evil empire". Reagan backed this rhetoric with a massive military build-up that ultimately the Soviets could not match.
- In 1983, Reagan implemented the Strategic Defense Initiative to deter a possible nuclear attack with lasers in space. The program was popularly known as "Star Wars," and proved to be a very expensive program that would never be used or had any assurance that it would even work.
- Meanwhile, in the Middle East, the U. intended to create a buffer zone that would neutralize the Soviet-friendly Iraq and Syria. In Afghanistan, the U.S. supported rebels who fought against Soviet rule. At the same time, the U.S. had struggles with Libya's Muammar Gaddafi for much of the eighties.
- In an attempt to free hostages in Lebanon, the U.S. secretly sold weapons to Iran who was at war with Iraq.
- In Latin America, the United States supported U.S.-friendly dictatorships until communist-influenced insurgents rose into power. Yet Congress passed the Boland Amendment to prohibit the U.S. from seeking to overthrow the communist government in Nicaragua.
- To secretly bypass this obstruction, Reagan aides used the money made from sales of arms to Iran and diverted it to anti-communists (Contras) in Nicaragua. By 1986, news of

this secret deal broke out and the incident quickly became known as the Iran-Contra affair. Although suspicions arose as to whether Reagan was involved in this affair, he was never officially implicated.

- Although the Iran-Contra Affair damaged Reagan's reputation, developments in the Soviet Union would lift him up again.
- In 1985, Mikhail Gorbachev became the new leader of the Soviet Union and implemented drastic changes to the Soviet political and economic system with the implementation of *glasnost* and *perestroika*. Reagan and Gorbachev established a personal bond and agreed to reduce intermediate-range nuclear forces. In essence, Reagan and Gorbachev helped to put the Cold War to an end.
- In the election of 1988, Reagan's vice president, George Herbert Walker Bush defeated Democrat, Michael Dukakis to win the presidency he had long sought.

THE CHANGING NATURE OF THE AMERICAN ECONOMY

- During the Reagan Era a dangerous pattern of investing had led values of stock to fall dramatically leading to Black Monday (1987). Fortunately, another Great Depression did not follow. Many savings and loans businesses became a victim to this plunge and either closed or had to be bailed out by the government.

CHANGES IN THE REST OF THE COUNTRY

- Music and technology began to dominate the eighties as seen with the Live Aid concert, the *We are the World* single, and the fast and cheap distribution of tapes and CDs.
- The eighties also featured numerous movies that packed the movie theaters such as the *Star Wars* Trilogy and *Raiders of the Lost Ark*. These could also be watched at home as well through the use of VCRs.
- To many, the entertainment of the eighties seemed completely immoral and thus the rise of the Religious Right emerged, with the Christian Coalition being its most powerful force. The Christian Coalition gained the full attention of the Republican Party and had numerous members gaining office.
- The Immigration Law of 1965 made a huge impact decades later as immigrants took advantage of the family reunion clause to enter the United States, many of which came from different places than during previous eras.
- Most of the migration made its way to California, Texas, Florida, New Jersey, Illinois, and New York.
- Reagan's amnesty law allowed many to stay, especially in California. At the same time, debates about immigration became heated.
- As the numbers of immigrants would rise during the eighties, so too would the prosperity of the Indian tribes that began to build casinos on their reservations.
- In 1981, the CDC reported AIDS for the first time and researchers later discovered that the agent of the disease was HIV. Originally thought to be a disease exclusive to gay men and intravenous drug users, the rapid spread of the disease among heterosexuals proved that the disease did not discriminate.
- The conservatism of the Reagan Administration influenced its decision to routinely deny requests for research funding.

- The early 1990s featured more funding towards AIDS research and through this research and education, AIDS ceased to be the death sentence that it had been in the early eighties.

MULTIPLE CHOICE

1. The features of the Reagan Revolution included all of the following *except*
   A. lower taxes.
   B. increased federal debt.
   C. more support for unions.
   D. end of Cold War.

2. Reagan's supply-side economics aimed to stimulate the economy by
   A. deficit spending.
   B. increasing aid to social programs.
   C. increasing the minimum wage.
   D. reducing taxes.

3. Reagan's plan to defend against a Soviet nuclear attack was known as
   A. Strategic Defense Initiative.
   B. Massive Retaliation.
   C. Big Stick Diplomacy.
   D. Nuclear Control Politics.

4. The Iran-Contra Affair involved the U.S. selling arms to Iran and secretly diverting the revenue from these sales to Contras in
   A. El Salvador.
   B. Cuba.
   C. Grenada.
   D. Nicaragua.

5. Reagan's use of the term, "the evil empire" was in reference to
   A. Iran.
   B. Syria.
   C. Soviet Union.
   D. Iraq.

6. Through Reagan's friendly negotiations with Soviet leader, Mikhail Gorbachev, the two agreed to
   A. completely eliminate nuclear weapons.
   B. dramatically reduce intermediate-range nuclear forces.
   C. eliminate the Strategic Defense Initiative.
   D. both evacuate forces from Berlin.

7. In the election of 1988, George Herbert Walker Bush easily defeated
   A. Walter Mondale.
   B. Jesse Jackson.
   C. Pat Buchanan.

D. Michael Dukakis.

8. Ivan Boesky made millions in the stock market because
   A. he was a shrewd investor.
   B. he had inside trading information.
   C. he studied the market obsessively.
   D. he was knowledgeable but lucky as well.

9. Technology and music came together in an epic concert featuring Madonna, Tina Turner and Michael Jackson known as
   A. Woodstock.
   B. Monterey Music Pop Festival.
   C. Monsters of Rock.
   D. Live Aid.

10. A frightening disease that the Center for Disease Control officially recognized in the eighties was
    A. AIDS.
    B. cancer.
    C. diabetes.
    D. heart disease.

Questions 11-12 refer to the following visual.

11. During his speech at the Berlin Wall, Ronald Reagan urged
    A. Gorbachev to maintain the safety of the wall zone.
    B. Gorbachev to allow workers into West Berlin.
    C. Gorbachev to end communism.
    D. Gorbachev to destroy the Berlin Wall.

12. The Berlin Wall was finally destroyed when
    A. the U.S. physically dismantled it.
    B. a new leadership controlled East Germany.
    C. the Soviets responded to repeated threats from the U.S.
    D. Gorbachev was ousted by Soviet hardliners.

Questions 13-15 refer to the following speech.

Ladies and Gentlemen, I'd planned to speak to you tonight to report on the state of the Union, but the events of earlier today have led me to change those plans. Today is a day for mourning and remembering. Nancy and I are pained to the core by the tragedy of the shuttle Challenger. We know we share this pain with all of the people of our country. This is truly a national loss.

Nineteen years ago, almost to the day, we lost three astronauts in a terrible accident on the ground. But, we've never lost an astronaut in flight; we've never had a tragedy like this. And perhaps we've forgotten the courage it took for the crew of the shuttle; but they, the Challenger Seven, were aware of the dangers, but overcame them and did their jobs brilliantly. We mourn seven heroes: Michael Smith, Dick Scobee, Judith Resnik, Ronald McNair, Ellison Onizuka, Gregory Jarvis, and Christa McAuliffe. We mourn their loss as a nation together.

For the families of the seven, we cannot bear, as you do, the full impact of this tragedy. But we feel the loss, and we're thinking about you so very much. Your loved ones were daring and brave, and they had that special grace, that special spirit that says, "give me a challenge and I'll meet it with joy." They had a hunger to explore the universe and discover its truths. They wished to serve, and they did. They served all of us.

We've grown used to wonders in this century. It's hard to dazzle us. But for twenty-five years the United States space program has been doing just that. We've grown used to the idea of space, and perhaps we forget that we've only just begun. We're still pioneers. They, the member of the Challenger crew, were pioneers.

And I want to say something to the schoolchildren of America who were watching the live coverage of the shuttle's takeoff. I know it is hard to understand, but sometimes painful things like this happen. It's all part of the process of exploration and discovery. It's all part of taking a chance and expanding man's horizons. The future doesn't belong to the fainthearted; it belongs to the brave. The Challenger crew was pulling us into the future, and we'll continue to follow them.

I've always had great faith in and respect for our space program, and what happened today does nothing to diminish it. We don't hide our space program. We don't keep secrets and cover things up. We do it all up front and in public. That's the way freedom is, and we wouldn't change it for a minute. We'll continue our quest in space. There will be more shuttle flights and more shuttle crews and, yes, more volunteers, more civilians, more teachers in space. Nothing ends here; our hopes and our journeys continue. I want to add that I wish I could talk to every man and woman who works for NASA or who worked on this mission and tell them: "Your dedication and professionalism have moved an impressed us for decades. And we know of your anguish. We share it."

There's a coincidence today. On this day 390 years ago, the great explorer Sir Francis Drake died aboard ship off the coast of Panama. In his lifetime the great frontiers were the oceans, and a historian later said, "He lived by the sea, died on it, and was buried in it." Well, today we can say of the challenger crew: Their dedication was, like Drake's, complete.

The crew of the space shuttle Challenger honored us by the manner in which they lived their lives. We will never forget them, nor the last time we saw them, this morning, as they prepared for the journey and waved goodbye and "slipped the surly bonds of earth" to "touch the face of God."

--Ronald Reagan, "Speech on the Challenger Disaster," January 28, 1986

13. When did the space program known as NASA begin?
    A. 1958
    B. 1969
    C. 1975
    D. 1985

14. According to Reagan, what NASA mission became the first in which astronauts died in flight?
    A. Space Shuttle Columbia
    B. Space Shuttle Endeavor
    C. Space Shuttle Challenger
    D. Space Shuttle Discovery

15. According to Reagan, what was the purpose of the space shuttle?
    A. to orbit the earth in record time.
    B. to land on the moon.
    C. to explore and discover.
    D. to test nuclear missiles.

Questions 16-18 refer to the following speech.

This morning at 7 a.m. the union representing those who man America's air traffic control facilities called a strike. This was the culmination of 7 months of negotiations between the Federal Aviation Administration and the union. At one point in these negotiations agreement was

311

reached and signed by both sides, granting a $40 million increase in salaries and benefits. This is twice what other government employees can expect. It was granted in recognition of the difficulties inherent in the work these people perform. Now, however, the union demands are 17 times what had been agreed to — $681 million. This would impose a tax burden on their fellow citizens which is unacceptable.

I would like to thank the supervisors and controllers who are on the job today, helping to get the nation's air system operating safely. In the New York area, for example, four supervisors were scheduled to report for work, and 17 additionally volunteered. At National Airport a traffic controller told a newsperson he had resigned from the union and reported to work because, ``How can I ask my kids to obey the law if I don't?" This is a great tribute to America.

Let me make one thing plain. I respect the right of workers in the private sector to strike. Indeed, as president of my own union, I led the first strike ever called by that union. I guess I'm maybe the first one to ever hold this office who is a lifetime member of an AFL - CIO union. But we cannot compare labor-management relations in the private sector with government. Government cannot close down the assembly line. It has to provide without interruption the protective services which are government's reason for being.

It was in recognition of this that the Congress passed a law forbidding strikes by government employees against the public safety. Let me read the solemn oath taken by each of these employees, a sworn affidavit, when they accepted their jobs: ``I am not participating in any strike against the Government of the United States or any agency thereof, and I will not so participate while an employee of the Government of the United States or any agency thereof."

It is for this reason that I must tell those who fail to report for duty this morning they are in violation of the law, and if they do not report for work within 48 hours, they have forfeited their jobs and will be terminated.

--Ronald Reagan, The Air Traffic Controllers Strike

16. The workers that went on strike were employed by
    A. various private airlines.
    B. the federal government.
    C. independent agencies.
    D. state agencies.

17. According to Reagan, he was the nation's first president who served as
    A. a strikebreaker.
    B. an arbitrator.
    C. a scab employee.
    D. a union member.

18. Ultimately, the air traffic controllers who went on strike were
    A. given an extension to return to work.
    B. given a raise.

C. given better health benefits.

D. fired.

Questions 19-21 refer to the following excerpt:

Supply-side economics brought a new perspective to fiscal policy. Instead of stressing the effects on spending, supply-siders showed that tax rates directly affect the supply of goods and services. Lower tax rates mean better incentives to work, to save, to take risks, and to invest. As people respond to the higher after-tax rewards, or greater profitability, incomes rise and the tax base grows, thus feeding back some of the lost revenues to the Treasury. The saving rate also grows, providing more financing for government and private borrowing. Since Keynesian analysis left out such effects, once supply-side economics appeared on the scene the Democrats could no longer claim that government spending stimulated the economy more effectively than tax cuts. Tax cuts were now competitive, and the House Republicans began to make the most of it. . . .

Many people also have the mistaken idea that taxes on personal income have no adverse consequences for business other than reducing the demand for products. They believe that higher tax rates on personal income help business by reducing the federal deficit and lowering interest rates. In actual fact, higher personal tax rates reduce private-sector saving and drive up both the cost of credit and the cost of labor to firms. When the Treasury examined the effects of the Kennedy tax cuts, it was found that the personal saving rate rose. This implies that the saving rate would fall if tax rates rise, and indeed the saving rate declined as bracket creep pushed savers into higher tax brackets.

We now have many decades of empirical evidence of the effects of disincentives on economic performance, ranging from China and the Soviet Union to the European welfare states. The effects of disincentives clearly thwart the intended results of central planning, government investment programs, and the maintenance of aggregate demand. On the other hand, there is an abundance of evidence of the positive effects of good incentives. Only free people are productive and forward-looking, but they cease to be free when their property rights are sacrificed to interest-group politics. Supply-side economics is the economics of a free society. It will prevail wherever freedom itself prevails.

--Paul Craig Roberts, *The Supply-Side Revolution* (1984)

19. The key to supply-side economics revolves around
    A. tax cuts.
    B. raising taxes.
    C. raising social spending.
    D. deficit spending.

20. According to Roberts, the tax cuts of Kennedy resulted in
    A. less saving.
    B. increased spending.
    C. increased saving.
    D. loss of jobs.

21. According to Roberts, lower taxes results in all of the following *except*
    A. better incentives to work.
    B. better incentives to save.
    C. better incentives to invest.
    D. better incentives to be less risky.

SHORT ANSWER QUESTIONS

The Cold War was basically over by the end of Reagan's presidency.

   a. Choose ONE of the following and explain why your choice represents the event that led to the end of the Cold War.
   - Strategic Defense Initiative goes into effect
   - Mikhail Gorbachev becomes the leader of the Soviet Union
   - INF Treaty is signed by Reagan and Gorbachev

   b. Contrast your choice against ONE of the other options, demonstrating why that option in not as significant as your choice.

LONG ESSAY QUESTION

What were the key features of the Reagan Revolution?

ANSWERS AND EXPLANATIONS

Multiple Choice Questions

1. C Reagan's handling of the air traffic controller strike displayed how he would deal with labor strife.
2. D Reducing taxes was a key component to supply-side economics or *Reaganomics*.
3. A Strategic Defense Initiative or SDI was designed to destroy incoming missiles in space.
4. D The secret diversion of money to Contras in Nicaragua eventually led to the Iran-Contra scandal.
5. C Reagan brought a new energy to fight communism and bring an end to the Cold War.
6. B The INF Treaty would be a major step in ending the Cold War.
7. D Dukakis was viewed as soft on crime and not a forceful candidate.
8. B Inside trading information allowed Boesky to buy and sell stock to his advantage.
9. D Live Aid featured simultaneous concerts in Philadelphia and London.
10. A A scourge known as AIDS made its presence felt beginning in the eighties.
11. D Reagan was quoted as saying, "Mr. Gorbachev, tear down this wall."

12. B The fall of communist regimes became a trend in Europe, including the end of communism in East Germany and the Soviet Union.
13. A NASA began shortly after the launching of Sputnik.
14. C Challenger exploded shortly after takeoff.
15. C The purpose of the space shuttle was to engage in exploration and discovery.
16. B Reagan believed the strike endangered federal safety regulations.
17. D Reagan was a member of the Screen Actors Guild.
18. D Reagan gave a 48 hour notice and then terminated the employment of the Strikers.
19. B Cutting taxes would allow for more spending, savings, and investment.
20. B Savings rose as a result of Kennedy's tax cuts.
21. D Tax cuts promoted taking risks with investments.

Long Essay Question

What were the key features of the Reagan Revolution?

(Key topics to focus and elaborate on)
- tax cuts
- decrease in social spending
- increase of defense spending
- increase of federal debt

Chapter 29
A NEW WORLD ORDER, 1989-2001

- As Bush took office, communist governments began to collapse.

THE BUSH ADMINISTRATION, 1989-1993

- Bush was well-prepared to handle foreign affairs upon entering the presidency.
- During his term, the Soviet Union dissolved in 1991 and Russia became its own republic. In essence, the Cold War was over because the prime enemy of the United States did not exist any longer.
- The same could not be said about China where the communist government suppressed a protest with tanks and killed thousands in the process.
- In August of 1990, Iraq invaded the neighboring country of Kuwait stirring much protest among UN nations. Despite an ultimatum, the dictator of Iraq, Saddam Hussein refused to withdraw troops from Kuwait, and thus Operation Desert Storm quickly annihilated Iraqi forces and freed Kuwait.
- In 1989, shortly before the Gulf War, Bush sent troops to remove the dictator of Panama, Manuel Noriega for drug trafficking.
- The Bush administration also dealt with numerous developments around the world including those in Somalia, Yugoslavia, and North America.
- On the domestic front, Bush pushed to improve education, reduce pollution, and end discrimination against those with disabilities.
- The Bush Administration also witnessed a major riot in Los Angeles after a jury acquitted four officers of severely beating an African American who resisted arrest.
- The O.J. Simpson trial displayed the tensions that still existed between blacks and whites as blacks cheered at Simpson's not guilty verdict and whites stood stunned.
- The economy went through a recession during Bush's presidency and Bush angered conservatives when he raised taxes. Consequently, Bush would struggle in the election of 1992 and ultimately lose to Bill Clinton.

The Clinton Presidency

- Although Clinton wanted to improve the economy, his first initiative dealt with universal health care, but ultimately the initiative was dropped.
- More struggle and criticism came after the tragic fallout at Waco that left over eighty people dead, including children.
- Success would come for Clinton with the Family Leave Act, Americorps, Goals 2000, a reduction in the federal debt, and the passage of NAFTA.
- In 1996, Clinton signed the Personal Responsibility and Work Opportunity. Reconciliation Act that prevented most people from receiving two years of assistance.
- During the 1990s, the political division between the Democrats and Republicans grew deeper and the notion of having respectful differences and moderation disappeared.

- Clinton dealt with or witnessed several issues pertaining to foreign policy: he assisted in the signing of the Oslo Accords between the PLO and Israel, tense moments in Somalia and Haiti, a civil war in Rwanda, ordered strikes against several Serbian positions in Yugoslavia, kept a watchful eye on both North Korea and Iraq, sought to recognize Vietnam, and worked for peace in Northern Ireland.
- Violence also struck the heartland when Timothy McVeigh bombed a federal building in Oklahoma City killing 168 Americans. Two angry students went on a shooting rampage at a school in Columbine, Colorado.
- At the same time, a terrorist group known as al-Qaeda formed and was led by Osama bin Laden, a Saudi Arabian who became infuriated when U.S. troops landed in Saudi Arabia during the Gulf War. This group participated in the bombing of the World Trade Center in 1993, bombings of U.S. Embassies in Africa, and an attack against the USS Cole.
- In 1998, Bill Clinton was accused of having an affair with a White House intern named Monica Lewinski. Clinton denied the accusation before the American people, but independent investigator, Kenneth Starr argued that Clinton had lied under oath about the incident and other similar incidents before a grand jury. Starr believed he had the necessary evidence to impeach the president and presented his finding before the House of Representatives.
- The House of Representatives obliged by impeaching the president under the charges of perjury and obstruction of justice. Subsequently, the Senate held a trial but the prosecution did not obtain enough votes to remove Clinton from office.
- As Clinton dealt with the consequences of the Monica Lewinski affair, the economy began to prosper with more Americans owning TVs, computers, etc.
- In the election of 2000, Clinton's vice president Al Gore ran against George W. Bush, son of former president, George Herbert Walker Bush. The election result hinged on the outcome in Florida which was too close to call. In fact, Gore demanded a recall because of the questionable ballots that were used. Ultimately, the Supreme Court ruled that a recount could not take place and George Bush won the election.
- No doubt, the results of this election were viewed on the internet by the American public through the use of computers, but the nation's very first computers were military in nature.
- Through a series of innovations throughout the mid-1900s, computers ultimately ended up in the homes of Americans. In the seventies, members of a group known as the Homebrew Club, including Steve Jobs and Steve Wozniak helped to launch the Apple Company which proved to be a huge success, and IBM introduced the PC and turned to Microsoft which was led by Bill Gates and Paul Allen for its software.
- While Microsoft would dominate the software industry, Jobs introduced the hand-held mouse which would revolutionize the operating systems of computers.
- By the turn of the century, American society had become heavily reliant on computers, so reliant that fears were widespread that the new millennium would trigger computer glitch disasters throughout the nation, if not the world. The fear became known as Y2K. Yet the world survived with very few malfunctions and glitches reported.
- The Internet revolutionized world society in numerous ways. The idea of "connection" stemmed from the military's fear that a nuclear assault could wipe out the nation's communications systems. The RAND Corporation led the research in producing the nation's first connection via computers.

- To add to this connection, Tim Berners-Lee introduced the World Wide Web in 1990, an innovation that revolutionized Internet connections. Some of the first software programs that allowed people to connect to the Internet included Netscape, AOL, and Yahoo.
- Entrepreneurs eager to make a profit from this new technology paved the way for the dot.com industry which saw soaring profits and an eventual bubble burst in 2000.
- The search engine known as Google was introduced in 1998 and became so popular that the term for looking up information was identified with Google.
- Despite the clear advantages of computer and Internet technology, there were losers during this period including record companies and newspapers, and numerous email users who had information "hacked."

MULTIPLE CHOICE

1. During the Bush administration, the Soviet Union would
   A. become stronger and more powerful.
   B. dissolve into independent republics.
   C. move forces into Afghanistan.
   D. renew its vows to spread communism.

2. During the Gulf War, Osama bin Laden became infuriated with the United States because
   A. Israel's support of the war.
   B. Bin Laden was from Iraq.
   C. American troops were on Saudi Arabian soil.
   D. the U.S. imposed economic sanctions on Afghanistan.

3. The U.S. attack against Iraqi forces during the Gulf War came to known as
   A. Operation Shock and Awe.
   B. Operation Desert Storm.
   C. Operation Desert Shield.
   D. Operation Free Iraqi.

4. During Bush's presidency, a violent riot broke out in the city of
   A. Detroit.
   B. New York.
   C. Oakland.
   D. Los Angeles.

5. The treaty that reduced all trade barriers between the United States, Canada, and Mexico was
   A. NATO.
   B. NAFTA.
   C. Hay-Bunau Varilla Treaty.
   D. Treaty of Tlatelolco.

6. A popular conservative radio show host who constantly criticized Clinton and called women activists "feminazis" was
   A. Tom Leikas.
   B. Rush Limbaugh.
   C. Larry King.
   D. G. Gordon Liddy.

7. Timothy McVeigh and Terry Nichols unleashed their own brand of American terrorism when they
   A. bombed in the World Trade Center.
   B. torpedoed the USS Cole   .
   C. bombed a federal building in Oklahoma.
   D. bombed a Spanish train.

8. The Pentagon co-worker who taped her conversations regarding the president's affair with Monica Lewinski was
   A. Linda Tripp.
   B. Kenneth Starr.
   C. Newt Gingrich.
   D. Paula Jones.

9. The scare of Y2K referred to
   A. fear of computer malfunction on New Year's Day 2000.
   B. hurricanes forecasted for the Gulf of Mexico.
   C. hacking into the accounts of online bankers.
   D. a terrorist attack on the World Trade Center.

10. Tim Berners-Lee revolutionized computer technology when he
    A. created Microsoft software.
    B. sent the first message via computers.
    C. introduced the World Wide Web.
    D. created the mouse for Apple.

Questions 11-12 refer to the following visual:

11. Which of the following did not occur under the presidency of George H.W. Bush?
    A. The Gulf War.
    B. invasion of Panama.
    C. passage of the Disability Act.
    D. the overthrow of Saddam Hussein.

12. Under the presidency of George H. W. Bush
    A. O.J. Simpson was acquitted of murder.
    B. NAFTA passed.
    C. the INF Treaty was signed.
    D. the Berlin Wall fell.

Questions 13-15 refer to the following articles.

House Resolution 611

Resolved, That William Jefferson Clinton, President of the United States, is impeached for high crimes and misdemeanors, and that the following articles of impeachment be exhibited to the United States Senate:

Articles of impeachment exhibited by the House of Representatives of the United States of America in the name of itself and of the people of the United States of America, against William Jefferson Clinton, President of the United States of America, in maintenance and support of its impeachment against him for high crimes and misdemeanors.

Article I

In his conduct while President of the United States, William Jefferson Clinton, in violation of his constitutional oath faithfully to execute the office of President of the United States and, to the best of his ability, preserve, protect, and defend the Constitution of the United States, and in violation of his constitutional duty to take care that the laws be faithfully executed, has willfully corrupted and manipulated the judicial process of the United States for his personal gain and exoneration, impeding the administration of justice, in that:

On August 17, 1998, William Jefferson Clinton swore to tell the truth, the whole truth, and nothing but the truth before a Federal grand jury of the United States. Contrary to that oath, William Jefferson Clinton willfully provided perjurious, false and misleading testimony to the grand jury concerning one or more of the following: (1) the nature and details of his relationship with a subordinate Government employee; (2) prior perjurious, false and misleading testimony he gave in a Federal civil rights action brought against him; (3) prior false and misleading statements he allowed his attorney to make to a Federal judge in that civil rights action; and (4) his corrupt efforts to influence the testimony of witnesses and to impede the discovery of evidence in that civil rights action.

In doing this, William Jefferson Clinton has undermined the integrity of his office, has brought disrepute on the Presidency, has betrayed his trust as President, and has acted in a manner subversive of the rule of law and justice, to the manifest injury of the people of the United States.

Wherefore, William Jefferson Clinton, by such conduct, warrants impeachment and trial, and removal from office and disqualification to hold and enjoy any office of honor, trust, or profit under the United States.

Article II

In his conduct while President of the United States, William Jefferson Clinton, in violation of his constitutional oath faithfully to execute the office of President of the United States and, to the best of his ability, preserve, protect, and defend the Constitution of the United States, and in violation of his constitutional duty to take care that the laws be faithfully executed, has prevented, obstructed, and impeded the administration of justice, and has to that end engaged personally, and through his subordinates and agents, in a course of conduct or scheme designed to delay, impede, cover up, and conceal the existence of evidence and testimony related to a Federal civil rights action brought against him in a duly instituted judicial proceeding.

--Impeachment Charges against William Jefferson Clinton

13. According to Article I, the exact nature of Clinton's offense was
    A. he brought disrepute on the Presidency.
    B. he refused to hand over tapes involving his investigation.
    C. he refused to discuss his relationship with Monica Lewinsky and Paula Jones.
    D. he committed an extra-marital affair.

14. According to Article II, the exact nature of Clinton's offense was
    A. he obstructed justice by convincing witnesses to give false testimony.
    B. he did not uphold his constitutional duty.
    C. he lied under oath.
    D. he committed an extra-marital affair.

15. The outcome of Clinton's impeachment proceedings was
    A. it never reached the Senate.
    B. there were not enough votes in the Senate to remove Clinton from office.
    C. Clinton resigned from office.
    D. a plea bargain was struck with the Senate that allowed Clinton to remain as president.

Questions 16-18 refer to the following document.

Just 2 hours ago, allied air forces began an attack on military targets in Iraq and Kuwait.

These attacks continue as I speak. Ground forces are not engaged.

This conflict started August 2d when the dictator of Iraq invaded a small and helpless neighbor. Kuwait-a member of the Arab League and a member of the United Nations-was crushed; its people, brutalized. Five months ago, Saddam Hussein [President of Iraq] Saddam Hussein started this cruel war against Kuwait. Tonight, the battle has been joined.

This military action, taken in accord with United Nations resolutions and with the consent of the Untied States Congress, follows months of constant and virtually endless diplomatic activity on the part of the United Nations, the United States, and many, many other countries. Arab leaders sought what became known as an Arab solution, only to conclude that Saddam Hussein was unwilling to leave Kuwait. Others traveled to Baghdad in a variety of efforts to restore peace and justice. Our Secretary of State, James Baker, held an historic meeting in Geneva, only to be totally rebuffed. This past weekend, in a last-ditch effort, the Secretary-General of the United Nations went to the Middle East with peace in his heart-his second such mission. And he came back from Baghdad with no progress at all in getting Saddam Hussein to withdraw from Kuwait...

As I report to you, air attacks are underway against military targets in Iraq. We are determined to knock out Saddam Hussein's nuclear-bomb potential. We will also destroy his chemical-weapons facilities. Much of Saddam's artillery and tanks will be destroyed. Our operations are designed to best protect the lives of all the coalition forces by targeting Saddam's vast military arsenal. Initial reports from General Schwarzkopf are that our operations are proceeding according to plan.

Our objectives are clear: Saddam Hussein's forces will leave Kuwait. The legitimate government of Kuwait will be restored to its rightful place, and Kuwait will once again be free. Iraq will eventually comply with all relevant United Nations resolutions, and then, when peace is restored, it is our hope that Iraq will live as a peaceful and cooperative member of the family of nations, thus enhancing the security and stability of the Gulf...

Tonight, as our forces fight, they and their families are in our prayers. May God bless each and every one of them, and the coalition forces at our side in the Gulf, and may He continue to bless our nation, the United States of America.

--George Bush, Address to the Nation Announcing Allied Military Action in the Persian Gulf (1991)

16. Kuwait was of major importance to the United States because
    A. it was a bastion of democracy.
    B. it was America's only ally in the Middle East.
    C. it was America's tourist capital in the Middle East.
    D. it was (and still is) an oil-rich nation.

17. The United States did not strike alone in this attack of Iraqi forces. The other members of this attacking coalition were
    A. Germany and Russia.
    B. France and Spain.
    C. Saudi Arabia and Iran.
    D. England and France.

18. The result of the Gulf War was
    A. Iraqi forces were removed from Kuwait but Saddam Hussein stayed in power.
    B. Iraqi forces remained in Kuwait and Saddam Hussein stayed in power.
    C. Iraqi forces were removed from Kuwait and Saddam Hussein was removed from power.
    D. Iraq was occupied by the U.S. military and Saddam Hussein was executed.

Questions 19-21 refer to the following speech.

My fellow citizens, today we celebrate the mystery of American renewal. This ceremony is held in the depth of winter, but by the words we speak and the faces we show the world, we force the spring, a spring reborn in the world's oldest democracy that brings forth the vision and courage to reinvent America. When our Founders boldly declared America's independence to the world and our purposes to the Almighty, they knew that America, to endure, would have to change; not change for change's sake but change to preserve America's ideals: life, liberty, the pursuit of happiness...

... This new world has already enriched the lives of millions of Americans who are able to compete and win in it. But when most people are working harder for less; when others cannot work at all; when the cost of health care devastates families and threatens to bankrupt our enterprises, great and small; when the fear of crime robs law-abiding citizens of their freedom; and when millions of poor children cannot even imagine the lives we are calling them to lead, we have not made change our friend...

To renew America, we must be bold... We must invest more in our own people, in their jobs, and in their future, and at the same time cut our massive debt. And we must do so in a world in which we must compete for every opportunity...

...We must do what America does best: offer more opportunity to all and demand more responsibility from all. It is time to break the bad habit of expecting something for nothing from our Government or from each other. Let us all take more responsibility not only for ourselves and our families but for our communities and our country.

To renew America, we must meet challenges abroad as well as at home. There is no longer a clear division between what is foreign and what is domestic. The world economy, the world environment, the world AIDS crisis, the world arms race: they affect us all. Today, as an older order passes, the new world is more free but less stable. Communism's collapse has called forth old animosities and new dangers. Clearly, America must continue to lead the world we did so much to make.

..When our vital interests are challenged or the will and conscience of the international community is defied, we will act, with peaceful diplomacy whenever possible, with force when necessary. The brave Americans serving our Nation today in the Persian Gulf, in Somalia, and wherever else they stand are testament to our resolve. ..

And so, my fellow Americans, as we stand at the edge of the 21st century, let us begin anew with energy and hope, with faith and discipline. And let us work until our work is done.

The Scripture says, "And let us not be weary in well doing: for in due season we shall reap, if we faint not." From this joyful mountaintop of celebration we hear a call to service in the valley. We have heard the trumpets. We have changed the guard. And now, each in our own way and with God's help, we must answer the call.

Thank you and God bless you all.

--Bill Clinton, Inauguration Address

19. In his Inaugural Address, Clinton speaks of lowering the national debt. During his presidency, the national debt
    A. actually skyrocketed to unprecedented levels.
    B. would increase moderately.
    C. would be completely eliminated.
    D. would see a major reduction.

20. The communist collapse Clinton spoke of led to old animosities especially in
    A. Iraq.
    B. Yugoslavia.
    C. Latin America.
    D. Germany.

21. When Clinton proclaims, "It is time to break the bad habit of expecting something *for nothing from* our Government or from each other, " he is mirroring the speech of his boyhood idol
    A. Franklin D. Roosevelt.
    B. Dwight D. Eisenhower.
    C. John F. Kennedy.
    D. Ronald Reagan.

SHORT ANSWER QUESTIONS

Despite an American victory against Iraq, George H.W. Bush loses his bid to be reelected.

a. Choose ONE of the following and explain why your choice represents the event that led Bush's loss.
- Americans faced unemployment and new taxes in the early 1990s
- The Los Angeles riots erupt
- Bill Clinton and Ross Perot run for the presidency

b. Contrast your choice against ONE of the other options, demonstrating why that option in not as significant as your choice.

LONG ESSAY QUESTION

How did the impeachment and subsequent acquittal of Bill Clinton unfold?

ANSWERS AND EXPLANATIONS

Multiple Choice Questions

1. B The Soviet Union dissolved in 1991.
2. C As part of Operation Desert Shield, the U.S placed soldiers in Saudi Arabia.
3. B Operation Desert Storm was led by General Norman Schwarzkopf.
4. D Rioting broke out in Los Angeles after four officers accused of beating Rodney were acquitted.
5. B NAFTA opened up free trade amongst the U.S., Canada, and Mexico.
6. B Rush Limbaugh was no friend to Clinton or his supporters.
7. C In protest to the tragedy at Waco, McVeigh and Nichols bombed the federal building in Oklahoma City.
8. A Linda Tripp gave her recorded messages to Kenneth Starr who was investigating Clinton on a sexual harassment lawsuit involving Paula Jones.
9. A Civilians and defense both worried about the outcome of computers switching to the time reference of 2000.
10. C World Wide Web made it possible for virtually anyone to use the Internet.
11. D Saddam Hussein was a target, but not a priority.

12. D The Berlin Wall was brought down in 1989.
13. A Clinton's perjury both brought disrepute to the presidency and a betrayal of trust.
14. A Clinton's second charge of impeachment was obstruction of justice.
15. B Clinton was well shy of votes required for his removal.
16. D Americans feared dictator rule in both Iraq and Kuwait.
17. D The U.S., France, and England provided forces to the UN to free Kuwait
18. A Bush's main objected was to remove Iraqi forces from Kuwait.
19. D The national debt decreased during Clinton's presidency.
20. B Ethnic cleansing in Yugoslavia became a consequence of the Cold War's end.
21. C Kennedy was a boyhood idol of Clinton.

Long Essay Question

How did the impeachment and subsequent acquittal of Bill Clinton unfold?

(Key topics to focus and elaborate on)
- Grand jury testimony of Monica Lewinski and Bill Clinton
- Starr Report given to House of Representatives/Articles of Impeachment charged against Bill Clinton
- Senate trial and acquittal

Chapter 30
ENTERING A NEW TIME, 2001-2013

- On the morning of September 11, 2001, four hijacked jetliners headed for the West Coast turned around and crashed into both towers of the World Trade Center, the Pentagon, and in the Pennsylvania countryside.
- Despite the tragedy of 9/11, many acts of heroism occurred on that eventful day.

THE IMPACT OF SEPTEMBER 11, 2001

- On the day of 9/11, Americans were stunned and shocked and by the events of the day and President Bush spoke of revenge for the perpetrators of the attack.
- By the end of the day, investigators determined that Osama bin Laden's al-Qaeda were behind the attack.
- Since Afghanistan harbored this terrorist network, that Middle Eastern country became a target of U.S. retaliation. In particular, the Taliban government who hosted al-Qaeda were subjects of U.S. attack.
- Bin Laden escaped to Pakistan and eluded capture for ten years until he was shot and killed by US forces.
- A commission reported that clearly the U.S. had not prepared itself well for such an attack.
- Before foreign policy became an obvious point of focus, Bush introduced No Child Left Behind that would utilized assessments to determine if schools made "adequate yearly progress."
- True to Republican form, Bush cut taxes and Americans received rebate checks.
- As plans for security emerged, Congress passed the USA Patriot act that allowed the Justice Department to search through personal information of those deemed as suspicious.
- Many believed that Iraq involved itself in the 9/11 attacks and many in the Bush Administration had ambitions to invade this country.
- Congress was divided over whether to invade Iraq. Nevertheless, authorization from Congress and the UN led to a swift victory over Saddam Hussein and his Iraqi forces in 2003.
- Maintaining control of Iraq would be a lot tougher than defeating its military. Hussein's staff was removed from their positions and chaos ensued with a country that was ill-prepared for new order. The dissolution of the military only exacerbated the post-war situation. Soon a religious war ensued and Iraq was close to a civil war with American forces caught in between.
- In the meantime, no weapons of mass destruction were ever found, but Hussein was found and executed by a U.S.-backed provisional government in 2006.
- Opposition to the war grew at home especially after American troops humiliated captured enemies at Abu Ghraib.
- Slowly, U.S.troops and their Iraqi allies would begin to take control of the nation.

Hurricane Katrina-August 29, 2005, and Its Aftermath

- In 2005 a deadly hurricane struck the Gulf Coast killing over 1800 people and causing $75 million worth of damage. Evacuation attempts were ignored or not called for in time.
- The storm proved to have both a disastrous and deadly effect in the city of New Orleans, especially in the poorest neighborhoods, especially those occupied by African Americans.
- Ironically, FEMA turned out to be a disaster in its ineffectiveness and inability to assist those in need.
- Hospitals were without generators and the Superdome contained scenes of death and horrifying primitive conditions.

The Financial Crisis of 2008

- In September of 2008, the stock market suffered a major jolt and the ensuing financial crisis of 2008 began.
- Risky mortgage loans coupled with low interest rates created a scenario where housing. prices went up, yet like other bubble investments would come down and defaults became all too common.
- Unemployment stayed high and teetered close to sixteen percent, and this had a ripple effect on the economy.
- Bernard Madoff contributed to the financial quagmire with a Ponzi scheme that lost investors between $10 and $17 billion.
- The federal government received much criticism with its bailouts of banks and the auto industry while unemployment stayed high.

New Liberals, New Conservatives

- Barack Obama's rise to the presidency began in 2004 when as a freshman senator, he was asked to run for the presidency. Hillary Clinton would've been the more obvious choice, but her track record and her husband's infidelity made many leading Democrats squeamish about her possible nomination.
- In 2008, during his bid to gain the Democratic presidential nomination, Obama took advantage of the latest internet social networking to build funds for his campaign. Indeed, the battle between Barack Obama and Hillary Clinton for the Democratic presidential nomination was extremely close.
- For the Republicans, John McCain, a Senate veteran and prisoner of war in Vietnam, gained the nomination for his party. For his running mate, McCain chose Sarah Palin.
- On Election Day, Obama won a solid victory over McCain and became the first African American to be elected as president.
- Upon entering the presidency, Obama pushed through Congress the American Recovery and Reinvestment Act as a means to "prime the pump" for the economy.
- In 2010, through much debate, Obama was able to push through Congress the Patient Protection and Affordable Care Act, a law that required every American to have health insurance.
- Government spending and bailouts prompted the rise of the National Tea Party Coalition. The coalition was strong but had its own contradictions as well.

- The Occupy Wall Street movement proved to be another movement that was dissatisfied with the direction of the government. The movement came in response to the financial crisis the nation faced and the growing gap between the nation's rich and poor, and quickly spread to other cities across the country.
- The Election of 2012 featured the incumbent, Barack Obama versus the Republican Mitt Romney. Obama defeated Romney but Congress was divided between Republicans and Democrats.

MULTIPLE CHOICE

1. On September 11, 2001, terrorist who hijacked four jetliners hit all of their targets except those aboard
   A. American Flight 11.
   B. United Flight 175.
   C. American Flight 77.
   D. United Flight 93.

2. In total, the number of people who were killed during the 9/11 terrorist attacks was
   A. 500.
   B. 1000.
   C. 2000.
   D. 3000.

3. The immediate response to the attacks by the Bush Administration was
   A. an invasion of Iraq.
   B. assassinating Osama bin Laden.
   C. invading Afghanistan.
   D. assassinating Saddam Hussein.

4. Bush's proposal for education reform came to be known as
   A. No Child Left Behind.
   B. National Defense Education Act.
   C. Common Core.
   D. A Nation at Risk.

5. Bush's legislation that he believed would boost the economy was
   A. creation of government jobs.
   B. implementation of tax cuts.
   C. raising the minimum wage.
   D. universal health care.

6. The USA Patriot Act allowed for
   A. a draft to mobilize for war against Iraq.
   B. easing of gun restrictions for protection.
   C. searching of personal records.
   D. pouring of funds to weapons research.

7. The premise for invading Iraq in 2006 was
   A. Iraq's hosting of terrorist networks.
   B. Osama bin Laden's refuge was in Iraq.
   C. Iraq's oil embargo against the U.S.
   D. Iraq's presumed possession of weapons of mass destruction.

8. The deadly hurricane that struck the Gulf Coast in 2005 was
   A. Hurricane Sandy.
   B. Hurricane Katrina.
   C. Hurricane Camille.
   D. Hurricane Audrey.

9. The election of 2008 was unprecedented in all of the following aspects *except*
   A. first African American elected as president.
   B. first female Republican vice-presidential candidate.
   C. first election utilizing Facebook and You-tube.
   D. first election that featured no campaign fundraising.

10. Obama's most notable law that passed during his first term dealt with
    A. tax relief reform.
    B. health care reform.
    C. education reform.
    D. campaign reform.

Questions 11-12 refer to the following image.

11. During the 9/11 attacks, the World Trade Center Towers collapsed as a result of
    A. bombs planted on the upper floors.
    B. car bombs detonated in the towers' parking lots.
    C. hijacked planes that struck the towers.
    D. missile attacks from al-Qaeda pilots.

12. As a result of the Twin Towers attack in New York City
    A. over 2500 were killed.
    B. less than 2500 were killed.
    C. over 3500 were killed.
    D. over 4000 were killed.

Questions 13-15 refer to the following excerpt.

The Arabian Peninsula has never - since Allah made it flat, created its desert, and encircled it with seas - been stormed by any forces like the crusader armies spreading in it like locusts, eating its riches and wiping out its plantations. All this is happening at a time in which nations are attacking Muslims like people fighting over a plate of food. In the light of the grave situation and the lack of support, we and you are obliged to discuss current events, and we should all agree on how to settle the matter.
No one argues today about three facts that are known to everyone; we will list them, in order to remind everyone:
First, for over seven years the United States has been occupying the lands of Islam in the holiest of places, the Arabian Peninsula, plundering its riches, dictating to its rulers, humiliating its people, terrorizing its neighbors, and turning its bases in the Peninsula into a spearhead through which to fight the neighboring Muslim peoples. If some people have in the past argued about the fact of the occupation, all the people of the Peninsula have now acknowledged it. The best proof of this is the Americans' continuing aggression against the Iraqi people using the Peninsula as a staging post, even though all its rulers are against their territories being used to that end, but they are helpless. Second, despite the great devastation inflicted on the Iraqi people by the crusader-Zionist alliance, and despite the huge number of those killed, which has exceeded 1

millionÉdespite all this, the Americans are once again trying to repeat the horrific massacres, as though they are not content with the protracted blockade imposed after the ferocious war or the fragmentation and devastation.

So here they come to annihilate what is left of this people and to humiliate their Muslim neighbors.

Third, if the Americans' aims behind these wars are religious and economic, the aim is also to serve the Jews' petty state and divert attention from its occupation of Jerusalem and murder of Muslims there. The best proof of this is their eagerness to destroy Iraq, the strongest neighboring Arab state, and their endeavor to fragment all the states of the region such as Iraq, Saudi Arabia, Egypt, and Sudan into paper statelets and through their disunion and weakness to guarantee Israel's survival and the continuation of the brutal crusade occupation of the Peninsula.

All these crimes and sins committed by the Americans are a clear declaration of war on Allah, his messenger, and Muslim And ulema have throughout Islamic history unanimously that the jihad is an individual duty...

On that basis, and in compliance with Allah's order, we issue the following fatwa to all Muslims: The ruling to kill the Americans and their allies - civilians and military - is an individual duty for every Muslim who can do it in any country in which it is possible to do it, in order to liberate the al-Aqsa Mosque and the holy mosque [Mecca] from their grip, and in order for their armies to move out of all the lands of Islam, defeated and unable to threaten any Muslim. This is in accordance with the words of Almighty Allah, "and fight the pagans all together as they fight you all together," and "fight them until there is no more tumult or oppression, and there prevail justice and faith in Allah."

This is in addition to the words of Almighty Allah: "And why should ye not fight in the cause of Allah and of those who, being weak, are ill-treated (and oppressed)? - women and children, whose cry is: 'Our Lord, rescue us from this town, whose people are oppressors; and raise for us from thee one who will help!'"

We - with Allah's help - call on every Muslim who believes in Allah and wishes to be rewarded to com-ply with Allah's order to kill the Americans and plunder their money wherever and whenever they find it. We also call on Muslims, leaders, youths, and soldiers to launch the raid on Satan's U.S. troops and the devil's supporters allying with them, and to displace those who are behind them so that they may learn a lesson.

Osama bin Laden, World Islamic Front Statement, 1998

13. According to Osama bin Laden, the U.S. used Saudi Arabia to
    A. launch its attacks against Iran.
    B. launch its attacks against Iraq.
    C. launch its attacks against Afghanistan.
    D. launch its attacks against Pakistan.

14. According to Osama bin Laden, America's wars in the Middle East were in part geared towards all of the following *except*
    A. diverting Israel's oppression and murder of Muslims.
    B. manipulating the leaders of Saudi Arabia.

C. fragmenting the states of the Middle East.
D. preserving and embracing the Muslim faith.

15. According to Osama bin Laden, the justification to murder Americans and its allies was
    A. retaliation for the attack on Saddam Hussein.
    B. America's lack of Muslim support in the U.S.
    C. the blessing and encouragement to do so by Allah.
    D. America's extraction of oil from the region.

Questions 16-18 refer to the following address.

ADDRESS TO THE NATION ON THE SEPTEMBER 11 ATTACKS
THE OVAL OFFICE
WASHINGTON, D.C.
SEPTEMBER 11, 2001

Good evening. Today, our fellow citizens, our way of life, our very freedom came under attack in a series of deliberate and deadly terrorist acts. The victims were in airplanes, or in their offices; secretaries, businessmen and women, military and federal workers; moms and dads, friends and neighbors. Thousands of lives were suddenly ended by evil, despicable acts of terror.

The pictures of airplanes flying into buildings, fires burning, huge structures collapsing, have filled us with disbelief, terrible sadness, and a quiet, unyielding anger. These acts of mass murder were intended to frighten our nation into chaos and retreat. But they have failed; our country is strong.

A great people has been moved to defend a great nation. Terrorist attacks can shake the foundations of our biggest buildings, but they cannot touch the foundation of America. These acts shattered steel, but they cannot dent the steel of American resolve.

America was targeted for attack because we're the brightest beacon for freedom and opportunity in the world. And no one will keep that light from shining.
Today, our nation saw evil, the very worst of human nature. And we responded with the best of America — with the daring of our rescue workers, with the caring for strangers and neighbors who came to give blood and help in any way they could.

Immediately following the first attack, I implemented our government's emergency response plans. Our military is powerful, and it's prepared. Our emergency teams are working in New York City and Washington, D.C. to help with local rescue efforts. Our first priority is to get help to those who have been injured, and to take every precaution to protect our citizens at home and around the world from further attacks.

The functions of our government continue without interruption. Federal agencies in Washington which had to be evacuated today are reopening for essential personnel tonight, and will be open for business tomorrow. Our financial institutions remain strong, and the American economy will be open for business, as well.

The search is underway for those who are behind these evil acts. I've directed the full resources of our intelligence and law enforcement communities to find those responsible and to bring them to justice. We will make no distinction between the terrorists who committed these acts and those who harbor them.

I appreciate so very much the members of Congress who have joined me in strongly condemning these attacks. And on behalf of the American people, I thank the many world leaders who have called to offer their condolences and assistance.
America and our friends and allies join with all those who want peace and security in the world, and we stand together to win the war against terrorism. Tonight, I ask for your prayers for all those who grieve, for the children whose worlds have been shattered, for all whose sense of safety and security has been threatened. And I pray they will be comforted by a power greater than any of us, spoken through the ages in Psalm 23: "Even though I walk through the valley of the shadow of death, I fear no evil, for You are with me."

This is a day when all Americans from every walk of life unite in our resolve for justice and peace. America has stood down enemies before, and we will do so this time. None of us will ever forget this day. Yet, we go forward to defend freedom and all that is good and just in our world.

Thank you. Good night, and God bless America.

--George W. Bush

16. The collapsing structures that Bush spoke of was
    A. Pentagon.
    B. Statue of Liberty.
    C. Washington Monument.
    D. World Trade Center.

17. One feature of the government's emergency response plan was
    A. to shut the nation's schools down.
    B. abort all flights throughout the nation.
    C. close all the freeways.
    D. air strike all suspected terrorists.

18. "We will make no distinction between the terrorists who committed these acts and those who harbor them." This warning by Bush was in particular in reference to
    A. Iraq.
    B. North Korea.
    C. Iran.
    D. Afghanistan.

Questions 19-21 refer to the following speech.

...And just as we keep our keep our promise to the next generation here at home, so must we keep America's promise abroad. If John McCain wants to have a debate about who has the temperament, and judgment, to serve as the next Commander-in-Chief, that's a debate I'm ready to have.

For while Senator McCain was turning his sights to Iraq just days after 9/11, I stood up and opposed this war, knowing that it would distract us from the real threats we face. When John McCain said we could just "muddle through" in Afghanistan, I argued for more resources and more troops to finish the fight against the terrorists who actually attacked us on 9/11, and made clear that we must take out Osama bin Laden and his lieutenants if we have them in our sights. John McCain likes to say that he'll follow bin Laden to the Gates of Hell - but he won't even go to the cave where he lives.

And today, as my call for a time frame to remove our troops from Iraq has been echoed by the Iraqi government and even the Bush Administration, even after we learned that Iraq has a $79 billion surplus while we're wallowing in deficits, John McCain stands alone in his stubborn refusal to end a misguided war.

That's not the judgment we need. That won't keep America safe. We need a President who can face the threats of the future, not keep grasping at the ideas of the past.

You don't defeat a terrorist network that operates in eighty countries by occupying Iraq. You don't protect Israel and deter Iran just by talking tough in Washington. You can't truly stand up for Georgia when you've strained our oldest alliances. If John McCain wants to follow George Bush with more tough talk and bad strategy, that is his choice - but it is not the change we need.

We are the party of Roosevelt. We are the party of Kennedy. So don't tell me that Democrats won't defend this country. Don't tell me that Democrats won't keep us safe. The Bush-McCain foreign policy has squandered the legacy that generations of Americans -- Democrats and Republicans - have built, and we are here to restore that legacy.

As Commander-in-Chief, I will never hesitate to defend this nation, but I will only send our troops into harm's way with a clear mission and a sacred commitment to give them the equipment they need in battle and the care and benefits they deserve when they come home.

I will end this war in Iraq responsibly, and finish the fight against al Qaeda and the Taliban in Afghanistan. I will rebuild our military to meet future conflicts. But I will also renew the tough, direct diplomacy that can prevent Iran from obtaining nuclear weapons and curb Russian aggression. I will build new partnerships to defeat the threats of the 21st century: terrorism and nuclear proliferation; poverty and genocide; climate change and disease. And I will restore our moral standing, so that America is once again that last, best hope for all who are called to the cause of freedom, who long for lives of peace, and who yearn for a better future.

--Barack Obama, Acceptance of Democratic Presidential Nomination

19. In terms of the U.S. invasion of Iraq in 2003, Barack Obama's stance was

A. he supported the war against Iraq.

B. he believed that the war against terrorism should be fought in both Iraq and Afghanistan.

C. he was opposed the war against Iraq.

D. he opposed the pursuit of Bin Laden.

20. "We are a party of Roosevelt....So don't tell me that Democrats won't defend this country." is in reference to

A. Roosevelt during the Spanish American War.

B. Roosevelt during period of Filipino resistance.

C. Roosevelt during World War II.

D. Roosevelt during the Great Depression.

21. During Obama's years as president, the United States

A. continued its war in Iraq.

B. would see a massive deployment of troops sent to Iraq.

C. saw US forces kill Osama Bin Laden.

D. saw the execution of Saddam Hussein.

SHORT ANSWER QUESTIONS

Barack Obama becomes the first African American to become the president of the United States.

a. Choose ONE of the following and explain why your choice represents the event that led to this election victory.

- Voting Rights Act of 1965 passed
- Jesse Jackson runs for president in 1988
- Obama approached by Democratic leaders to consider a run for the presidency

b. Contrast your choice against ONE of the other options, demonstrating why that option in not as significant as your choice.

LONG ESSAY QUESTION

Explain the events that led to the terrorist attacks on September 11, 2001

ANSWERS AND EXPLANATIONS

Multiple Choice Questions

1. D United Flight 93 crashed in Pennsylvania before reaching Washington D.C. before reaching Washington D.C.

2. D 9/11 was the deadliest attack of Americans on U.S. soil.

3. C   The U.S. invaded the base of al-Qaeda which was in Afghanistan.
4. A   No Child Left Behind was the basis of education until Common Core emerged.
5. B   Early in his presidency, tax rebate checks were distributed.
6. C   The government viewed this power as necessary to fight terrorism in the U.S.
7. D   Weapons of mass destruction were never found in Iraq.
8. B   Close to two thousand died as a result of Hurricane Katrina.
9. D   Massive campaign funding was raised during the election of 2008.
10. B   Obamacare as it was labeled went into effect in 2014.
11. C   Hijacked planes were used as gasoline-filled missiles.
12. A   Over 2500 were killed as a result of the attack on the Twin Towers.
13. B   Desert Shield in Saudi Arabia turned into Desert Storm.
14. D   Bin Laden believed the U.S. committed blasphemy against the Islam faith with its actions in the Middle East.
15. C   Bin Laden believed that terrorism against Americans was supported by Allah.
16. D   Both towers collapsed as a result of the terrorist strikes.
17. B   All flights were cancelled and planes in the air were ordered to land.
18. D   Since the Taliban government harbored the terrorists camps of al-Qaeda, it became a target of the U.S.
19. C   Obama opposed the war from the beginning.
20. C   Roosevelt guided the U.S. throughout most of WWII.
21. C   Osama Bin Laden was killed by U.S. forces in Pakistan in 2011.

Long Essay Question

Explain the events that led to the terrorist attacks on September 11, 2001

(Key points to cover)
- Operation Desert Shield begins
- Al-Qaeda terrorist camps established
- Terrorist attacks against U.S. in Africa and Yemen
- Osama bin Laden declares war on the U.S.

PART III

PRACTICE DOCUMENT-BASED QUESTIONS WITH SAMPLE ESSAYS

The practice Document-based Questions in Part III mirror the actual section in the AP exam in format and question type. Set aside a time to write essay responses to these questions, timing yourself as you will be timed when you take the actual exam. This will help you prepare for your test-taking experience.

DOCUMENT-BASED QUESTION 1

> **Analyze the relationship between the British North American colonies and the government back in England.**

DOCUMENT 1 Navigation Act of September 13, 1660

For the increase of shipping and encouragement of the navigation of this nation wherein, under the good providence and protection of God, the wealth, safety, and strength of this kingdom is so much concerned; (2) be it enacted by the king's most excellent Majesty, and by the Lords and Commons in this present Parliament assembled, and by the authority thereof, that from and after the first day of December, one thousand six hundred and sixty, and from thence forward, no goods or commodities whatsoever shall be imported into or exported out of any lands, islands, plantations, or territories to his Majesty belonging or in his possession, or which may hereafter belong unto or be in the possession of his Majesty, his heirs, and successors, in Asia, Africa, or America, in any other ship or ships, vessel or vessels whatsoever, but in such ships or vessels as do truly and without fraud belong only to the people of England or Ireland, dominion of Wales or town of Berwick upon Tweed, or are of the built of and belonging to any the said lands, islands, plantations, or territories, as the proprietors and right owners thereof, and whereof the master and three fourths of the mariners at least are English; (3) under the penalty of the forfeiture and loss of all the goods and commodities which shall be imported into or exported out of any the aforesaid places in any other ship or vessel, as also of the ship or vessel, with all its guns, furniture, tackle, ammunition, and apparel; one third part thereof to his Majesty, his heirs and successors; one third part to the governor of such land, plantation, island, or territory where such default shall be committed, in case the said ship or goods be there seized, or otherwise that third part also to his Majesty, his heirs and successors; and the other third part to him or them who shall seize, inform, or sue for the same in any court of record, by bill, information, plaint, or other action, wherein no session, protection, or wager of law shall be allowed; (4) and all admirals and other commanders at sea of any the ships of war or other ship having commission from his Majesty or from his heirs or successors, are hereby authorized and strictly required to seize and bring in as prize all such ships or vessels as shall have offended contrary hereunto, and deliver them to the court of admiralty, there to be proceeded against; and in case of condensation, one moiety of such forfeitures shall be to the use of such admirals or commanders and their companies, to be divided and proportioned amongst them according to the rules and orders of the sea in case of ships taken prize; and the other moiety to the use of his Majesty, his heirs and successors XVIII. And it is further enacted by the authority aforesaid, that from and after the first day of April, which shall be in the year of our Lord one thousand six hundred sixty-one, no sugars, tobacco, cotton-wool, indigoes, ginger, rustic, or other dyeing wood, of the growth, production, or manufacture of any English plantations in America, Asia, or Africa, shall be shipped, carried, conveyed, or transported from any of the said English plantations to any land, island, territory, dominion, port, or place whatsoever, other than to such other English plantations as do belong to his Majesty, his heirs and successors, or to the kingdom of England or Ireland, or principality of Wales, or town of Berwick upon Tweed, there to be laid on shore; (2) under the penalty of the forfeiture of the said goods, or the full value thereof, as also of the ship, with all her guns, tackle, apparel, ammunition, and furniture; the one moiety to the king's Majesty, his heirs and successors, and the other moiety to him or them that shall seize, inform, or sue for the same in any court of record, by bill, plaint, or information, wherein no ession, protection, or wager of law shall be allowed.

DOCUMENT 2   Nathaniel Bacon's Challenge to William Berkeley, 1676

The Declaracion of the People.
1. For haveing upon specious pretences of publiqe works raised greate unjust taxes upon the Comonality for the advancement of private favorites and other sinister ends, but noe visible effects in any measure adequate, For not haveing dureing this long time of his Gouvernement in any measure advanced this hopefull Colony either by fortificacons Townes or Trade.
2. For haveing abused and rendred contemptable the Magistrates of Justice, by advanceing to places of Judicature, scandalous and Ignorant favorites....
4. For haveing, protected, favoured, and Imboldned the Indians against his Majesties loyall subjects, never contriveing, requireing, or appointing any due or proper meanes of sattisfaction for theire many Invasions, robberies, and murthers comitted upon us.
5. For haveing when the Army of English, was just upon the track of those Indians, who now in all places burne, spoyle, murther and when we might with ease have destroyed them: who then were in open hostillity, for then haveing expressly countermanded, and sent back our Army, by passing his word for the peaceable demeanour of the said Indians, who imediately prosecuted theire evill intentions, comitting horred murthers and robberies in all places, being protected by the said engagement and word past of him the said Sir William Berkeley, haveing ruined and laid desolate a greate part of his Majesties Country, and have now drawne themselves into such obscure and remote places, and are by theire success soe imboldned and confirmed, by theire confederacy soe strengthned that the cryes of blood are in all places, and the terror, and constimation of the people soe greate, are now become, not onely a difficult, but a very formidable enimy, who might att first with ease have beene destroyed.
6. And lately when upon the loud outcryes of blood the Assembly had with all care raised and framed an Army for the preventing of further mischeife and safeguard of this his Majesties Colony....
These are therefore in his majesties name to command you forthwith to seize the persons above mentioned as Trayters to the King and Country and them to bring to Midle plantacon, and there to secure them untill further order, and in case of opposition, if you want any further assistance you are forthwith to demand itt in the name of the people in all the Counties of Virginia.

Nathaniel Bacon
Generall by Consent of the people.

DOCUMENT 3   William Berkeley's Response to Nathaniel Bacon, 1676

The declaration and Remonstrance of Sir William Berkeley his most sacred Majesties Governor and Captain Generall of Virginia...

And now I will state the Question betwixt me as a Governor and Mr. Bacon, and say that if any enimies should invade England, any Councellor Justice of peace or other inferiour officer, might raise what forces they could to protect his Majesties subjects, But I say againe, if after the Kings knowledge of this invasion, any the greatest peere of England, should raise forces against the kings prohibition this would be now, and ever was in all ages and Nations accompted treason. Nay I will goe further, that though this peere was truly zealous for the preservation of his King, and subjects, and had better and greater abibitys then all the rest of his fellow subjects, doe his King and Country service, yett if the King (though by false information) should suspect the contrary, itt were treason in this Noble peere to proceed after the King's prohibition, and for the truth of this I appeale to all the laws of England, and the Laws and constitutions of all other Nations in the world, And yett further itt is declared by this Parliament that the takeing up Armes for the King and Parliament is treason, for the event shewed that what ever the pretence was to seduce ignorant and well affected people, yett the end was ruinous both to King and people, as this will be if not prevented, I doe therefore againe declair that Bacon proceedeing against all Laws of all Nations modern and ancient, is Rebell to his sacred Majesty and this Country, nor will I insist upon the sweareing of men to live and dye togeather, which is treason by the very words of the Law.

To conclude, I have don what was possible both to friend and enimy, have granted Mr. Bacon three pardons, which he hath scornefully rejected, suppoaseing himselfe stronger to subvert then I and you to maineteyne the Laws, by which onely and Gods assisting grace and mercy, all men mwt hope for peace and safety. I will add noe more though much more is still remaineing to Justifie me and condenme Mr. Bacon, but to desier that this declaration may be read in every County Court in the Country, and that a Court be presently called to doe itt, before the Assembly meet, That your approbation or dissattisfaction of this declaration may be knowne to all the Country, and the Kings Councell to whose most revered Judgments itt is submitted, Given the xxixth day of May, a happy day in the xxv"ith yeare of his most sacred Majesties Reigne, Charles the second, who God grant long and prosperously to Reigne, and lett all his good subjects say
Amen.
Sir William Berkeley
Governor

DOCUMENT 4 Edward Randolph Describes King Philip's War, 1685

That notwithstanding the ancient law of the country, made in the year 1633, that no person should sell any armes or ammunition to any Indian upon penalty of £10 for every gun, £5 for a pound of powder, and 40s. for a pound of shot, yet the government of the Massachusets in the year 1657, upon designe to monopolize the whole Indian trade did publish and declare that the trade of furrs and peltry with the Indians in their jurisdiction did solely and properly belong to their commonwealth and not to every indifferent person, and did enact that no person should trade with the Indians for any sort of peltry, except such as were authorized by that court, under the penalty of £100 for every offence, giving liberty to all such as should have licence from them to sell, unto any Indian, guns, swords, powder and shot, paying to the treasurer 3d. for each gun and for each dozen of swords; 6d. for a pound of powder and for every ten pounds of shot, by which means the Indians have been abundantly furnished with great store of armes and ammunition to the utter ruin and undoing of many families in the neighbouring colonies to enrich some few of their relations and church members.

DOCUMENT 5   William Penn's Charter of Privileges, 1701

WILLIAM PENN, Proprietary and Governor of the Province of Pensilvania and Territories thereunto belonging, To all to whom these Presents shall come, sendeth Greeting. WHEREAS King CHARLES the Second, by His Letters Patents, under the Great Seal of England, bearing Date the Fourth Day of March in the Year One Thousand Six Hundred and Eighty-one, was graciously pleased to give and grant unto me, and my Heirs and Assigns for ever, this Province of Pennsilvania, with divers great Powers and Jurisdictions for the well Government thereof. AND WHEREAS the King's dearest Brother, JAMES Duke of YORK and ALBANY, &c. by his Deeds of Feoffment, under his Hand and Seal duly perfected, bearing Date the Twenty-Fourth Day of August, One Thousand Six Hundred Eighty and Two, did grant unto me, my Heirs and Assigns, all that Tract of Land, now called the Territories of Pensilvania, together with Powers and Jurisdictions for the good Government thereof. AND WHEREAS for the Encouragement of all the Freemen and Planters, that might be concerned in the said Province and Territories, and for the good Government thereof, I the said WILLIAM PENN, in the Year One Thousand Six Hundred Eighty and Three, for me, my Heirs and Assigns, did grant and confirm unto all the Freemen Planters and Adventurers therein, divers Liberties, Franchises and Properties, as by the said Grant, entitled, The FRAME of the Government of the Province of Pensilvania, and Territories thereunto belonging, in America, may appear; which Charter or Frame being found in some Parts of it, not so suitable to the present Circumstances of the Inhabitants, was in the Third Month, in the Year One Thousand Seven Hundred, delivered up to me, by Six Parts of Seven of the Freemen of this Province and Territories, in General Assembly met, Provision being made in the said Charter, for that End and Purpose. AND WHEREAS I was then pleased to promise, That I would restore the said Charter to them again, with necessary Alterations, or in lieu thereof, give them another, better adapted to answer the present Circumstances and Conditions of the said Inhabitants; which they have now, by their Representatives in General Assembly met at Philadelphia, requested me to grant. KNOW YE THEREFORE, That for the further Well-being and good Government of the said Province, and Territories; and in Pursuance of the Rights and Powers before mentioned, I the said William Penn do declare, grant and confirm, unto all the Freemen, Planters and Adventurers, and other Inhabitants of this Province and Territories, these following Liberties, Franchises and Privileges, so far as in me lieth, to be held, enjoyed and kept, by the Freemen, Planters and Adventurers, and other Inhabitants of and in the said Province and Territories "hereunto annexed, forever.

DOCUMENT 6   The Closing of the Frontier, 1763

October 7, 1763

BY THE KING. A PROCLAMATION

Whereas We have taken into Our Royal Consideration the extensive and valuable Acquisitions in America, secured to our Crown by the late Definitive Treaty of Peace, with all convenient Speed, of the great Benefits and Advantages which must accrue therefrom to their Commerce, Manufactures, and Navigation, We have thought fit, with the Advice of our Privy Council, to issue this our Royal Proclamation, hereby to publish and declare to all our loving Subjects, that we have, with the Advice of our Said Privy Council, granted our Letters Patent, under our Great Seal of Great Britain, to erect, within the Countries and Islands ceded and confirmed to Us by the said Treaty, Four distinct and separate Governments, styled and called by the names of Quebec, East Florida, West Florida and Grenada, and limited and bounded as follows, viz....

We have also thought fit, with the advice of our Privy Council as aforesaid, to give unto the Governors and Councils of our said Three new Colonies, upon the Continent full Power and Authority to settle and agree with the Inhabitants of our said new Colonies or with any other Persons who shall resort thereto, for such Lands, Tenements and Hereditaments, as are now or hereafter shall be in our Power to dispose of; and them to grant to any such Person or Persons upon such Terms, and under such moderate Quit-Rents, Services and Acknowledgments, as have been appointed and settled in our other Colonies, and under such other Conditions as shall appear to us to be necessary and expedient for the Advantage of the Grantees, and the Improvement and settlement of our said Colonies.

DOCUMENT-BASED QUESTION 2

Explain the process by which slavery was created in North America.

DOCUMENT 1

DOCUMENT 2

Approximately 6,600,000 Africans taken to the Americas, 1700-1800

Mozambique 2%
Senegambia 6%
Windward Coast 8%
Gold Coast 11%
Bight of Benin 18%
Bight of Biafra 18%
West Central Africa 37%

DOCUMENT 3   Alexander Falconbridge, The African Slave Trade, 1788

. . . About eight o'clock in the morning the Negroes are generally brought upon deck. Their irons being examined, a long chain, which is locked to a ring-bolt, fixed in the deck, is run through the rings of the shackles of the men, and then locked to another ring-bolt, fixed also in the deck. By this means fifty or sixty, and sometimes more, are fastened to one chain, in order to prevent them from rising, or endeavoring to escape. If the weather proves favorable, they are permitted to remain in that situation till four or five in the afternoon, when they are disengaged from the chain, and sent down. . . . Upon the Negroes refusing to take sustenance, I have seen coals of fire, glowing hot, put on a shovel, and placed so near their lips, as to scorch and burn them. And this has been accompanied with threats, of forcing them to swallow the coals, if they any longer persisted in refusing to eat. These means have generally had the desired effect. I have also been credibly informed that a certain captain in the slave trade poured melted lead on such of the Negroes as obstinately refused their food. Exercise being deemed necessary for the preservation of their health, they are sometimes obligated to dance, when the weather will permit their coming on deck. If they go about it reluctantly, or do not move with agility, they are flogged; a person standing by them all the time with at cat-o'-nine-tails in his hand for that purpose.

DOCUMENT 4   Olaudah Equiano, The Middle Passage, 1788

. . . I and some few more slaves, that were not saleable amongst the rest, from very much fretting, were shipped off in a sloop for North America. . . . While I was in this plantation [in Virginia] the gentleman, to whom I suppose the estate belonged, being unwell, I was one day sent for to his dwelling house to fan him; when I came into the room where he was I was very much affrighted at some things I saw, and the more so as I had seen a black woman slave as I came through the house, who was cooking the dinner, and the poor creature was cruelly loaded with various kinds of iron machines; she had one particularly on her head, which locked her mouth so fast that she could scarcely speak; and could not eat nor drink. I was much astonished and shocked at this contrivance, which I afterwards learned was called the iron muzzle . . . .

DOCUMENT 5   An Act Concerning Servants and Slaves

IV. And also be it enacted, by the authority aforesaid, and it is hereby enacted, That all servants imported and brought into this country, by sea or land, who were not Christians in their native country, (except Turks and Moors in amity with her majesty, and others that can make due proof of their being free in England, or any other Christian country, before they were shipped, in order to transportation hither) shall be accounted and be slaves, and as such be here bought and sold notwithstanding a conversion to Christianity afterwards.

V. And be it enacted, by the authority aforesaid, and it is hereby enacted, That if any person or persons shall hereafter import into this colony, and here sell as a slave, any person or persons that shall have been a freeman in any Christian country, island, or plantation, such importer and seller as aforesaid, shall forfeit and pay, to the party from whom the said freeman shall recover his freedom, double the sum for which the said freeman was sold. To be recovered, in any court of record within this colony, according to the course of the common law, wherein the defendant shall not be admitted to plead in bar, any act or statute for limitation of actions.

VI. Provided always, That a slave's being in England, shall not be sufficient to discharge him of his slavery, without other proof of his being manumitted there.

DOCUMENT 6   James Oglethorpe: The Stono Rebellion, 1739

Sometime since there was a Proclamation published at Augustine, in which the King of Spain (then at Peace with Great Britain) promised Protection and Freedom to all Negroes Slaves that would resort thither. Certain Negroes belonging to Captain Davis escaped to Augustine, and were received there. They were demanded by General Oglethorpe who sent Lieutenant Demere to Augustine, and the Governour assured the General of his sincere Friendship, but at the same time showed his Orders from the Court of Spain, by which he was to receive all Run away Negroes… On the 9th day of September last being Sunday which is the day the Planters allow them to work for themselves, Some Angola Negroes assembled, to the number of Twenty; and one who was called Jemmy was their Captain, they surprised a Warehouse belonging to Mr. Hutchenson at a place called Stonehow [sicÑ]; they there killed Mr. Robert Bathurst, and Mr. Gibbs, plundered the House and took a pretty many small Arms and Powder, which were there for Sale. Next they plundered and burnt Mr. Godfrey's house, and killed him, his Daughter and Son. They then turned back and marched Southward along Pons Pons, which is the Road through Georgia to Augustine, they passed Mr. Wallace's Taxern towards day break, and said they would not hurt him, for he was a good Man and kind to his Slaves, but they broke open and plundered Mr. Lemy's House, and killed him, his wife and Child. They marched on towards Mr. Rose's resolving to kill him; but he was saved by a Negroe, who having hid him went out and pacified the others. Several Negroes joyned them, they calling out Liberty, marched on with Colours displayed, and two Drums beating, pursuing all the white people they met with, and killing Man Woman and Child when they could come up to them…The Lieutenant Governour sent an account of this to General Oglethorpe, who met the advices on his return form the Indian Nation He immediately ordered a Troop of Rangers to be ranged, to patrole through Georgia, placed some Men in the Garrison at Palichocolas, which was before abandoned, and near which the Negroes formerly passed, being the only place where Horses can come to swim over the River Savannah for near 100 miles, ordered out the Indians in pursuit, and a Detachment of the Garrison at Port Royal to assist the Planters on any Occasion, and published a Proclamation ordering all the Constables &c. of Georgia to pursue and seize all Negroes, with a Reward for any that should be taken. It is hoped these measures will prevent any Negroes from getting down to the Spaniards.

DOCUMENT 7 Jefferson the Slave-owner; Thomas Jefferson, advertisement, Virginia Gazette, September 14, 1769

Run away from the subscriber in Albemarle, a Mulatto slave called Sandy, about 35 years of age, his stature is rather low, inclining to corpulence, and his complexion light; he is a shoemaker by trade, in which he uses his left hand principally, can do coarse carpenters work, and is something of a horse jockey; he is greatly addicted to drink, and when drunk is insolent and disorderly, in his conversation he swears much, and in his behavior is artful and knavish. He took with him a white horse, much scarred with traces, of which it is expected he will endeavor to dispose; he also carried his shoemakers tools, and will probably endeavor to get employment that way. Whoever conveys the said slave to me, in Albemarle, shall have 40 s. reward, if taken up within the county, 4 l. if elsewhere within the colony, and 10 l. if in any other colony, from Thomas Jefferson.

DOCUMENT-BASED QUESTION 3

> **Defend or refute the following statement: Differing patterns of immigration and migration created different social and political climates in the various regions of the Americas.**

DOCUMENT 1 J. Hector St. John Crèvecoeur, "What Is an American?" 1782

The next wish of this traveller will be to know whence came all these people? They are a mixture of English, Scotch, Irish, French, Dutch, Germans, and Swedes. From this promiscuous breed, that race now called Americans have arisen. The eastern provinces must indeed be excepted, as being the unmixed descendants of Englishmen. I have heard many wish that they had been more intermixed also: for my part, I am no wisher, and think it much better as it has happened. They exhibit a most conspicuous figure in this great and variegated picture; they too enter for a great share in the pleasing perspective displayed in these thirteen provinces. I know it is fashionable to reflect on them, but I respect them for what they have done, for the accuracy and wisdom with which they have settled their territory; for the decency of their manners; for their early love of letters; their ancient college, the first in this hemisphere; for their industry; which to me who am but a farmer, is the criterion of everything. There never was a people, situated as they are, who with so ungrateful a soil have done more in so short a time. Do you think that the monarchical ingredients which are more prevalent in other governments, have purged them from all foul stains? Their histories assert the contrary.

DOCUMENT 2 Benjamin Franklin, "Observations Concerning the Increase of Mankind, Peopling of Countries, &c.," 1751

There is in short, no Bound to the prolific Nature of Plants or Animals, but what is made by their crowding and interfering with each others Means of Subsistence. Was the Face of the Earth vacant of other Plants, it might be gradually sowed and overspread with one Kind only; as, for Instance, with Fennel; and were it empty of other Inhabitants, it might in a few Ages be replenish'd from one Nation only; as, for Instance, with Englishmen. Thus there are suppos'd to be now upwards of One Million English Souls in North-America, (tho' 'tis thought scarce 80,000 have been brought over Sea) and yet perhaps there is not one the fewer in Britain, but rather many more, on Account of the Employment the Colonies afford to Manufacturers at Home. This Million doubling, suppose but once in 25 Years, will in another Century be more than the People of England, and the greatest Number of Englishmen will be on this Side the Water. What an Accession of Power to the British Empire by Sea as well as Land! What Increase of Trade and Navigation! What Number of Ships and Seamen! We have been here but little more than 100 Years, and yet the Force of our Privateers in the late War, united, was greater, both in Men and Guns, than that of the whole British Navy in Queen Elizabeth's Time. . . .

And since Detachments of English from Britain sent to America, will have their Places at Home so soon supply'd and increase so largely here; why should the Palatine Boors be suffered to swarm into our Settlements, and by herding together establish their Language and Manners to the Exclusion of ours? Why should Pennsylvania, founded by the English, become a Colony of Aliens, who will shortly be so numerous as to Germanize us instead of our Anglifying them, and will never adopt our Language or Customs, any more than they can acquire our Complexion.

DOCUMENT 3

DOCUMENT 4

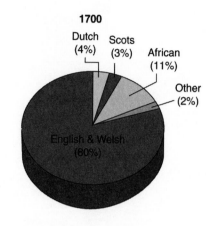

1700

Dutch
(4%)

Scots
(3%)

African
(11%)

Other
(2%)

English & Welsh
(80%)

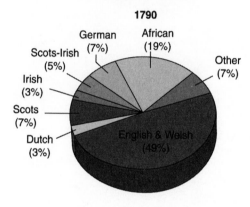

1790

German
(7%)

African
(19%)

Scots-Irish
(5%)

Other
(7%)

Irish
(3%)

Scots
(7%)

Dutch
(3%)

English & Welsh
(49%)

DOCUMENT 5

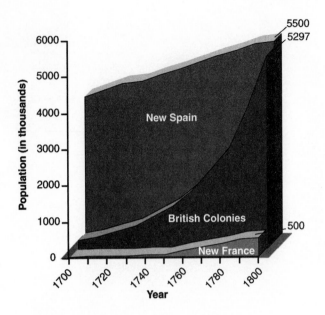

DOCUMENT 6

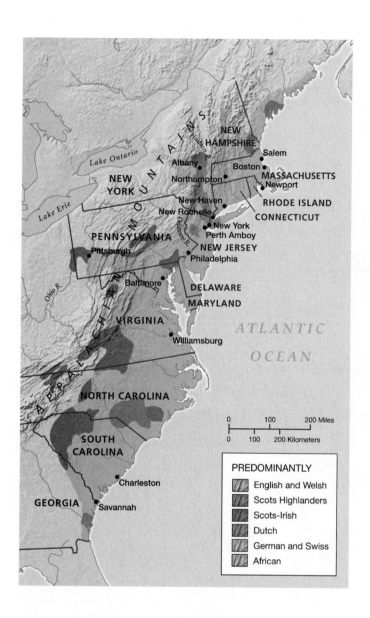

Lake Ontario

Lake Erie

Ohio R.

NEW HAMPSHIRE

Salem
Albany •
Northampton •
Boston •
MASSACHUSETTS
Newport

NEW YORK

New Haven •
New Rochelle •
New York •
Perth Amboy •
RHODE ISLAND
CONNECTICUT

PENNSYLVANIA

Pittsburgh •

Delaware R.

NEW JERSEY
Philadelphia •

Baltimore •

DELAWARE

MARYLAND

VIRGINIA

Williamsburg •

ATLANTIC

OCEAN

NORTH CAROLINA

SOUTH CAROLINA

Charleston •

GEORGIA
Savannah •

A P P A L A C H I A N   M O U N T A I N S

| 0 | 100 | 200 Miles |
| 0 | 100 | 200 Kilometers |

PREDOMINANTLY

English and Welsh
Scots Highlanders
Scots-Irish
Dutch
German and Swiss
African

DOCUMENT 7

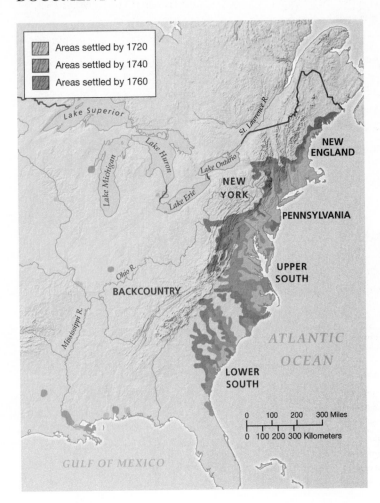

Areas settled by 1720
Areas settled by 1740
Areas settled by 1760

Lake Superior

St. Lawrence R.

NEW ENGLAND

Lake Michigan

Lake Huron

Lake Ontario

NEW YORK

Lake Erie

PENNSYLVANIA

Ohio R.

BACKCOUNTRY

UPPER SOUTH

Mississippi R.

ATLANTIC OCEAN

LOWER SOUTH

0   100   200   300 Miles

0 100 200 300 Kilometers

GULF OF MEXICO

DOCUMENT-BASED QUESTION 4

Analyze the circumstances leading up to the Missouri Compromise.

DOCUMENT 1   Letter from Benjamin Banneker to Thomas Jefferson, 1791

SIR,
...Sir, if these are sentiments of which you are fully persuaded, I hope you cannot but
acknowledge, that it is the indispensable duty of those, who maintain for themselves
the rights of human nature, and who possess the obligations of Christianity, to extend their power
and influence to the relief of every part of the human race, from whatever burden or oppression

they may unjustly labor under; and this, I apprehend, a full conviction of the truth and obligation of these principles should lead all to. Sir, I have long been convinced, that if your love for yourselves, and for those inestimable laws, which preserved to you the rights of human nature, was founded on sincerity, you could not but be solicitous, that every individual, of whatever rank or distinction, might with you equally enjoy the blessings thereof; neither could you rest satisfied short of the most active effusion of your exertions, in order to their promotion from any state of degradation, to which the unjustifiable cruelty and barbarism of men may have reduced them…

And now, Sir, I shall conclude, and subscribe myself, with the most profound respect,

Your most obedient humble servant,

BENJAMIN BANNEKER.

DOCUMENT 2 Letter from Thomas Jefferson to Benjamin Banneker, 1791

SIR,

I THANK you, sincerely, for your letter of the 19th instant, and for the Almanac it contained. No body wishes more than I do, to see such proofs as you exhibit, that nature has given to our black brethren talents equal to those of the other colors of men; and that the appearance of the want of them, is owing merely to the degraded condition of their existence, both in Africa and America. I can add with truth, that no body wishes more ardently to see a good system commenced, for raising the condition, both of their body and mind, to what it ought to be, as far as the imbecility of their present existence, and other circumstances, which cannot be neglected, will admit. I have taken the liberty of sending your Almanac to Monsieur de Condozett, Secretary of the Academy of Sciences at Paris, and Member of the Philanthropic Society, because I considered it as a document, to which your whole color had a right for their justification, against the doubts which have been entertained of them.

I am with great esteem, Sir, Your most obedient Humble Servant,

THOMAS JEFFERSON.

DOCUMENT 3 Thomas Jefferson Reacts to the "Missouri Question," 1820

…The cession of that kind of property, for so it is misnamed, is a bagatelle which would not cost me a second thought, if, in that way, a general emancipation and expatriation could be effected; and gradually, and with due sacrifices, I think it might be. But as it is, we have the wolf by the ears, and we can neither hold him, nor safely let him go. Justice is in one scale, and self-preservation in the other. Of one thing I am certain, that as the passage of slaves from one state to another would not make a slave of a single human being who would not be so without it, so their diffusion over a greater surface would make them individually happier, and proportionally facilitate the accomplishment of their emancipation, by dividing the burden on a greater number of coadjutors. An abstinence too, from this act of power, would remove the jealousy excited by the undertaking of Congress to regulate the condition of the different descriptions of men composing a state. This certainly is the exclusive right of every state, which nothing in the Constitution has taken from them and given to the general government. Could Congress, for example, say that the non-freemen of Connecticut shall be freemen, or that they shall not emigrate into any other state?

DOCUMENT 4

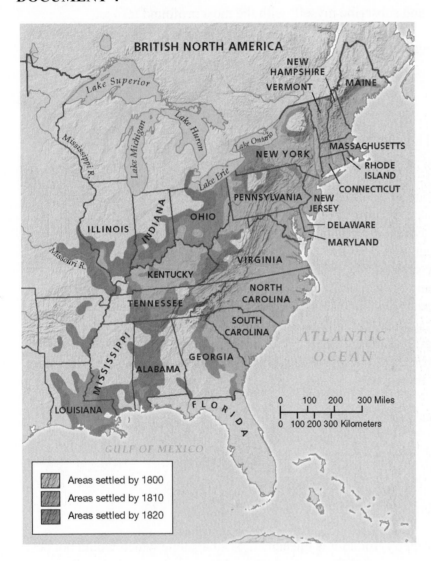

DOCUMENT 5 "Memoirs of a Monticello Slave, as Dictated to Charles Campbell by Isaac," 1847

… Mr. Jefferson had a clock in his kitchen at Monticello; never went into the kitchen except to wind up the clock.

He never would have less than eight covers at dinner if nobody at table but himself. Had from eight to thirty-two covers for dinner. Plenty of wine, best old Antigua rum and cider; very fond of wine and water. Isaac never heard of his being disguised in drink. He kept three fiddles; played in the arternoons and sometimes arter supper. This was in his early time. When he begin to git so old, he didn't play. Kept a spinnet made mostly in shape of a harpsichord; his daughter played on it. Mr. Fauble, a Frenchman that lived at Mr. Walker's, a music man, used to come to Monticello and tune it. There was a fortepiano and a guitar there. Never seed anybody play on them but the French people. Isaac never could git acquainted with them; could hardly larn their names. Mr. Jefferson always singing when ridin' or walkin'; hardly see him anywhar outdoors but what he was a-singin'. Had a fine clear voice, sung minnits (minuets) and sich; fiddled in the parlor. Old Master very kind to servants.

DOCUMENT 6

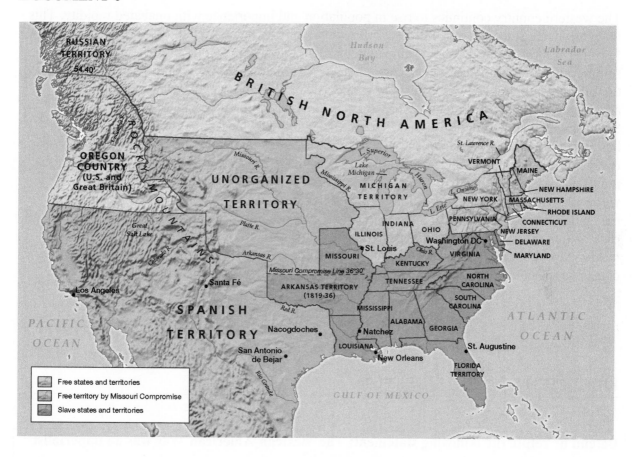

DOCUMENT 7   Thomas Jefferson on the Constitutionality of the Louisiana Purchase, 1803

…Our information as to the country is very incompleat; we have taken measures to obtain it in full as to the settled part, which I hope to receive in time for Congress. The boundaries, which I deem not admitting question, are the high lands on the western side of the Mississippi enclosing all it's waters, the Missouri of course, and terminating in the line drawn from the northwestern point of the Lake of the Woods to the nearest source of the Missipi, as lately settled between Gr Britain and the U S. We have some claims to extend on the sea coast Westwardly to the Rio Norte or Bravo, and better, to go Eastwardly to the Rio Perdido, between Mobile & Pensacola, the antient boundary of Louisiana. These claims will be a subject of negociation with Spain, and if, as soon as she is at war, we push them strongly with one hand, holding out price in the other, we shall certainly obtain the Floridas, and all in good time. In the meanwhile, without waiting for permission, we shall enter into the exercise of the natural right we have always insisted on with Spain, to wit, that of a nation holding the upper part of streams, having a right of innocent passage thro' them to the ocean. We shall prepare her to see us practise on this, & she will not oppose it by force.

Document 8 "The Western Country," Extracts from Letters Published *in Niles' Weekly Register*, 1816

The western country continues to rise in population and importance with unabated rapidity. This town has been, since the war, full to overflowing; many being obliged to leave it after coming from the Eastern states, not being able to get a room to dwell in. More houses will be built this summer than during the last three years together. Manufactories of several important kinds are establishing, among which is a steam grist and saw mill. The surveyor general is making arrangements for laying out, agreeably to late acts of Congress, towns at the Lower Rapids of Sandusky, and at the Rapids of the Miami of the Lakes. The local situation of the latter cannot but render it a most important place. It will be situated at some point within the reservation of twelve miles square, to which vessels of a small tonnage can ascend, and as near the foot of the rapids as may be. I believe the time not very distant when the wealth and resources of the western country will be brought almost to your doors, by means of an extensive inland navigation through the lakes and the grand canal proposed to be made in New York. It will be an easy matter to connect the Miami of the Lakes and the Miami of the Ohio by a canal, the face of the country between the head of the navigation of each of those rivers being quite level. What an extensive inland navigation would then be opened!-from New Orleans to the Hudson!

DOCUMENT-BASED QUESTION 5

Defend or refute the following statement: The Mexican-American War was an imperialist war.

DOCUMENT 1 The Treaties of Velasco, 1836

ARTICLES OF AGREEMENT AT SAN JACINTO

Whereas, The President Santa Anna, with divers officers of his late army, is a prisoner of war in charge of the army of Texas, and is desirous of terminating the contest now existing between the Government of Texas and that of Mexico, in which desire the Generals above named do fully concur, and Whereas, The President of the Republic of Texas, and the Cabinet, are also willing to stay the further effusion of blood, and to see the two neighboring Republics placed in relations of friendship, on terms of reciprocal advantage;

Therefore, it is agreed by the President Santa Anna, and the Generals Don Vicente Filisola, Don Jose Urea, Don Joaquin Ramires y Sesma, and Don Antonio Gaona…

5th. That the following be, and the same are hereby established and made the lines of demarcation between the two Republics of Mexico and of Texas, to wit: The line shall commence at the estuary or mouth of the Rio Grande, on the western bank thereof, and shall pursue the same bank up the said river, to the point where the river assumes the name of the Rio Bravo del Norte, from which point it shall proceed on the said western bank to the head waters, or source of said river, it being understood that the terms Rio Grande and Rio Bravo del Norte, apply to and designate one and the same stream. From the source of said river, the principal head branch being taken to ascertain that source, a due north line shall be run until it shall intersect the boundary line established and described in the Treaty negotiated by and between the Government of Spain and the Government of the United States of the North; which line was subsequently transferred to, and adopted in the Treaty of limits made between the Government of Mexico and that of the United States; and from this point of intersection the line shall be the same as was made and established in and by the several Treaties above mentioned, to continue to the mouth or outlet of the Sabine river, and from thence to the Gulf of Mexico.

DOCUMENT 2 John L. O'Sullivan, "The Great Nation of Futurity," 1845

America is destined for better deeds. It is our unparalleled glory that we have no reminiscences of battlefields, but in defense of humanity, of the oppressed of all nations, of the rights of conscience, the rights of personal enfranchisement. Our annals describe no scenes of horrid carnage, where men were led on by hundreds of thousands to slay one another, dupes and victims to emperors, kings, nobles, demons in the human form called heroes. We have had patriots to defend our homes, our liberties, but no aspirants to crowns or thrones; nor have the American people ever suffered themselves to be led on by wicked ambition to depopulate the land, to spread desolation far and wide, that a human being might be placed on a seat of supremacy.

DOCUMENT 3 Thomas Corwin, Against the Mexican War, 1847

What is the territory, Mr. President, which you propose to wrest from Mexico? It is consecrated to the heart of the Mexican by many a well-fought battle with his old Castilian master. His Bunker Hills, and Saratogas, and Yorktowns are there! The Mexican can say, "There I bled for liberty! and shall I surrender that consecrated home of my affections to the Anglo-Saxon invaders? What do they want with it? They have Texas already. They have possessed themselves of the territory between the Nueces and the Rio Grande. What else do they want? To what shall I point my children as memorials of that independence which I bequeath to them, when those battlefields shall have passed from my possession?"

Sir, had one come and demanded Bunker Hill of the people of Massachusetts, had England's lion ever showed himself there, is there a man over thirteen and under ninety who would not have been ready to meet him? Is there a river on this continent that would not have run red with blood? Is there a field but would have been piled high with the unburied bones of slaughtered Americans before these consecrated battlefields of liberty should have been wrested from us?

But this same American goes into a sister republic, and says to poor, weak Mexico, "Give up your territory, you are unworthy to possess it; I have got one half already, and all I ask of you is to give up the other!"....

DOCUMENT 4

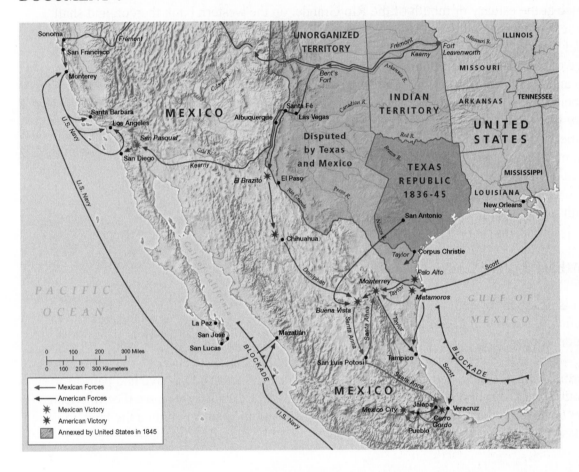

DOCUMENT 5   President Polk Sends a Message to Congress

Mexico has passed the boundary of the United States, has invaded our territory and shed American blood upon American soil. . . . War exists, and, notwithstanding all our efforts to avoid it, exists by the act of Mexico herself.

DOCUMENT 6

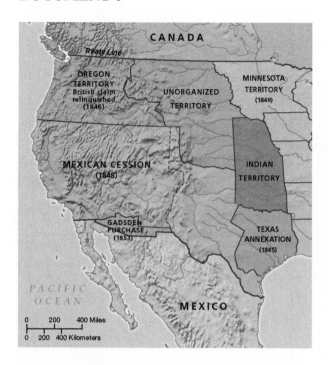

DOCUMENT 7

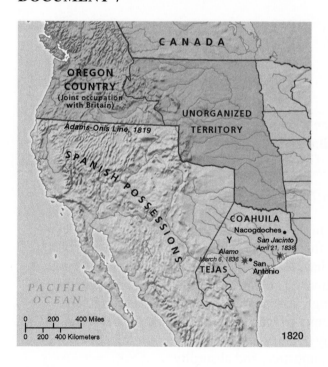

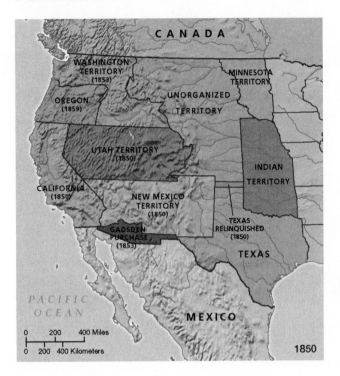

DOCUMENT-BASED QUESTION 6

> The ultimate "cause" of the Civil War has been a matter of intense debate among
> historians. Evaluate the various factors contributing to the outbreak of war and determine
> which was the most significant and why.

DOCUMENT 1   William Lloyd Garrison, from *The Liberator*, 1831

Assenting to the "self-evident truth" maintained in the American Declaration of Independence
"that all men are created equal, and endowed by their Creator with certain inalienable rights-
among which are life, liberty, and the pursuit of happiness," I shall strenuously contend for the
immediate enfranchisement of our slave population. . . . In Park Street Church, on the Fourth of
July, 1829, in an address on slavery, I unreflectingly assented to the popular but pernicious
doctrine of gradual abolition. I seize this opportunity to make a full and unequivocal recantation,
and thus publicly to ask pardon of my God, of my country, and of my brethren the poor slaves,
for having uttered a sentiment so full of timidity, injustice, and absurdity. . . .
I am aware that many object to the severity of my language; but is there not cause for severity? I
will be as harsh as truth, and as uncompromising as justice. On this subject I do not wish to
think, or speak, or write, with moderation. No! No! Tell a man whose house is on fire to give a

moderate alarm; tell him to moderately rescue his wife from the hands of the ravisher; tell the mother to gradually extricate her babe from the fire into which it has fallen-but urge me not to use moderation in a cause like the present. I am in earnest-will not equivocate-I will not excuse-I will not retreat in a single inch-and I will be heard.

DOCUMENT 2   Harriet Beecher Stowe, from *Uncle Tom's Cabin*, 1852

"Well, here's a pious dog, at last, let down among us sinners-a saint, a gentleman, and no less, to talk to us sinners about our sins! Powerful holy crittur, he must be! Here, you rascal, you make believe to be so pious-didn't you never hear, out of yer Bible, 'Servants, obey yer masters'? An't I yer master? Didn't I pay down twelve hundred dollars, cash, for all there is inside yer old cussed black shell? An't yer mine, now, body and soul?" he said, giving Tom a violent kick with his heavy boot; "tell me!"
In the very depth of physical suffering, bowed by brutal oppression, this question shot a gleam of joy and triumph through Tom's soul. He suddenly stretched himself up, and, looking earnestly to heaven, while the tears and blood that flowed down his face mingled, he exclaimed, " No! no! no! my soul an't yours, Mas'r! You haven't bought it-ye can't buy it! It's been bought and paid for by One that is able to keep it. No matter, no matter, you can't harm me!"
"I can't!" said Legree, with a sneer; "we'll see-we'll see! Here Sambo, Quimbo, give this dog such a breakin' in as he won't get over this month!"

DOCUMENT 3   A Dying Statesman Speaks Out against the Compromise of 1850

The result of the whole of these causes combined is that the North has acquired a decided ascendancy over every department of this government, and through it a control over all the powers of the system. A single section, governed by the will of the numerical majority, has now in fact the control of the government and the entire powers of the system. What was once a constitutional federal republic is now converted, in reality, into one as absolute as that of the Autocrat of Russia, and as despotic in its tendency as any absolute government that ever existed. As, then, the North has the absolute control over the government, it is manifest that on all questions between it and the South, where there is a diversity of interests, the interests of the latter will be sacrificed to the former, however oppressive the effects may be, as the South possesses no means by which it can resist through the action of the government. But if there was no question of vital importance to the South, in reference to which there was a diversity of views between the two sections, this state of things might be endured without the hazard of destruction to the South. There is a question of vital importance to the Southern section, in reference to which the views and feelings of the two sections are as opposite and hostile as they can possibly be.
I refer to the relation between the two races in the Southern section, which constitutes a vital portion of her social organization. Every portion of the North entertains views and feelings more or less hostile to it. Those most opposed and hostile regard it a sin, and consider themselves under most sacred obligation to use every effort to destroy it. Indeed, to the extent that they conceive they have power, they regard themselves as implicated in the sin and responsible for suppressing it by the use of all and every means. Those less opposed and hostile regard it as a crime—an offense against humanity, as they call it—and, although not so fanatical, feel themselves bound to use all efforts to effect the same object; while those who are least opposed

and hostile regard it as a blot and a stain on the character of what they call the nation, and feel themselves accordingly bound to give it no countenance or support. On the contrary, the Southern section regards the relation as one which cannot be destroyed without subjecting the two races to the greatest calamity and the section to poverty, desolation, and wretchedness; and accordingly they feel bound by every consideration of interest and safety to defend it.

This hostile feeling on the part of the North toward the social organization of the South long lay dormant, but it only required some cause to act on those who felt most intensely that they were responsible for its continuance to call it into action. The increasing power of this government and of the control of the Northern section over all its departments furnished the cause. It was this which made an impression on the minds of many that there was little or no restraint to prevent the government from doing whatever it might choose to do. This was sufficient of itself to put the most fanatical portion of the North in action for the purpose of destroying the existing relation between the two races in the South.

DOCUMENT 4

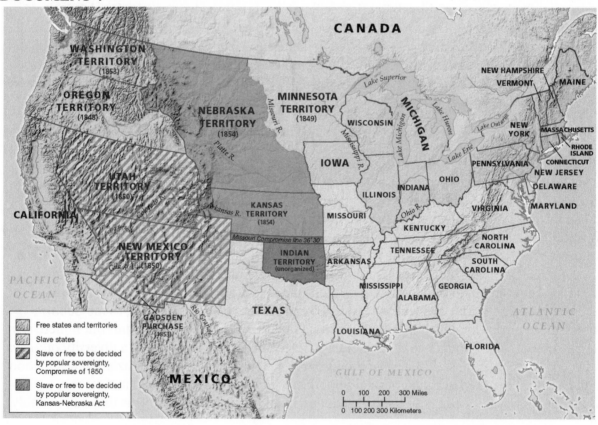

DOCUMENT 5

DOCUMENT 6

365

DOCUMENT 7 *Dred Scott v. Sandford*, 1857

The Question is simply this: Can a negro, whose ancestors were imported into this country, and sold as slaves, become a member of the political community formed and brought into existence by the Constitution of the United States, and as such become entitled to all the rights, and privileges, and immunities, guarantied [sic] by that instrument to the citizen? One of which rights is the privilege of suing in a court of the United States in the cases specified in the constitution. . . . The only matter in issue before the Court, therefore, is, whether the descendants of such slaves, when they shall be emancipated, or who are born of parents who had become free before their birth, are citizens of a State, in the sense which the word citizen is used in the Constitution. . . .

The words "people of the United States" and "citizens" are synonymous terms. . . . They both describe the political body who, according to our republican institutions, form the sovereignty, and who hold the power and conduct the government through their representatives. . . . The question before us is, whether the class of persons described in the plea in abatement compose a portion of this people, and are constituent members of this sovereignty? We think they are not, under the word "citizens" in the Constitution, and can therefore claim none of the rights and privileges which that instrument provides for and secures to citizens of the United States. On the contrary, they were at that time considered as a subordinate and inferior class of beings, who had been subjugated by the dominant race, and whether emancipated or not, yet remained subject to their authority, and had no rights or privileges but such as those who held the power and the government might choose to grant them. . . .

In discussing the question, we must not confound the rights of citizenship which a State may confer within its own limits, and the rights of citizenship as a member of the Union. It does not by any means follow, because he has all the rights and privileges of a citizen of a State, that he must be a citizen of the United States. . . .

In the opinion of the court, the legislation and histories of the times, and the language used in the Declaration of Independence, show, that neither the class of persons who had been imported as slaves, nor their descendants, whether they had become free or not, were then acknowledged as a part of the people, nor intended to be included in the general words used in that memorable instrument. . . .

They had for more than a century before been regarded as beings of an inferior order, and altogether unfit to associate with the white race, either in social or political relations, and so far inferior, that they had no rights which the white man was bound to respect; and that the negro might justly and lawfully be reduced to slavery for his benefit. . . .

. . . there are two clauses in the constitution which point directly and specifically to the negro race as a separate class of persons, and show clearly that they were not regarded as a portion of the people or citizens of the government then formed.

. . . upon full and careful consideration of the subject, the court is of opinion, that, upon the facts stated. . . , Dred Scott was not a citizen of Missouri within the meaning of the constitution of the United States and not entitled as such to sue in its courts. . . .

DOCUMENT 8

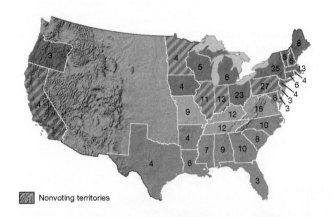

Nonvoting territories

	Electoral Vote (%)	Popular Vote (%)
ABRAHAM LINCOLN (Republican)	180 (59)	1,865,593 (40)
John C. Breckinridge (Southern Democrat)	72 (24)	848,356 (18)
John Bell (Constitutional Union)	39 (13)	592,906 (13)
Stephen A. Douglas (Northern Democrat)	12 (4)	1,382,713 (29)
States that Republicans lost in 1856, won in 1860		

Document 9   Abraham Lincoln, "A House Divided," 1858

If we could first know where we are, and whither we are tending, we could better judge what to do and how to do it. We are now far into the fifth year since a policy was initiated with the avowed object, and confident promise, of putting an end to slavery agitation. Under the operation of that policy, that agitation has not only not ceased but has constantly augmented. In my opinion, it will not cease until a crisis shall have been reached and passed. "A house divided against itself cannot stand." I believe this government cannot endure permanently half-slave and half-free. I do not expect the Union to be dissolved-I do not expect the house to fall-but I do expect it will cease to be divided. It will become all one thing or all the other. Either the opponents of slavery will arrest the further spread of it and place it where the public mind shall rest in the belief that it is in the course of ultimate extinction or its advocates will push it forward, till it shall become alike lawful in all the states, old as well as new-North as well as South.

DOCUMENT-BASED QUESTION 7

Many forces contributed to the rapid transformation of the North American West following 1850. Identify, compare, and contrast the various motivations for western settlement and decide which factor was the most decisive in transforming the West.

DOCUMENT 1

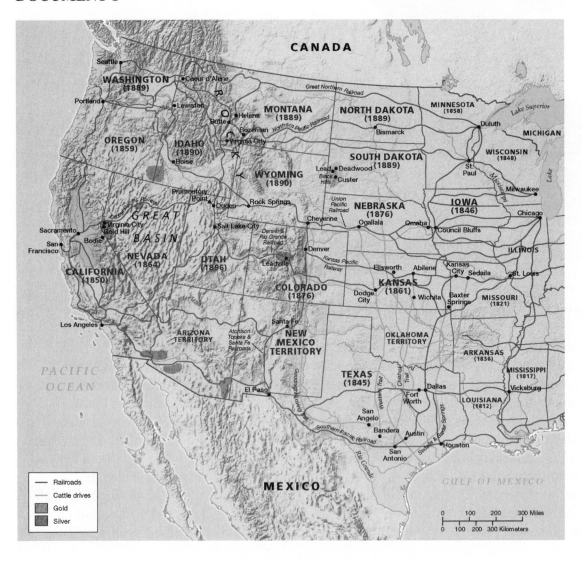

DOCUMENT 2   Lydia Allen Rudd, Diary of Westward Travel, 1852

May 14 Just after we started this morning we passed four men dig[g]ing a grave. They were packers. The man that had died was taken sick yesterday noon and died last night. They called it cholera morbus. The corpse lay on the ground a few feet from where they were dig[g]ing. The grave it was a sad sight. . . .

On the bank of the stream waiting to cross, stood a dray with five men harnessed to it bound for California. They must be some of the persevering kind I think. Wanting to go to California more than I do. . . . We passed three more graves this afternoon. . . .

Sept. 5 Traveled eighteen miles today encamped on a slough of powder river poor camp not much grass water nor wood. I am almost dead tonight. I have been sick two or three days with the bowel complaint and am much worse tonight.

Sept. 6 We have not been able to leave this miserable place today. I am not as well as yesterday and no physician to be had. We got a little medicine from a train tonight that has checked the disease some, the first thing that has done me any good.

Sept. 7 . . . I am some better today so much so that they ventured to move me this for the sake of a better camp. Mrs. Girtman is also sick with the same disease. Our cattle are most all of them ailing-there are two more that we expect will die every day. . . .

Oct. 8 started early this morning without any breakfast for the very good reason that we had nothing to eat still three miles from the falls safely landed about eight o'clock tired hungry and with a severe cold from last nights exposure something like civilization here in the shape of three or four houses there is an excuse here for a railroad of a mile and half on which to convey bag[g]age below the falls where they can again take water for the steamboat landing. Harry packed our bag[g]age down the railroad and the rest of us walked the car is drawn across the railroad by a mule and they will car[r]y no persons but sick. We again hired an Indian with his canoe to take us from the falls to the steamboat landing ar[r]ived about sundown a great many emigrants waiting for a chance to leave the steamboat and several flat boats lying ready to start out in the morning encamped on the shore for the night. We have made but eleven miles of travel encamped on the prairie no water for our stock and not much for ourselves.

October 26 . . . we reached Burlington about two o'clock. There is one store one blacksmith shop and three or four dwelling houses. We encamped close by found Mr. Donals in his store an old acquaintance of my husband's. I do not know what we shall yet conclude on doing for the winter. There is no house in town that we can get to winter in. We shall probably stay here tomorrow and by the time know what we are to do for a while at least.

October 27 . . . Our men have been looking around for a house and employment and have been successful for which I feel very thankful. Harry has gone into copartnership with Mr. Donals in the mercantile business and we are to live in the back part of the store for this winter. Henry and Mary are going into Mr. D—-house on his farm for the winter one mile from here. Mr. D—-will also find him employment if he wants. I expect that we shall not make a claim after all our trouble in getting here on purpose for one. I shall have to be poor and dependent on a man my life time.

DOCUMENT 3

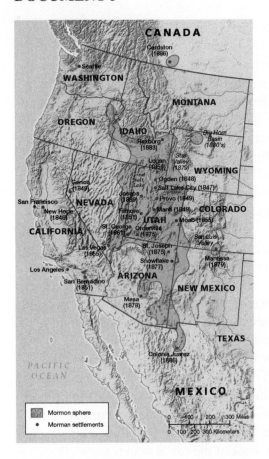

DOCUMENT 4   Horace Greeley, An Overland Journey, 1860

Men and brethen! let us resolve to have a railroad to the Pacific-to have it soon. It will add more to the strength and wealth of our country than would the acquisition of a dozen Cubas. It will prove a bond of union not easily broken, and a new spring to our national industry, prosperity and wealth. It will call new manufactures into existence, and increase the demand for the products of those already existing. It will open new vistas to national and to individual aspiration, and crush out filibusterism by giving a new and wholesome direction to the public mind. My long, fatiguing journey was undertaken in the hope that I might do something toward the early construction of the Pacific Railroad; and I trust that it has not been made wholly in vain.

DOCUMENT 5   Joseph G. McCoy, Historic Sketches of the Cattle Trade of the West and Southwest, 1874

We have in a former paper said that Texan drovers, as a class, were clannish, and easily gulled by promises of high prices for their stock. As an illustration of these statements we cite a certain secret meeting of the drovers held at one of the camps in 1867, whereat they all, after talking the matter over, pledged themselves to hold their cattle for 3 cents per pound gross and to sell none for less. One of the principal arguments used was that their cattle must be worth that price or those Illinoisans would not be expending so much money and labor in preparing facilities for shipping them. To this resolution they adhered persistently, refusing $2.75 per 100 pounds for fully 10,000 head; and afterwards, failing to get their 3 cents on the prairie for their cattle, shipped them to Chicago on their own account and sold them there at $2.25 to $2.50 per 100 pounds; and out of that paid a freight of $150 per car, realizing from $10 to $15 per head less than they had haughtily refused upon the prairie. Some of them refused to accept these prices and packed their cattle upon their own account. Their disappointment and chagrin at their failure to force a buyer to pay 3 cents per pound for their cattle was great and bitter, but their refusal to accept the offer of 23/4 cents per pound was great good fortune to the would-be buyers, for at that price $100,000 would have been lost on 10,000 head of cattle. An attempt was made the following year to form a combination to put up prices; but a burnt child dreads the fire, and the attempted combination failed, and every drover looked out sharply for himself.

DOCUMENT 6 Helen Hunt Jackson, from *A Century of Dishonor*, 1881

There is not among these three hundred bands of Indians one which has not suffered cruelly at the hands either of the Government or of white settlers. The poorer, the more insignificant, the more helpless the band, the more certain the cruelty and outrage to which they have been subjected. This is especially true of the bands on the Pacific slope. These Indians found themselves of a sudden surrounded by and caught up in the great influx of gold-seeking settlers, as helpless creatures on a shore are caught up in a tidal wave. There was not time for the Government to make treaties; not even time for communities to make laws. The tale of the wrongs, the oppressions, the murders of the Pacific-slope Indians in the last thirty years would be a volume by itself, and is too monstrous to be believed.
It makes little difference, however, where one opens the record of the history of the Indians; every page and every year has its dark stain. The story of one tribe is the story of all, varied only differences of time and place; but neither time nor place makes any difference in the main facts. Colorado is as greedy and unjust in 1880 as was Georgia in 1830, and Ohio in 1795; and the United States Government breaks promises now as deftly as then, and with an added ingenuity from long practice.
One of its strongest supports in so doing is the wide-spread sentiment among the people of dislike to the Indian, of impatience with his presence as a "barrier to civilization" and distrust of it as a possible danger. The old tales of the frontier life, with its horrors of Indian warfare, have gradually, by two or three generations' telling, produced in the average mind something like an hereditary instinct of questioning and unreasoning aversion which it is almost impossible to dislodge or soften. . . .

DOCUMENT 7 Benjamin Harrison, Report on Wounded Knee Massacre and the Decrease in Indian Land Acreage, 1891

Since March 4, 1889, about 23,000,000 acres have been separated from Indian reservations and added to the public domain for the use of those who desired to secure free homes under our beneficent laws. It is difficult to estimate the increase of wealth which will result from the conversion of these waste lands into farms, but it is more difficult to estimate the betterment which will result to the families that have found renewed hope and courage in the ownership of a home and the assurance of a comfortable subsistence under free and healthful conditions. It is also gratifying to be able to feel, as we may, that this work has proceeded upon lines of justice toward the Indian, and that he may now, if he will, secure to himself the good influences of a settled habitation, the fruits of industry, and the security of citizenship.

DOCUMENT-BASED QUESTION 8

There are both internationalist and Isolationist streams in the history of American thought. Discuss the role that this continuing debate played in the period surrounding World War I.

DOCUMENT 1

DOCUMENT 2

THE WORLDS CONSTABLE.

DOCUMENT 3   Woodrow Wilson, The Fourteen Points, 1918

We entered this war because violations of right had occurred which touched us to the quick and made the life of our own people impossible unless they were corrected and the world secure once for all against their recurrence.

What we demand in this war, therefore, is nothing peculiar to ourselves. It is that the world be made fit and safe to live in; and particularly that it be made safe for every peace-loving nation which, like our own, wishes to live its own life, determine its own institutions, be assured of justice and fair dealing by the other peoples of the world as against force and selfish aggressions…

14. A general association of nations must be formed under specific covenants for the purpose of affording mutual guarantees of political independence and territorial integrity to great and small states alike.

DOCUMENT 4   Boy Scouts of America from, "Boy Scouts Support the War Effort," 1917

This patriotic service will be rendered under the slogan: "EVERY SCOUT TO BOOST AMERICA" AS A GOVERNMENT DISPATCH BEARER. The World War is for liberty and democracy.

America has long been recognized as the leader among nations standing for liberty and democracy. American entered the war as a sacred duty to uphold the principles of liberty and democracy.

As a democracy, our country faces great danger-not so much from submarines, battleships and armies, because, thanks to our allies, our enemies have apparently little chance of reaching our shores.

Our danger is from within. Our enemies have representatives everywhere; they tell lies; they mispresent the truth; they deceive our own people; they are a real menace to our country.

DOCUMENT 5   Francis Whiting Halsey, The Great War, 1920

Observers felt that the President, while reading his address, did not know how thoroughly the whole country not only sympathized with him in the great crisis, but voiced its sincere determination to support him, until he had heard the cheers that greeted a later passage as he delivered it slowly, almost haltingly at times, but with deep emphasis, as follows:
"With a profound sense of the solemn and even tragical character of the step I am taking, and of the grave responsibilities which it involves, but in unhesitating obedience to what I deem my constitutional duty, I advise that the Congress declare the recent course of the Imperial German Government to be in fact nothing less than war against the Government and People of the United States; that it formally accept the status of belligerent which has thus been thrust upon it; and that it take immediate steps not only to put the country in a more thorough state of defense, but also to exert all its power and employ all its resources to bring the Government of the German Empire to terms and end the war."

DOCUMENT 6   Warren G. Harding, Campaign Speech at Boston, 1920

This republic has its ample tasks. If we put an end to false economics which lure humanity to utter chaos, ours will be the commanding example of world leadership today. If we can prove a representative popular government under which a citizenship seeks what it may do for the government rather than what the government may do for individuals, we shall do more to make democracy safe for the world than all armed conflict ever recorded. The world needs to be reminded that all human ills are not curable by legislation, and that quantity of statutory enactment and excess of government offer no substitute for quality of citizenship. . . .
My best judgment of America's needs is to steady down, to get squarely on our feet, to make sure of the right path. Let's get out of the fevered delirium of war, with the hallucination that all the money in the world is to be made in the madness of war and the wildness of its aftermath. Let us stop to consider that tranquility at home is more precious than peace abroad, and that both our good fortune and our eminence are dependent on the normal forward stride of all the American people.

DOCUMENT 7   American Troops in the Trenches, 1918

July 21.—What a week this has been in the world's history! A week ago, while the French were celebrating Bastille Day, the Germans, strong in hope because of two preceding drives, were making ready for another great effort. On the 15th they launched an attack from Château-Thierry to north of Châlons on a 100-kilometer front. They crossed the Marne and moved a short distance toward their objectives. Then, out of a clear sky, July 18, came Foch's blow from

Soissons to Château-Thierry. On Thursday and Friday French and Americans fought ahead, and then today they hit Ludendorff a body blow south of the Marne. The week started with a formidable German offensive. The week ends with a great allied offensive.

Americans, French, English—all the Allies—now face the fury of the German high command, with its great military machine. That machine is big and powerful, but it is not the machine it used to be. The morale of the German Army is weakening from day to day. The size of the German Army is growing surely less day by day.

The morale of the allied armies is getting better every day, and because of America the size of the allied armies is growing day by day. The defeat of Germany is but a matter of time. How much time no one can say. America should rejoice, but America should not be overconfident. But for what France has to be thankful for America has a just right to be thankful for, too.

DOCUMENT-BASED QUESTION 9

Defend or refute the following statement: The Marshall Plan was motivated by Cold War considerations.

DOCUMENT 1   George F. Kennan, "Long Telegram," 1946

We have here a political force committed fanatically to the belief that with US there can be no permanent modus vivendi, that it is desirable and necessary that the internal harmony of our society be disrupted, our traditional way of life be destroyed, the international authority of our state be broken, if Soviet power is to be secure. This political force has complete power of disposition over energies of one of world's greatest peoples and resources of world's richest national territory, and is borne along by deep and powerful currents of Russian nationalism. In addition, it has an elaborate and far flung apparatus for exertion of its influence in other countries, and apparatus of amazing flexibility and versatility, managed by people whose experience and skill in underground methods are presumably without parallel in history. Finally, it is seemingly inaccessible to considerations of reality in its basic reactions. For it, the vast fund of objective fact about human society is not, as with us, the measure against which outlook is constantly being tested and re-formed, but a grab bag from which individual items are selected arbitrarily and tendentiously to bolster an outlook already preconceived. This is admittedly not a pleasant picture. Problem of how to cope with this force in [is] undoubtedly greatest task our diplomacy has ever faced and probably greatest it will ever have to face. It should be point of departure from which our political general staff work at present juncture should proceed. It should be approached with same thoroughness and care as solution of major strategic problem in war, and if necessary, with no smaller outlay in planning effort. I cannot attempt to suggest all answers here. But I would like to record my conviction that problem is within our power to solve-and that without recourse to any general military conflict.

DOCUMENT 2   Kenneth McFarland, "The Unfinished Work," 1946

One who traveled about over the country a year ago this month, talking with taxi drivers, bell hops, policemen, business employees, and others who reflect the thinking of the man-on-the-street, found the conversation all to be along the same lines. The war was over, the boys would be coming home now, rationing would end. Truman was doing better than expected, we must resolutely work together to build one world in which war would be outlawed and the principles of the Atlantic Charter would hold sway. The keynote a year ago was one of joyous relief that the bloodiest conflict in all history had ended in complete victory over the enemy, and a feeling of faith that we had at last learned our lesson sufficiently well to outlaw war. There was confidence that an effective United Nations organization would be developed.
But today, one year after, that buoyant faith has turned to cynicism. Hope in the United Nations is largely gone. The average American has already resigned himself to a future in which there will be at least two worlds instead of one. Having given up his hope for a better world, the average man has ceased to realize how terribly important it is that we keep striving, and he has settled down to bickering over a myriad of minor issues here on the domestic scene. . . .
There is a strange fear and insecurity in America today. The people fear that in winning the war we introduced a new power into the world which may in turn engulf us.

DOCUMENT 3   George Marshall, The Marshall Plan, 1947

Aside from the demoralizing effect on the world at large and the possibilities of disturbances arising as a result of the desperation of the people concerned, the consequences of the economy of the United States should be apparent to all. It is logical that the United States should do whatever it is able to do to assist in the return of normal economic health in the world, without which there can be no political stability and no assured peace. Our policy is directed not against any country or doctrine but against hunger, poverty, desperation, and chaos. Its purpose should be the revival of a working economy in the world so as to permit the emergence of political and social conditions in which free institutions can exist.

DOCUMENT 4   Containment, 1947

This means that we are going to continue for a long time to find the Russians difficult to deal with. It does not mean that they should be considered as embarked upon a do-or-die program to overthrow our society by a given date. The theory of the inevitability of the eventual fall of capitalism has the fortunate connotation that there is no hurry about it. The forces of progress can take their time in preparing the final coup de grâce. Meanwhile, what is vital is that the "Socialist fatherland"—that oasis of power which has been already won for Socialism in the person of the Soviet Union—should be cherished and defended by all good Communists at home and abroad, its fortunes promoted, its enemies badgered and confounded. The promotion of premature, "adventuristic" revolutionary projects abroad which might embarrass Soviet power in any way would be an inexcusable, even a counter-revolutionary act. The cause of Socialism is the support and promotion of Soviet power, as defined in Moscow...

These considerations make Soviet diplomacy at once easier and more difficult to deal with than the diplomacy of individual aggressive leaders like Napoleon and Hitler. On the one hand it is more sensitive to contrary force, more ready to yield on individual sectors of the diplomatic front when that force is felt to be too strong, and thus more rational in the logic and rhetoric of power. On the other hand it cannot be easily defeated or discouraged by a single victory on the part of its opponents. And the patient persistence by which it is animated means that it can be effectively countered not by sporadic acts which represent the momentary whims of democratic opinion but only by intelligent long-range policies on the part of Russia's adversaries—policies no less steady in their purpose, and no less variegated and resourceful in their applications, than those of the Soviet Union itself.

In these circumstances it is clear that the main element of any United States policy toward the Soviet Union must be that of a long-term, patient but firm and vigilant containment of Russian expansive tendencies. It is important to note, however, that such a policy has nothing to do with outward histrionics: with threats or blustering or superfluous gestures of outward "toughness." While the Kremlin is basically flexible in its reaction to political realities, it is by no means unamenable to considerations of prestige. Like almost any other government, it can be placed by tactless and threatening gestures in a position where it cannot afford to yield even though this might be dictated by its sense of realism. The Russian leaders are keen judges of human psychology, and as such they are highly conscious that loss of temper and of self-control is never a source of strength in political affairs. They are quick to exploit such evidences of weakness. For these reasons, it is a sine qua non of successful dealing with Russia that the foreign government in question should remain at all times cool and collected and that its demands on Russian policy should be put forward in such a manner as to leave the way open for a compliance not too detrimental to Russian prestige.

DOCUMENT 5   Harry S Truman, The Truman Doctrine, 1947

At the present moment in world history nearly every nation must choose between alternative ways of life. The choice is too often not a free one.

One way of life is based upon the will of the majority, and is distinguished by free institutions, representative government, free elections, guaranties of individual liberty, freedom of speech and religion, and freedom from political oppression.

The second way of life is based upon the will of a minority forcibly imposed upon the majority. It relies upon terror and oppression, a controlled press and radio, fixed elections, and the suppression of personal freedoms.

I believe that it must be the policy of the United States to support free peoples who are resisting attempted subjugation by armed minorities or by outside pressures.

I believe that we must assist free peoples to work out their own destinies in their own way.

I believe that our help should be primarily through economic and financial aid, which is essential to economic stability and orderly political processes.

The world is not static, and the status quo is not sacred. But we cannot allow changes in the status quo in violation of the Charter of the United Nations by such methods as coercion, or by such subterfuges as political infiltration. In helping free and independent nations to maintain their freedom, the United States will be giving effect to the principles of the Charter of the United Nations. . . .

The seeds of totalitarian regimes are nurtured by misery and want. They spread and grow in the evil soil of poverty and strife. They reach their full growth when the hope of a people for a better life has died. We must keep that hope alive.

The free peoples of the world look to us for support in maintaining their freedoms.

If we falter in our leadership, we may endanger the peace of the world-and we shall surely endanger the welfare of our own Nation.

DOCUMENT 6   National Security Council Memorandum Number 68, 1950

In the light of present and prospective Soviet atomic capabilities, the action which can be taken under present programs and plans, however, becomes dangerously inadequate, in both timing and scope, to accomplish the rapid progress toward the attainment of the United States political, economic, and military objectives which is now imperative.

A continuation of present trends would result in a serious decline in the strength of the free world relative to the Soviet Union and its satellites. This unfavorable trend arises from the inadequacy of current programs and plans rather than from any error in our objectives and aims. These trends lead in the direction of isolation, not by deliberate decision but by lack of the necessary basis for a vigorous initiative in the conflict with the Soviet Union.

Our position as the center of power in the free world places a heavy responsibility upon the United States for leadership. We must organize and enlist the energies and resources of the free world in a positive program for peace which will frustrate the Kremlin design for world domination by creating a situation in the free world to which the Kremlin will be compelled to adjust. Without such a cooperative effort, led by the United States, we will have to make gradual withdrawals under pressure until we discover one day that we have sacrificed positions of vital interest.

It is imperative that this trend be reversed by a much more rapid and concerted build-up of the actual strength of both the United States and the other nations of the free world. The analysis shows that this will be costly and will involve significant domestic financial and economic adjustments.

The execution of such a build-up, however, requires that the United States have an affirmative program beyond the solely defensive one of countering the threat posed by the Soviet Union. This program must light the path to peace and order among nations in a system based on freedom and justice, as contemplated in the Charter of the United Nations. Further, it must envisage the political and economic measures with which and the military shield behind which the free world can work to frustrate the Kremlin design by the strategy of the cold war; for every consideration of devotion to our fundamental values and to our national security demands that we achieve our objectives by the strategy of the cold war, building up our military strength in order that it may not have to be used. The only sure victory lies in the frustration of the Kremlin design by the steady development of the moral and material strength of the free world and its projection into the Soviet world in such a way as to bring about an internal change in the Soviet system. Such a positive program-harmonious with our fundamental national purpose and our objectives-is necessary if we are to regain and retain the initiative and to win and hold the necessary popular support and cooperation in the United States and the rest of the free world.

> **Identify and assess the impact of three major events that were responsible for undermining American public support for the Vietnam War.**

DOCUMENT 1   Account of Brinsley Tyrrell, Kent State Faculty, 1970

[We] watched the Guard go up the hill and vanish over the top of the hill at which point they were invisible to us. And then I, in my innocence, heard a group of firecrackers go off. And I suppose it wasn't 'til ten, fifteen minutes later that at least the part of the crowd I was in sort of realized what had happened. We saw the Guard come down in a rather hurried fashion. But then, people from the other side of the hill came down, in tears, incoherent, crying. I remember a Vietnam veteran coming down—big, hulking guy, crew cut—screaming at the Guard, calling them toy soldiers, calling them a disgrace to their uniform. And in a very chaotic way, I think everybody left campus.

DOCUMENT 2   Lyndon Johnson, Comments on the Tet Offensive, 1968

I am not a great strategist and tactician. I know that you are not. Let us assume that the best figures we can have are from our responsible military commanders. They say 10,000 [enemy soldiers] died and we lost 249 and the South Vietnamese lost 500. That does not look like a Communist victory. I can count. It looks like somebody has paid a very dear price for the temporary encouragement that some of our enemies had. Is that a great enemy victory?

DOCUMENT 3

DOCUMENT 4   Joint Resolution of Congress, 1964 (Tonkin Gulf Resolution)

Resolved by the Senate and House of Representatives of the United States of America in Congress assembled. That the Congress approves and supports the determination of the President, as the Commander in Chief, to take all necessary measures to repel any armed attack against the forces of the United States and to prevent further aggression.

DOCUMENT 5 Congressional Debate over the Tonkin Gulf Resolution, 1964

MR. GRUENING: [Ernest Gruening, Dem.-Alaska] . . . Regrettably, I find myself in disagreement with the President's Southeast Asian policy. . . The serious events of the past few days, the attack by North Vietnamese vessels on American warships and our reprisal, strikes me as the inevitable and foreseeable concomitant and consequence of U.S. unilateral military aggressive policy in Southeast Asia.... We now are about to authorize the President if he sees fit to move our Armed Forces . . . not only into South Vietnam, but also into North Vietnam, Laos, Cambodia, Thailand, and of course the authorization includes all the rest of the SEATO nations. That means sending our American boys into combat in a war in which we have no business, which is not our war, into which we have been misguidedly drawn, which is steadily being escalated. This resolution is a further authorization for escalation unlimited. I am opposed to sacrificing a single American boy in this venture. We have lost far too many already....

DOCUMENT 6 Johnson to Congress on Tonkin Gulf Attack, 1964

Last night I announced to the American people that the North Vietnamese regime had conducted further deliberate attacks against U.S. naval vessels operating in international waters, and I had therefore directed air action against gunboats and supporting facilities used in these hostile operations. This air action has now been carried out with substantial damage to the boats and facilities. Two U.S. aircraft were lost in the action.

DOCUMENT 7 Testimony of Dennis Conti, My Lai Trial, 1970

Lieutenant Calley came out and said take care of these people. So we said, okay, so we stood there and watched them. He went away, then he came back and said, "I thought I told you to take care of these people. We said, "We are. He said, "I mean, kill them. I was a little stunned and I didn't know what to do....There were bursts and single shots for two minutes. It was automatic. The people screamed and yelled and fell. I guess they tried to get up, too. They couldn't... Lots of heads was shot off, pieces of heads and pieces of flesh flew off the sides and arms. They were all messed up.

DOCUMENT 8 Lyndon B. Johnson, "Address to the Nation," 1968

I have concluded that I should not permit the Presidency to become involved in the partisan divisions that are developing in this political year.

With America's sons in the fields far away, with America's future under challenge right here at home, with our hopes and the world's hopes for peace in the balance every day, I do not believe that I should devote an hour or a day of my time to any personal partisan causes or to any duties other than the awesome duties of this office--the Presidency of your country.

Accordingly, I shall not seek, and I will not accept, the nomination of my party for another term as your President.

DOCUMENT 9

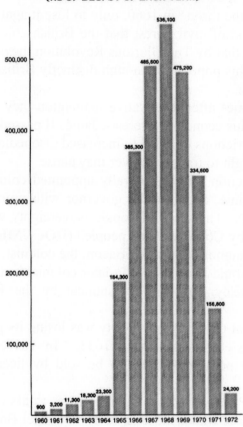

U.S. TROOP LEVELS IN VIETNAM
(AS OF DEC. 31 OF EACH YEAR)

Source: U.S. Department of Defense.

SAMPLE ANSWERS

Analyze the relationship between the British North American colonies and the government back in England in the light of the following documents.

The seventeenth century saw many changes in British religion and government. The death of Queen Elizabeth in 1603 saw the rise of the Stuarts to the British throne. They were deposed by Oliver Cromwell in 1649, but restored to the throne in 1660, only to lose it again to William of Orange in 1688. It was during this period of civil unrest that the British colonial project in North America was born and matured, such that by The Glorious Revolution they had a population of 225,000 people (**DOCUMENT 7**). This population, though distinctly British in character, was not always obedient to the British crown.

In 1660, in order to restore order in the colonies after the relative inattention they had received during the Interregnum, as well as to protect his economic interests, James II passed the Navigation Act (**DOCUMENT 1**). The increased restrictions only led to increased disobedience and smuggling, as the colonists felt that they had the right to trade wherever they chose.

By the 1670s there was substantial dissatisfaction with the royally appointed colonial governments. Nathanial Bacon led a revolt in Virginia, charging the governor with unjustly taxing the people and not protecting them sufficiently. The seeds of popular sovereignty were already sown, as he signed his declaration "Generall by Consent of the people" (**DOCUMENT 2**). The fundamental disagreement about the roots of authority between Bacon, the colonist, and Berkeley, the Royal governor, is a stark one, which would have echoes in later colonial history. Bacon derived his authority from the people, Berkeley from his appointment by the King (**DOCUMENT 3**).

In New England there were also clear signs that the King's authority was losing its grip. A law against selling weapons to Indians had passed Parliament in 1633. In 1657, the Commonwealth of Massachusetts had passed a law permitting them to be sold by licensed dealers (**DOCUMENT 4**).

In 1701 William Penn issued his charter for Pennsylvania, granting various rights to its inhabitants. His effort was less subversive than those of Massachusetts, or of Nathaniel Bacon. Penn appealed to the King's authority, and was very clear that he had the land only through that authority. However, the very existence of the charter, granting rights to Englishman above those given by the crown, is subversive to royal power (**DOCUMENT 5**).

By 1763, at the end of the French and Indian War, the King was through with this disobedience. He issued a declaration that reaffirmed the power of the Royal governors in the colonies, as well as establishing governors in the newly acquired colonies (**DOCUMENT 6**).

The British North American colonies took advantage of the varying states of governmental disarray over the course of the seventeenth century to pull away from Royal control. By the mid-eighteenth century the Crown would no longer tolerate this, which would soon lead to a conflict.

DOCUMENT-BASED QUESTION 2

Explain the process by which slavery was created in North America.

Though the presence of household slaves had existed in Mediterranean Europe prior to colonial expansion, slavery in North America developed over time and was influenced by a variety of factors. Through colonial expansion, Europeans had developed economies in North America that were dependent on an ever-increasing need for labor. At first, they filled this need with indentured servants and slaves purchased from African traders, who captured Africans, forced them on brutal marches to the west coast of Africa, and sold them to Europeans in exchange for European goods (**DOCUMENT 1**). These captured men, women, and children were then shipped to North America via the Middle Passage of the trade pattern between Europe, Africa, and America called Triangular Trade (**DOCUMENT 2**). Conditions on the slave ships that traveled the Middle Passage were abysmal, and though Africans often rebelled in a variety of ways against such treatment, they were abused, starved, and susceptible to serious illness on the long journey (**DOCUMENT 3**). The shock of enslavement and the savage treatment of the slaves on their forced migration to America did not end upon arrival; slavery was early characterized by various forms of oppression and brutality that were employed as a way to maintain control over slaves (**DOCUMENT 4**). Slavery soon became encoded in laws that defined the difference between indentured servants and slaves and outlined the process by which such a system would be upheld (**DOCUMENT 5**). Nonetheless, there were many ways in which slaves rebelled and tried to achieve freedom from an increasingly institutionalized system. Large-scale group attempts at retaliation and escape, such as the Stono Rebellion, are clear evidence that slavery was not established without rebellion and struggle, though most attempts to achieve freedom were met with harsh reprisals designed to quell future rebellions (**DOCUMENT 6**). This was true even for those who attempted individual acts of rebellion as slavery became increasingly institutionalized as part of the American system. Escaped slaves could expect that they would be pursued in order to maintain the system (**DOCUMENT 7**).

DOCUMENT-BASED QUESTION 3

Defend or refute the following statement: Differing patterns of immigration and migration created different social and political climates in the various regions of the Americas.

Each region in the North American colonies had its own pattern of settlement, which was a component in its cultural development. The colonies of the French Crescent differed from those of Puritan New England, which differed from the Spanish colonies of New Mexico or the British Mid-Atlantic colonies. Each was shaped by its own particular settlers. However, no colony was identical in culture to the mother country of its settlers, but each one had its own American culture.

Many of the colonies were peopled by immigrants from different countries, as opposed to a homogenous group of settlers. The primary exception, were the eastern colonies, which were peopled mostly by English colonists, at least in the 1780's (**DOCUMENT 1**). However, even the British Colonies were not exclusively English. Farther south and west they had, German, Scottish, Dutch, Swiss and Irish settlers, as well as a significant number of Africans, brought over as slaves (**DOCUMENT 6**). Over the course of the eighteenth century the population of

British North America had gone from being 80 percent English to being barely half English. This large demographic switch was partially due to an influx of African slaves (they increased from 11 to 19 percent of the population), but also to a large amount of European immigration. (**DOCUMENT 4**).

Benjamin Franklin was of the belief that despite this non-English immigration, the English population was so large that they would dominate North America, politically and culturally (**DOCUMENT 2**). While he turned out to be largely correct, he was basing his hypothesis on false data. At the time, the largest population group in North America was in New Spain (**DOCUMENT 5**). It was not only large, it was also diverse. The particular character of New Spain, where ethnic mixing was frequent, led to a highly stratified society, in a way that was very distinct from the British and French colonies (**DOCUMENT 3**).

At the same time that the population of the colonies was growing, it was also moving. Over the course of the middle of the eighteenth century, there was a steady stream of expansion from the east coast westwards, into the backcountry. By the 1760's there was settlement as far west as the Ohio river (**DOCUMENT 7**).

The demographic shifts over the course of the eighteenth century changed the characters of the North American colonies, but they did so in different ways. Each colony had its own demographics, consequently they differed culturally.

DOCUMENT-BASED QUESTION 4
Analyze the circumstances leading up to the Missouri Compromise.

A number of important changes took place in the period leading up to the Missouri Crisis of 1819 and its subsequent resolution in 1820. Changing attitudes about the morality of slavery raised questions about its legality, causing the eventual abolition of slavery in the north. Meanwhile, the continuation of westward expansion raised the question of whether to expand slave-owning territories.

Already by the 1790s there was pressure to abolish slavery. Letters were being written on the subject to prominent politicians, urging them to do what is right (**DOCUMENT 1**). This pressure, however, was implied mostly in vain. Though this letter, and presumably others, received a cautiously positive response (**DOCUMENT 2**), the system did not change, even in the houses of those who gave lip service to abolition (**DOCUMENT 5**).

At the same times as the pressure was beginning to be brought to bear by northerners, westward expansion continued at a breakneck pace. The appeal of the west was powerful because of the draw of its open spaces and cheap land (**DOCUMENT 8**). Jefferson's Louisiana purchase of 1803 increased the territory into which settlers could move, doubling the size of the country (**DOCUMENT 7**). These pull factors, along with the push factors of decreasing space and opportunity in the east, created a massive wave of westward migration in the period between 1800 and 1820 (**DOCUMENT 4**). By 1820 there were settlers well on the far side of the Mississippi River, up the Missouri (**DOCUMENT 6**).

When it became time to admit this newly populated territory as a state, the question of slavery was a major one. Missouri requested admission as a slave state, but the northern states were concerned about upsetting the balance between free and slave states. This tension was so severe that an aging Jefferson thought it might mean the end of the union (**DOCUMENT 3**).

The westward expansion coupled with new, abolitionist leaning tendencies in the north were the important factors in the period leading up to the Missouri Crisis and its resolution in the Missouri Compromise.

Defend or refute the following statement: The Mexican-American War was started essentially to steal land from Mexico.

The Mexican-American War was driven primarily by a desire for territorial expansion. It was started on false pretenses by a president who had based his campaign on expanding U.S. territory. However, it was not a straightforward "land grab." American expansionism was driven by idealism as well as greed. The Mexican-American War was a product of both.

The roots of the war can be traced back to the American settlement of Mexican Texas. Americans were invited in by the Mexican government, and settled there in droves. They eventually won their independence, and settled that the border between the Republic of Texas and Mexico would be at the Rio Grande River (**DOCUMENT 1**); however, Mexico did not respect the southern boundary set by the treaty, disputing the territory between the Nueces River and the Rio Grande. Texas attempted to be admitted to the United States. However, its annexation was disputed, and it did not gain statehood until 1845, after the election of President James K. Polk.

President Polk's election was widely viewed as a mandate for territorial expansion, and he did not disappoint. In the summer of 1845 he sent an army to defend Texas, and made provisions to take California in the case of war.

The war was not long in coming. Polk sent the Army south, into the disputed territory, without any provocation, though he claimed that the Mexicans had attacked (**DOCUMENT 5**). This claim is crucial to understanding the climate of opinion in the U.S. The American people would not fight a war as an aggressor. Indeed, this idealistic view, that America had only ever fought defensive wars, was an important part of American identity (**DOCUMENT 2**). The idea that America might be a conquering nation was so repugnant to some of Polk's political opponents that some even argued that, should the U.S. win the war, they should not take any Mexican territory (**DOCUMENT 3**).

Despite these anti-expansionist voices, the war continued, and the president did intend to take territory from Mexico. Not a single battle was fought on American soil, and only one was fought in disputed territory (**DOCUMENT 4**). At the end of the war Mexico was forced to cede massive amounts of land to the U.S. (**DOCUMENT 6**). The end to which Polk had started the war had been achieved.

The Mexican-American War was fought for territorial expansion. In 1820 a contemporary American would not recognize the western outline of the United States (**DOCUMENT 7**). By 1850, after the war, it had taken its current shape (**DOCUMENT 8**).

The ultimate "cause" of the Civil War has been a matter of intense debate among historians. Evaluate the various factors contributing to the outbreak of war and determine which was the most significant and why.

America in the 1850s was a larger, richer and more diverse nation than it had been in 1800. It was also a nation in crisis. Though many Americans believed it was their "manifest destiny" to spread the nation's boundaries from coast to coast, such expansion created problems for the delicate political balance that existed between states with divergent cultures, economic systems, and political goals. The expansion of American territory particularly hinged on the issue of slavery and whether that institution would also spread into the new western territories. Northern opponents of slavery, organized into the antislavery and abolition movements, not only opposed its expansion but called for its outright abolition, creating a powerful movement that exercised influence through the use of moral arguments and impassioned rhetoric (**DOCUMENT 1**). Cultural differences between the North and South also emerged and were evident in the powerful abolitionist literature distributed throughout society, culminating in Harriet Beecher Stowe's stark condemnation of slavery in the hugely successful novel *Uncle Tom's Cabin* (**DOCUMENT 2**).

Of the many attempts to reduce sectional tension by settling issues surrounding the creation of new states, the Compromise of 1850 was made necessary by the hardening of sectional lines and the clear differences between the way northern and southern politicians regarded the relationship between congressional representation and power and the increasing regulatory power of the federal government (**DOCUMENT 3**). But as the 1850s wore on, compromise floundered in the face of increased challenges to the political balance between free and slave states. The Kansas-Nebraska Act hoped to settle the issue by introducing popular sovereignty with regard to the expansion of slavery (**DOCUMENT 4**), but the resulting violence there demonstrated that the issue had become the most divisive the nation had ever seen, as pro-slavery and antislavery advocates clashed in bloody battles in Kansas (**DOCUMENT 5**). This was further proved when northerners fully realized the horrors of slavery with the institution of the Fugitive Slave Act (**DOCUMENT 6**), which spread antislavery sentiments even more. The movement continued to grow despite the Dred Scott decision, in which the Supreme Court decided that blacks in America were not citizens, which also struck a blow for states' rights (**DOCUMENT 7**). The real division in the nation that had was revealed in the Election of 1860, which centered on the issue of slavery. The new Republican Party captured the presidency (**DOCUMENT 8**). Recognizing that his triumph in the election signaled a break in the Union, as southern states made plans to secede, newly elected President Abraham Lincoln established his commitment to the Union (**DOCUMENT 9**). Now there was no turning back; the crises caused by the various tensions of the 1850s had reached a head, and the North and the South prepared to meet each other in battle.

DOCUMENT-BASED QUESTION 7

Many forces contributed to the rapid transformation of the North American West following 1850. Identify, compare and contrast the various motivations for western settlement and decide which factor was the most decisive in transforming the West.

From 1850 to 1900, the North American West underwent a series of changes that completely transformed that area from a rural, unsettled and vast landscape into a settled region bustling with commercial and industrial energy (**DOCUMENT 1**). It also became a land dominated by Americans of European ancestry, as the expansion of the United States, aided by military strength, defeated the traditional Native American population of the region. Various motivations for western settlement fostered these changes. While many traveled west with the hope that they could share in the fabulous gold and silver claims of some successful pioneers, many had more modest dreams, hoping to purchase or claim land for themselves and their families and thereby gain a measure of economic independence (**DOCUMENT 2**). Yet others yearned for more independence from the power of state and federal governments over their beliefs and values **(DOCUMENT 3)**. At the root of these motives, some believe, is a specific desire for a more individualized experience of freedom, helping to establish the West's image as a home for rugged individualists.

However, many larger forces expanded westward in order to take advantage of the resources of the area. Industry viewed the wealth of natural resources as a valuable boon to trade, and soon the expansion of the railroad into the West was viewed as a necessary step in the ongoing development of the American economy **(DOCUMENT 4)**. Similarly, new and old Westerners alike participated in the transformation of the West as they developed regionally specific industries and markets **(DOCUMENT 5)**. However, western settlers and expansionists believed that the Native Americans were an impediment to the achievement of their goals. In addition, many Americans viewed the native tribes as examples of "uncivilized" peoples who would prevent the achievement of a greater United States **(DOCUMENT 7)**. The ongoing conflict between the United States and the native peoples of the land quickly became a losing battle for the Native Americans, as the United States marshaled its forces to defeat them in the name of national wealth and power **(DOCUMENT 6)**.

DOCUMENT-BASED QUESTION 8

There are both internationalist and isolationist streams in the history of American thought. Discuss the role that this continuing debate played in the period surrounding World War I.

The United States has always had an ambiguous relationship with the rest of the world. Though Washington warned against entangling foreign alliances in his farewell address, there have always been those who saw benefits in working with foreign governments. At the beginning of the twentieth century internationalist thinking was on the upswing, culminating with the American participation in World War I, but afterward war weariness pushed the country back into an isolationist perspective.

Theodore Roosevelt's presidency was one that stressed internationalism. Aside from his imperial adventures in the Philippines and Cuba, Roosevelt also won the Nobel Peace Prize for helping to end the Russo-Japanese war. However, his efforts were not viewed by every American as appropriate. He was mocked by some as "the world's constable," a busybody interfering where he had no business **(DOCUMENT 2)**.

Woodrow Wilson continued Roosevelt's internationalist policies. He interfered frequently in South American politics, attempting to sow liberty there, in his view. He was also mocked **(DOCUMENT 1)**, though others approved of his efforts, When the war in Europe started, he kept the United States neutral. In fact, he ran for a second term with the slogan, "I Kept America Out of the War." However, he was looking for a way to get involved, and he soon had one. Germany's policy of unrestricted submarine warfare was considered sufficient excuse to declare war. When Wilson did so, he had the whole nation behind him **(DOCUMENT 5)**.

The entire country threw itself into the war effort. Men signed up for the newly instituted draft in droves (though the fact that they needed to be drafted may be a sign that they were less enthusiastic than they liked to pretend). Women were co-opted into the workforce. Even children did what they could **(DOCUMENT 4)**. The soldiers in the trenches were confident of success **(DOCUMENT 7)**. The spirit of international cooperation was high.

At the end of the war, Wilson continued his internationist policies. At the Versailles conferences he pushed an agenda that promoted national determination for the citizens of the now defunct German and Ottoman empires. He also wanted to create an international body to adjudicate disputes between countries, a League of Nations (**DOCUMENT 3**). However, at this point America's isolationist streak asserted itself. The Senate refused to ratify a treaty that subjected America's foreign policy to foreign approval. They would not join the League. At the end of the war, Americans wanted to turn inward. They were tired of getting involved in Europe's troubles. Instead, they wanted to heal their wounds and deal with American issues (**DOCUMENT 6**).

The beginning of the twentieth century was a period of strong internationalist tendencies in the United States. However, the trauma of the First World War caused Americans to rethink these policies and return to a more traditional isolationist perspective.

DOCUMENT-BASED QUESTION 9

Defend or refute the following statement: The Marshall Plan was motivated by Cold War considerations.

The Marshall Plan, a 1947 plan for economic aid to Europe, was motivated by Cold War considerations. In the aftermath of World War II, Europe was being cut up into US and Soviet spheres of influence. Emerging U.S. strategy coming out of the Truman administration was one of containment. The Marshall Plan was a part of that strategy.

After the Second World War, Europe was devastated. Most of its economic infrastructure was a casualty of the war. At the same time, it was being split up between U.S. and Soviet spheres of influence (**DOCUMENT 7**). Europe needed help, and in order to encourage cooperation with its agenda, the United States offered it.

A year before the plan was offered, it had become abundantly clear to even U.S. civilians that the world was being split in two (**DOCUMENT 2**). U.S. policy makers were certain that the USSR had no desire for coexistence. There would be no sharing the world with the communists (**DOCUMENT 1**). It was necessary to form a strategy to deal with them.

The strategy became known as containment. As the Soviets were willing to be patient in their battle with the United States, America would also have to be willing to be deliberate. The plan would be to prevent the USSR from expanding, while waiting for its inevitable collapse (**DOCUMENT 4**). One of the ways in which this plan was to be executed was to give aid to "free peoples," so that they would be able to keep off "the communist yoke" (**DOCUMENT 5**). Though Marshall claimed that the goal of the plan was to alleviate suffering in Europe (**DOCUMENT 3**), it was part of this larger scheme of containment. By giving aid to European countries the United States was attempting to prevent them from falling to communism.

By 1950, the United States had changed course in its strategy for fighting communism in the world. A decision had been made to be more aggressive in combating communist interests (**DOCUMENT 6**). However, the Marshall Plan belongs to an earlier time, and was firmly a part of early containment strategy.

DOCUMENT-BASED QUESTION 10

Identify and assess the impact of three major events that were responsible for undermining American public support for the Vietnam War.

President Johnson, Secretary of Defense Robert McNamara, and the various members of the Joint Chiefs of Staff had been reassuring the American people that victory in Vietnam was only a short distance ahead when in January 1968 disaster suddenly and unexpectedly struck during the Tet Lunar New Year armistice. Although the Vietcong had agreed to a ceasefire for this traditional Vietnamese holiday, they launched a massive attack against thirty-six of the forty-four provincial capitals in Vietnam and even against the U.S. embassy in Saigon. Almost immediately President Johnson attempted to put a positive spin on this military disaster. The Vietcong had caught the South Vietnamese forces and their American allies completely by surprise. The communists had prepared a military offense about which thousands of Vietnamese civilians had to be aware, but none informed their government or its American allies. Johnson focused his February 2nd comments on the 10,000 enemy troops killed against the 249 American and 500 South Vietnamese soldiers lost. The president argued that the communists had paid dearly for battle gains which were only "temporary encouragement" to their cause (**DOCUMENT 2**). Johnson completely ignored the fact that the communists still remained in control of the Vietnam countryside. The American people who had been told to expect news of military victories could not help but see this as an American defeat. Johnson continued to argue in a March 31st speech that Tet had been a communist defeat. It had been a communist defeat. As Johnson said in March, the communists had taken heavy casualties, but he admitted they remain capable to mount more rounds of heavy attack. Then, a weary Johnson informed the American people that he was unwilling to continue in the presidency and that he was withdrawing from the 1968 campaign (**DOCUMENT 8**). Johnson's withdrawal was a clear signal to the American people that the many years of war in Vietnam had been wasted. Public support for the war began to ebb with Johnson's admission of personal defeat.

SAMPLE PRACTICE AP® EXAM

On the following pages is a complete sample exam. This practice test mirrors the actual AP exam in format and question types. Set aside a time to take this exam, timing yourself as you will be timed when you take the real test to prepare you for the actual test-taking experience.

PART IV

SAMPLE
PRACTICE AP® EXAM

SAMPLE AP EXAM

Questions 1.1-1.3 refer to the following excerpt.

And of all the infinite universe of humanity, these people are the most guileless, the most devoid of wickedness and duplicity, the most obedient and faithful to their native masters and to the Spanish Christians whom they serve. They are by nature the most humble, patient, and peaceable, holding no grudges, free from embroilments, neither excitable nor quarrelsome. These people are the most devoid of rancors, hatreds, or desire for vengeance of any people in the world. And because they are so weak and complaisant, they are less able to endure heavy labor and soon die of no matter what malady. The sons of nobles among us, brought up in the enjoyments of life's refinements, are no more delicate than are these Indians, even those among them who are of the lowest rank of laborers. They are also poor people, for they not only possess little but have no desire to possess worldly goods. For this reason they are not arrogant, embittered, or greedy...

--Bartolomé de las Casas "The Devastation of the Indies, 1565

1.1. The lack of what Europeans considered civilization allowed the Spanish conquistadors to
    A. teach the Indians the essence of European civilization without any pretensions.
    B. dominate the Indians with their advanced weaponry.
    C. control the daily activities of the Indians but with guilt.
    D. bring in African slaves from advanced civilizations.

1.2. The frailty of the Indians that Bartolome de Las Casas describes eventually led the Spanish to
    A. provide more nourishment to the Indians to be stronger workers.
    B. bring in Spanish indentured servants.
    C. import slaves from Africa.
    D. bring in wage laborers from throughout Europe.

1.3. The fact that the Indians possessed little or had no desire to do so differed from the Spanish in that
    A. the Spanish came merely for scholarship and discovery.
    B. the Spanish sought to gain gold, land, and other valuable possessions.
    C. the Spanish came merely to convert the Indians to Christianity.
    D. the Spanish wanted nothing more than to share farm land with the natives.

Questions 2.1-2.3 refer to the following excerpt.

There is an herb called uppowoc, which sows itself. In the West Indies it has several names, according to the different places where it grows and is used, but the Spaniards generally call it tobacco. Its leaves are dried, made into powder, and then smoked by being sucked through clay pipes into the stomach and head. The fumes purge superfluous phlegm and gross humors from the body by opening all the pores and passages. Thus its use not only preserves the body, but if there are any obstructions it breaks them up. By this means the natives keep in excellent health, without many of the grievous diseases which often afflict us in England...
While we were there we used to suck in the smoke as they did, and now that we are back in England we still do so. We have found many rare and wonderful proofs of the uppowoc's virtues, which would themselves require a volume to relate. There is sufficient evidence in the fact that it is used by so many men and women of great calling, as well as by some learned physicians...

2.1 The tobacco of the West Indies became significant to the British colonies in North America in that
   A. it gave them energy needed for the hardships of colonizing.
   B. it could be grown anywhere in the colonies.
   C. it did not require outside labor.
   D. it became an invaluable cash crop to the Chesapeake colonies.

2.2 The "stinking weed" as it eventually became known
   A. was banned for health reasons.
   B. was used throughout the colonies and Europe as well.
   C. lost its value and was replaced by other forms of drugs.
   D. lost its addictive nature through cross-planting.

2.3 Physicians of the twenty-first century would find the description of tobacco in this excerpt
   A. enlightening and empowering.
   B. completely inaccurate in terms of tobacco's health benefits.
   C. agreeable in tobacco's ability to preserve the body.
   D. beneficial to make smokers abstain from using tobacco.

Questions 3.1-3.3 refer to the following excerpt.

...They tell us, sir, that we are weak-unable to cope with so formidable an adversary. But when shall we be stronger? Will it be the next week, or the next year? Will it be when we are totally disarmed, and when a British guard shall be stationed in every house? Shall we gather strength by irresolution and inaction? Shall we acquire the means of effectual resistance by lying supinely on our backs, and hugging the delusive phantom of hope until our enemies shall have bound us hand and foot? Sir, we are not weak, if we make a proper use of those means which the God of nature hath placed in our power. Three millions of people, armed in the holy cause of liberty, and in such a country as that which we possess, are invincible by any force which our enemy can send against us. Besides, sir, we shall not fight our battles alone. There is a just God who presides over the destinies of nations; and who will raise up friends to fight our battles for us. The battle, sir, is not to the strong alone; it is to the vigilant, the active, the brave. Besides, sir,

we have no election. If we were base enough to desire it, it is not too late to retire from the contest. There is no retreat but in submission and slavery! Our chains are forged; their clanking may be heard on the plains of Boston! The war is inevitable-and let it come! I repeat it, sir, let it come!

It is in vain, sir, to extenuate the matter. Gentlemen may cry, Peace, peace; but there is no peace. The war is actually begun. The next gale that sweeps from the north will bring to our ears the clash of resounding arms. Our brethren are already in the field. Why stand we here idle? What is it that gentlemen wish? What would they have? If life so dear, or peace sweet, as to be purchased at the price of chains and slavery? Forbid it Almighty God-I know not what course others may take; but as for me, give me liberty or give me death!

3.1 Patrick Henry's speech mirrored the thoughts of those in the colonies that wanted to
    A. send an olive branch to the mother country.
    B. seek independence from British rule in the colonies.
    C. stay loyal to England but on equal terms.
    D. maintain the essence of virtual representation.

3.2 The inspiration that Henry invokes is reminiscent of
    A. Thomas Paine's views.
    B. Benjamin Franklin's views.
    C. George III's views.
    D. Benedict Arnold's views.

3.3 Henry's views on liberty would later be used against
    A. the ratification of the Constitution.
    B. the signing of the Declaration of Independence.
    C. the election of Thomas Jefferson.
    D. the practice of British impressment.

Questions 4.1-4.3 refer to the following legislative act.

An Act to authorize the people of the Missouri territory to form a constitution and state government, and for the admission of such state into the Union on an equal footing with the original states, and to prohibit slavery in certain territories.

Be it enacted That the inhabitants of that portion of the Missouri territory included within the boundaries hereinafter designated, be, and they are hereby, authorized to form for themselves a constitution and state government, and to assume such name as they shall deem proper; and the said state, when formed, shall be admitted into the Union, upon an equal footing with the original states, in all respects whatsoever.

SEC. 8. That in all that territory ceded by France to the United States, under the name of Louisiana, which lies north of thirty-six degrees and thirty minutes north latitude, not included within the limits of the state, contemplated by this act, slavery and involuntary servitude, otherwise than in the punishment of crimes, whereof the parties shall have been duly convicted, shall be, and is hereby, forever prohibited: Provided always, That any person escaping into the same, from whom labour or service is lawfully claimed, in any state or territory of the United

States, such fugitive may be lawfully reclaimed and conveyed to the person claiming his or her labour or service as aforesaid.

4.1 The purpose of the 36' 30 boundary line was to keep slavery from
   A. moving beyond the South.
   B. moving north of this line in the event that the U.S .expanded west.
   C. moving South of the border line.
   D. moving beyond Missouri.

4.2 The controversy surrounding the admission of Missouri as a state was
   A. Texas was about to be added as a state as well.
   B. that abolitionists were calling for an immediate end to slavery.
   C. James Monroe was a fierce opponent of slavery.
   D. the balance of power in Congress would tilt towards the slave-owning South.

4.3 Despite the compromise that allowed Missouri's statehood, Thomas Jefferson was correct in labeling this incident a "fire bell in the night" because
   A. the expansion west would create similar controversies.
   B. a mini-civil war would break out in Missouri.
   C. Mexico's opposition to slavery would create tension with the United States.
   D. North and South relations would sour over the admission of Maine as state.

Questions 5.1-5.3 refer to the following excerpt.

The real indictment against the Roman Church is that it is, fundamentally and irredeemably, in its leadership, in politics, in thought, and largely in membership, actually and actively alien, un-American and usually anti-American. The old stock Americans, with the exception of the few such of Catholic faith...see in the Roman Church today the chief leader of alienism, and the most dangerous alien power with a foothold inside our boundaries. It is this and nothing else that has revived hostility to Catholicism...
The hierarchical government of the Roman Church is equally at odds with Americanism. The Pope and the whole hierarchy have been for centuries almost wholly Italian. It is nonsense to suppose that a man, by entering a church, loses his race or national loyalties. The Roman Church today, therefore, is just what its name says - Roman; and it is impossible for its hierarchy or the policies they dictate to be in real sympathy with Americanism. Worse, the Italians have proven to be one of the least assimilable of people. The autocratic nature of the Catholic Church organization, and its suppression of free conscience or free decision, need not be discussed; they are unquestioned. Thus it is fundamental to the Roman Church to demand a supreme loyalty, overshadowing national or race loyalty, to a power that is inevitably alien, and which at the best must inevitably inculcate ideals un-American if not actively anti-American.... The facts are that almost everywhere, and especially in the great industrial centers where the Catholics are strongest, they vote almost as a unit, under control of leaders of their own faith, always in support of the interests of the Catholic Church and of Catholic candidates without regard to other interests, and always also in support of alienism whenever there is an issue

raised. They vote, in short, not as American citizens, but as aliens and Catholics! They form the biggest, strongest, most cohesive of all the alien blocs.

--Hiram Evans "Klan's Fight For Americanism"

5.1. The context in which this article was written was
A. the looming threat of war with Nazi Germany and the expansion of Japan.
B. the massive presence of southern and eastern European immigrants within a post WWI era.
C. a period of decreasing Protestant church membership.
D. the expansion of America's presence in the Caribbean.

5.2 Evans' attack on Catholicism largely stems from his believe that Catholics can't be completely loyal to the United States and thus embrace 100% Americanism since
A. many Catholics were immigrants.
B. the Pope is centered in Rome, Italy.
C. more Protestants fought for the U.S. during World War I.
D. there were more Protestants elected into public office.

5.3 The Klan's attack on Catholics in the twenties mirrors similar attacks from
A. The Know-Nothing Party.
B. Knights of Columbus.
C. Knights of Equity.
D. supporters of Al Smith.

Questions 6.1-6.3 refer to the following excerpt.

The advocates of Black Power reject the old slogans and meaningless rhetoric of previous years in the civil rights struggle. The language of yesterday is indeed irrelevant: progress, non-violence, integration, fear of "white backlash," coalition. . . .
One of the tragedies of the struggle against racism is that up to this point there has been no national organization which could speak to the growing militancy of young black people in the urban ghettos and the black-belt South. There has been only a "civil rights" movement, whose tone of voice was adapted to an audience of middle-class whites. It served as a sort of buffer zone between that audience and angry young blacks. It claimed to speak for the needs of a community, but it did not speak in the tone of that community. None of its so-called leaders could go into a rioting community and be listened to. In a sense, the blame must be shared-along with the mass media-by those leaders for what happened in Watts, Harlem, Chicago, Cleveland, and other places. Each time the black people in those cities saw Dr. Martin Luther King get slapped they became angry. When they saw little black girls bombed to death in a church and civil rights workers ambushed and murdered, they were angrier; and when nothing happened, they were steaming mad. We had nothing to offer that they could see, except to go out and be beaten again. We helped to build their frustration. We had only the old language of love and suffering. And in most places-that is, from the liberals and middle class-we got back the old language of patience and progress. . . .

Such language, along with admonitions to remain non-violent and fear the white backlash, convinced some that that course was the only course to follow. It misled some into believing that a black minority could bow its head and get whipped into a meaningful position of power. The very notion is absurd. . . .

--Stokely Carmichael and Charles V. Hamilton, from *Black Power: The Politics of Liberation in America*, 1967

6.1 The writing of *Black Power* came after the violence in 1965 that struck the neighborhood of
   A. Harlem.
   B. Watts.
   C. Southwestern Atlanta.
   D. Seventh Ward.

6.2 *Black Power* reflected a shift of the civil rights movement from non-violent and peaceful aims to all of the following EXCEPT
   A. the use of Black militancy in speeches.
   B. violent protests.
   C. the push for separately controlled black neighborhoods.
   D. the continued push for integration.

6.3 Carmichael and Hamilton were particularly frustrated that King's style of protest
   A. didn't lead to a civil rights act.
   B. didn't lead to a voting rights act.
   C. didn't protect blacks against white violence.
   D. didn't lead to desegregation in schools or public places.

Questions 7.1-7.3 refer to the following article excerpt.

JAKARTA, Indonesia (CNN) — Allegations that Sen. Barack Obama was educated in a radical Muslim school known as a "madrassa" are not accurate, according to CNN reporting.
Insight Magazine, which is owned by the same company as The Washington Times, reported on its Web site last week that associates of Sen. Hillary Rodham Clinton, D-New York, had unearthed information the Illinois Democrat and likely presidential candidate attended a Muslim religious school known for teaching the most fundamentalist form of Islam.
Obama lived in Indonesia as a child, from 1967 to 1971, with his mother and stepfather and has acknowledged attending a Muslim school, but an aide said it was not a madrassa...
Insight stood by its story in a response posted on its Web site Monday afternoon...
But reporting by CNN in Jakarta, Indonesia and Washington, D.C., shows the allegations that Obama attended a madrassa to be false. CNN dispatched Senior International Correspondent John Vause to Jakarta to investigate.
He visited the Basuki school, which Obama attended from 1969 to 1971.
"This is a public school. We don't focus on religion," Hardi Priyono, deputy headmaster of the Basuki school, told Vause. "In our daily lives, we try to respect religion, but we don't give preferential treatment."

Vause reported he saw boys and girls dressed in neat school uniforms playing outside the school, while teachers were dressed in Western-style clothes.

"I came here to Barack Obama's elementary school in Jakarta looking for what some are calling an Islamic madrassa ... like the ones that teach hate and violence in Pakistan and Afghanistan," Vause said on the "Situation Room" Monday. "I've been to those madrassas in Pakistan this school is nothing like that."

Vause also interviewed one of Obama's Basuki classmates, Bandug Winadijanto, who claims that not a lot has changed at the school since the two men were pupils. Insight reported that Obama's political opponents believed the school promoted Wahhabism, a fundamentalist form of Islam, "and are seeking to prove it."

"It's not (an) Islamic school. It's general," Winadijanto said. "There is a lot of Christians, Buddhists, also Confucian. ... So that's a mixed school."...

Obama has noted in his two books, "Dreams From My Father" and "The Audacity of Hope," that he spent two years in a Muslim school and another two years in a Catholic school while living in Indonesia from age 6 to 10.

--CNN Report, False Report about Obama, January 23, 2007

7.1 The context of this article that makes this story volatile and controversial is
    A. the occupation of Iraq and Afghanistan.
    B. the aura of fear caused by 9/11.
    C. a rise of the Moral Majority.
    D. the executions of Americans in the Middle East.

7.2 A political candidate running against Obama could use this accusation to
    A. affirm his/her own Christian values.
    B. accuse Obama of not being loyal to the United States.
    C. criticize Obama's upbringing.
    D. promote Christian education.

7.3 The danger of the article is that it's reminiscent of all of the following EXCEPT
    A. the accusations of McCarthyism.
    B. the fear caused by the Red Scare.
    C. the hysteria of the Salem Witch Hunts.
    D. the creation of the First Amendment.

Questions 8.1-8.3 refer to the following cartoon visual.

8.1 The tar and feathering by angry Bostonians reflected the colonists' anger over
   A. the British attempt at selling Dutch imported tea.
   B. the British attempt at making the colonists buy taxed tea that was actually
      cheaper than smuggled Dutch tea.
   C. Loyalists during the Battle of Bunker Hill.
   D. British colonial governors.

8.2 The practice of tarring and feathering was also seen
   A. after the passage of the Quartering Act.
   B. after the passage of the Stamp Act.
   C. during ratification of the Constitution.
   D. in protest to the Proclamation Line of 1763.

8.3 The resort to using tar and feathers during the American Revolution reflected
   A. the quick tempered nature of the colonists.
   B. the violent nature common in the colonies.
   C. the lack of intellectualism inherent in the colonial protests.
   D. a deep concern of British oppression.

Questions 9.1-9.3. refer to the following cartoon visual.

9.1 The depiction of Uncle Sam as the teacher reflects the cartoonists belief that
   A. democracy would be guaranteed.
   B. the "lesser peoples" needed America's guidance to be civilized.
   C. the darker skinned people were advanced students sitting in the front.
   D. America had no interest in spreading its customs to outsiders.

9.2 The term that best describes the context in which this cartoon was drawn would be
   A. Manifest Destiny.
   B. New Frontier.
   C. American Imperialism.
   D. New Nationalism.

9.3 The event that established the United States as a world power was
   A. War of 1812.
   B. U.S./Mexican War.
   C. Civil War.
   D. Spanish-American War.

Questions 10.1-10.3 refer to the following cartoon visual.

10.1 As part of John D. Rockefeller's domination of the oil industry, he did all of the following EXCEPT
    A. cause the outlaw of secret rebates.
    B. buy out his competitors.
    C. use spies to track his competitor's customers.
    D. force competitors out of business.

10.2 A trend of the Industrial Revolution that Rockefeller followed was the
    A. establishment of trusts that monopolized industries.
    B. drive to maximize competition.
    C. advocating of business regulation by government.
    D. move away from railroads for transportation.

10.3 Rockefeller's oil company kingdom dissolved under the pressure of
    A. Chevron and Texaco.
    B. foreign oil countries.
    C. an anti-trust lawsuit.
    D. Theodore Roosevelt.

Questions 11.1-11.3 refer to the following poster.

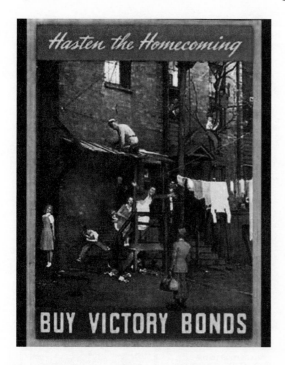

11.1 The main purpose of buying victory bonds was to
    A. finance the war effort of the United States.
    B. make unlimited profits.
    C. fight the Great Depression.
    D. create pensions for returning soldiers.

11.2 During World War II, Americans experienced
    A. lower taxes and inflation.
    B. higher taxes and price ceilings.
    C. high unemployment.
    D. prolonged stagflation.

11.3 Americans faced the advertising of war bonds everywhere EXCEPT
    A. at the movie theaters.
    B. on billboards and posters.
    C. in newspapers and magazines.
    D. during television commercials.

Questions 12.1 to 12.3 refer to the following map.

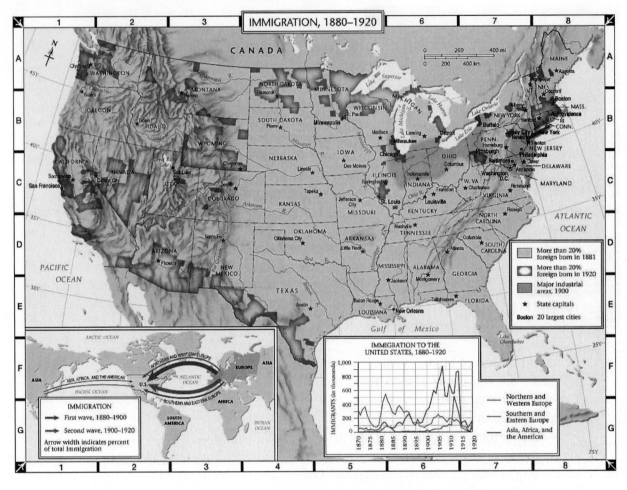

Copyright © 2003 by Pearson Education, Inc.

12.1 Most of the immigrants that came during the second wave of migration were from
  A. Northern and Western Europe.
  B. Southern and Eastern Europe.
  C. Asia.
  D. Africa.

12.2 The second wave of immigrants arrived and worked largely in the
  A. Southwest.
  B. Northwest.
  C. Southeast.
  D. Northeast.

12.3 As the anti-immigration laws of the 1920s went into effect, what group was exempt from these laws?
A. Italians
B. Russians
C. Polish
D. Mexicans

Question 13 is based on the following two passages.

"They hate our ways. They are hostile to our ideas. Our religion, language, institutions, and manners offend them. They like their own ways, and if we appear amongst them as rulers, there will be social discord in all the great departments of social interest. The most important thing which we shall inherit from the Spaniards will be the task of suppressing rebellions...
Now, the great reason why all these enterprises which begin by saying to somebody else, "We know what is good for you better than you know yourself and we are going to make you do it," are false and wrong is that they violate liberty; or, to turn the same statement into other words, the reason why liberty, of which we Americans talk so much, is a good thing is that it means leaving people to live out their own lives in their own way, while we do the same.
If we believe in liberty, as an American principle, why do we not stand by it? Why are we going to throw it away to enter upon a Spanish policy of dominion and regulation?"

--William Graham Sumner, "On Empire and the Philippines," 1898

"When next I realized that the Philippines had dropped into our laps, I confess I did not know what to do with them...
And one night late it came to me this way - I don't know how it was, but it came:
(1) That we could not give them back to Spain - that would be cowardly and dishonorable;
(2) That we could not turn them over to France or Germany, our commercial rivals in the Orient - that would be bad business and discreditable;
(3) The we could not leave them to themselves - they were unfit for self-government, and they would soon have anarchy and misrule worse then Spain's was; and
(4) That there was nothing left for us to do but to take them all, and to educated the Filipinos, and uplift and civilize and Christianize them and by God's grace do the very best we could by them, as our fellow men for whom Christ also died."

--William McKinley, "Decision on the Philippines," 1900

13. Based on the two interpretations above of the annexation of the Philippines, complete the following three tasks.

   A) Briefly explain the main point made by Passage 1.
   B) Briefly explain the main point made by Passage 2.
   C) Provide *one* piece of evidence from the era of the Age of American Imperialism that is not included in the passages, and explain how it supports the interpretation in either passage.

Question 14 is based on the following image.

Great Depression breadline

14. Use the image above and your knowledge of United States history to answer parts A, B, and C.

    A) Explain the point of view reflected in the image above regarding *one* of the following:
        -unemployment
        -hunger
        -homelessness
    B) Explain how *one* element of the image expresses the point of view you identified in Part A.
    C) Explain how the point of view you identified in Part A helped to shape *one* specific United States government action between 1929 and 1935.

Long Essay Questions (Choose one)

1) Historians commonly argue that the Civil Rights Act of 1964 marked a turning point of progress for African Americans. Support, modify, or refute this contention using specific evidence.

2) Some contemporary historians argue that the election of Barack Obama as the president of the United States marked a turning point of progress for African Americans. Support, modify, or refute this contention using specific evidence.

Document Based Question

What were some of the issues involved in the debate surrounding the composition and ratification of the Constitution?

DOCUMENT 1 Constitution of Pennsylvania, 1776

I. That all men are born equally free and independent, and have certain natural inherent and inalienable rights, amongst which are the enjoying and defending life and liberty, acquiring, possessing and protecting property, and pursuing and obtaining happiness and safety.

II. That all men have a natural and unalienable right to worship Almighty God according to the dictates of their own consciences and understanding: And that no man ought or of right can be compelled to attend any religious worship, or erect or support any place of worship, or maintain any ministry, contrary to, or against, his own free will and consent: Nor can any man, who acknowledges the being of a God, be justly deprived or abridged of any civil right as a citizen, on account of his religious sentiments or peculiar mode of religious worship: And that no authority can or ought to be vested in, or assumed by any power whatever, that shall in any case interfere with, or in any manner controul, the right of conscience in the free exercise of religious worship…

XI. That in controversies respecting property, and in suits between man and man, the parties have a right to trial by jury, which ought to be held sacred.

XII. That the people have a right to freedom of speech, and of writing, and publishing their sentiments; therefore the freedom of the press ought not to be restrained.

XIII. That the people have a right to bear arms for the defence of themselves and the state; and as standing armies in the time of peace are dangerous to liberty, they ought not to be kept up; And that the military should be kept under strict subordination to, and governed by, the civil power.

DOCUMENT 2 A Declaration of the Rights of the Inhabitants of the Commonwealth of Massachusetts (1780)

CHAPTER I

THE LEGISLATIVE POWER SECTION I. THE GENERAL COURT

ARTICLE I. The department of legislation shall be formed by two branches, a Senate and House of Representatives; each of which shall have a negative on the other.

The legislative body shall assemble every year [on the last Wednesday in May, and at such other times as they shall judge necessary; and shall dissolve and be dissolved on the day next preceding the said last Wednesday in May;] and shall be styled, THE GENERAL COURT OF MASSACHUSETTS.

DOCUMENT 3 Henry Knox, Letter to George Washington (1786)

Our political machine, composed of thirteen independent sovereignties, has been perpetually operating against each other and against the federal head ever since the peace. The powers of Congress are totally inadequate to preserve the balance between the respective States, and oblige them to do those things which are essential for their own welfare or for the general good. The frame of mind in the local legislatures seems to be exerted to prevent the federal constitution from having any good effect. The machine works inversely to the public good in all its parts: not only is State against State, and all against the federal head, but the States within themselves possess the name only without having the essential concomitant of government, the power of preserving the peace, the protection of the liberty and property of the citizens. On the very first impression of faction and licentiousness, the fine theoretic government of Massachusetts has given way, and its laws [are] trampled under foot. Men at a distance, who have admired our systems of government unfounded in nature, are apt to accuse the rulers, and say that taxes have been assessed too high and collected too rigidly. This is a deception equal to any that has been hitherto entertained. That taxes may be the ostensible cause is true, but that they are the true cause is as far remote from truth as light from darkness. The people who are the insurgents have never paid any or but very little taxes. But they see the weakness of government: they feel at once their own poverty compared with the opulent, and their own force, and they are determined to make use of the latter in order to remedy the former.

DOCUMENT 4 Marquis de Chastellux, Travels in North America (1786)

The government [of Virginia] may become democratic, as it is at the present moment; but the national character, the very spirit of the government, will always be aristocratic. Nor can this be doubted when one considers that another cause is still operating to produce the same result. I am referring to slavery, not because it is a mark of distinction or special privilege to possess Negroes, but because the sway held over them nourishes vanity and sloth, two vices which accord wonderfully with established prejudices. It will doubtless be asked how these prejudices have been reconciled with the present revolution, founded on such different principles. I shall answer that they have perhaps contributed to it; that while New England revolted through reason and calculation, Virginia revolted through pride. . . .

DOCUMENT 5 Thomas Jefferson to James Madison

Paris, January 30th, 1787
Dear Sir,

...Societies exist under three forms, sufficiently distinguishable: (1) without government, as among our Indians; (2) under governments, wherein the will of everyone has a just influence, as is the case in England, in a slight degree, and in our states, in a great one; (3) under governments of force, as is the case in all other monarchies, and in most of the other republics.
To have an idea of the curse of existence under these last, they must be seen. It is a government of wolves over sheep. It is a problem, not clear in my mind, that the first condition is not the best. But I believe it to be inconsistent with any great degree of population. The second state has a

great deal of good in it. The mass of mankind under that enjoys a precious degree of liberty and happiness. It has its evils, too, the principal of which is the turbulence to which it is subject. But weigh this against the oppressions of monarchy, and it becomes nothing. *Malo periculosam libertatem quam quietam servitutem.* Even this evil is productive of good. It prevents the degeneracy of government and nourishes a general attention to the public affairs.

I hold it that a little rebellion now and then is a good thing, and as necessary in the political world as storms in the physical. Unsuccessful rebellions, indeed, generally establish the encroachments on the rights of the people which have produced them. An observation of this truth should render honest republican governors so mild in their punishment of rebellions as not to discourage them too much. It is a medicine necessary for the sound health of government. . . .

Yours affectionately,

Th. Jefferson

DOCUMENT 6 The "Distracting Question" in Philadelphia (1787)

Wednesday July 11, 1787

IN CONVENTION

. . .Mr. WILLIAMSON was for making it the duty of the Legislature to do what was right & not leaving it at liberty to do or not do it. He moved that Mr. Randolph's proposition be postponed. in order to consider the following "that in order to ascertain the alterations that may happen in the population & wealth of the several States, a census shall be taken of the free white inhabitants and 3/5 ths. of those of other descriptions on the 1st. year after this Government shall have been adopted and every year thereafter; and that the Representation be regulated accordingly."

DOCUMENT 7 Patrick Henry Speaks against Ratification of the Constitution (1788)

. . .And here I would make this inquiry of those worthy characters who composed a part of the late federal Convention. I am sure they were fully impressed with the necessity of forming a great consolidated government, instead of a confederation. That this is a consolidated government is demonstrably clear; and the danger of such a government is, to my mind, very striking I have the highest veneration for those gentlemen; but, sir, give me leave to demand, What right had they to say, We, the people? My political curiosity, exclusive of my anxious solicitude for the public welfare, leads me to ask, Who authorized them to speak the language of, We, the people, instead of, We, the states? States are the characteristics and the soul of a confederation. If the states be not the agents of this compact, it must be one great, consolidated, national government, of the people of all the states . . . It is not mere curiosity that actuates me: I wish to hear the real, actual, existing danger, which should lead us to take those steps, so dangerous in my conception.

DOCUMENT 8   James Madison Defends the Constitution (1788)

...Give me leave to say something of the nature of the government, and to show that it is safe and just to vest it with the power of taxation. There are a number of opinions; but the principal question is, whether it be a federal or consolidated government. In order to judge properly of the question before us, we must consider it minutely in its principal parts. I conceive myself that it is of a mixed nature; it is in a manner unprecedented; we cannot find one express example in the experience of the world. It stands by itself. In some respects it is a government of a federal nature; in others, it is of a consolidated nature. Even if we attend to the manner in which the Constitution is investigated, ratified, and made the act of the people of America, I can say, notwithstanding what the honorable gentleman has alleged, that this government is not completely consolidated, nor is it entirely federal. Who are parties to it? The people but not the people as composing one great body; but the people as composing thirteen sovereignties. Were it, as the gentleman asserts, a consolidated government, the assent of a majority of the people would be sufficient for its establishment; and, as a majority have adopted it already, the remaining states would be bound by the act of the majority, even if they unanimously reprobated it. Were it such a government as is suggested, it would be now binding on the people of this state, without having had the privilege of deliberating upon it. But, sir, no state is bound by it, as it is, without its own consent. Should all the states adopt it, it will be then a government established by the thirteen states of America, not through the intervention of the legislatures, but by the people at large. In this particular respect, the distinction between the existing and proposed governments is very material. The existing system has been derived from the dependent derivative authority of the legislatures of the states; whereas this is derived from the superior power of the people.

ANSWERS AND EXPLANATIONS

Multiple Choice Questions

1.1 B The Spanish saw the Indians as an easy group to conquer.
1.2 C African slaves eventually replaced Indian workers.
1.3 B The Europeans in general believed in the acquisition of material goods.
2.1 D Tobacco became extremely profitable especially for growers in Virginia.
2.2 B Tobacco became enormously popular in Europe.
2.3 B Tobacco hinders health instead of improves it.
3.1 B Many were inspired for independence after Henry's "Give me liberty or give me death" speech.
3.2 A Thomas Paine also urged for liberty and freedom.
3.3 A Henry became a leading Anti-Federalist.
4.1 B The line would ultimately be ruled unconstitutional by the Supreme Court.
4.2 D The admission of Maine kept the balance between free and slave states.
4.3 A The addition of more territory would stir heated passions once again.
5.1 B 100% Americanism was a backlash to industrial immigration.
5.2 B According to the Klan, Catholics were only loyal to a foreign leader.
5.3 A This party was very anti-Catholic in the 1840s and 1850s.
6.1 B In 1965, Watts suffered a deadly riot.
6.2 D Advocates of Black Power opposed mixing with whites.
6.3 C Blacks were still being attacked despite civil rights legislation.
7.1 B Fear of terrorism produced its own sense of McCarthyism.
7.2 B Some rumors circulated about Obama's religious background.
7.3 D The First Amendment protects religious freedom.
8.1 B The victim in the picture purchased imported tea.
8.2 B Tax collectors suffered from tar and feathering.
8.3 D British oppression led to dramatic consequences in the colonies.
9.1 B America had the burden of civilizing much of the world from its "darkness."
9.2 C The age of American Imperialism was filled with a sense of racial superiority.
9.3 D The victory over Spain with its new navy launched the U.S. into a world power.
10.1 A Rockefeller manipulated the railroads to give him secret rebates.
10.2 A Trusts in virtually every industry formed during this period.
10.3 C Under Taft's presidency, Standard Oil was dissolved.
11.1 A The federal government relied on bonds to pay for war expenses.
11.2 B Taxes went up to pay for the war and price ceilings were established.
11.3 D Television was not common in the forties.
12.1 B Many Italians and Russians migrated to America during this second wave.
12.2 D The factories and coal mines were filled with second wave immigrants.
12.3 D Mexicans continued to migrate into the US without restrictions during the twenties.

Document-Based Question

What were some of the issues involved in the debate surrounding the composition and ratification of the Constitution?

The ratification of the U.S. Constitution was not a universally celebrated measure, and its composition was a controversial process. There were powerful concerns, determined both by regional politics and larger ideological issues, that shaped the document. Even once those had been resolved, its ratification was not guaranteed.

In the 1780s a number of problems forced the governments of the United States to reassess the Articles of Confederation. There was a feeling that the federal government was too weak, and that the states were pulling away from each other. Congress seemed unable to maintain the balance between the states (**DOCUMENT 3**). It was in this context that the Constitutional convention was called. However, not everybody believe that these problems were worth address. Thomas Jefferson, for example, thought that they were actually the signs of a free, healthy society (**DOCUMENT 5**).

There were a few early models on which the convention was able to base its discussion. For example, Pennsylvania had a constitution that guaranteed the basic rights of free speech, freedom of religion, and the right to a fair trial (**DOCUMENT 1**), which were eventually adopted as the first amendments to the Consitution. Massachusetts had a bicameral legislature (**DOCUMENT 2**), a feature that became part of the US constitution.

It was not easy for the members of the convention to come to an agreement on how to organize the government. For example, the question of how slaves were to be counted in the population for the purposes of representation was controversial. Southern states wanted them to count as full citizens, though they did not vote, as this would give them greater representation in Congress, due to the large number of slaves in the South. The Northern states, with far fewer slaves, did not want them to count. Eventually, a compromise was proposed, that they should count as three fifths of a citizen (**DOCUMENT 6**).

Even once this and other compromises were reached, the Constitution's ratification was not certain. There were those who argued against it, saying that it was creating a central government that was too powerful, and was illegitimate (**DOCUMENT 7**). Others defended the Constitution, arguing that it balanced central power with federal concerns (**DOCUMENT 8**).

Though the Constitution was ratified, this tension continued to be a part of American discourse. The tug-of-war between artistocracy and democracy, nowhere as sharply embodied as in the slave Virginia's arguments for liberty (**DOCUMENT 4**), is an essential part of the American national heritage, as enshrined in the U.S. Constitution.